TEXAS DEATH ROW

Edited by
Bill Crawford

PENGUIN BOOKS

PENGUIN BOOKS

Published by the Penguin Group
Penguin Books Ltd, 80 Strand, London WC2R ORL, England
Penguin Group (USA) Inc., 375 Hudson Street, New York, New York 10014, USA
Penguin Group (Canada), 90 Eglinton Avenue East, Suite 700, Toronto, Ontario, Canada M4P 2Y3
(a division of Pearson Penguin Canada Inc.)
Penguin Ireland, 25 St Stephen's Green, Dublin 2, Ireland (a division of Penguin Books Ltd)
Penguin Group (Australia), 250 Camberwell Road, Camberwell, Victoria 3124, Australia
(a division of Pearson Australia Group Pty Ltd)
Penguin Books India Pvt Ltd, 11 Community Centre, Panchsheel Park, New Delhi – 110 017, India
Penguin Group (NZ), 67 Apollo Drive, Rosedale, North Shore 0632, New Zealand
(a division of Pearson New Zealand Ltd)
Penguin Books (South Africa) (Pty) Ltd, 24 Sturdee Avenue, Rosebank, Johannesburg 2196, South Africa

Penguin Books Ltd, Registered Offices: 80 Strand, London WC2R ORL, England

www.penguin.com

First published in the United States of America by Plume,
a member of Penguin Group (USA) Inc. 2008
Previously published in a Mapache edition
First published in Great Britain by Penguin Books 2008

3

Designed by Bill Carson Design, Austin
Printed in England by Clays Ltd, St Ives plc

ISBN: 978-0-141-03866-7

www.greenpenguin.co.uk

Penguin Books is committed to a sustainable future
for our business, our readers and our planet.
The book in your hands is made from paper
certified by the Forest Stewardship Council.

Texas Death Row: Executions in the Modern Era presents the factual record preserved by the Texas Department of Criminal Justice for each of the individual offenders executed by the State of Texas in the modern era. I refer to the modern era as the era of executions by the State of Texas by lethal injection, beginning on December 7, 1982. Since that date, Texas has executed more inmates by lethal injection than all other states combined.

In the present volume, I have listed the executed inmates in order of their execution by the State of Texas, beginning with Charlie Brooks and ending with James Lee Clark, the last execution to occur before this book went to press.

The Texas Department of Criminal Justice (TDCJ) provided all of the information in this book, except for some of the introductory material. Those seeking more information are encouraged to visit the TDCJ website at http://www.tdcj.state.tx.us/stat/deathrow.htm.

We wish to thank the public relations office at the TDCJ in Huntsville, Texas: Michelle Lyons, the public information officer; Byron Hays, the former public information officer; and Rebecca Blanton, administrative assistant. Ms. Lyons, Mr. Hays, and Ms. Blanton went out of their way to be open, honest, and cooperative. They are true professionals. We also wish to thank former TDCJ employees Larry Fitzgerald, former public information officer; and Tracy Espinoza, former public information associate. Without the helpful assistance of the dedicated TDCJ employees, this book would not have been possible to produce.

In the past few years the debate over the death penalty has increased in volume and vehemence. It is our hope that the information presented in this book will assist readers in framing informed opinions about the execution process.

Death Row Facts

(Source: Texas Department of Criminal Justice website http://www.tdcj.state.tx.us/stat/ drowfacts.htm)

Texas Capital Offenses

The following crimes are capital murder in Texas: murder of a public safety officer or firefighter; murder during the commission of kidnapping, burglary, robbery, aggravated sexual assault, arson, or obstruction or retaliation; murder for remuneration; murder during prison escape; murder of a correctional employee; murder by a state prison inmate who is serving a life sentence for any of five offenses (murder, capital murder, aggravated kidnapping, aggravated sexual assault, or aggravated robbery); multiple murders; murder of an individual under six years of age. (Editor's note: a person convicted of capital murder may be sentenced to one of two sentences—death or life imprisonment. A person must serve at least thirty-five calendar years of a life sentence if the offense is committed prior to September 1, 1993, or at least forty years if the offense is committed after this date.)

Death Row Location

Death row is located in the Polunsky Unit of the Texas Department of Criminal Justice in Livingston, Texas. Death row offenders are housed separately in single-person cells measuring sixty square feet, with each cell having a window. Death row offenders are also re-created individually. Offenders on death row receive a regular diet, and have access to reading, writing, and legal materials. Depending upon their custody level, some death row offenders are allowed to have a radio. The women on death row are housed at the Mountain View Unit. Offenders on death row do not have regular TDCJ ID numbers but have special death row numbers. (Editor's note: Executions do not occur at death row. The death house, where all executions take place, is located in the northeast corner of the Walls Unit in Huntsville, Texas.)

History of Execution in Texas

• Hanging was the means of execution between 1819 and 1923.

• The State of Texas authorized the use of the electric chair in 1923, and ordered all executions to be carried out by the state in Huntsville. Prior to 1923, Texas counties were responsible for their own executions.

• The State of Texas executed the first offender, Charles Reynolds from Red River County, by electrocution on February 8, 1924. On that same date, four additional offenders, Ewell Morris, George Washington, Mack Matthews, and Melvin Johnson were executed.

• The State of Texas executed the last offender, Joseph Johnson from Harris County, by electrocution on July 30, 1964.

• The State of Texas executed brothers on six occasions:
    Frank and Lorenzo Noel electrocuted July 3, 1925
    S. A. and Forest Robins electrocuted April 6, 1926
    Oscar and Mack Brown electrocuted July 1, 1936
    Roscoe and Henderson Brown electrocuted May 6, 1938

Curtis (July 1, 1993) and Danny (July 30, 1993) Harris (both by lethal injection) Jessie (September 16, 1994) and Jose (November 18, 1999) Gutierrez (both by lethal injection).

• A total of 361 inmates were electrocuted in the State of Texas

• When capital punishment was declared "cruel and unusual punishment" by the U.S. Supreme Court on June 29, 1972, there were forty-five men on death row in Texas and seven in county jails with a death sentence. All of the sentences were commuted to life sentences by the Governor of Texas, and death row was clear by March 1973.

• In 1973, revision to the Texas Penal Code once again allowed assessment of the death penalty and allowed for executions to resume effective January 1, 1974. Under the new statute, the first man John Devries was placed on death row on February 1, 1974. Devries committed suicide on July 1, 1974, by hanging himself with bed sheets.

• The State of Texas adopted lethal injection as means of execution in 1977. The state's first execution by lethal injection occurred on December 7, 1982. Charlie Brooks of Tarrant County was executed for the kidnap-murder of a Fort Worth auto mechanic.

• Lethal injection consists of:
    Sodium thiopental (lethal dose—sedate person)
    Pancuronium bromide (muscle relaxant—collapses diaphram and lungs)
    Potassium chloride (stops heartbeat)

• The Lethal injection process takes approximately seven minutes and the cost per execution for the drugs used is $86.08.

• Witnesses: reporters from the community where the crime was committed have first choice to witness execution. Members of the Kelley family were the first victims' family allowed to witness an execution on February 9, 1996, under the adoption preamble effective September 26, 1995. The offender executed was Leo Jenkins, who shot the brother and sister of the Kelley family during a robbery at the family owned Golden Nugget Pawn Shop, in Houston, August 29, 1988.

Executions carried out by the State of Texas since death penalty was reinstated

Executions
*December 7, 1982 through October 25, 2006**

RACE	1982	1984	1985	1986	1987	1988	1989	1990	1991	1992	1993	1994	1995	1996	1997	1998†	1999	2000†	2001	2002	2003	2004	2005	2006	Total
White	0	3	3	6	2	1	2	2	2	5	6	9	8	1	21	13	17	19	10	17	14	7	11	5	184
	0%	100%	50%	60%	33.3%	33.3%	50%	50%	40%	41.7%	35.3%	64.3%	42.1%	33.3%	56.8%	65.0%	48.6%	47.5%	58.8%	51.5%	58.3%	30.4%	57.9%	20.0%	49%
Black	1	0	1	2	2	2	1	2	2	5	7	4	8	1	13	2	11	16	6	11	7	13	5	12	134
	100%	0%	17%	20%	33.3%	66.7%	25%	50%	40%	41.7%	41.2%	28.6%	42.1%	33.3%	35.1%	10.0%	31.4%	40.0%	35.3%	33.3%	29.2%	56.5%	26.3%	55.0%	36%
Hispanic	0	0	2	2	2	0	1	0	1	2	4	1	2	1	2	5	7	5	1	5	3	3	3	5	57
	0%	0%	33%	20	33.3%	0%	25%	0%	20%	16.7%	23.5%	7.1%	10.5%	33.3%	5.4%	25.0%	20.0%	12.5%	5.9%	15.2%	12.5%	13.0%	15.8%	25.0%	15%
Other	0	0	0	0	0	0	0	0	0	0	0	0	1	0	1	0	0	0	0	0	0	0	0	0	2
	0%	0%	0%	0%	0%	0%	0%	0%	0%	0%	0%	0%	5.3%	0%	2.7%	0%	0%	0%	0%	0%	0%	0%	0%	0%	1%
TOTAL	1	3	6	10	6	3	4	4	5	12	17	14	19	3	37	20	35	40	17	33	24	23	19	22	377

* Last Execution October 25, 2006.

† 1 White Female Offender Executed in 1998, 1 White Female Offender Executed in 2000 and 1 Black Female Offender Executed in 2005.

Texas Execution Statistics
Average Time on Death Row: 10.43 years

Shortest Time on Death Row prior to Execution

	Name	County	TDCJ Number	Time on Death Row	Execution Date
1.	Joe Gonzales	Potter	999177	252 days	9/18/96
2.	Steven Renfro	Harrison	999229	263 days	2/9/98

Longest Time on Death Row prior to Execution

	Name	County	TDCJ Number	Time on Death Row	Execution Date
1.	Excell White	Collin	511	8982 days (24 years)	3/30/99
2.	Sammie Felder Jr.	Harris	550	8569 days (23 years)	12/15/99

Average Age of Executed Offenders

39

Youngest at Time of Execution

Name	County	TDCJ Number	Age	Execution Date
Jay Pinkerton	Nueces	686	24	5/15/1986
Jesse De La Rosa	Bexar	713	24	5/15/1985

Oldest at Time of Execution

Name	County	TDCJ Number	Age	Execution Date
William Chappell	Tarrant	960	66	11/20/2002
Hilton Crawford	Montgomery	999200	64	7/2/2003

Execution Procedures of Inmates Sentenced to Death
(Source: Texas Department of Criminal Justice)

Male inmates under the sentence of death will be housed at the Polunsky Unit of the Texas Department of Criminal Justice Institutional Division located east of Huntsville on FM 350 in Livingston, Texas. Female death row inmates will be housed at the Mountain View Unit located in Gatesville, Texas.

• Visitors at the Polunsky/Mountain View Units:
MEDIA — Press interviews of condemned prisoners shall be scheduled by the Public Information Office and conducted at the Polunsky Unit and Mountain View Unit during specified times. Any media requesting an interview with death row inmate-sat Polunsky Unit or Mountain View Unit should submit names to the Public Information Office prior to the interview date. Requests will not be accepted at the Polunsky/Mountain View Units on the day of the interview. The number of inmates requested to be interviewed should be kept within reason.

The inmate may have the following visitors at the Polunsky/Mountain View Units: family member(s) and friend(s) on the list of approved visitors.

An inmate scheduled for execution shall be transported from the Polunsky/Mountain View Unit to the Huntsville Unit prior to the scheduled execution. Transportation arrangements shall be known only to the unit wardens involved, and no public announcement to either the exact time, method, or route of transfer shall be made. The Director's Office and the Public Information Office will be notified immediately after the inmate arrive at the Huntsville Unit.

During transportation and after arrival at the Huntsville Unit, the inmate shall be constantly observed and supervised by security personnel.

The inmate may have the following visitors at the Huntsville Unit:
TDCJ Institutional Division Chaplain(s)
Minister(s)
Attorney(s)

All visits must be approved by the warden. With the exception of chaplain's visits, all visits will be terminated by 12:30 PM on the day of the execution. No media visits will be allowed at the Huntsville Unit.

The last meal will be served at approximately 3:30–4:00 PM.

Prior to 6:00 PM, the inmate may shower and dress in clean clothes.
The Huntsville Unit Warden's office will serve as the communications command post and only operations personnel will be allowed entry to this area. All other individuals, including witnesses to the execution, will assemble at approximately 5:54 PM in the lounge adjacent to the visiting room. All necessary arrangements to carry out the execution shall be completed at the predetermined time. Shortly after 6:00 PM, the door will be unlocked, and the inmate will be removed from the holding cell.

The inmate will be taken from the cell area into the execution chamber and secured to a gurney. A medically trained individual (not to be identified) shall insert an intravenous catheter into the condemned person's arms and cause a saline solution to flow.

At a predetermined time, the witnesses shall be escorted to the execution chamber.

Witnesses shall include:

MEDIA – One Texas Bureau representative designated by the Associated Press, one Texas Bureau representative designated by the United Press International, one representative for the Huntsville Item, and one representative each from established separate rosters of print and broadcast media will be admitted to the execution chamber as witnesses, provided those designated agree to meet with all media representatives present, immediately subsequent to the execution. No recording devices, either audio or video, shall be permitted in the unit or in the execution chamber.

Policy allows for up to five pre-approved witnesses requested by the condemned and up to five immediate family members or close friends of the victim to attend.

Once the witnesses are in place, the warden shall allow the condemned person to make a last statement. Upon completion of the statement, if any, the warden shall signal for the execution to proceed. At the time, the designee(s) of the Director, shall induce by syringe, substance and/or substances necessary to cause death. The individual(s) shall be visually separated from the execution by a wall and locked door, and shall also not be identified. After the inmate is pronounced dead, the body shall be immediately removed from the execution chamber, taken to an awaiting vehicle, and delivered to a local funeral home for burial by the family or state. The inmate may request that his body be donated to the state anatomical board for medical research purposes. Arrangements for the body, are to be concluded prior to the execution, shall be made per Vernon's Ann. C.C.P., Article 43.25.

The Director of the Texas Department of Criminal Justice Institutional Division in accordance with Article 43.23 shall return the death warrant and certificate with a statement of any such act and his proceedings endorsed thereon, together with a statement showing what disposition was made of the body of the convict, to the clerk of the court in which the sentence was passed.

United States Capital Punishment
(Information from the Death Penalty Information Center and Amnesty International)

• Texas leads the nation in number of executions since the use of the death penalty in the United States was resumed in 1977.

• California has the largest death row population (660 in 2007). Texas's death row population at the same time was 393.

• In 2005, sixty persons in sixteen states were executed—nineteen in Texas; five each in Indiana, Missouri, and North Carolina; four each in Ohio, Alabama, and Oklahoma; three each in Georgia, and South Carolina; two in California; and one each in Connecticut, Arkansas, Delaware, Florida, Maryland, and Mississippi. All executions in 2005 were by lethal injection.

• As of 2007, thirty-seven states, the U.S. military, and the U.S. federal government provided for the death penalty by law by lethal injection. Ten states allow for execution by electrocution. Five states allow for execution by the gas chamber. Two states allow for execution by hanging. Two states allow for execution by firing squad. Utah allows for execution by firing squad only for those inmates who chose this option prior to its being outlawed by the State of Utah.

Every attempt has been made to report all information for each executed offender. Information not available at the time of publication is indicated by "n/a." Lengthy written and spoken last statements have been included in the Appendix. An alphabetical index of inmates is displayed in the Index.

Charlie Brooks Jr.

Executed: December 7, 1982

Personal data: *Born:* September 1, 1942. *Race:* Black. *Height:* n/a. *Weight:* n/a. *Education:* n/a. *Prior occupation:* n/a. *County of conviction:* Tarrant. *Age at time of execution:* 40.

Sentenced to death for: The December 14, 1976, kidnapping and murder of used car lot mechanic David Gregory.
Codefendant: Woodie Lourdes was also charged with capital murder in connection with the slaying.

Received at death row: April 15, 1978. *Time on death row:* 1,697 days (4.65 years).

Last meal: T-bone steak, french fries, ketchup, Worcestershire sauce, rolls, peach cobbler, iced tea, and a toothpick.

Last statement: [To witness Vanessa Sapp, his girlfriend] "I love you. Be strong."

Pronounced dead: 12:16 A.M.
Note: Brooks was the first person to be executed by lethal injection in the United States and the first person executed in Texas following the reinstatement of the death penalty in 1974. He was the sixth person in the United States to be executed after the reinstatement.

2

James David Autry

Executed: March 14, 1984

Personal data: *Born:* September 27, 1954. *Race:* White. *Height:* n/a. *Weight:* n/a. *Education:* n/a. *Prior occupation:* n/a. *County of conviction:* Jefferson. *Age at time of execution:* 29.

Sentenced to death for: Shot and killed Shirley Crouet, a convenience store clerk, during a robbery on April 20, 1980. The robbery netted one six-pack of beer.

Received at death row: October 10, 1980. *Time on death row:* 1,251 days (3.43 years).

Last meal: Hamburger, french fries, and Dr Pepper.

Last statement: None.

Pronounced dead: 12:40 A.M.

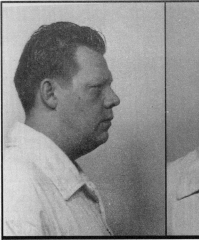

3

Ronald Clark O'Bryan

Executed: March 31, 1984

Personal data: *Born:* October 19, 1944. *Race:* White. *Height:* 5'10". *Weight:* 215 pounds. *Education:* 14 years. *Prior occupation:* Optician. *County of conviction:* Harris. *Age at time of execution:* 39.

Sentenced to death for: Convicted in the murder of his son, Timothy O'Bryan. O'Bryan poisoned the boy's Halloween candy with cyanide.
Note: Ronald O'Bryan was nicknamed the Candy Man in the press.

Received at death row: July 14, 1975. *Time on death row:* 3,183 days (8.72 years).

Last meal: T-bone steak (medium to well-done), french fries and ketchup, whole-kernel corn, sweet peas, lettuce and tomato salad with egg and French dressing, iced tea (sweet), saltines, ice cream, Boston cream pie, and rolls.

Last statement: See Appendix.

Pronounced dead: 12:48 A.M.

4

Thomas Andy Barefoot

Executed: October 30, 1984

Personal data: *Born:* February 23, 1945. *Race:* White. *Height:* n/a. *Weight:* n/a. *Education:* 10 years. *Prior occupation:* Cement finisher, oil field worker, derrick man. *County of conviction:* Bell. *Age at time of execution:* 39.

Sentenced to death for: Convicted in the August 7, 1978, capital murder of police officer Carl Levin near Killeen. Barefoot shot Officer Levin with a .25 caliber pistol to avoid arrest. Barefoot was apprehended in Beaumont after bragging about the murder.
Note: Prior to the murder of Levin, Barefoot had been arrested for the rape of the three-year-old daughter of his estranged girlfriend. He escaped from jail by digging himself out with a spoon.

Received at death row: November 21, 1978. *Time on death row:* 2,170 days (5.95 years).

Last meal: Chef salad with crackers, chili with beans, steamed rice, seasoned pinto beans, corn O'Brien, seasoned mustard greens, hot spiced beets, and iced tea.

Last statement: "I hope that one day we can look back on the evil that we're doing right now like the witches we burned at the stake. I want everybody to know that I hold nothing against them. I forgive them all. I hope everybody I've done anything to will forgive me. I've been praying all day for Carl Levin's wife to drive the bitterness from her heart, because the bitterness that's in her heart will send her to hell just as surely as any other sin. I'm sorry for everything that I've ever done to anybody. I hope they'll forgive me. Sharon, tell all my friends good-bye, you know who they are: Charles Bass, David Powell . . ."

Pronounced dead: 12:24 A.M.

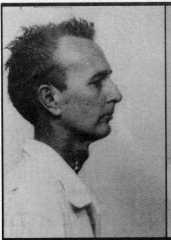

Doyle Skillern

Executed: January 16, 1985

TEXAS
EX 5 1 8
1975

Personal data: *Born:* April 8, 1936. *Race:* White. *Height:* 5'7". *Weight:* 125 pounds. *Education:* 12 years. *Prior occupation:* Sales. *County of conviction:* Lubbock. *Age at time of execution:* 48.

Sentenced to death for: Convicted of capital murder in the October 23, 1974, shooting death of Texas Department of Public Safety narcotics officer Patrick Allen Randel during an undercover drug buy near the town of George West.

Received at death row: March 3, 1975. *Time on death row:* 3,607 days (9.88 years).

Last meal: Sirloin steak, baked potato, peas, a roll, banana pudding, and coffee. *Note:* At the end of the meal Skillern said, "My compliments to the chef."

Last statement: "I pray that my family will rejoice and will forgive, thank you."

Pronounced dead: 12:23 A.M.

6

**Stephen
Peter
Morin**

Executed:
March 13,
1985

TEXAS
EX 7 1 2
1982

Personal data: *Born:* February 19, 1951. *Race:* White. *Height:* n/a. *Weight:* n/a. *Education:* n/a. *Prior occupation:* n/a. *County of conviction:* Jefferson and Nueces. *Age at time of execution:* 34.

Sentenced to death for: Convicted in the December 11, 1981, murder of Carrie Marie Scott, 21, who police said was shot in a robbery attempt outside a San Antonio restaurant. This crime was made a capital offense when Morin stole Scott's car after shooting her.

Received at death row: April 16, 1982. *Time on death row:* 1,062 days (2.91 years).

Last meal: Bread without yeast (unleavened).

Last statement: "Heavenly Father, I give thanks for this time, for the time that we have been together, the fellowship of your world, the Christian family presented to me [he called the names of the personal witnesses]. Allow your holy spirit to flow as I know your love has been showered upon me. Forgive them for they know not what they do as I know that you have forgiven me, as I have forgiven them. Lord Jesus I commit my soul to you, I praise you, and I thank you."

Pronounced dead: 12:55 A.M.

7

Jesse de la Rosa

Executed: May 15, 1985

Personal data: *Born:* September 22, 1960. *Race:* Hispanic. *Height:* 5'9". *Weight:* 220 pounds. *Education:* 9 years. *Prior occupation:* Laborer. *County of conviction:* Bexar. *Age at time of execution:* 24.

Sentenced to death for: Convicted in the slaying of Masaoud Ghazali, a former captain in the Iranian Air Force, who was shot twice in the head during a robbery at a San Antonio convenience store August 22, 1979. The robbery netted only one six-pack of beer; the cash register could not be opened.

Received at death row: May 18, 1982. *Time on death row:* 1,093 days (2.99 years).

Last meal: Spanish rice, refried beans, flour tortillas, a T-bone steak, tea, chocolate cake, and jalapeño peppers.

Last statement: Gave last statement in Spanish. No record kept.

Pronounced dead: 12:17 A.M.

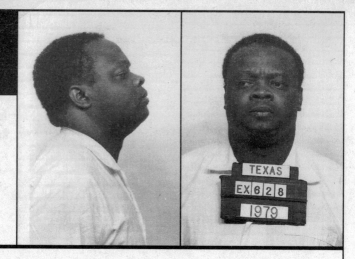

8

Charles Milton

Executed:
June 25,
1985

Personal data: *Born:* March 15, 1951. *Race:* Black. *Height:* 5'6". *Weight:* 165 pounds. *Education:* 7 years. *Prior occupation:* Cook. *County of conviction:* Tarrant. *Age at time of execution:* 34.

Sentenced to death for: Convicted of capital murder for the robbery and murder of liquor store owner Menaree Denton in Fort Worth. Her husband, Leonard Denton, was also shot but survived to testify against Milton.

Received at death row: January 18, 1979. *Time on death row:* 2,350 days (6.44 years).

Last meal: T-bone steak, french fries, tossed salad with French dressing, ketchup, hot rolls, and chocolate cake.

Last statement: "There's no god but Allah, and unto thee I belong and unto thee I return. I want to continue to tell my brothers and sisters to be strong."

Pronounced dead: 1:33 A.M.

9

Henry Martinez Porter

Executed: July 9, 1985

Personal data: *Born:* December 12, 1941. *Race:* Hispanic. *Height:* 5'6".
Weight: 125 pounds. *Education:* 9 years. *Prior occupation:* Painter's helper.
County of conviction: Tarrant. *Age at time of execution:* 43.

Sentenced to death for: Convicted of capital murder in the November 29, 1975, shooting death of Henry P. Malloux, a Fort Worth police officer who had stopped Porter on an investigation of three armed robberies.

Received at death row: July 28, 1976. *Time on death row:* 3,268 days (8.95 years).

Last meal: Flour tortillas, a T-bone steak, refried beans, tossed salad, jalapeño peppers, ice cream, and chocolate cake.

Last statement: "I want to thank Father Walsh for his spiritual help. I want to thank Bob Ray [Sanders] and Steve Blow for their friendship. What I want people to know is that they call me a cold-blooded killer, when I shot a man that shot me first. The only thing that convicted me was that I am a Mexican and that he was a police officer. People hollered for my life, and they are to have my life tonight. The people never hollered for the life of the policeman that killed a 13-year-old boy who was handcuffed in the backseat of a police car. The people never hollered for the life of a Houston police officer who beat up and drowned Jose Campo Torres and threw his body in the river. You call that equal justice. This is your equal justice. This is America's equal justice. A Mexican's life is worth nothing. When a policeman kills someone he gets a suspended sentence or probation. When a Mexican kills a police officer, this is what you get. From there you call me a cold-blooded murderer. I didn't tie anybody to a stretcher. I don't pump any poison into anybody's veins from behind a locked door. You call this justice. I call this and your society a bunch of cold-blooded murderers. I don't say this with any bitterness or anger. I just say this with truthfulness. I hope God forgives me for all my sins. I hope that God will be as merciful to society as he has been to me. I'm ready, Warden."

Pronounced dead: 12:31 A.M.

10

Charles Francis Rumbaugh

Executed: September 11, 1985

Personal data: *Born:* June 23, 1957. *Race:* White. *Height:* n/a. *Weight:* n/a. *Education:* n/a. *Prior occupation:* n/a. *County of conviction:* Potter. *Age at time of execution:* 28.

Sentenced to death for: Convicted in the April 4, 1975, slaying of Michael Fiorillo, 58, during a jewelry store robbery. Rumbaugh was 17 years old at the time of the offense.

Note: After being sentenced to death in 1976, Rumbaugh threatened to kill the judge, D.A., bailiff, and his attorney. In February 1983, Rumbaugh was critically wounded in a courtroom after he lunged at a deputy U.S. marshal with a makeshift weapon and shouted, "Shoot me."

Received at death row: August 25, 1976. *Time on death row:* 3,304 days (9.05 years).

Last meal: One flour tortilla and water.

Last statement: "D.J., Laurie, Dr. Wheat, about all I can say is good-bye, and for the rest of you, although you don't forgive me for my transgressions, I forgive yours against me. I am ready to begin my journey and that's all I have to say." See Appendix for written last statement.

Pronounced dead: 12:27 A.M.

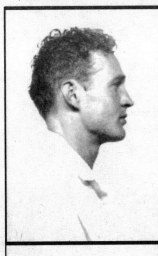

11

Charles William Bass

Executed: March 12, 1986

Personal data: *Born:* January 10, 1957. *Race:* White. *Height:* 5'6". *Weight:* 135 pounds. *Education:* 9 years. *Prior occupation:* Sheet and metal mechanic. *County of conviction:* Harris. *Age at time of execution:* 29.

Sentenced to death for: Capital murder. On August 16, 1979, Bass robbed a lounge at gunpoint and fled. Half a mile from the robbery, he was seen coincidentally by two Houston city marshals who had a traffic warrant on him. Bass was stopped by the officers, who noticed his pockets stuffed with rolled coins and dollar bills. Bass pulled out an automatic pistol and shot Officer Baker in the stomach, then shot at Baker's partner and missed. He then shot Baker again as Baker lay on the pavement. Bass fled and was arrested four days later in Covington, Kentucky. Officer Baker died.

Received at death row: September 9, 1980. *Time on death row:* 2,010 days (5.51 years).

Last meal: A plain cheese sandwich.

Last statement: "I deserve this. Tell everyone I said good-bye."

Pronounced dead: 12:21 A.M.

12

Jeffery Allen Barney

Executed:
April 16, 1986

Photographs Not Available

Personal data: *Born:* March 1, 1958. *Race:* White. *Height:* 5'8". *Weight:* 145 pounds. *Education:* n/a. *Prior occupation:* n/a. *County of conviction:* Harris. *Age at time of execution:* 28.

Sentenced to death for: Convicted in the rape-strangulation death of a Pasadena, Texas, game room manager, Ruby Mock Longsworth, whose husband, a clergyman, had befriended Barney. Mrs. Longsworth was murdered in her home, strangled with a microphone cord.

Received at death row: June 17, 1982. *Time on death row:* 1,399 days (3.83 years).

Last meal: Two boxes of Frosted Flakes and one pint of milk.

Last statement: "I'm sorry for what I've done. I deserve this. Jesus forgive me."

Pronounced dead: 12:22 A.M.

13

Jay Kelly Pinkerton

Executed:
May 15, 1986

Personal data: *Born:* February 14, 1962. *Race:* White. *Height:* 6'0". *Weight:* 159 pounds. *Education:* 10 years (GED). *Prior occupation:* Truck driver. *County of conviction:* Nueces and Potter. *Age at time of execution:* 24.

Sentenced to death for: Convicted of capital murder for the death of Sarah Donn Lawrence on October 26, 1979, during a robbery (or burglary) with intent to rape. Lawrence suffered thirty or more stab wounds to her body and face. Pinkerton was also convicted of capital murder for the stabbing death of Sherry Welch, a furniture store employee in Amarillo. Ms. Welch was stabbed approximately thirty times and raped.
Note: Pinkerton was 17 years of age at the time of the offense.

Received at death row: June 29, 1981. *Time on death row:* 1,781 days (4.88 years).

Last meal: Fish sandwich, french fries, and milk.
Note: Pinkerton did not eat during the day in honor of Ramadan, the Muslim fasting month.

Last statement: [To his father, who witnessed the execution] "Be strong for me. I want you to know I'm at peace with myself and with my God. I bear witness that there is not God but Allah. With your praise I ask for forgiveness and I return unto you. I love you, Dad."

Pronounced dead: 12:25 A.M.

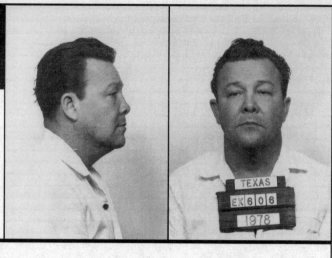

14

Rudy Ramos Esquivel

Executed: June 9, 1986

Personal data: *Born:* n/a. *Race:* Hispanic. *Height:* n/a. *Weight:* n/a. *Education:* n/a. *Prior occupation:* n/a. *County of conviction:* Harris. *Age at time of execution:* 50.

Sentenced to death for: Convicted in the June 8, 1978, slaying of Houston narcotics officer Tim Hearn.

Received at deathrow: August 30, 1978. *Time on death row:* 2,840 days (7.78 years).

Last meal: Fried breast of chicken, corn on the cob, french fries, jalapeño peppers, and pecan pie.

Last statement: "Good-bye to all my friends. Be cool. Thank you for being my friends. Give my love to everybody."

Pronounced dead: 12:21 A.M.

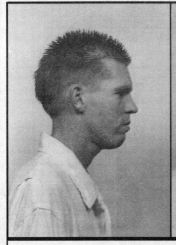

Kenneth Brock

Executed: June 19, 1986

Personal data: *Born:* n/a. *Race:* White. *Height:* n/a. *Weight:* n/a. *Education:* n/a. *Prior occupation:* n/a. *County of conviction:* Harris. *Age at time of execution:* 37.

Sentenced to death for: Convicted in the 1974 robbery and shooting death of 7-Eleven store manager Michael Sedita.

Received at death row: March 27, 1975. *Time on death row:* 4,102 days (11.24 years).

Last meal: Large double-meat cheeseburger with mustard, and Dr Pepper.

Last statement: "I have no last words. I am ready."

Pronounced dead: 12:18 A.M.

16

Randy Lynn Woolls

Executed: August 20, 1986

TEXAS
EX646
1979

Personal data: *Born:* November 21, 1949. *Race:* White. *Height:* 5'11".
Weight: 182 pounds. *Education:* 10 years. *Prior occupation:* Carpenter.
County of conviction: Tom Green. *Age at time of execution:* 36.

Sentenced to death for: Convicted of capital murder in the death of Betty Stotts,
age 43, a ticket teller at the Bolero Drive-In in Kerrville. On June 16, 1979,
Woolls entered the ticket booth of the drive-in, hit Ms. Stotts on the head
with a blunt instrument, stabbed her repeatedly, and then set her on fire.
Woolls took $600 from the cash register, stole Ms. Stotts's car, and drove it
into the drive-in. Stotts's car was recognized and Woolls was arrested on-site;
the stolen cash was in his pocket. Woolls was said to be under the influence
of Valium and beer.

Received at death ow: November 15, 1979. *Time on death row:* 2,470 days
(6.77 years).

Last meal: Two cheeseburgers, fries, and iced tea. He later requested chocolate cake.

Last statement: "Good-bye to my family. I love all of you. I'm sorry for the
victim's family. I wish I could make it up to them. I want those out there to
keep fighting the death penalty."

Pronounced dead: 12:23 A.M.

17

Larry Smith

Executed:
August 22, 1986

Personal data: *Born:* August 26, 1955. *Race:* Black. *Height:* n/a. *Weight:* n/a. *Education:* n/a. *Prior occupation:* Laborer. *County of conviction:* Dallas. *Age at time of execution:* 30.

Sentenced to death for: Convicted of killing Mike Mason, a night manager of a 7-Eleven store in Dallas, on February 3, 1978. Mason and Fred Norris were working the midnight shift when Larry Smith and Gloster Ray Smith entered the store at 3:15 A.M. and demanded the safe be opened. Mason did not have the two keys needed to open the safe. Smith then took the cash drawer and shot Mason once in the back of the head as he lay facedown on the floor.

Received at death row: September 19, 1979. *Time on death row:* 2,529 days (6.93 years).

Last meal: Smothered steak and gravy, french fries, lemon pie, and Coke.

Last statement: "Tell my mother I love her and continue on without me. Tell the guys on death row to continue their struggle to get off death row. That's about it."

Pronounced dead: 12:24 A.M.

18

Chester Wicker

Executed:
August 26, 1986

Photographs Not Available

Personal data: *Born:* August 28, 1948. *Race:* White. *Height:* 6'1". *Weight:* n/a. *Education:* 10 years. *Prior occupation:* Shrimper. *County of conviction:* Galveston. *Age at time of execution:* 37.

Sentenced to death for: Convicted in the April 1980 slaying of Suzanne C. Kruth, 22. Kruth was abducted from a Beaumont shopping center and taken to an isolated location near Galveston Beach. Wicker choked her, then buried her alive. Wicker confessed to the crime and led officials to the location of the body.

Received at death row: March 5, 1981. *Time on death row:* 2,000 days (5.48 years).

Last meal: Lettuce and tomatoes.

Last statement: "I love you."

Pronounced dead: 12:20 A.M.

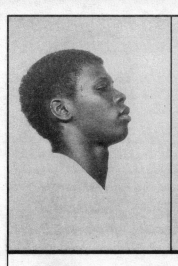

Michael Wayne Evans

Executed: December 4, 1986

Personal data: *Born:* November 13, 1956. *Race:* Black. *Height:* n/a. *Weight:* n/a. *Education:* n/a. *Prior Occupation:* Auto mechanic. *County of conviction:* Dallas. *Age at time of execution:* 30.

Sentenced to death for: Convicted of capital murder in the June 1977 shooting death of 36-year-old Elvira Guerrero during a robbery in the Oak Cliff area of Dallas. Guerrero, a pianist with the Second Mexican Baptist Church in Oak Cliff, was leaving church with friend Mario Garza when they were abducted by Evans and his codefendant, Earl Stanley Smith. In a statement to police, Evans admitted robbing Guerrero of $40, shooting her twice, and then cutting her face with a carpet knife as she prayed to God to forgive her attacker. Garza was also found shot to death.
Codefendant: Earl Stanley Smith received a life sentence for murder.

Received at death row: September 8, 1978. *Time on death row:* 3,009 days (8.24 years).

Last meal: Declined last meal.

Last statement: "I want to say I'm sorry for the things I've done and I hope I'm forgiven. I don't hold nothing against no one. Everyone has treated me well and I know it's not easy for them. That's all, I'm sorry."

Pronounced dead: 12:21 A.M.

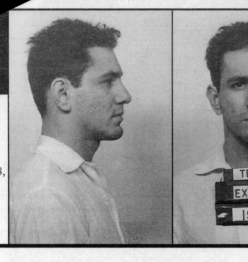

20

Richard Andrade

Executed: December 18, 1986

Personal data: *Born:* April 4, 1961. *Race:* Hispanic. *Height:* 5'10". *Weight:* 169 pounds. *Education:* 7 years. *Prior occupation:* House leveler, forklift operator. *County of conviction:* Nueces. *Age at time of execution:* 25.

Sentenced to death for: Convicted of stabbing Cordelia Mae Guevara more than fourteen times in the course of sexually assaulting her in Corpus Christi on March 20, 1984.

Received at death row: November 9, 1984. *Time on death row:* 769 days (2.11 years).

Last meal: Pizza, pinto beans, Spanish rice, and cake.

Last statement: None.

Pronounced dead: 12:32 A.M.

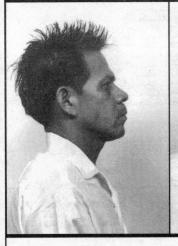

Ramon Hernandez

Executed: January 30, 1987

Personal data: *Born:* March 2, 1942. *Race:* Hispanic. *Height:* 5'3". *Weight:* 130 pounds. *Education:* 9 years. *Prior occupation:* Welder. *County of conviction:* El Paso. *Age at time of execution:* 44.

Sentenced to death for: Convicted of capital murder in the June 20, 1980, shooting death of Oscar Martin Frayre, a mechanic at a gas station in El Paso. Frayre, who was staying overnight at the station, was shot three times after Hernandez broke in and robbed the station.

Received at death row: September 30, 1980. *Time on death row:* 2,313 days (6.34 years).

Last meal: Beef tacos, beef enchiladas, jalapeño peppers, salad, onions, hot sauce, shredded cheese, and coffee.

Last statement: "Only to my wife: I love her. Only to my kids: I love my kids. [Looking at his wife] I will always love you. You know that."

Pronounced dead: 1:13 A.M.

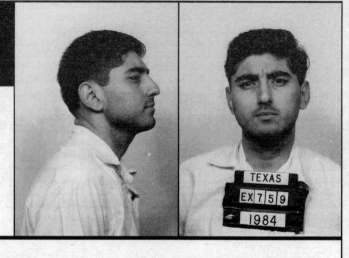

22

Eliseo Hernandez Moreno

Executed:
March 4, 1987

TEXAS
EX 7 5 9
1984

Personal data: *Born:* September 15, 1959. *Race:* Hispanic. *Height:* 5'9". *Weight:* 155 pounds. *Education:* 10 years. *Prior occupation:* Mechanic. *County of conviction:* Fort Bend. *Age at time of execution:* 27.

Sentenced to death for: Convicted of capital murder in the October 11, 1983, shooting death of Texas Department of Public Safety trooper Russell Lynn Boyd near Hempstead. Boyd, 25, was one of six people prosecutors said Moreno killed during a 160-mile crime spree that started in College Station with the slaying of his brother-in-law, Juan Garza, and Garza's wife, Esther Garza. Boyd was shot to death after stopping Moreno on Texas 6 north of Hempstead for a traffic violation. Moreno was also charged with the shooting deaths of James Bennatte, 62, Allie Wilkins, 79, and Ann Bennatt, 70, in Hempstead. Moreno later kidnapped a family of five and forced them to drive him to Pasadena, Texas. He then abducted a Friendswood man, who, at gunpoint, drove Moreno south on U.S. 59 toward the Rio Grande Valley. DPS officers stopped the car at a roadblock in Wharton County and arrested Moreno. In October 1985, Moreno pleaded guilty to murder in the Garza killings and was given a forty-five-year sentence. Prosecutors said Moreno killed the Garzas because they wouldn't help him find his estranged wife.

Received at death row: February 14, 1984. *Time on death row:* 1,114 days (3.05 years).

Last meal: Four cheese enchiladas, two fish patties, french fries, milk, ketchup, and lemon pie.

Last statement: "I'm here because I'm guilty. I have no grudges against anyone. I am paying according to the laws of the State of Texas."

Pronounced dead: 12:19 A.M.

23

Anthony Charles Williams

Executed: May 28, 1987

TEXAS
EX 6 1 9
1978

Personal data: *Born:* November 8, 1959. *Race:* Black. *Height:* 5'9". *Weight:* 169 pounds. *Education:* 11 years. *Prior occupation:* Carpenter. *County of conviction:* Harris. *Age at time of execution:* 27.

Sentenced to death for: Convicted in the June 1978 death of Vickie Lynn Wright, 13, who was abducted from a bowling alley, sexually assaulted, and then beaten to death with a board.

Received at death row: November 8, 1978. *Time on death row:* 3,123 days (8.56 years).

Last meal: Fish, tartar sauce, french fries, ketchup, white bread, and milk.

Last statement: "Mother, I am sorry for all the pain I've caused you. Please forgive me. Take good care of yourself. Ernest and Otis, watch out for the family. Thank all of you who have helped me."

Pronounced dead: 12:22 A.M.

24

**Elliot
Rod
Johnson**

Executed:
June 24,
1987

Personal data: *Born:* August 17, 1958. *Race:* Black. *Height:* 5'7". *Weight:* 164 pounds. *Education:* n/a. *Prior occupation:* n/a. *County of conviction:* Jefferson. *Age at time of execution:* 28.

Sentenced to death for: Convicted of capital murder in the April 1982 execution-style shooting death of 67-year-old Joseph Granado during a robbery at Granado's jewelry store. Store clerk Arturo Melendez, 45, was also killed in the robbery. Both victims were shot in the head at close range after being ordered to lie on the floor. A quantity of jewelry taken in the robbery was later found at the home of Johnson's codefendant, Maurice Andrews, of Port Arthur.

Received at death row: May 27, 1983. *Time on death row:* 1,489 days (4.08 years).

Last meal: A cheeseburger and fries.

Last statement: "I am very sorry for bringing all the pain and hurt to the family. I hope you find it in your heart to forgive me. Try not to worry too much about me. Remember one thing, Mother, I love you."

Pronounced dead: 12:55 A.M.

25

John R. Thompson

Executed: July 8, 1987

Personal data: *Born:* January 27, 1955. *Race:* White. *Height:* n/a. *Weight:* n/a. *Education:* n/a. *Prior occupation:* Laborer. *County of conviction:* Bexar. *Age at time of execution:* 32.

Sentenced to death for: Convicted of capital murder in the May 1977 shooting death of 70-year-old Mary Kneupper during a robbery attempt at her mini-storage business in San Antonio. Kneupper was shot in the neck with a .45 caliber pistol and later died at a San Antonio hospital.

Received at death row: September 25, 1978. *Time on death row:* 3,208 days (8.79 years).

Last meal: Fresh-squeezed orange juice.

Last statement: None.

Pronounced dead: 12:20 A.M.

26

Joseph Starvaggi

Executed: September 10, 1987

Personal data: *Born:* November 1, 1952. *Race:* White. *Height:* 5'9" *Weight:* 154 pounds. *Education:* n/a. *Prior occupation:* n/a. *County of conviction:* Montgomery. *Age at time of execution:* 34.

Sentenced to death for: Convicted in the November 19, 1976, shooting death of 43-year-old John Denson, a Montgomery County juvenile probation officer and reserve deputy sheriff, during a burglary at the officer's home in Magnolia. Starvaggi admitted during his trial that he went to Denson's home with two accomplices to steal his gun collection. Starvaggi shot Denson when the officer struggled with one of the intruders and wrestled his gun away. Starvaggi said he then shot Denson two more times to "keep him from suffering." Denson's 13-year-old daughter, who was taken upstairs with her mother, testified that she heard her father beg for mercy after he was shot once, saying, "I beg of you, don't do this." The accomplices reportedly urged Starvaggi to kill Denson's wife and daughter, but he refused, saying he only killed "dopers and pigs." *Codefendants:* Glenn Earl Martin and G. W. Green were convicted of capital murder in Montgomery County. Martin was sentenced to life in prison; Green was given the death penalty and executed on November 12, 1991. (See entry 42, G. W. Green.)

Received at death row: March 17, 1978. *Time on death row:* 3,464 days (9.49 years).

Last meal: Declined last meal.

Last statement: None.

Pronounced dead: 12:30 A.M.

Robert Streetman

Executed: January 7, 1988

Personal data: *Born:* n/a. *Race:* White. *Height:* 5'11". *Weight:* 150 pounds. *Education:* 9 years. *Prior occupation:* Derrick hand. *County of conviction:* Hardin. *Age at time of execution:* 27.

Sentenced to death for: Convicted in the December 1982 robbery-slaying of 44-year-old Christine Baker, of Kountze. Baker was shot in the head with a .22 caliber rifle while she sat knitting and watching television in the living room of her home, four miles south of Kountze. The fatal shot was fired through a window from outside the residence. Streetman and three other men had planned to rob Baker and her husband, Nyle, of $180,000 they believed the couple had in the home. Court records indicate the couple kept about $50,000 in cash and cashier's checks in the residence, but only Mrs. Baker's purse and the dollar in change inside were taken. Streetman, who began a life of crime upon becoming involved with drugs at age 8, reportedly told an accomplice on the way to the Baker home that he was "going to do something I've always wanted to do—kill another human being." Streetman's accomplice Gary Wayne Holden pleaded guilty to theft and was given ten years of probation for testimony against Streetman. Accomplice David Kirkindoll was given forty-five years for burglary of a habitation. Johnny Johnson, Kirkindoll's stepfather, who helped plan the robbery, was given immunity in the case.

Received at death row: August 11, 1983. *Time on death row:* 1,610 days (4.41 years).

Last meal: Six scrambled eggs, flour tortillas, french fries, and ketchup.

Last statement: None.

Pronounced dead: 3:26 A.M.

28

Donald Gene Franklin

Executed: November 3, 1988

TEXAS
EX 546
1976

Personal data: *Born:* September 21, 1951. *Race:* Black. *Height:* 6'0". *Weight:* 198 pounds. *Education:* n/a. *Prior occupation:* n/a. *County of conviction:* Nueces. *Age at time of execution:* 37.

Sentenced to death for: Convicted of capital murder in connection with the death of Mary Margaret Moran, of San Antonio, on July 25, 1975. Moran was kidnapped as she approached her car in the parking lot of the Audie L. Murphy Memorial Veteran's Administration Hospital following her shift. Two witnesses saw Franklin driving his car at a high rate of speed from the parking lot, where Moran's car was later found. Franklin was found at his home several hours later, after police traced the license plate number of his car. Police found his pants soaking in a pail of bloody water and found several of the nurse's personal items in a trash can. Five days later, Moran was found nude and barely alive in a field near the hospital. She suffered from irreversible shock and died the next morning.

Received at death row: May 5, 1976. *Time on death row:* 4,565 days (12.51 years).

Last meal: A hamburger, french fries, and ketchup.

Last statement: None.

Pronounced dead: 12:30 A.M.

29

Raymond Landry

Executed: December 13, 1988

Personal data: *Born:* n/a. *Race:* Black. *Height:* 6'10". *Weight:* 198 pounds. *Education:* n/a. *Prior occupation:* n/a. *County of conviction:* Harris. *Age at time of execution:* 39.

Sentenced to death for: Convicted of capital murder in the August 6, 1982, shooting death of 33-year-old Kosmas Prittis, owner of the Dairy Maid restaurant in the 7100 block of East Bellfort in Houston. Prittis was robbed of more than $2,300 and then shot in the head while he and his family were closing up the restaurant. Witnesses testified that Landry slapped Prittis's wife and pointed a gun at the children before fleeing. Landry was arrested at his home in the 7300 block of Eisenhower three days after the shooting. Police found a bank bag from the restaurant at the house.

Received at death row: May 24, 1983. *Time on death row:* 2,030 days (5.56 years).

Last meal: Declined last meal.

Last statement: None.

Pronounced dead: 12:45 A.M.
Note: Two minutes into the procedure, the tube attached to his right arm sprang a leak, spraying solution into the air and halting the execution. It took fourteen minutes to reinsert the lethal injection needle and restart the execution. Officials blamed the delay on a mechanical problem caused by Landry's muscular arms and previous drug use.

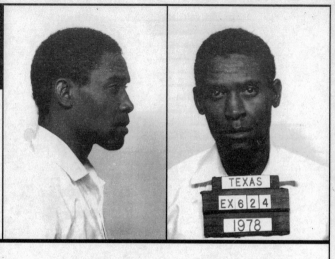

30

Leon Rutherford King

Executed: March 22, 1989

Personal data: *Born:* May 22, 1944. *Race:* Black. *Height:* 6'2". *Weight:* 176 pounds. *Education:* 10 years. *Prior occupation:* Bricklayer. *County of conviction:* Harris. *Age at time of execution:* 44.

Sentenced to death for: King and Allan Ray Carter abducted Michael Clayton Underwood, 26, and his 19-year-old girlfriend at gunpoint from a Houston nightclub on April 10, 1976. King and Carter took Underwood and his girlfriend to a remote area, where Underwood was beaten to death with the butt of a shotgun as the young girl was forced to watch. The woman was raped and sodomized. She later identified King and Carter as her attackers. *Codefendant:* Allan Ray Carter was sentenced to life in prison because he was 16 years old at the time of the crime.

Received at death row: December 5, 1978. *Time on death row:* 3,760 days (10.30 years).

Last meal: Declined last meal.

Last statement: "I would like to tell Mr. Richard [Richard Wells, a witness] I appreciate what you've done for me. I love you."

Pronounced dead: 12:27 A.M.

31

Stephen A. McCoy

Executed: May 24, 1989

Personal data: *Born:* December 17, 1948. *Race:* White. *Height:* 6'0". *Weight:* 175 pounds. *Education:* 7 years (GED). *Prior occupation:* Electrician. *County of conviction:* Harris. *Age at time of execution:* 40.

Sentenced to death for: Convicted of capital murder in the January 1, 1981, rape-strangulation death of 18-year-old Cynthia Johnson, in Houston. Johnson was abducted by McCoy and codefendants James Emery Paster and Gary Louis LeBlanc after her car broke down returning from a New Year's Eve party. Evidence showed that McCoy raped the woman and then held her legs while Paster and LeBlanc strangled her with electrical wire. The three men were tied to the October 1980 murder-for-hire of Robert Edward Howard and the November 1980 rape and stabbing of Diane Trevino Oliver. Paster was sentenced to death for the shooting of Howard and life in prison for Johnson's murder. LeBlanc testified for the state and was given a thirty-five-year sentence for murder. McCoy, who was in prison on a five-year sentence for burglary when charged in the Johnson murder, was also charged with accessory to murder and given a concurrent thirty-year prison term. Courtroom testimony indicated that Johnson was killed because McCoy and his codefendants agreed that they would each kill someone in front of each other and thus seal their mutual trust in blood.
Note: Paster was executed on September 20, 1989. (See entry 32, James Emery Paster.)

Received at death row: August 2, 1984. *Time on death row:* 1,756 days (4.81 years).

Last meal: A cheeseburger, french fries, and a strawberry milk shake.

Last statement: None.

Pronounced dead: 12:25 A.M.

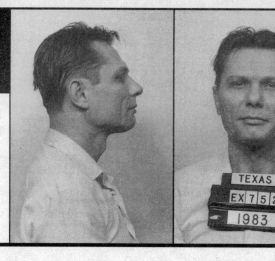

32

James Emery Paster

Executed: September 20, 1989

Personal data: *Born:* January 30, 1945. *Race:* White. *Height:* 5'8". *Weight:* 156 pounds. *Education:* 12 years. *Prior occupation:* Cook. *County of conviction:* Harris. *Age at time of execution:* 44.

Sentenced to death for: Convicted of capital murder in the shooting death of 38-year-old Robert Edward Howard in Houston on October 25, 1980. Howard was shot in the head outside a southeast Houston lounge where Paster worked. Testimony supported allegations that Howard's ex-wife, Trudy, hired Paster to kill her former husband for $1,000. She was convicted of murder with a deadly weapon and sentenced to life in prison. Along with Paster, 40-year-old Gary L. LeBlanc and 38-year-old Stephen McCoy were implicated in the contract slaying of Howard as well as the January 1981 rape-strangulation death of 18-year-old Cynthia Johnson, of Conroe, and the November 1980 rape-stabbing death of 27-year-old Diane Trevino Oliver near Channelview.

Received at death row: November 22, 1983. *Time on death row:* 2,129 days (5.83 years).

Last meal: T-bone steak, dinner salad, french fries, and watermelon.

Last statement: "I hope Mrs. Howard can find peace in this."

Pronounced dead: 12:17 A.M.

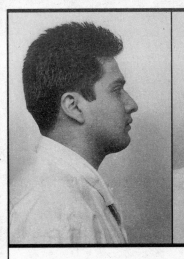

33

Carlos De Luna

Executed: December 7, 1989

Personal data: *Born:* March 15, 1962. *Race:* Hispanic. *Height:* 5'8". *Weight:* 185 pounds. *Education:* 9 years. *Prior occupation:* Electrician. *County of conviction:* Nueces. *Age at time of execution:* 27.

Sentenced to death for: Convicted in the February 2, 1983, robbery-slaying of 24-year-old Wanda Jean Lopez, a Corpus Christi service station clerk. Police said Lopez was stabbed to death minutes after she phoned police and attempted to describe her assailant to the dispatcher. Her final words recorded by police were, "You want it {money}. I'll give it to you. I'll give it to you. I'm not going to do nothing to you. Please." De Luna took an undetermined amount of money and fled on foot. Police found him hiding under a truck parked in the area. De Luna contended that another person killed Lopez and that he ran so he would not be implicated.

Received at death row: July 6, 1983. *Time on death row:* 2,346 days (6.43 years).

Last meal: Declined last meal.

Last statement: "I want to say that I hold no grudges. I hate no one. I love my family. Tell everyone on death row to keep the faith and don't give up."

Pronounced dead: 12:24 A.M.

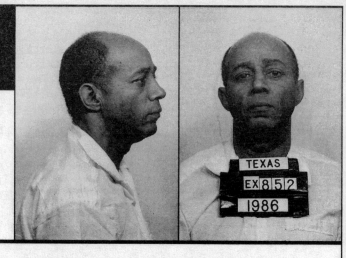

34

Jerome Butler

Executed:
April 21,
1990

Personal data: *Born:* April 7, 1936. *Race:* Black. *Height:* 5'6". *Weight:* 141 pounds. *Education:* 9 years (GED). *Prior occupation:* Delivery driver. *County of conviction:* Harris. *Age at time of execution:* 54.

Sentenced to death for: Convicted of capital murder in the shooting death of 67-year-old Nathan Oakley, a Houston cab driver, on June 17, 1986. Butler hailed Oakley's cab at the intersection of Blodgett and Scott at 4 P.M. After riding a short distance, Butler pulled out a pistol and shot Oakley three times in the back of the head. The prosecutor said Oakley's pockets were turned inside out and all his money was missing. Oakley, who drove a Skyjack cab, was believed to have been carrying more than $300. Prosecutors said Butler may have killed Oakley because the cab driver recognized him as the man who killed his good friend A. C. Johnson in 1973. Ironically, State District Judge Wallace Moore presided over both the Johnson murder case and the Oakley capital murder case.

Received at death row: November 26, 1986. *Time on death row:* 1,242 days (3.40 years).

Last meal: T-bone steak, four pieces of chicken (two breasts and two legs), fresh corn, and iced tea.

Last statement: "I wish everybody a good life. Everything is OK."

Pronounced dead: 12:26 A.M.

35

Johnny Anderson

Executed: May 17, 1990

TEXAS
EX 732
1983

Personal data: *Born:* December 28, 1959. *Race:* White. *Height:* 5'9". *Weight:* 185 pounds. *Education:* 6 years. *Prior occupation:* Mechanic. *County of conviction:* Jefferson. *Age at time of execution:* 30.

Sentenced to death for: Shot and killed his brother-in-law, Ronald Gene Goode, 22, of Kountze, in a scheme to collect insurance money. Anderson, his sister, the victim's wife, and her mother conspired to kill Goode to collect $67,000. The victim's widow and Anderson's sister were both convicted of capital murder and sentenced to life in prison.
Note: Anderson was named as a suspect in a December 1984 stabbing incident on death row. Inmate Kenneth D. Dunn was stabbed seven times in a dayroom after he and Anderson allegedly argued over a television program. Dunn, stabbed with a fan guard, was treated at the unit and released back to his cell.

Received at death row: February 15, 1983. *Time on death row:* 2,648 days (7.25 years).

Last meal: Three hamburgers, french fries, chocolate ice cream with nuts, and iced tea.

Last statement: "I would like to point out that I have written a statement and the warden will give you a copy. I still proclaim I am innocent, and that's all I have to say." See Appendix for written statement.

Pronounced dead: 12:30 A.M.

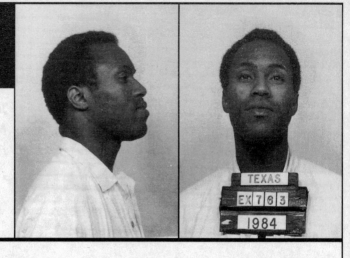

36

James Smith

Executed:
June 26, 1990

TEXAS
EX 7 6 3
1984

Personal data: *Born:* October 19, 1952. *Race:* Black. *Height:* 5'10". *Weight:* 158 pounds. *Education:* 14 years. *Prior occupation:* Retail merchant. *County of conviction*: Harris. *Age at time of execution:* 37.

Sentenced to death for: Convicted in the March 1983 shooting death of Larry Don Rohus during a robbery of offices inside the International Trade Center Building, in Houston. Rohus, district manager for the Union Life Insurance Company, and another employee were in the company's cashier's office when Smith approached with a pistol and demanded money. When the second employee fled and hid behind a filing cabinet, Rohus complied with Smith's instructions and placed an undetermined amount of money inside a small trash can and put it on a table near the robber. As Rohus began to walk away, Smith called him back and fired a shot as Rohus pleaded for his life. Rohus ran but was shot through the heart and killed. Smith was arrested a short time later in a nearby apartment complex after being pursued on foot by one of Rohus's coworkers, a businessman on the street, and a crew of workers at the apartment complex.
Note: At one point during the jury selection of his trial, Smith ran from the courthouse. He was captured several blocks away by a police officer.

Received at death row: April 5, 1984. *Time on death row:* 2,273 days (6.23 years).

Last meal: Yogurt.

Last statement: See Appendix.

Pronounced dead: 12:31 A.M.
Note: The U.S. Supreme Court voted in the case. The court had enough votes to support review of the inmate's case (4) but not enough votes to grant a stay (5). Court rules allowed the execution to proceed.

37

Mikel James Derrick

Executed: July 18, 1990

Personal data: *Born:* February 10, 1957. *Race:* White. *Height:* 5'11". *Weight:* 201 pounds. *Education:* 8 years. *Prior occupation:* Laborer. *County of conviction:* Harris. *Age at time of execution:* 33.

Sentenced to death for: Convicted in the October 1980 robbery-slaying of 32-year-old Edward Sonnier, of Houston. Sonnier reportedly took Derrick home with him to his Montrose apartment, where the two smoked marijuana. Derrick told authorities he stabbed Sonnier fifteen times when the victim allegedly made an unwelcome homosexual advance toward him. Derrick stole Sonnier's car, which he later stripped down with the help of friends. Police had no suspect in the killing until Derrick wrote to Harris County District Attorney John Holmes saying, "I killed a man to get his car." Derrick wrote from prison, where he was serving time for robbery. He said in the letter that he had heard his brother might be wrongly charged in the theft of Sonnier's car.

Received at death row: January 19, 1982. *Time on death row:* 3,102 days (8.50 years).

Last meal: Rib-eye steak, tossed green salad with blue cheese dressing, and baked potato with sour cream.

Last statement: "I just ask everybody I ever hurt or done anything wrong to, to just forgive me for whatever wrongs I done to them."

Pronounced dead: 12:17 A.M.

38

Lawrence Lee Buxton

Executed: February 26, 1991

Personal data: *Born:* September 16, 1952. *Race:* Black. *Height:* 5'10". *Weight:* 230 pounds. *Education:* 10 years. *Prior occupation:* Truck driver/meat cutter. *County of conviction:* Harris. *Age at time of execution:* 38.

Sentenced to death for: Convicted of capital murder in the September 19, 1980, shooting death of Joel Slotnik during a grocery store robbery in Houston. Buxton and two unknown codefendants robbed the Safeway store at Fry Road and Interstate 10 West. After the robbers had taken money from a cash register and left for the getaway car, Buxton shot Slotnik, a customer, because Slotnik's 5-year-old son, Aaron, would not get down on the floor as ordered. Slotnik died on September 23, 1980, from a neck wound.

Received at death row: July 5, 1983. *Time on death row:* 2,793 days (7.65 years).

Last meal: Filet mignon, pineapple upside-down cake, tea, punch, and coffee.

Last statement: "I'm ready, Warden."

Pronounced dead: 12:21 A.M.

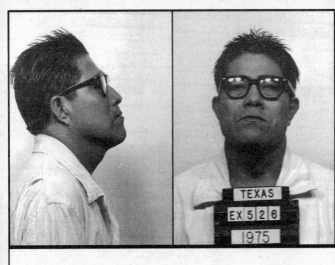

39

Ignacio Cuevas

Executed: May 23, 1991

Personal data: *Born:* July 31, 1931. *Race:* Hispanic. *Height:* 5'2". *Weight:* 140 pounds. *Education:* None. *Prior occupation:* House mover. *County of conviction:* Harris. *Age at time of execution:* 59.

Sentenced to death for: Cuevas and his two codefendants (Fred Carrasco and Rudy Dominquez) shot and killed two hostages, Julia Standley and Elizabeth Beseda, in an escape attempt from the Huntsville Unit Library. Cuevas admits that he helped Carrasco in the escape attempt but denies that he was armed at the time the murders occurred. Cuevas was convicted for the murder of Julia Standley. He escaped injury of any type during the last moments of the siege (reportedly, he fainted). Cuevas had been convicted twice of capital murder and twice sentenced to death.
Note: To make their escape, Cuevas and his codefendants rigged a four-sided shield made of rolling chalkboards lined with thick library books, and they handcuffed eight hostages to the outside. Officials at first turned fire hoses on the shield, then gunfire erupted. Carrasco was said to have shot Elizabeth Beseda and then himself.

Received at death row: May 30, 1975. *Time on death row:* 5,837 days (15.99 years).

Last meal: Chicken and dumplings, steamed rice, black-eyed peas, sliced bread, and iced tea.

Last statement: "I am going to a beautiful place. OK, Warden, roll 'em."

Pronounced dead: 12:18 A.M.

40

**Jerry
Joe
Bird**

Executed:
June 17,
1991

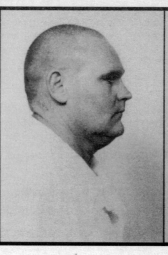

Personal data: *Born:* April 2, 1937. *Race:* White. *Height:* 5'11". *Weight:* 214 pounds. *Education:* 14 years. *Prior occupation:* Machinist. *County of conviction:* Cameron. *Age at time of execution:* 54.

Sentenced to death for: Convicted of capital murder in the January 1974 slaying of Victor Trammel in Corpus Christi. Trammel and his wife, Jo Ellen, were robbed of a valuable antique gun collection by Bird and accomplice Emmett L. Korges. The two men, who gained entrance to the Trammels' house with claims they had guns to sell, handcuffed and bound the husband and wife and placed them in separate bedrooms. Mrs. Trammel testified she heard a muffled gunshot before she managed to slip from her restraints and flee the house through a rear window. She hid in a drainage ditch until realizing her home had been set afire. Her husband's badly burned body was found inside the house. He had been shot twice with a .22 caliber pistol fitted with a silencer.

Received at death row: September 16, 1974. *Time on death row:* 6,118 days (16.76 years).

Last meal: Double cheeseburger with mustard, mayonnaise, pickles, onions, and tomatoes, and iced tea.

Last statement: "I don't think so. That's all. Go ahead. Start things rolling." [Mouthed "Hi Mom" to his mother.]

Pronounced dead: 12:21 A.M.

TEXAS
EX 5 7 9
1977

41

James Russell

Executed: September 19, 1991

Personal data: *Born:* March 5, 1949. *Race:* Black. *Height:* 5'9". *Weight:* 150 pounds. *Education:* 10 years. *Prior occupation:* Musician. *County of conviction:* Fort Bend. *Age at time of execution:* 42.

Sentenced to death for: Convicted in the March 1974 abduction and shooting death of 24-year-old Thomas Robert Stearns, of Houston. Stearns, manager of a Radio Shack store at 10810 W. Bellfort, was abducted after leaving his home and driven to a wooded area near Arcola, where he was shot twice in the head. Trial testimony indicated Russell killed Stearns because Stearns was a witness to an April 1972 robbery of the same Radio Shack store by Russell. Russell was out of jail on bond when Stearns was killed. He had been convicted in March 1977 of robbery and given a fifty-year prison sentence based on testimony given by Stearns during a 1972 examining trial.

Received at death row: November 30, 1977. *Time on death row:* 5,041 days (13.81 years).

Last meal: An apple.

Last statement: His exact final statement was not recorded, but it lasted three minutes. He thanked everybody who fought against his sentence. He spoke to his family and said he would carry their love with him.

Pronounced dead: 12:20 A.M.

42

G. W. Green

Executed:
November 12, 1991

TEXAS
EX 576
1977

Personal data: *Born:* November 21, 1936. *Race:* White. *Height:* 5'5".
Weight: 130 pounds. *Education:* 14 years. *Prior occupation:* Cement mason.
County of conviction: Montgomery. *Age at time of execution:* 54.

Sentenced to death for: Convicted in the November 1976 shooting death of
43-year-old John Denson, a Montgomery County juvenile probation officer
and reserve deputy sheriff, during a burglary at the officer's home in
Magnolia. Green and accomplices Joseph Starvaggi and Glenn Earl Martin
went to Denson's home to steal his gun collection. Starvaggi shot Denson
when the officer struggled with one of the intruders and wrestled his gun
away. Starvaggi then shot Denson two more times but declined Green's
alleged urgings to kill the officer's wife and 13-year-old daughter.
Note: Starvaggi was executed on September 10, 1987. (See entry 26, Joseph
Starvaggi.)

Received at death row: October 13, 1977. *Time on death row:* 5,143 days
(14.09 years).

Last meal: Pizza, coffee, and tea.

Last statement: "Let's do it, man. Lock and load. Ain't life a [expletive deleted]?"

Pronounced dead: 12:17 A.M.

43

Joe Angel Cordova

Executed:
January 22, 1992

Personal data: *Born:* March 29, 1952. *Race:* Hispanic. *Height:* 5'7". *Weight:* 143 pounds. *Education:* 14 years. *Prior occupation:* Carpenter. *County of conviction:* Harris. *Age at time of execution:* 39.

Sentenced to death for: Convicted in the February 27, 1982, murder-robbery of Masel Williams, 32. Williams was abducted from a phone booth on Little York near the Eastex Freeway and taken to a wooded area, where he was stripped and shot in the chest at close range with a shotgun.
Codefendant: Paul Guillory was convicted of aggravated robbery, sentenced to 15 years, and paroled in March 1987.

Received at death row: December 30, 1982. *Time on death row:* 3,310 days (9.07 years).

Last meal: Fried chicken, french fries, hot sauce, rolls, salad with thousand island dressing, and ice cream.

Last statement: None.

Pronounced dead: 12:18 A.M.

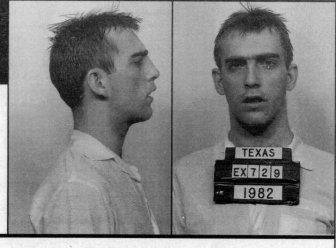

44

Johnny Frank Garrett

Executed: February 11, 1992

TEXAS
EX 7 2 9
1982

Personal data: *Born:* December 24, 1963. *Race:* White. *Height:* 5'11".
Weight: 152 pounds. *Education:* 7 years. *Prior occupation:* Laborer. *County of conviction:* Potter. *Age at time of execution:* 28.

Sentenced to death for: Convicted in the October 1981 murder of Sister Tadea Benz, a 76-year-old nun of the St. Francis Convent in Amarillo. Sister Benz was raped, strangled, beaten, and stabbed in her second-floor room at the convent. Garrett's fingerprints were found at the convent, located across the street from his home. In a statement to police, Garrett admitted breaking in to the convent and said he strangled and raped the nun after she awoke and found him in her room.
Note: Garrett was 17 years of age at the time of the offense.

Received at death row: December 15, 1982. *Time on death row:* 3,345 days (9.16 years).

Last meal: Ice cream.

Last statement: None.

Pronounced dead: 12:18 A.M.

45

David M. Clark

Executed: February 28, 1992

Personal data: *Born:* March 5, 1959. *Race:* White. *Height:* 5'8". *Weight:* 145 pounds. *Education:* 10 years (GED). *Prior occupation:* Construction. *County of conviction:* Brazos. *Age at time of execution:* 32.

Sentenced to death for: Convicted in the murders of Beverly Benninghoff and Charles Gears at their residence on February 18, 1987. Investigative reports indicate that the victims were shot, stabbed, and clubbed to death. A .25 caliber gun, a club, and a knife were used in the slayings. Clark and three codefendants were arrested for the murders on February 20, 1987. *Codefendants:* Mary Copeland was convicted of murder and sentenced to life. Gary Penuel was convicted of burglary and sentenced to thirty years.

Received at death row: June 30, 1987. *Time on death row:* 1,704 days (4.67 years).

Last meal: Clark told officials he wanted to fast.

Last statement: None. But as he lay there he said, "Praise the Lord," and he seemed to be praying.

Pronounced dead: 1:38 A.M.

46

Edward Ellis

Executed:
March 3,
1992

Personal data: *Born:* June 15, 1953. *Race:* White. *Height:* 5'8". *Weight:* 133 pounds. *Education:* 10 years. *Prior occupation:* Welder/maintenance man. *County of conviction:* Harris. *Age at time of execution:* 38.

Sentenced to death for: Convicted of capital murder in the February 27, 1983, death of 74-year-old Bertie Elizabeth Eakens, of Houston. Eakens's body was found on March 1, 1983, in the bathtub of her apartment in the 2200 block of Eighteenth Street. Her hands were handcuffed, and a pillowcase had been tied around her neck so she suffocated. Her jewelry, checks, furs, and car were taken from the residence. Ellis had formerly worked as a maintenance man at Eakens's apartment complex and reportedly used a passkey to gain entrance to her apartment. The killing of Eakens and two other Houston women found in bathtubs came to be called the "bathtub slayings."

Received at death row: September 12, 1983. *Time on death row:* 3,095 days (8.48 years).

Last meal: Steak, baked potato with butter, salad, biscuits, pineapple pie, and iced tea.

Last statement: "I just want everyone to know that the prosecutor and Bill Scott are some sorry sons of bitches." [To his family he added that he loved them all.]
Note: Bill Scott was an inmate who testified against Ellis. Exact last statement was not recorded.

Pronounced dead: 3:39 A.M.
Note: Execution was delayed until the U.S. Supreme Court refused a stay at approximately 3:00 A.M.

47

Billy Wayne White

Executed: April 23, 1992

Personal data: *Born:* October 13, 1957. *Race:* Black. *Height:* 5'11". *Weight:* 167 pounds. *Education:* 10 years. *Prior occupation:* Dump truck driver. *County of conviction:* Harris. *Age at time of execution:* 34.

Sentenced to death for: Convicted in the August 1976 robbery-slaying of 65-year-old Martha Spinks, co-owner of a Houston furniture store. Spinks and her husband, Alge, were closing their store when White entered, pulled a pistol, and demanded money. Without provocation, he then shot Mrs. Spinks once in the face at point-blank range. White ordered Mr. Spinks to open the safe and then lie on the floor. When White dropped his pistol while attempting to steal rings and a watch from Mrs. Spinks's body, her husband grabbed the pistol and managed to fire two shots, striking White in the groin. White ran from the store but was captured by police a quarter of a mile away after a car lot attendant who heard the shots flagged down a patrol car. Police found $269 in stolen money in White's pants pocket.

Received at Death Row: February 24, 1978. *Time on death row:* 5,172 days (14.17 years).

Last meal: T-bone steak, french fries, and ice cream.

Last statement: None.

Pronounced dead: 12:58 A.M.

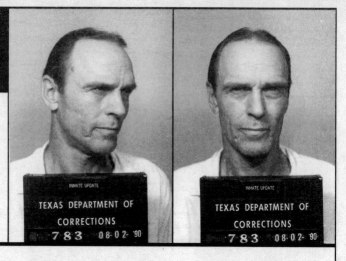

48

Justin Lee May

Executed: May 7, 1992

INMATE UPDATE

TEXAS DEPARTMENT OF CORRECTIONS

7 8 3   0 8-0 2- '90

INMATE UPDATE

TEXAS DEPARTMENT OF CORRECTIONS

7 8 3   0 8-0 2- '90

Personal data: *Born:* April 26, 1946. *Race:* White. *Height:* 6'1". *Weight:* 185 pounds. *Education:* 11 years. *Prior occupation:* Welder. *County of conviction:* Brazoria. *Age at time of execution:* 46.

Sentenced to death for: Convicted in the shooting death of 43-year-old Jeanetta Murdaugh during a robbery of the Western Auto Store she and her husband, Frank, owned and operated in Freeport. Mrs. Murdaugh died from two gunshot wounds to the head. Her husband was killed by four gunshots to the neck, chest, and back. Police believed the Murdaughs were two of five people robbed and killed by May during a two-week crime spree.
Codefendant: Richard Allen Miles was convicted of robbery and murder, sentenced to forty-two years, and paroled on December 5, 1990.

Received at death row: February 20, 1985. *Time on death row:* 2,633 days (7.21 years).

Last meal: Two cheeseburgers, ketchup, french fries, and a shake.

Last statement: He thanked his family.

Pronounced dead: 12:18 A.M.

49

Jesus Romero Jr.

Executed:
May 20,
1992

Personal data: *Born:* February 3, 1965. *Race:* Hispanic. *Height:* 5'6". *Weight:* 128 pounds. *Education:* 11 years. *Prior occupation:* Laborer. *County of conviction:* Cameron. *Age at time of execution:* 27.

Sentenced to death for: Convicted in the December 1984 rape-slaying of 15-year-old Olga Perales near San Benito. Romero and three codefendants drove Perales to a remote location 1.3 miles west of State Highway 2520, where she was raped repeatedly, beaten around the head with a pipe, and stabbed twice in the chest with a knife. Her nude body was found the same day in a brushy area off Kilgore Road.
Codefendants: Davis Losada was convicted of capital murder, received the death penalty, and was executed on June 4, 1997. (See entry 127, Davis Losada.) Jose F. Cardenas was convicted of capital murder and received a life sentence. Rafael Leyva Jr. was convicted of sexual assault and given a twenty-year sentence.

Received at death row: July 24, 1985. *Time on death row:* 2,492 days (6.83 years).

Last meal: T-bone steak, baked potato, salad, a vanilla shake, and chocolate ice cream.

Last statement: None.

Pronounced dead: 1:40 A.M.

50

Robert Black Jr.

Executed:
May 22,
1992

TEXAS
EX 819
1986

Personal data: *Born:* January 31, 1947. *Race:* White. *Height:* 5'9". *Weight:* 200 pounds. *Education:* 14 years. *Prior occupation:* Insurance salesman/electrician. *County of conviction:* Brazos. *Age at time of execution:* 45.

Sentenced to death for: Hired John Wayne Hearn to murder his wife, Sandra Black, for insurance money. The victim was found dead with two bullet wounds to the head. The house appeared to have been burglarized. During the investigation, evidence came to light that Robert Black had increased his wife's life insurance by $100,000 shortly before her death.
Codefendant: John Wayne Hearn received life in prison concurrent with two life sentences in Florida.
Note: Black hired Hearn after Hearn responded to an ad Black had placed in *Soldier of Fortune* magazine. The magazine was later ordered to pay $1.5 million in actual damages to Mrs. Black's son Gary W. Black and $400,000 to her mother.

Received at death row: February 26, 1986. *Time on death row:* 2,277 days (6.24 years).

Last meal: T-bone steak, baked potato, a bowl of lettuce, corn, a roll, a chocolate milk shake, and tea.

Last statement: None. Black began to recite the poem "High Flight" as the lethal injection began. After he recited the line "And done a hundred things you have not thought of…" he gasped and stopped breathing.

Pronounced dead: 12:20 A.M.

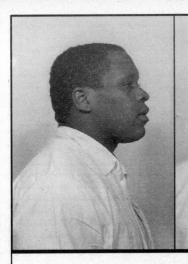

51

Curtis L. Johnson

Executed: August 11, 1992

Personal data: *Born:* April 22, 1954. *Race:* Black. *Height:* 5'9". *Weight:* 230 pounds. *Education:* 10 years. *Prior occupation:* Laborer. *County of conviction:* Harris. *Age at time of execution:* 38.

Sentenced to death for: Shot and killed Murray Dale Sweat, 25, in Houston. Sweat was shot once in the chest with a .38 caliber revolver when he returned to his apartment at 603 W. Saulnier and found Johnson and an accomplice in the kitchen. The two intruders were arrested six days later while committing aggravated robbery.
Codefendant: Roy Junior Jones was convicted of burglary of a habitation with intent to commit theft and aggravated robbery and sentenced to forty-five years.

Received at death row: March 21, 1984. *Time on death row:* 3,065 days (8.40 years).

Last meal: Scrambled eggs, bacon, toast, jelly, butter, and a strawberry milk shake.

Last statement: "I want to thank my mother and my aunt for sticking by me and to tell them that I love them very much. Everybody who participated in this is forgiven."

Pronounced dead: 12:16 A.M.

52

James Demouchette

Executed:
September
22, 1992

Personal data: *Born:* n/a. *Race:* Black. *Height:* 5'10". *Weight:* 150 pounds. *Education:* 9 years. *Prior occupation:* Painter. *County of conviction:* Harris. *Age at time of execution:* 37.

Sentenced to death for: Convicted in the October 17, 1976, shooting deaths of Scott Sorrell, 19, assistant manager, and his roommate Robert White, 20, at a Pizza Hut restaurant on Antoine Road, in northwest Houston. Both Sorrell and White were shot in the head with a .38-caliber revolver as they and restaurant manager Geoff Hambrick, 18, sat at a table with Demouchette and his brother, Christopher, after closing. Hambrick was also shot in the head by James Demouchette but survived his wound. Hambrick, who slumped over the table and played dead, testified that the Demouchette brothers ransacked the back office, taking a sack of change and a piece of stereo equipment. Before leaving the restaurant, James Demouchette heard Sorrell choking on his own blood and shot him a second time. James then turned the gun on Hambrick a second time but found it empty when he pulled the trigger. Christopher Demouchette surrendered to police the next morning and gave a written statement implicating himself and his brother in the shootings. James was arrested at his home that afternoon.

Note: James's capital-murder and death sentence were overturned in 1981 by the Texas Court of Criminal Appeals on grounds that he had not been warned of his right to remain silent by the court-appointed psychologist prior to his competency examination in 1977. He was again convicted of capital murder in April 1983 and given the death penalty.

Codefendant: Christopher Demouchette was convicted of capital murder and sentenced to life in prison.

Received at death row: August 3, 1977. *Time on death row:* 5,529 days (15.15 years).

Last meal: Grilled steak, baked potato, any vegetable except squash or okra, dessert, and anything to drink except punch or milk.

Last statement: None.

Pronounced dead: 12:22 A.M.

53

Jeffery Griffin

Executed: November 19, 1992

Personal data: *Born:* January 3, 1955. *Race:* Black. *Height:* 5'6". *Weight:* 165 pounds. *Education:* 4 years. *Prior occupation:* Laborer. *County of conviction:* Harris. *Age at time of execution:* 37.

Sentenced to death for: Convicted in the March 1979 abduction and stabbing death of 19-year-old David Sobotik, a night manager at the One Stop Drive-In grocery, at 3814 Fulton, in Houston. Sobotik and 7-year-old Horatio DeLeon, who worked as an errand boy at the store, were abducted and led to an area about ten blocks from the store, where both were repeatedly stabbed in a concise pattern around the heart. Sobotik was also robbed of personal items. The bodies of the two victims were found inside Sobotik's car the next morning. Griffin himself alerted the store's owner to the incident, saying he had seen the two victims abducted. When discrepancies were found in his story, he confessed to the murders. He was never tried in the death of DeLeon, nor was he ever tried after being charged with the murder of 20-year-old Silvia Mendoza, whose slashed body was found inside a dumpster in Houston in July 1978.

Received at death row: November 30, 1979. *Time on death row:* 4,738 days (12.98 years).

Last meal: T-bone steak (medium to well-done), french fries and ketchup, whole-kernel corn, sweet peas, lettuce and tomato salad with egg and French dressing, iced tea (sweet), saltines, ice cream, Boston cream pie, and rolls.

Last statement: See Appendix.

Pronounced dead: 12:48 A.M.

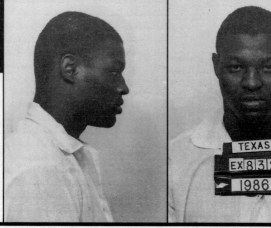

54

Kavin Lincecum

Executed: December 10, 1992

Personal data: *Born:* June 17, 1963. *Race:* Black. *Height:* 5'10". *Weight:* 178 pounds. *Education:* 10 years. *Prior occupation:* Laborer. *County of conviction:* Brazoria. *Age at time of execution:* 29.

Sentenced to death for: Convicted in the August 1985 abduction, attempted rape, and strangulation of Kathy Coppedge, a 35-year-old Brenham schoolteacher. Coppedge and her 11-year-old son, Casey, were abducted from a Brenham church parking lot and driven in their car to an isolated area about thirteen miles west of Brenham. There, Lincecum attempted to rape Mrs. Coppedge and then strangled her with a cord or rope when she resisted. At some point, he bound her hands behind her back with her purse strap. Her son's hands were also bound behind his back before he was placed into the trunk of the car, where he suffocated. Both bodies were found in the trunk of the car, which Lincecum abandoned. He took jewelry from Mrs. Coppedge and gave them to his girlfriend. He also took the boy's shoes and later sold them to a friend for $7.

Received at death row: June 5, 1986. *Time on death row:* 2,380 days (6.52 years).

Last meal: Declined last meal.

Last statement: None.

Pronounced dead: 12:18 A.M.

55

Carlos Santana

Executed: March 23, 1993

Personal data: *Born:* October 10, 1952. *Race:* Hispanic. *Height:* 5'9". *Weight:* 147 pounds. *Education:* 11 years. *Prior occupation:* Electrician. *County of conviction:* Harris. *Age at time of execution:* 40.

Sentenced to death for: Convicted in connection with the failed $1.1 million robbery of a Purolator Armored, Inc., van and the killing of 29-year-old security guard Oliver Flores in Houston on April 21, 1981. Testimony showed that Santana and accomplice James Ronald Meanes wore matching green military-like uniforms for a noon attack on the van in a department store parking lot in the 8500 block of the Gulf Freeway. A second security guard, who survived the attack, said Flores was shot even though he had not gone for his gun. Santana and Meanes were arrested shortly after the robbery in the 8900 block of Winkler. Police found a getaway car parked nearby and recovered two weapons, two green jumpsuits, and the money from the van.
Codefendant: James Ronald Meanes was convicted of capital murder, sentenced to death, and executed on December 15, 1998. (See entry 164, James Ronald Meanes.)

Received at death row: November 9, 1981. *Time on death row:* 4,152 days (11.38 years).

Last meal: Requested "justice, temperance, with mercy."

Last statement: "Love is the answer, not hatred. I love all of you guys. I will see some of you in the state of heaven. Bye."

Pronounced dead: 2:54 A.M.

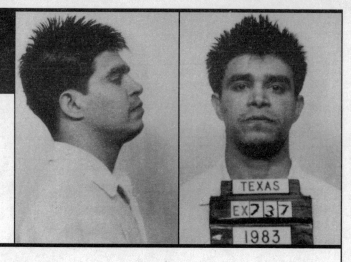

56

Ramon Montoya

Executed: March 25, 1993

TEXAS
EX737
1983

Personal data: *Born:* January 15, 1954. *Race:* Hispanic. *Height:* 5'3". *Weight:* 125 pounds. *Education:* 7 years. *Prior occupation:* Laborer. *County of conviction:* Dallas. *Age at time of execution:* 38.

Sentenced to death for: Convicted of capital murder in the shooting death of Dallas police officer John R. Pasco. Pasco was shot once in the head after chasing Montoya in the vicinity of the Spanish Villa Apartments at 1818 Park Avenue. He had gone to the apartments to check out residents' complaints about an armed man. Police said Montoya fired at Pasco's squad car as it pulled in to the complex but did not hit the officer. Pasco called for help on the car radio and then gave chase on foot. Montoya said he ran from the patrolman to avoid being arrested for carrying a weapon. He said he fell during the chase and the gun fired while he was attempting to throw the weapon away.
Note: U.S. immigration officials said Montoya had earlier been deported on a weapons charge but had reentered the country illegally.

Received at death row: May 19, 1983. *Time on death row:* 3,598 days (9.86 years).

Last meal: A cheeseburger, french fries, ice cream, and Coke.

Last statement: None.

Pronounced dead: 12:18 A.M.

57

Darryl Elroy Stewart

Executed: May 4, 1993

Personal data: *Born:* April 2, 1955. *Race:* Black. *Height:* 5'7". *Weight:* 148 pounds. *Education:* 12 years. *Prior occupation:* Auto mechanic. *County of conviction:* Harris. *Age at time of execution:* 38.

Sentenced to death for: Convicted in the February 1980 shooting death of 22-year-old Donna Kate Thomas inside her south Houston apartment. Stewart and Kelvin Kelly, who lived in the same apartment complex as the victim at 11710 Algonquin, were walking through the complex when they noticed Thomas's door open. Stewart asked Kelly for his .25 caliber pistol, because he wanted to go in and see what he could steal. Kelly heard Thomas scream, "Oh, my God," and rushed in to see what was happening. Kelly said Stewart and Thomas were in a bedroom and that Stewart told her to undress. After she complied, Stewart placed her in a closet, where she was joined by her 4-year-old daughter when she entered the apartment. Stewart eventually removed the two from the closet and demanded sex from Thomas. When she refused and started crying, he became upset, put his pistol to her head, covered it with a pillow, and shot her twice. Stewart reportedly left the apartment with $50.

Received at death row: August 20, 1980. *Time on death row:* 4,640 days (12.71 years).

Last meal: Steak, baked potato, garden salad, and tea.

Last statement: None.

Pronounced dead: 12:25 A.M.

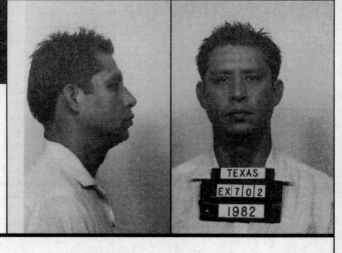

58

Leonel Torres Herrera

Executed: May 12, 1993

Personal data: *Born:* September 17, 1947. *Race:* Hispanic. *Height:* 5'11". *Weight:* 188 pounds. *Education:* 11 years (GED). *Prior occupation:* Roofer. *County of conviction:* Cameron. *Age at time of execution:* 45.

Sentenced to death for: Convicted in the September 1981 shooting death of Enrique Carrisalez, a Los Fresnos police officer. Carrisalez was shot after stopping Herrera for speeding. Before the police officer died, he identified a police mug shot of Herrera as the man who shot him.

Received at death row: January 22, 1982. *Time on death row:* 4,128 days (11.31 years).

Last meal: Declined last meal.

Last statement: "I am innocent, innocent, innocent. Make no mistake about this, I owe society nothing. Continue the struggle for human rights, helping those who are innocent, especially Mr. Graham [death row inmate Gary Lee Graham, executed June 22, 2000; see entry 222]. I am an innocent man, and something very wrong is taking place tonight. May God bless you all. I am ready."

Pronounced dead: 4:49 A.M.

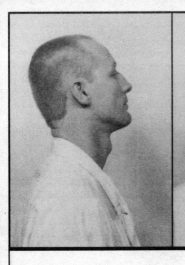

59

John Sawyers

Executed: May 18, 1993

TEXAS EX 7 4 2 1983

Personal data: *Born:* July 30, 1955. *Race:* White. *Height:* 5'10". *Weight:* 165 pounds. *Education:* 12 years. *Prior occupation:* Millwright. *County of conviction:* Harris. *Age at time of execution:* 37.

Sentenced to death for: Convicted in the February 1983 robbery-slaying of 67-year-old Ethyl Delaney at her Houston home. Delaney, who lived alone at 1834 Ojeman and worked as a notary public and property manager, was beaten to death with a cast-iron frying pan and robbed of her cash, jewelry (three rings), and car. Sawyers, a neighbor of Delaney's who had been to her home previously to have her notarize his personal papers, told police he ripped off the woman's pants, slapped her, put her on her bed, and hit her four times over the head with the skillet. He said the fourth blow broke the handle of the skillet. Testimony showed Sawyers later showed the stolen car and jewelry to friends and then pawned the jewelry for about $200. The pawn ticket and an accident Sawyers was involved in while driving Delaney's car led to his arrest.

Received at death row: June 21, 1983. *Time on death row:* 3,619 days (9.92 years).

Last meal: A cheeseburger, french fries, and a strawberry shake.

Last statement: None.

Pronounced dead: 12:23 A.M.

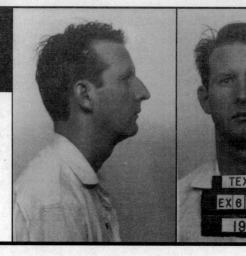

60

Markum Duff-Smith

Executed: June 29, 1993

Personal data: *Born:* January 14, 1947. *Race:* White. *Height:* 5'9". *Weight:* 146 pounds. *Education:* 14 years. *Prior occupation:* Insurance investor. *County of conviction:* Harris. *Age at time of execution:* 46.

Sentenced to death for: Convicted in the October 15, 1975, strangulation death of his wealthy adoptive mother, Getrude Duff-Smith Zabolio, at her home in the River Oaks neighborhood of Houston. Through two accomplices, Duff-Smith hired Allen Wayne Janecka to kill his mother so he could collect his inheritance. Duff-Smith promised to pay Janecka and coconspirator Paul MacDonald a total of $10,000 for the murder. Court records show that Duff-Smith also wanted his stepfather, Dow Zabolio, killed at the same time, but Zabolio had traveled to Austria on business. Mrs. Zabolio's death was originally ruled a suicide based on two suicide notes found in her bedroom. Duff-Smith was not arrested in the case until 1979, when he was suspected of masterminding the murders of his sister and brother-in-law, Diana and John Wanstrath, and their 14-month-old son, Kevin, to gain control of their estate. The probe into Gertrude Zabolio's death was reopened and police learned that Duff-Smith had bragged to a friend about having his mother killed.
Codefendants: Paul MacDonald testified against Duff-Smith in his mother's murder trial, served a sixteen-year sentence for murder, and was paroled in November 1984. Allen Wayne Janecka was executed on July 24, 2003. (See entry 309, Allen Wayne Janecka.)

Received at death row: October 20, 1981. *Time on death row:* 4,270 days (11.70 years).

Last meal: Declined last meal.

Last statement: "I am the sinner of all sinners. I was responsible for the '75 and '79 cases. My trial was not just; it was not fair; they lied against me. I love all those on death row, and I will always hold them in my hands. Those who stood by me, I will always love you. Jim and Judy Peterson and Chaplain Lopez, I thank you for staying by my side."

Pronounced dead: 12:16 A.M.

61

Curtis Paul Harris

Executed: July 1, 1993

Personal data: *Born:* August 31, 1961. *Race:* Black. *Height:* 5'5". *Weight:* 144 pounds. *Education:* 8 years. *Prior occupation:* Laborer. *County of conviction:* Brazos. *Age at time of execution:* 31.

Sentenced to death for: Convicted of capital murder in the December 11, 1978, killing of Timothy Michael Merka, 27, who was beaten to death with a tire iron and robbed after rendering assistance to Harris and three companions in rural Brazos County.

Note: Harris was 17 years of age at the time of the offense.

Codefendants: Danny Ray Harris, Harris's brother, was convicted of capital murder, sentenced to death, and executed on July 30, 1993. (See entry 62, Danny Ray Harris.) James Charles Manuel was convicted of burglary and murder with a deadly weapon, sentenced to twenty-five years, and released on October 27, 1989. Valarie Denise Rencher turned state's evidence and was not sentenced to prison. She was 16 years old at the time of the crime.

Received at death row: June 7, 1979. *Time on death row:* 5,138 days (14.08 years).

Last meal: A cheeseburger, ice cream, and water.

Last statement: None.

Pronounced dead: 12:27 A.M.

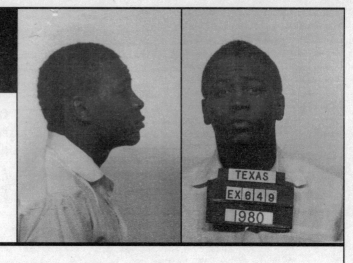

62

Danny Ray Harris

Executed: July 30, 1993

Personal data: *Born:* July 31, 1960. *Race:* Black. *Height:* 5'10". *Weight:* 156 pounds. *Education:* 9 years. *Prior occupation:* Laborer. *County of conviction:* Brazos. *Age at time of execution:* 32.

Sentenced to death for: Convicted of capital murder in the December 11, 1978, killing of Timothy Michael Merka, 27, who was beaten to death with a tire iron and robbed after rendering assistance to Harris and three companions in rural Brazos County.
Note: Harris was 18 years of age at the time of the offense.
Codefendants: Curtis Harris, Harris's brother, was convicted of capital murder, sentenced to death, and executed on July 1, 1993. (See entry 61, Curtis Paul Harris.) James Charles Manuel was convicted of burglary and murder with a deadly weapon, sentenced to twenty-five years, and released on October 27, 1989. Valarie Denise Rencher, 16, turned state's evidence and was not sentenced to prison.

Received at death row: February 25, 1980. *Time on death row:* 4,904 days (13.44 years).

Last meal: "God's saving grace, love, truth, peace, and freedom."

Last statement: "I would like to tell my family I love them very dearly, and I know they love me. I love all of the people who supported me all of these years. I would like to tell the Merka family I love them, too. I plead with all the teenagers to stop the violence and accept Jesus Christ and find victory. Today I have victory in Christ and I thank Jesus for taking my spirit into His precious hands. Thank you, Jesus."

Pronounced dead: 12:18 A.M.

63

Joseph Paul Jernigan

Executed: August 5, 1993

Personal data: *Born:* January 31, 1954. *Race:* White. *Height:* 5'10". *Weight:* 152 pounds. *Education:* 13 years. *Prior occupation:* Mechanic. *County of conviction:* Navarro. *Age at time of execution:* 39.

Sentenced to death for: Convicted in the July 3, 1981, murder of Edward Hale, 75, of Dawson, a community near Corsicana. Authorities said Hale was stabbed several times, then shot three times with his single-shot .410-gauge shotgun. Jernigan said he killed Hale with a knife and a shotgun after the robbery because he feared the man would be able to identify him.
Codefendant: Roy Dean Lamb was convicted of murder with a deadly weapon and sentenced to thirty years.

Received at death row: November 20, 1981. *Time on death row:* 4,276 days (11.72 years).

Last meal: Two cheeseburgers, french fries, tossed salad with thousand island dressing, and iced tea.

Last statement: None.

Pronounced dead: 12:31 A.M.

64

David Holland

Executed: August 12, 1993

Personal data: *Born:* July 7, 1935. *Race:* White. *Height:* 5'11". *Weight:* 190 pounds. *Education:* 13 years. *Prior occupation:* Dispatcher for trucking company. *County of conviction:* Jefferson. *Age at time of execution:* 58.

Sentenced to death for: Convicted in the July 16, 1985, robbery-slaying of Helen Jean Barnard, 29, a branch manager at Jefferson Savings and Loan in Beaumont. A teller at the office, Dianna Joy Jackson, 23, was also slain in the robbery.

Received at death row: February 26, 1986. *Time on death row:* 2,724 days (7.46 years).

Last meal: A cheeseburger, french fries, and coffee.

Last statement: None.

Pronounced dead: 12:16 A.M.

65

Carl E. Kelly

Executed: August 20, 1993

Personal data: *Born:* March 27, 1959. *Race:* Black. *Height:* 6'2". *Weight:* 186 pounds. *Education:* 11 years. *Prior occupation:* Laborer. *County of conviction:* McLennan. *Age at time of execution:* 34.

Sentenced to death for: Convicted of capital murder for his role in a September 1980 overnight robbery, abduction, and murder spree in Waco. Victims were Steven Pryon (convenience store clerk) and David Wade Riley (transient). Kelly allegedly shot both men, then threw their bodies over a cliff.
Codefendant: Thomas Graves was convicted of murder with a deadly weapon and sentenced to life in prison.

Received at death row: July 22, 1981. *Time on death row:* 4,412 days (12.09 years).

Last meal: "Wild game or whatever is on the menu and cold lemonade." He was served a cheeseburger and french fries.

Last statement: "I am an African warrior, born to breathe, and born to die."

Pronounced dead: 12:22 A.M.

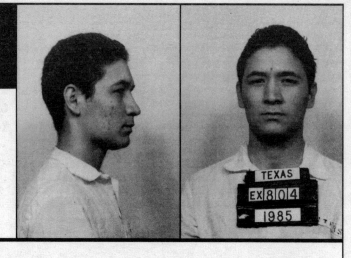

66

Ruben Montoya Cantu

Executed: August 24, 1993

Personal data: *Born:* December 5, 1966. *Race:* Hispanic. *Height:* 5'10". *Weight:* 142 pounds. *Education:* 9 years. *Prior occupation:* Laborer. *County of conviction:* Bexar. *Age at time of execution:* 26.

Sentenced to death for: Convicted of capital murder for the shooting-robbery of Pedro Gomez and Juan Moreno. Moreno survived the gunshot wounds and testified in the case. Gomez, 35, died as a result of multiple rimfire rifle wounds. Approximately $600 and a watch were taken.
Codefendant: David Garza was 15 years old at the time of the incident. He was certified to stand trial as an adult, convicted of robbery, and sentenced to twenty years.

Received at death row: September 10, 1985. *Time on death row:* 2,905 days (7.96 years).

Last meal: Barbecue chicken, refried beans, brown rice, sweet tea, and bubble gum (bubble gum is not permitted under TDCJ regulations).

Last statement: None.

Pronounced dead: 12:22 A.M.

Richard J. Wilkerson

Executed: August 31, 1993

Personal data: *Born:* April 18, 1964. *Race:* Black. *Height:* 5'11". *Weight:* 191 pounds. *Education:* 10 years. *Prior occupation:* Laborer. *County of conviction:* Harris. *Age at time of execution:* 29.

Sentenced to death for: Convicted in the July 1983 robbery-slaying of 18-year-old Anil Varughese, a night manager of the Malibu Grand Prix Race Track amusement center, in Houston. Varughese, a premed student at Houston Baptist University, and three other amusement center employees were fatally stabbed during a robbery that netted about $2,000. Also killed were Roddy Harris, 22, and brothers Arnold Pequeno, 19, and Joerene Pequeno, 18. All four victims died of multiple stab wounds to the upper body, neck, and head. Wilkerson had been fired from his job as a pit attendant at the raceway and amusement center in the 6100 block of the Southwest Freeway about two weeks before the murders.
Codefendant: Kenneth Ray Ransom was convicted of capital murder, sentenced to death, and executed on October 28, 1997. (See entry 139, Kenneth Ray Ransom.) James Edward Randall was convicted of capital murder and given a life sentence. Randall, who was Wilkerson's cousin, was 16 years old at the time of the murders.

Received at death row: January 17, 1984. *Time on death row:* 3,514 days (9.63 years).

Last meal: Two double-meat cheeseburgers, french fries, and ice cream (chocolate or chocolate chip).

Last statement: See Appendix.

Pronounced dead: 12:16 A.M.

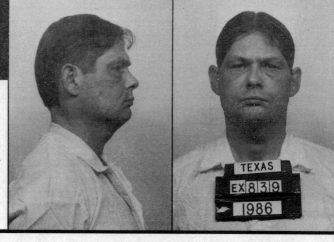

68

Johnny James

Executed: September 3, 1993

TEXAS
EX 8 3 9
1986

Personal data: *Born:* January 30, 1954. *Race:* White. *Height:* 5'9". *Weight:* 185 pounds. *Education:* 9 years. *Prior occupation:* Truck driver. *County of conviction:* Chambers. *Age at time of execution:* 39.

Sentenced to death for: Convicted in the October 1985 abduction and shooting death of 47-year-old Barbara Harrington Mayfield, owner of a High Island lounge where James once tended bar. Mayfield was abducted from BJ's Lounge and shot twice in the head with a .38 caliber pistol after being forced to drive James around three southeast Texas counties while he raped a 23-year-old convenience store clerk he had earlier robbed of $300 and kidnapped. The clerk, a black female who worked at Porter's Get It & Go store in Winnie, was shot three times in the head but survived to identify James. Both women were found lying on Russell's Landing Road, in Jefferson County.

Received at death row: July 17, 1986. *Time on death row:* 2,605 days (7.14 years).

Last meal: Double-meat cheeseburgers, double order of french fries, Dr Pepper, and a pint of banana nut ice cream.

Last statement: None.

Pronounced dead: 12:17 A.M.

Antonio Nathaniel Bonham

Executed: September 28, 1993

Personal data: *Born:* February 6, 1960. *Race:* Black. *Height:* 5'6". *Weight:* 165 pounds. *Education:* 9 years. *Prior occupation:* Laborer. *County of conviction:* Harris. *Age at time of execution:* 33.

Sentenced to death for: Convicted in the July 9, 1981, abduction and murder of 62-year-old Marie Jones McGowen, a key-punch instructor at Massey Business College, in Houston. McGowen was abducted outside the college, raped, and then run over by her own car. Prosecutors also said the woman had been hit over the head with a brick and locked in the trunk of her car before being run over. Her crushed body was found underneath her car on a secluded road in southeast Houston about eleven hours after her abduction. Bonham was arrested by Houston police on July 17, 1981. He had been on parole less than two months before committing the crime.

Received at death row: November 25, 1981. *Time on death row:* 4,325 days (11.85 years).

Last meal: Hamburgers, french fries, and water.

Last statement: None.

Pronounced dead: 12:28 A.M.

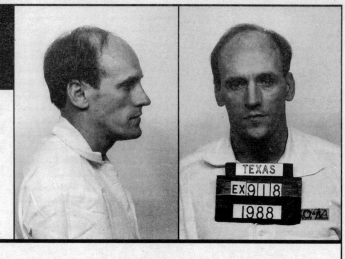

70

Anthony Quinn Cook

Executed: November 10, 1993

Personal data: *Born:* January 4, 1959. *Race:* White. *Height:* 5'6". *Weight:* 150 pounds. *Education:* 9 years. *Prior occupation:* Construction worker. *County of conviction:* Milam. *Age at time of execution:* 34.

Sentenced to death for: Convicted in the June 1988 abduction and slaying of 35-year-old David Dirck VanTassel Jr., a University of Texas law student. Cook and codefendant Robert Brian Moore abducted VanTassel from outside the Sheraton Crest Hotel in Austin, where he had just completed a state bar test review. Cook and Moore drove VanTassel in his car to a roadside park fourteen miles west of Cameron on Highway 36 and tied him with his shirt and belt. After taking his watch and wallet, Cook shot VanTassel four times in the head with a .22 caliber pistol. Cook and Moore stole VanTassel's car and sold it to a man who later identified them in a police lineup. When arrested, Cook was wearing VanTassel's watch and had the victim's wallet in his pocket. *Codefendant:* Robert Brian Moore was awaiting trial for capital murder at the time of Cook's execution.

Received at death row: October 28, 1988. *Time on death row:* 1,839 days (5.04 years).

Last meal: A double-meat cheeseburger and a strawberry shake.

Last statement: "I just want to tell my family I love them; and I thank the Lord Jesus for giving me another chance and for saving me."

Pronounced dead: 12:15 A.M.

Clifford X. Phillips

Executed: December 15, 1993

Personal data: *Born:* December 2, 1934. *Race:* Black. *Height:* 5'7". *Weight:* 155 pounds. *Education:* 7 years. *Prior occupation:* General contractor. *County of conviction:* Harris. *Age at time of execution:* 59.

Sentenced to death for: Convicted in the January 1982 strangulation death of 58-year-old Iris Siff, managing director of the Alley Theater in Houston. Phillips, a former security guard at the theater, said he had gone to Siff's office on January 13 to rob her but was forced to kill her in self-defense when she allegedly attacked him. Siff was found dead in her office. She had been strangled to death with a telephone cord. Testimony showed Phillips stole Siff's television, fur coat, jewelry, tote bag, and Lincoln Continental after the killing. He was arrested in Los Angeles about three weeks after the slaying.

Received at death row: September 28, 1982. *Time on death row:* 4,096 days (11.22 years).

Last meal: Declined last meal.

Last statement: "I want to express my feelings regarding the mishap of the deceased Mrs. Iris Siff. That was a very unfortunate incident and only God knows it was an unintentional situation that took place. I want to express my remorse to the family and the discomfort and pain I caused in their lives. Only God will determine if I am truly guilty or innocent of being the type of person I have been drawn up to be by the press and the media. I have given my wife the power and energy to be a disciple of Islam. I rescued her from a wretched life in Ireland. I thank Allah for sending her to me. Certainly murder cannot be an instrument of Allah. My wife is very devoted and a very pious wife. I am very grateful Allah has chosen me to teach the greatness of Allah through her. I am grateful to Allah for allowing me to touch other people's lives through Allah. In spite of what the newspapers have said of me, my wife, I love you very deeply. May Allah continue to bless you and shower you with his glory." [Prayer and chanting]

Pronounced dead: 12:53 A.M.

72

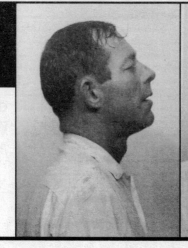

Harold Amos Barnard

Executed: February 2, 1994

Personal data: *Born:* November 1, 1942. *Race:* White. *Height:* 5'8". *Weight:* 155 pounds. *Education:* 12 years. *Prior occupation:* Carpenter. *County of conviction:* Galveston. *Age at time of execution:* 51.

Sentenced to death for: Convicted for killing Tuan Nguyen, 16, a clerk at a Galveston 7-Eleven store managed by his family. Nguyen was shot once in the heart with a sawed-off .22 caliber rifle fired by Barnard during a robbery. Barnard and three codefendants fled in a stolen car following the shooting and were arrested about thirty minutes later on Interstate 45, north of Galveston. The murder weapon was found inside the car, along with a buck knife and a 12-gauge shotgun. Although Nguyen and his father were forced to put the money from the cash register into a bag, Barnard and his codefendants left the store empty-handed after the shooting.
Note: The three codefendants were convicted of aggravated robbery and sentenced to prison terms of fifteen years, twelve years, and seven years.

Received at death row: May 14, 1981. *Time on death row:* 4,647 days (12.73 years).

Last meal: Steak, french fries, and wine (water was substituted).

Last statement: "God, please forgive me of my sins. Look after my people. Bless and protect all people. I am sorry for my sins. Lord, take me home with you. Amen." [Barnard said several other sentences prison officials could not understand.]

Pronounced dead: 12:27 A.M.

**Freddie
Lee
Webb**

Executed:
March 31,
1994

Personal data: *Born:* August 17, 1960. *Race:* Black. *Height:* 5'8". *Weight:* 165 pounds. *Education:* 11 years. *Prior occupation:* Construction worker. *County of conviction:* Nueces. *Age at time of execution:* 33.

Sentenced to death for: Convicted in the December 1985 abduction and slaying of 26-year-old Leopoldo Cantu, of Corpus Christi. Cantu and his wife, Elizabeth, a supervisor at Ship Ahoy restaurant in Corpus Christi, were abducted from a car wash after closing the restaurant. They were driven back to the restaurant, where Elizabeth was forced to open the safe and turn over the day's receipts. She was tied up and left inside the restaurant. Her husband was driven to an isolated location and shot five times with a .45 caliber pistol. Webb and an accomplice were arrested in George West on March 29, 1986, following the armed robbery of a convenience store there.

Received at death row: October 27, 1986. *Time on death row:* 2,712 days (7.43 years).

Last meal: Declined last meal.

Last statement: "Peace."

Pronounced dead: 12:20 A.M.

74

Richard Lee Beavers

Executed:
April 4,
1994

TEXAS
EX 9116
1988
MD-2

Personal data: *Born:* December 9, 1955. *Race:* White. *Height:* 5'11". *Weight:* 200 pounds. *Education:* 5 years. *Prior occupation:* Laborer. *County of conviction:* Harris. *Age at time of execution:* 38.

Sentenced to death for: Convicted in the August 1986 abduction and slaying of Douglas G. Odle, a 24-year-old Houston restaurant manager. Odle and his wife, Jenny, also 24 at the time, were abducted from their apartment at gunpoint and forced to drive to several banks and withdraw money from automatic teller machines. They were then forced to drive to the restaurant Odle managed and return with the money. Beavers then forced the couple to drive to a field in Galveston County, where Doug Odle was shot through the throat after being forced to kneel before Beavers. Beavers drove away from the scene with Odle's wife, who was later raped, shot in the head, and left for dead. She survived a destroyed left eye and brain damage to testify against Beavers, who was arrested by the FBI in Virginia following the crime.

Received at death row: October 18, 1988. *Time on death row:* 1,994 days (5.46 years).

Last meal: Six pieces of French toast with syrup, jelly, and butter; six barbecue spare ribs; six pieces of well-cooked bacon; four scrambled eggs; five well-cooked sausage patties; french fries with ketchup; three slices of cheese; two pieces of yellow cake with chocolate fudge icing; and four cartons of milk.

Last statement: "Jesus Christ, the way of truth and light. I thank you, Lord Jesus, for giving me the way."

Pronounced dead: 12:29 A.M.

75

Larry Norman Anderson

Executed: April 26, 1994

Personal data: *Born:* August 30, 1952. *Race:* White. *Height:* 6'4". *Weight:* 180 pounds. *Education:* 12 years. *Prior occupation:* Electrician. *County of conviction:* Harris. *Age at time of execution:* 41.

Sentenced to death for: Convicted in the March 28, 1982, stabbing death of 28-year-old Zelda Webster, a northwest Houston bar manager. Webster was abducted as she was closing Shelee's Club in the 7700 block of Long Point. About $1,000 was taken from the club. Two bank bags, along with a bloodstained knife, were found in Anderson's truck when it was stopped near the Addicks reservoir that night for traveling without headlights. Anderson admitted to the killing and told police he left Webster's body in a ditch on Clay Road.

Received at death row: March 25, 1983. *Time on death row:* 4,050 days (11.10 years).

Last meal: Barbecue ribs, chef salad, baked potato, peach cobbler, and tea.

Last statement: None.

Pronounced dead: 12:42 A.M.

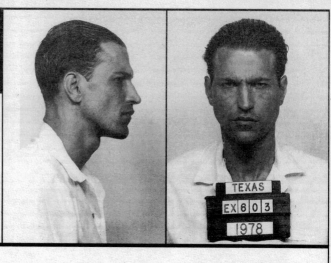

76

Paul Rougeau

Executed:
May 3, 1994

Personal data: *Born:* December 22, 1947. *Race:* Black. *Height:* 6'1". *Weight:* 160 pounds. *Education:* 9 years. *Prior occupation:* Carpenter. *County of conviction:* Harris. *Age at time of execution:* 46.

Sentenced to death for: Convicted in the January 1978 slaying of Albert C. Wilkins, a 50-year-old Harris County deputy constable. Wilkins was killed at the Stock Exchange Lounge in the 5400 block of Griggs Road while working an off-duty security job. The murder reportedly occurred during an attempted robbery. Prosecutors said Rougeau cursed the officer as he begged for his life and then shot him in the head with a .38 caliber pistol. Rougeau's younger brother Joseph was reportedly killed at the scene of the shooting during a gun battle with police. Paul Rougeau was arrested twelve hours after the killing, reportedly after being shot while fleeing police.

Received at death row: August 16, 1978. *Time on death row:* 5,739 days (15.72 years).

Last meal: Declined last meal.

Last statement: No last statement was given, but greeted three of his sisters and a niece who witnessed with, "Love you all. Peace be with you all."

Pronounced dead: 12:20 A.M.

77

Stephen Ray Nethery

Executed: May 27, 1994

Personal data: *Born:* June 2, 1960. *Race:* White. *Height:* 5'11". *Weight:* n/a. *Education:* 12 years. *Prior occupation:* Laborer. *County of conviction:* Dallas. *Age at time of execution:* 33.

Sentenced to death for: Convicted in the February 1981 shooting death of 24-year-old John T. McCarthy, a Dallas police officer. Nethery was raping a 22-year-old woman in his car parked near White Rock Lake when McCarthy and his partner, Phillip Brown, pulled up in their squad car. Not knowing the woman was being raped, the officers told the two to leave the area. As the officers started to walk away, Nethery stepped from the car, said, "Officers, I'm sorry," and fired three shots at McCarthy, striking him in the back of the head. Brown fired three shots at Nethery before chasing him into the lake, where Nethery swam a few yards before surrendering when Brown fired a fourth shot at him. Nethery was not hit by any of the shots. McCarthy was rushed to a Dallas hospital, where he died two days later.

Received at death row: November 13, 1981. *Time on death row:* 4,578 days (12.54 years).

Last meal: Two cheeseburgers with lettuce, tomato, and onion; french fries; and milk.

Last statement: "Well, I just wanted to ask people to pray for two families, my family and the family of Officer McCarthy. I appreciate the prayers. Lord Jesus, receive my spirit."

Pronounced dead: 12:30 A.M.

78

Denton Crank

Executed: June 14, 1994

Personal data: *Born:* October 10, 1955. *Race:* White. *Height:* 5'9". *Weight:* 161 pounds. *Education:* 12 years. *Prior occupation:* Construction worker. *County of conviction:* Harris. *Age at time of execution:* 38.

Sentenced to death for: Convicted in the murder of grocery store manager Terry Oringderff, 31. Crank and his half brother, Truman Moffett Jr., kidnapped Oringderff, wired him with dynamite, robbed his store, and shot him to death.
Codefendant: Truman O. Moffett Jr. was convicted of aggravated robbery with a deadly weapon and sentenced to life in prison.

Received at death row: August 6, 1985. *Time on death row:* 3,234 days (8.86 years).

Last meal: Double-meat cheeseburger, lettuce, pickles, tomato, onions, mayonnaise, onion rings, and two chocolate shakes.

Last statement: "To my family, who has kept me strong, I give my love."

Pronounced dead: 12:22 A.M.

79

Robert Nelson Drew

Executed: August 2, 1994

Personal data: *Born:* April 8, 1959. *Race:* White. *Height:* 5'5". *Weight:* 140 pounds. *Education:* 10 years. *Prior occupation:* Carpenter. *County of conviction:* Harris. *Age at time of execution:* 35.

Sentenced to death for: Convicted in the February 22, 1983, stabbing death of Jeffrey Leon Mays, a 17-year-old runaway from Alabama. According to court records, Drew stabbed Mays after a fight. Drew allegedly took Mays's watch and wallet after the slaying.
Note: Earnest Purleauski, 37, originally charged with capital murder, signed a statement after pleading guilty to murder and received a sixty-year sentence. He later recanted his testimony, stating, "I alone committed the murder of Jeffrey Mays. Robert Drew did not assist me in any way. Robert Drew is innocent."

Received at death row: January 5, 1984. *Time on death row:* 3,862 days (10.58 years).

Last meal: Steak (cooked rare), ham, two hamburgers, two pieces of fish, and chocolate milk.

Last statement: "[First two or three words were unintelligible] I don't know why Marta Glass wasn't allowed in here. I love you all. Keep the faith. Remember the death penalty is murder. They are taking the life of an innocent man. My attorney will read my letter at a press conference after this is over. [See Appendix.] That is all I have to say. I love you all."

Pronounced dead: 12:22 A.M.

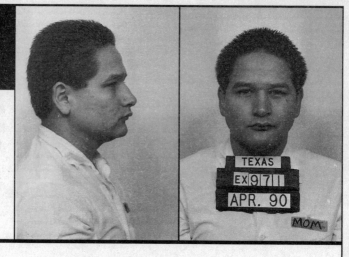

80

Jessie Gutierrez

Executed:
September
16, 1994

Personal data: *Born:* April 30, 1965. *Race:* Hispanic. *Height:* 5'5". *Weight:* 155 pounds. *Education:* 8 years. *Prior occupation:* Welder. *County of conviction:* Brazos. *Age at time of execution:* 29.

Sentenced to death for: Convicted in the September 1989 robbery and murder of 42-year-old Dorothy McNew, a College Station store clerk. McNew was working the counter at the Texas Coin Exchange, 404 University, when Jessie Gutierrez and his brother Jose entered shortly after 10 A.M. McNew attempted to flee into an office when she saw one of the men pull a handgun from his coat; she was shot in the head. The Gutierrez brothers fled the store with gems and jewelry worth approximately $500,000. Both were traced to Houston, where they were arrested on September 13, 1989. Approximately $375,000 worth of the stolen merchandise was recovered.
Codefendant: Jose Gutierrez, Jessie's brother, was convicted of capital murder, sentenced to death, and executed November 18, 1999. (See entry 195, Jose Gutierrez.)

Received at death row: April 27, 1990. *Time on death row:* 1,603 days (4.39 years).

Last meal: Declined last meal.

Last statement: "I just love everybody, and that's it."

Pronounced dead: 12:20 A.M.

81

George Douglas Lott

Executed: September 20, 1994

Personal data: *Born:* June 7, 1947. *Race:* White. *Height:* 5'4". *Weight:* 144 pounds. *Education:* 16 years. *Prior occupation:* Computer programmer. *County of conviction:* Potter. *Age at time of execution:* 47.

Sentenced to death for: Convicted in the random shooting of 41-year-old Clyde Christopher Marshall, an assistant district attorney, inside the old Tarrant County Court House at 100 W. Weatherford in Fort Worth. Lott entered a fourth-floor courtroom carrying a 9mm automatic handgun shortly before 10 A.M. and opened fire. Marshall died at the scene from multiple gunshot wounds. Another man, John Edwards, was also killed, and Judge John Hill was wounded. Lott fled from the courthouse to the studios of WFAA-TV, in Dallas, where he confessed to the crime. Police arrested him while he was being interviewed by a reporter.

Received at death row: March 18, 1993. *Time on death row:* 551 days (1.51 years).

Last meal: Three pieces of French toast with syrup, baked sweet potato with butter, two sausage patties, and one fried egg.

Last statement: None.

Pronounced dead: 12:19 A.M.

82

Walter Key Williams

Executed: October 5, 1994

Personal data: *Born:* January 30, 1962. *Race:* Black. *Height:* 5'5". *Weight:* 130 pounds. *Education:* 12 years. *Prior occupation:* Laborer. *County of conviction:* Bexar. *Age at time of execution:* 32.

Sentenced to death for: Convicted in the February 11, 1981, murder of San Antonio convenience store clerk Daniel Liepold. Williams shot Liepold in the back with a .38 caliber pistol during a robbery attempt at the Circle K Food Store, where Williams had once worked. At his trial, eyewitnesses testified that they had seen Williams and his accomplice, Theodore Roosevelt Edwards, in the store at the time of the robbery; prosecutors introduced a confession signed by Williams some eight hours after the crime. Authorities found the gun used in the store robbery at his parents' home on a nightstand next to the bed Williams was sleeping in. Williams had married at age 17 and was separated from his wife when the crime took place. He had worked as a clerk at the Circle K Food Store for about a year, taking home $180 a week, and knew Liepold casually, he said. Edwards was later convicted of murder in another robbery and sentenced to life in prison.

Received at death row: September 3, 1982. *Time on death row:* 4,415 days (12.10 years).

Last meal: A double-meat cheeseburger, chocolate cake, peas and corn, and tea.

Last statement: He mumbled something about wishing his whole life had been spent as Islamic.

Pronounced dead: 12:21 A.M.

83

Warren Eugene Bridge

Executed: November 22, 1994

Personal data: *Born:* July 3, 1960. *Race:* White. *Height:* 5'7". *Weight:* 135 pounds. *Education:* 11 years. *Prior occupation:* Cashier/restaurant worker. *County of conviction:* Galveston. *Age at time of execution:* 34.

Sentenced to death for: Convicted in the February 10, 1980, robbery-shooting of Walter Rose, a 62-year-old convenience store clerk, in Galveston. Rose was shot four times with a .38 caliber pistol as Bridge and codefendant Robert Joseph Costa robbed the Stop & Go store at 710 Fourth Street of $24. Rose died of his wounds on February 24, 1980, four days following the arrests of Bridge and Costa.
Codefendant: Robert Joseph Costa was convicted of aggravated robbery and sentenced to thirteen years in prison.

Received at death row: October 1, 1980. *Time on death row:* 5,165 days (14.15 years). *Note:* While on death row, Bridge was implicated in the bombing of another inmate's cell in September 1984 and the nonfatal stabbing of another inmate in March 1985.

Last meal: A double-meat cheeseburger.

Last statement: [To stepfather Bill Mathis, a witness] "I'll see you. I would like to tell the surviving victims here, society, my family, and friends, that I ask that they forgive me for anything I have done. I beg for your forgiveness. I would like to ask Lord Jesus Christ's forgiveness and say that in spite of my circumstances I have been blessed by him. My first thought is that Jesus Christ came down and separated the humans from God. I would like to see the wall that separates these groups here tonight brought down and that we would all have love and compassion for one another, and that you all build a future for all of us. There are a lot of men on the row that need to be remembered. I love all of you all the same."

Pronounced dead: 12:25 A.M.

84

Herman Robert Charles Clark Jr.

Executed: December 6, 1994

Personal data: *Born:* July 26, 1946. *Race:* Black. *Height:* 5'11". *Weight:* 188 pounds. *Education:* 14 years. *Prior occupation:* Manager, Houston Plastic Products. *County of conviction:* Harris. *Age at time of execution:* 48.

Sentenced to death for: Convicted in the April 4, 1981, murder of bartender Joseph Edward McClain. At approximately 3 A.M. Clark broke into McClain's apartment in the 3200 block of Clarewood and awoke the victim, his girlfriend, Paulette Spies, and her son. He burglarized the apartment and was attempting to rape Spies when a three-way fight over Clark's pistol ensued. During the struggle, Spies was shot in the arm and McClain was fatally shot in the chest. Court records show that approximately two weeks after this incident, Clark burglarized another apartment, robbing the male victim and raping the female victim. He also raped and sodomized the female victim's 10-year-old daughter. Several months later Clark again burglarized an apartment and raped and sodomized both the complainant and her 11-year-old daughter. Clark admitted terrorizing more than one hundred families during late-night burglaries and often sexually assaulting the women.

Received at death row: June 17, 1982. *Time on death row:* 4,555 days (12.48 years).

Last meal: Declined last meal.

Last statement: "I told the daughter not to come. Discontinue. Be quiet please. Specifically, I want to say that the bad man I was when I came to death row thirteen years ago is nowhere—by the power of God, Jesus Christ, God Almighty Holy Spirit he has transformed me as a new creature of Christ. I know that I am a Christ child and that my Lord will welcome me into his arms. Jesus Christ is the Lord of Lords and the King of Kings. I love all of you, those I can and can't see, with the love of Christ. My love for you is secure and I love you purely and wholeheartedly in the name of the Almighty God . . ." [Record ends here]

Pronounced dead: 12:28 A.M.

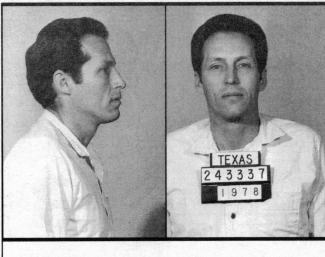

85

Raymond Kinnamon

Executed: December 11, 1994

Personal data: *Born:* November 20, 1941. *Race:* White. *Height:* 5'10". *Weight:* 180 pounds. *Education:* 11 years. *Prior occupation:* Mechanic. *County of conviction:* Harris. *Age at time of execution:* 53.

Sentenced to death for: Convicted in the December 1984 robbery and slaying of 41-year-old Ronald Charles Longmire at NJ's, a bar in the 3800 block of Magnum in Houston. Kinnamon was in the bar drinking when he pulled a pistol and demanded money from customers and employees. He took more than $1,500, including $250 from Longmire. Longmire was shot once in the back when he reportedly slapped Kinnamon's hand away when the robber touched his back pocket and asked what was in it. Kinnamon fled and was arrested about two weeks later as a result of a tip from a police informant.

Received at death row: October 10, 1985. *Time on death row:* 3,349 days (9.18 years).

Last meal: Fish, salad, vanilla ice cream, and tea.

Last statement: See Appendix.
Note: Press reports noted that Kinnamon staged a filibuster in an attempt to talk until sunrise, because his death warrant called for the execution to occur before dawn. Among statements recorded by the press: "Wherever I'm buried, I'd like it to say, 'Here lies a man who loved women.' I've always been that way." Kinnamon finally tried to slip out of his leather straps on the gurney that kept him connected to the intravenous tubes carrying the solution of lethal drugs. As he tried to free himself, he said, "I can see no reason for my death." Warden Morris Jones and prison chaplain Alex Taylor helped control the inmate, and the lethal dose was begun.

Pronounced dead: 5:56 A.M.

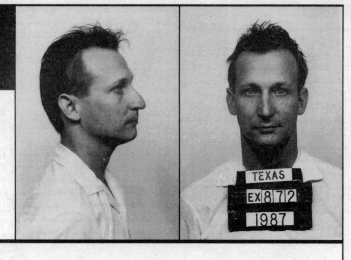

86

Jesse Dewayne Jacobs

Executed: January 4, 1995

Personal data: *Born:* February 12, 1950. *Race:* White. *Height:* 5'5". *Weight:* 131 pounds. *Education:* 12 years. *Prior occupation:* Auto mechanic. *County of conviction:* Walker. *Age at time of execution:* 44.

Sentenced to death for: Convicted in the February 1986 abduction and shooting death of Etta Ann Urdiales, the ex-wife of his sister's boyfriend. Jacobs told police his sister, Bobbie Jean Hogan, offered him $500 and a place to stay if he would kill Urdiales. He said Urdiales, 25, was supposedly pestering her ex-husband, Michael Urdiales, about child-support payments and custody. Jacobs, posing as a coworker of Urdiales's boyfriend, abducted the victim from her Conroe apartment, drove her to an area south of Sawdust Road near the Woodlands, and shot her once in the head with a .38 caliber pistol after blindfolding her with a towel. He then wrapped her body in a sleeping bag and buried her in a wooded area. Her body was not discovered until September 13, 1986. Meanwhile, Jacobs went on a six-month crime spree, during which he committed nine robberies and stole six vehicles. He was finally stopped in a stolen car at a checkpoint near Sierra Blanca on September 9, 1986, and arrested for armed robbery. He was returned to Conroe three days later and gave an oral confession of the Urdiales murder.

Received at death row: June 17, 1987. *Time on death row:* 2,758 days (7.56 years).

Last meal: T-bone steak, french fries, ketchup, and milk.

Last statement: See Appendix.

Pronounced dead: 12:19 A.M.

Mario Marquez

Executed: January 17, 1995

Personal data: *Born:* August 22, 1958. *Race:* Hispanic. *Height:* 5'8". *Weight:* 165 pounds. *Education:* 6 years. *Prior occupation:* Drywaller. *County of conviction:* Bexar. *Age at time of execution:* 36.

Sentenced to death for: Convicted of capital murder in the January 27, 1984, rape-strangulation death of 14-year-old Rachel Gutierrez, of San Antonio. Gutierrez and Rebecca Marquez, the defendant's 18-year-old estranged wife, were both strangled to death after being sexually assaulted in their home. Gutierrez and Rebecca Marquez were sisters and lived with their mother, Rosa Gutierrez, in the Villa Veramendi Courts.

Received at death row: November 28, 1984. *Time on death row:* 3,702 days (10.14 years).

Last meal: Fried chicken, baked potato, and cinnamon roll.

Last statement: "Thank you for being my Lord Jesus and savior and I am ready to come home. Amen."

Pronounced dead: 12:21 A.M.

88

Clifton Charles Russell Jr.

Executed:
January 31, 1995

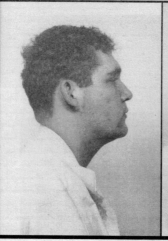

Personal data: *Born:* August 5, 1961. *Race:* White. *Height:* 6'1". *Weight:* 210 pounds. *Education:* 7 years. *Prior occupation:* Laborer. *County of conviction:* Taylor. *Age at time of execution:* 33.

Sentenced to death for: Convicted in the December 1979 robbery-slaying of 41-year-old Hubert Otha Tobey in Abilene. Tobey, an air-traffic controller, was found dead outside an abandoned house. He had been stabbed repeatedly and had his skull crushed with a rock. Russell and an accomplice, William Battee Jr., stole Tobey's car and drove to Hobbs, New Mexico, where they were arrested. *Codefendant:* William Battee Jr. was convicted of burglary and murder and given a sixty-year sentence.

Received at death row: April 30, 1980. *Time on death row:* 5,389 days (14.76 years).

Last meal: He asked for whatever was on the menu (chili dogs, baked beans, corn, and peanut butter cookies).

Last statement: "I would like to thank my friends and family for sticking with me through all of this. I would like to encourage my brothers to continue to run the race. I thank my Father, God in heaven, for the grace he has granted me. I am ready."

Pronounced dead: 12:19 A.M.
Note: This was the first time in almost forty-five years that Texas officials executed two men in a single night. Russell was executed first because his death row number, 658, was lower than Willie Williams's death row number, 677. (See entry 89, Willie Ray Williams.)

89

Willie Ray Williams

Executed: January 31, 1995

Personal data: *Born:* February 12, 1956. *Race:* Black. *Height:* 6'0". *Weight:* 210 pounds. *Education:* 11 years. *Prior occupation:* Laborer. *County of conviction:* Harris. *Age at time of execution:* 38.

Sentenced to death for: Convicted in the October 1980 murder of Claude Schaffer Jr. during the robbery of a Houston delicatessen. Williams's accomplice, Joseph Bennard Nichols, was also sentenced to death in connection with the robbery and shooting. Lawyers for Nichols claimed Williams went back inside the store after the robbery and shot Schaffer as he crouched behind a counter.

Received at death row: February 27, 1981. *Time on death row:* 5,086 days (13.93 years).

Last meal: Two double-meat cheeseburgers, onion rings, cheesecake, and root beer.

Last statement: "There's love and peace in Islam."

Pronounced dead: 1:57 A.M.
Note: This was the first time in almost forty-five years that Texas officials executed two men in a single night. Williams was executed second because his death row number, 677, was higher than Clifton Russell's death row number, 658. (See entry 88, Clifton Charles Russell Jr.)

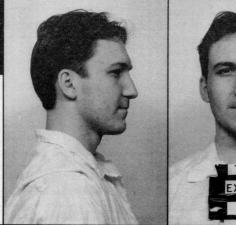

90

Jeffery Dean Motley

Executed: February 7, 1995

TEXAS
EX 789
1985

Personal data: *Born:* September 17, 1965. *Race:* White. *Height:* 6'2". *Weight:* 194 pounds. *Education:* 9 years. *Prior occupation:* Air-conditioner repairman. *County of conviction:* Harris. *Age at time of execution:* 29.

Sentenced to death for: Court records reflect the fact that Motley abducted Marie Edelia Duron, 30, at gunpoint and forced her to take him to a bank, where she withdrew funds totaling $300. He either immediately shot her in the back, causing her death, or waited until later in the day to shoot her; the exact time is unknown. Her decomposed body was found in a field in La Porte August 1, 1984.

Received at death row: April 17, 1985. *Time on death row:* 3,583 days (9.82 years).

Last meal: Declined last meal.

Last statement: "I love you, Mom, good-bye."

Pronounced dead: 12:20 A.M.

91

Billy Conn Gardner

Executed: February 16, 1995

Personal data: *Born:* July 28, 1943. *Race:* White. *Height:* 5'11". *Weight:* 157 pounds. *Education:* 12 years. *Prior occupation:* Welder. *County of conviction:* Dallas. *Age at time of execution:* 51.

Sentenced to death for: Convicted in the May 1983 shooting death of Thelma Catherine Row, cafeteria supervisor at Lake Highlands High School, in the Richardson Independent School District. Row was shot twice in the chest with a .357 caliber pistol during a robbery of the cafeteria office that netted $1,600. She died nine days later. Gardner was arrested in his home on July 26, 1984, and was later picked out of a lineup by witnesses who saw him at the school the day of the murder.

Received at death row: November 3, 1983. *Time on death row:* 4,123 days (11.30 years).

Last meal: A hamburger, french fries, tea, and any dessert (no preference).

Last statement: "I forgive all of you and hope God forgives all of you too."

Pronounced dead: 12:30 A.M.

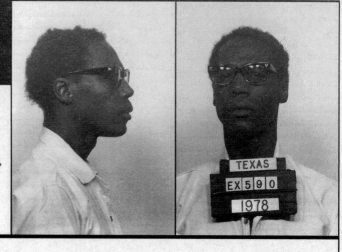

92

Samuel Hawkins

Executed:
February 21, 1995

TEXAS
EX 5 9 0
1978

Personal data: *Born:* September 1, 1943. *Race:* Black. *Height:* 5'10". *Weight:* 140 pounds. *Education:* 12 years. *Prior occupation:* Meat trimmer. *County of conviction:* Lubbock. *Age at time of execution:* 51.

Sentenced to death for: Convicted in the slaying of Abbe Rogus Hamilton, 19, of Borger. She was six months pregnant when she was raped and stabbed to death with a hunting knife.

Received at death row: April 8, 1978. *Time on death row:* 6,163 days (16.88 years).

Last meal: A double-meat cheeseburger, french fries, and tea.

Last statement: None.

Pronounced dead: 12:21 A.M.

93

Noble Mays

Executed: April 6, 1995

Personal data: *Born:* August 15, 1953. *Race:* White. *Height:* 6'1". *Weight:* 185 pounds. *Education:* 15 years. *Prior occupation:* Roughneck. *County of conviction:* Denton. *Age at time of execution:* 41.

Sentenced to death for: Convicted in the April 7, 1979, stabbing death and robbery of Jerry Lamb in Wichita Falls. Lamb was stabbed three times with a knife after being robbed of his money and chased from his car by Mays and codefendant, James Thomas Moore, 27.
Codefendant: Moore was convicted of murder and sentenced to forty-five years.

Received at death row: November 7, 1980. *Time on death row:* 5,263 days (14.42 years).

Last meal: Four to five fried eggs (sunny-side up), three sausage links, three biscuits, and coffee.

Last statement: None.

Pronounced dead: 1:42 A.M.
Note: Mays offered to stop his appeals in exchange for a payment of $10,000 for his family.

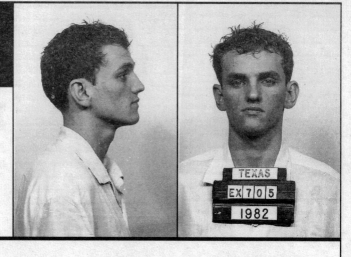

94

**Fletcher
Thomas
Mann**

Executed:
June 1,
1995

TEXAS
EX 7 0 5
1982

Personal data: *Born:* April 7, 1961. *Race:* White. *Height:* 5'6". *Weight:* 135 pounds. *Education:* 8 years. *Prior occupation:* Laborer. *County of conviction:* Dallas. *Age at time of execution:* 34.

Sentenced to death for: Convicted of capital murder in the September 11, 1980, shooting death of Christopher Lee Bates in Dallas County. Mann and a companion entered an apartment where Bates, his roommate Robert Matzig, and a woman, Barbara Hoppe, were watching a football game. Both Bates and Matzig were robbed; Hoppe was raped before being strangled and stabbed to death. Bates and Matzig were driven to grocery stores, where they cashed two checks and gave the money to the intruders. They were then driven to a secluded area, where Bates was shot in the head. Matzig was shot in the neck but survived. Mann said he and his accomplice went to the victims' apartment because he and his accomplice "needed the money and knew they had cocaine." *Codefendant:* Martin David Verbrugge was convicted of attempted murder and sentenced to life in prison.

Received at death row: February 22, 1982. *Time on death row:* 4,847 days (13.28 years).

Last meal: Two hamburger steaks, sliced onions, four pieces of toast, french fries, mustard, ketchup, fruit cocktail, and Coke.

Last statement: "I would like to tell my family I love them. My attorneys did their best. All of my brothers on death row—those who died and those who are still there—to hang in there, and that's all I have to say."

Pronounced dead: 12:20 A.M.

95

Ronald Keith Allridge

Executed: June 8, 1995

Personal data: *Born:* September 27, 1960. *Race:* Black. *Height:* 6'4". *Weight:* n/a. *Education:* 10 years (GED). *Prior occupation:* Unemployed. *County of conviction:* Tarrant. *Age at time of execution:* 34.

Sentenced to death for: Convicted of shooting and killing customer Carla McMillen during a robbery of a What-a-Burger restaurant in Fort Worth on March 25, 1985.

Received at death row: February 20, 1986. *Time on death row:* 3,395 days (9.30 years).

Last meal: Declined last meal.

Last statement: None.

Pronounced dead: 12:21 A.M.
Note: Officials had trouble finding a vein in Allridge's left arm. They went ahead with only one IV in the right arm.

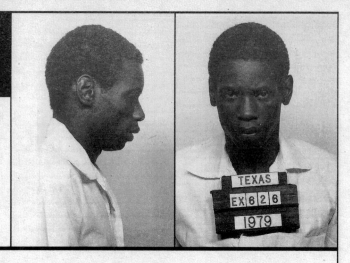

96

John W. Fearance

Executed: June 20, 1995

Personal data: *Born:* October 27, 1954. *Race:* Black. *Height:* 5'8". *Weight:* 157 pounds. *Education:* 8 years. *Prior occupation:* Auto body repairman. *County of conviction:* Dallas. *Age at time of execution:* 40.

Sentenced to death for: Convicted in the December 1977 stabbing death of Larry Faircloth, in Dallas. Faircloth was stabbed repeatedly after Fearance broke in to burglarize his north Dallas home. The victim's wife identified Fearance as the intruder, and he was arrested about three hours later. In 1980, the Texas Court of Criminal Appeals ruled that a prospective juror was improperly excluded from the jury and granted a new trial. Fearance was again convicted of capital murder in October 1981 and sentenced to death a second time.

Received at death row: January 5, 1979. *Time on death row:* 6,010 days (16.47 years).

Last meal: A double-meat cheeseburger, french fries, vanilla ice cream, and milk.

Last statement: "I would like to say that I have no animosity towards anyone. I made a mistake eighteen years ago. I lost control of my mind but I didn't mean to hurt anyone. I have no hate towards humanity. I hope He will forgive me for what I done. I didn't mean to."

Pronounced dead: 12:22 A.M.

Karl Hammond

Executed: June 21, 1995

TEXAS
EX 865
1987

Personal data: *Born:* July 4, 1964. *Race:* Black. *Height:* 5'10". *Weight:* 170 pounds. *Education:* 9 years. *Prior occupation:* Construction worker. *County of conviction:* Bexar. *Age at time of execution:* 30.

Sentenced to death for: Convicted of capital murder in the death of 21-year-old Donna Lynn Vetter in San Antonio on September 4, 1986. Vetter, an FBI secretary, was raped and stabbed to death after Hammond broke in to her apartment at 4848 Goldfield sometime between 9:30 P.M. and 10:55 P.M. Police said Hammond pulled the screen from the front window and surprised Vetter. She was stabbed once in the chest with a knife from her kitchen and sexually assaulted. Hammond's prints were found on an end table and on the murder weapon. *Note:* A few hours after he was convicted of capital murder on March 30, 1987, Hammond escaped from the Bexar County jail when a jailer left open a door separating a second-floor holding area and a visitation area. He was recaptured the following evening when police spotted him running across a street. Two jailers and two sergeants were fired for allowing Hammond to escape.

Received at death row: April 7, 1987. *Time on death row:* 2,997 days (8.21 years).

Last meal: A double-meat cheeseburger, french fries, chocolate milk, and cake or pie.

Last statement: n/a.

Pronounced dead: 12:23 A.M.

98

Vernon Lamar Sattiewhite

Executed: August 15, 1995

Personal data: *Born:* September 1, 1955. *Race:* Black. *Height:* 5'7". *Weight:* 209 pounds. *Education:* 10 years. *Prior occupation:* Forklift operator. *County of conviction:* Bexar. *Age at time of execution:* 39.

Sentenced to death for: Convicted in the June 1986 abduction and shooting death of his ex-girlfriend, Sandra Sorrell, in San Antonio. Sorrell was walking to nursing school near downtown San Antonio when Sattiewhite grabbed her in a headlock, dragged her several hundred feet across a parking lot, and then shot her twice in the head with a .22 caliber pistol. Sattiewhite then turned the gun on himself and attempted to commit suicide; the gun misfired. For more than a month before the murder, Sorrell had been calling police and the Bexar County District Attorney's Office in an effort to keep Sattiewhite away from her.

Received at death row: December 16, 1986. *Time on death row:* 3,164 days (8.67 years).

Last meal: Six scrambled eggs with cheese, seven pieces of buttered white toast, fifteen pieces of bacon, three hash browns, a bowl of grits with butter and jelly, and orange juice.

Last statement: "I would like to say I just hope Ms. Tielden is happy now. I would like to thank my lawyer Nancy for her help on my case and for being with me now."

Pronounced dead: 12:25 A.M.

Carl Johnson

Executed: September 19, 1995

Personal data: *Born:* March 5, 1955. *Race:* Black. *Height:* 5'8". *Weight:* 150 pounds. *Education:* 8 years. *Prior occupation:* Ironworker. *County of conviction:* Harris. *Age at time of execution:* 40.

Sentenced to death for: Convicted of murdering 75-year-old Ed Thompson, a security guard, during an armed robbery at Wayne's Food Store at 9210 W. Montgomery in Houston on October 6, 1978. His accomplice, Carl Baltimore, allegedly held a gun to the store owner's head; Johnson shot Thompson five times with a .38 caliber revolver.
Codefendant: Carl Baltimore was convicted of murder, sentenced to forty years, and paroled on August 17, 1987.

Received at death row: May 4, 1979. *Time on death row:* 5,982 days (16.39 years).

Last meal: T-bone steak, green salad, baked potato, banana nut ice cream, and Coke.

Last statement: "I want the world to know I'm innocent and that I've found peace. Let's ride."

Pronounced dead: 12:24 A.M.

100

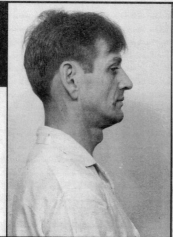

Harold Lane

Executed: October 4, 1995

TEXAS EX 7 4 5 1983

Personal data: *Born:* August 30, 1945. *Race:* White. *Height:* 5'10". *Weight:* 160 pounds. *Education:* 9 years (GED). *Prior occupation:* Electrician. *County of conviction:* Dallas. *Age at time of execution:* 50.

Sentenced to death for: Convicted in the November 20, 1982, shooting death of Tammy Davis, 17, a high school senior who was employed at a Dallas Winn-Dixie store. According to testimony, Lane robbed the store's cashier's office of $3,300, then tried to flee through the entrance side of the store's electronic doors. Davis, apparently unaware that a robbery had taken place, tried to explain that Lane was going through the wrong doors, when he raised his gun and shot her in the head.

Received at death row: July 28, 1983. *Time on death row:* 4,451 days (12.19 years).

Last meal: Two double-meat cheeseburgers, french fries, and a strawberry shake.

Last statement: "I wish you eternal happiness and everlasting peace. I have found everlasting peace with God. I wish the guys on the row peace. I have everlasting peace now and I am ready."

Pronounced dead: 6:28 P.M.

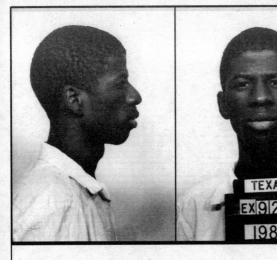

Bernard Eugene Amos

Executed: December 6, 1995

Personal data: *Born:* December 22, 1961. *Race:* Black. *Height:* 6'0". *Weight:* 150 pounds. *Education:* 11 years. *Prior occupation:* Mechanic. *County of conviction:* Dallas. *Age at time of execution:* 33.

Sentenced to death for: Convicted in the shooting death of 34-year-old James Joe at a Dallas apartment complex. Joe was investigating a burglary in progress in an apartment near his home when he confronted Amos and an unknown accomplice. Shots were exchanged before Joe fell with a fatal chest wound. Amos, wounded in the arm and leg, fled with his accomplice in a car that was later spotted by a police helicopter. Amos was arrested while attempting to crawl from the vehicle after it had been stopped. His accomplice apparently escaped.

Received at death row: December 15, 1988. *Time on death row:* 2,547 days (6.98 years).

Last meal: Two turkey sandwiches.

Last statement: "The State of Texas is making a mistake tonight. It does not do any good to have lawyers; they hold you to procedural law. Fifty percent of the cases before the CCA. They only hear the white ones. The State of Texas will take my life with eleven unanswered claims. May the grace of God have mercy on them."

Pronounced dead: 6:31 P.M.

102

Hai Hai Vuong

Executed: December 7, 1995

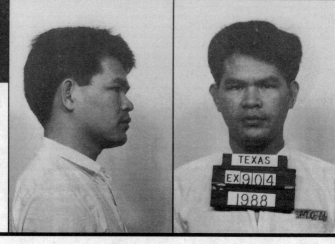

Personal data: *Born:* September 12, 1955. *Race:* Asian. *Height:* 5'5". *Weight:* 154 pounds. *Education:* 7 years. *Prior occupation:* Shrimper. *County of conviction:* Jefferson. *Age at time of execution:* 40.

Sentenced to death for: Convicted in the December 1986 shooting deaths of 16-year-old Hien Quang Tran and 27-year-old Tien Van Nguyen at a Port Arthur game room. The two victims were shot with a rifle inside the Tam Game Room at 648 Ninth Avenue. Three other men were wounded during the shooting, which reportedly stemmed from a prior argument.
Note: Court records indicate a capital murder indictment returned against Thien Huu Nguyen, but TDCJ has no record of incarceration as of July 1988.

Received at death row: May 27, 1988. *Time on death row:* 2,750 days (7.53 years).

Last meal: Steak, french fries, beans, and water.

Last statement: "I thank God that he died for my sins on the cross. And I thank Him for saving my soul so I will know when my body lays back in the grave my soul goes to be with the Lord. Praise God. I hope whoever hears my voice tonight will turn to the Lord. I give my spirit to Him. Praise the Lord. Praise Jesus. Hallelujah."

Pronounced dead: 6:22 P.M.

Esequel Banda

Executed: December 11, 1995

Personal data: *Born:* December 19, 1963. *Race:* Hispanic. *Height:* 5'5". *Weight:* 140 pounds. *Education:* 9 years. *Prior occupation:* Laborer. *County of conviction:* Hamilton. *Age at time of execution:* 31.

Sentenced to death for: Convicted of capital murder in the stabbing death of Merle Laird, a Hamilton housewife, on August 3, 1986. Laird was sexually assaulted and then stabbed several times inside her home at 620 South Bell Street. Banda reportedly told friends he stabbed a woman and sucked the blood that was coming from her mouth.

Received at death row: March 25, 1987. *Time on death row:* 3,183 days (8.72 years).

Last meal: Declined last meal.

Last statement: None.

Pronounced dead: 6:21 P.M.

104

James Michael Briddle

Executed:
December 12, 1995

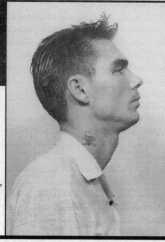

Personal data: *Born:* April 7, 1955. *Race:* White. *Height:* 5'11". *Weight:* 160 pounds. *Education:* 7 years. *Prior occupation:* Laborer. *County of conviction:* Harris. *Age at time of execution:* 40.

Sentenced to death for: Convicted of capital murder in the February 24, 1980, slaying of Robert Banks, a 30-year-old oil company worker in Houston. Banks and a friend, 26-year-old Bob Skeens, were found strangled in Banks's home in the 2900 block of Hepburn. Missing from the home were $800 in cash, credit cards, a car, a camera, and several weapons. Testimony showed that Briddle, his ex-wife, Linda Briddle Fletcher, and a companion, Pamela Lynn Perillo, were picked up by Banks while they were hitchhiking near the Houston Astrodome and offered a ride and a place to spend the night. Banks and Skeens, who was visiting at Banks's home from Louisiana, were both strangled with a rope after returning with coffee and doughnuts for their guests. The three suspects drove Skeens's car to Dallas and then took a bus to Colorado, where they were arrested in early March 1980 after Perillo gave a statement to authorities in Denver. *Codefendants:* Linda Briddle Fletcher was convicted of robbery and placed on five years probation. Pamela Lynn Perillo was convicted of capital murder in Skeens's death and sentenced to die by injection.

Received at death row: April 15, 1982. *Time on death row:* 4,989 days (13.67 years).

Last meal: T-bone steak (cooked rare), six fried eggs, hash browns, buttered toast, milk, and orange juice.

Last statement: "I love you. You all take care of Mom and Dad. I'm ready [when needle reinserted]. I'm leaving you. I can taste it. I'll see you later on."
Note: Officials removed the needle from the left arm because of poor flow. At 6:15, the left arm blew out, and officials had to start over. At 6:23, officials set the needle in the left forearm.

Pronounced dead: 6:35 P.M.

Leo Ernest Jenkins Jr.

Executed: February 9, 1996

TEXAS
EX967
FEB. 90

Personal data: *Born:* October 12, 1957. *Race:* White. *Height:* 5'10". *Weight:* 182 pounds. *Education:* 10 years. *Prior occupation:* Mechanic. *County of conviction:* Harris. *Age at time of execution:* 38.

Sentenced to death for: Convicted in the August 1988 shooting deaths of Kara Denise Voss and her brother Mark Brandon Kelley during the robbery of a Houston pawnshop. The brother and sister were working at the Golden Nugget at 9822 Airline Drive when Jenkins and his codefendant, Eugene Hart, entered around 2:00 P.M. Jenkins approached the counter and told Voss he was interested in placing a rifle on layaway. As Voss was preparing the layaway slip, Jenkins pulled out a .22 caliber pistol and shot her in the head. Jenkins then shot Kelley in the face and head. The codefendants took several trays of jewelry before fleeing. Jenkins confessed the crime to police following his and Hart's arrests on September 1, 1988.
Codefendant: Hart was convicted of murder (two) and credit card abuse and sentenced to life in prison.
Note: Jenkins was identified in part because of his extensive tattoos. Each tear tattooed on his face denoted a trip to prison for burglary.

Received at death row: March 1, 1990. *Time on death row:* 2,171 days (5.95 years).

Last meal: Two bacon cheeseburgers, french fries, and Coke.

Last statement: "I would like to say that I believe that Jesus Christ is my Lord and savior. I am sorry for the loss of the Kelleys but my death won't bring them back. I believe that the State of Texas is making a mistake tonight. Tell my family I love them. I'm ready."

Pronounced dead: 6:29 P.M.

106

Kenneth Granviel

Executed: February 27, 1996

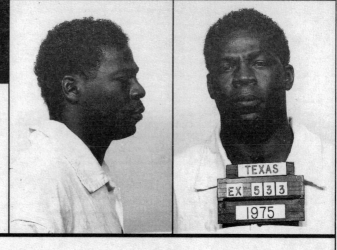

TEXAS
EX 533
1975

Personal data: *Born:* August 4, 1950. *Race:* Black. *Height:* 6'2". *Weight:* 190 pounds. *Education:* 12 years. *Prior occupation:* Machinist. *County of conviction:* Tarrant. *Age at time of execution:* 45.

Sentenced to death for: Convicted of capital murder in the October 1974 stabbing death of 2-year-old Natasha McClendon in Fort Worth. The young girl was one of seven people Granviel killed during two separate murder sprees. Also killed on October 7 inside a Fort Worth apartment complex were Martha McClendon, the young girl's mother; Linda McClendon; and Laura McClendon and her 3-year-old son, Steven. All of the victims were murdered with a butcher knife. All were friends of Granviel's. Granviel surrendered to police on February 8, 1975. He later admitted to the killings of two other personal friends, Betty Williams and Vera Hill. Both women were raped and stabbed to death with a knife. Granviel led authorities to their bodies.
Note: The Fifth U.S. Circuit Court of Appeals in New Orleans set aside the death penalty in Granviel's case because at least one prospective juror was improperly disqualified after members of the jury panel were questioned about their views on the death penalty. Granviel was again tried in May 1983 and sentenced to death upon conviction.

Received at death row: November 21, 1975. *Time on death row:* 7,403 days (20.28 years).

Last meal: A double-meat cheeseburger, french fries, chocolate cake, and punch.

Last statement: None.

Pronounced dead: 6:20 P.M.

Joe Fedelfido Gonzales Jr.

Executed: September 18, 1996

Personal data: *Born:* November 17, 1960. *Race:* Hispanic. *Height:* 5'10". *Weight:* 253 pounds. *Education:* 11 years (GED). *Prior occupation:* General contractor. *County of conviction:* Potter. *Age at time of execution:* 35.

Sentenced to death for: Convicted in the October 19, 1992, shooting death of 50-year-old William J. Veader in Amarillo. Veader died from a single gunshot wound to the head, which initially appeared to have been self-inflicted. A subsequent investigation revealed that Gonzales killed Veader and then arranged the crime scene to make it look like a suicide. Police also discovered that Gonzales had stolen a number of items, including cash, from the rental home Veader owned at 1001 S. Hodges.

Received at death row: January 10, 1996. *Time on death row:* 252 days (0.69 year).

Last meal: A strawberry shake and cheesecake.

Last statement: "There are people all over the world who face things worse than death on a daily basis, and in that sense I consider myself lucky. I cannot find the words to express the sadness I feel for bringing this hurt and pain on my loved ones. I will not ask forgiveness for the decisions I have made in this judicial process, only acceptance. God bless you all."

Pronounced dead: 6:19 P.M.

108

Richard Brimage Jr.

Executed:
February 10,
1997

TEXAS
433730
1986

Personal data: *Born:* December 5, 1955. *Race:* White. *Height:* 5'8". *Weight:* 153 pounds. *Education:* 12 years. *Prior occupation:* Electrician. *County of conviction:* Kleberg. *Age at time of execution:* 41.

Sentenced to death for: Convicted in the October 1987 abduction and slaying of Mary Beth Kunkel, of Kingsville. Kunkel was reportedly lured to Brimage's residence, where she was sexually assaulted, strangled, and suffocated with a sock.
Codefendant: Leonel Molina was convicted of murder and sentenced to 50 years in prison.

Received at death row: April 20, 1988. *Time on death row:* 3,218 days (8.82 years).

Last meal: Pepperoni pizza (medium) and Dr Pepper.

Last statement: "Not from me but I have a message to you from God. Save the children. Find one who needs help and make a small sacrifice of your own wealth and save the innocent ones. They are the key for making the world a better place."

Pronounced dead: 6:20 P.M.

109

John Kennedy Barefield

Executed: March 12, 1997

Personal data: *Born:* March 30, 1964. *Race:* Black. *Height:* 5'8". *Weight:* 168 pounds. *Education:* 8 years. *Prior occupation:* Carpenter. *County of conviction:* Harris. *Age at time of execution:* 32.

Sentenced to death for: Convicted in the April 1986 rape and execution-style slaying of Cindy Rounsaville, a 25-year-old Rice University student. Rounsaville was abducted by Barefield and two other men as she was walking to her car in the parking lot of her southwest Houston apartment complex. She was forced into her car and driven to her bank, where she was forced to withdraw $70 from an automatic teller machine. Rounsaville was then taken to a remote field in southwest Houston, where she was sexually assaulted by all three men and shot twice in the back of the head by Barefield after she tried to run. After the shooting, the suspects reportedly drove the victim's car to the other side of Houston and robbed another woman at gunpoint. They then drove back to near where Rounsville was killed and set her car afire.
Codefendants: Perry J. Barefield was convicted of aggravated robbery and sentenced to forty-five years in prison. Earnest Lee Sonnier is serving a life sentence for an unrelated aggravated kidnapping of a 24-year-old Houston woman.

Received at death row: September 26, 1986. *Time on death row:* 3,820 days (10.47 years).

Last meal: A double-meat cheeseburger and french fries.

Last statement: [Mumbled] "Tell Mama I love her."

Pronounced dead: 6:18 P.M.

110

**David
Lee
Herman**

Executed:
April 2, 1997

Personal data: *Born:* November 7, 1957. *Race:* White. *Height:* 6'4". *Weight:* 235 pounds. *Education:* 14 years. *Prior occupation:* Stockbroker. *County of conviction:* Tarrant. *Age at time of execution:* 39.

Sentenced to death for: Convicted in the December 1989 shooting death of 21-year-old Jennifer E. Burns during the robbery of the LACE topless nightclub in Arlington. Burns, a club employee, was shot three times after fighting off an attempted sexual assault by Herman. She and club manager Harold "Clay" Griffin and club hostess Sally Fogle were forced into the club office, where Herman stole $20,000 from a safe and then shot all three employees. Griffin and Fogle survived. Approximately $8,500 of the stolen money was recovered following Herman's arrest in Kennedale on December 30, 1989. Herman had been employed as manager of the LACE nightclub in 1987.

Received at death row: June 21, 1991. *Time on death row:* 2,112 days (5.78 years).

Last meal: A hamburger, pizza, root beer, and vanilla ice cream.

Last statement: "It was horrible and inexcusable for me to take the life of your loved one and to hurt so many mentally and physically. I am here because I took a life, and killing is wrong by an individual and by the state, and I am sorry we are here, but if my death gives you peace and closure then this is all worthwhile. To all of my friends and family, I love you and I am going home."

Pronounced dead: 7:09 P.M.

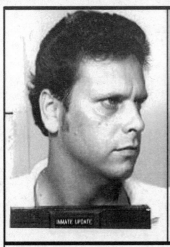
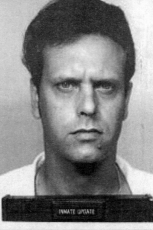

David Wayne Spence

Executed: April 3, 1997

Personal data: *Born:* July 18, 1956. *Race:* White. *Height:* 5'9". *Weight:* 176 pounds. *Education:* 9 years (GED). *Prior occupation:* Roofer. *County of conviction:* McLennan. *Age at time of execution:* 40.

Sentenced to death for: Twice convicted of capital murder in the July 1982 mistaken-identity killings of three teenagers in a botched murder-for-hire scheme. Accomplice Muneer Mohammed Deeb reportedly hired Spence and two other codefendants to kill his girlfriend, Gayle Kelley, for a share of the benefits to be paid on a life insurance policy he had taken out on her. However, Spence and his accomplices apparently mistook 17-year-old Jill Montgomery, of Waxahachie, for Kelley, who friends said closely resembled Montgomery. Montgomery and friends Raylene Rice, 17, and Kenneth Franks, 18, were stabbed to death at a Waco lakeside park. Both women were sexually assaulted before being killed. Spence was convicted of capital murder and given the death penalty for the slayings of Montgomery and Franks.
Codefendants: Muneer Mohammad Deeb was convicted of capital murder and sentenced to death. His case was retried and dismissed in 1996. Anthony Melendez was convicted of murder (two) and sentenced to ninety-nine years in prison. Gilbert Melendez was convicted of murder and sentenced to life in prison.

Received at death row: October 11, 1984. *Time on death row:* 4,557 days (12.48 years).

Last meal: Fried chicken, french fries, chocolate ice cream, Coke, tea, and coffee.

Last statement: "Yes, I do. First of all, I want you to understand I speak the truth when I say I didn't kill your kids, anyone. Honestly, I have not killed anyone. I wish you could get the rage from your hearts and you could see the truth and get rid of the hatred. I love you all [names of children, other names garbled]. This is very important. I love you and I miss you. OK. Now I'm finished."

Pronounced dead: 6:32 P.M.

112

Billy Joe Woods

Executed:
April 14, 1997

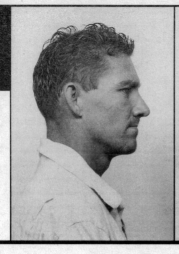

Personal data: *Born:* December 20, 1946. *Race:* White. *Height:* 5'11". *Weight:* 150 pounds. *Education:* 10 years. *Prior occupation:* Laborer. *County of conviction:* Harris. *Age at time of execution:* 50.

Sentenced to death for: Convicted in the beating and strangulation death of Mabel E. Ehatt, a 62-year-old disabled woman. Woods broke into Ehatt's second-story apartment in the 2000 block of Fairmont in Houston and brutally beat her before raping her. Woods then ransacked the apartment and was in the process of stealing her television set when police arrived. Woods was a suspect in a similar attack on a Louisiana woman, who survived.

Received at death row: July 30, 1976. *Time on death row:* 7,563 days (20.72 years).

Last meal: A hamburger, french fries, banana pudding, and coffee.

Last statement: None.

Pronounced dead: 6:30 P.M.

Kenneth Edward Gentry

Executed: April 16, 1997

Personal data: *Born:* January 28, 1961. *Race:* White. *Height:* 6'2". *Weight:* 157 pounds. *Education:* 9 years (GED). *Prior occupation:* Mechanic. *County of conviction:* Denton. *Age at time of execution:* 36.

Sentenced to death for: Convicted in the September 1983 capital murder of 23-year-old Jimmy Don Ham, whose body was found in a park on the shore of Lake Lewisville. Ham had been shot once in the chest and once in the head. Prosecutors said Gentry, who escaped from a Georgia prison in 1982, killed Ham in a scheme to assume Ham's identity because Gentry was wanted. He was arrested in Austin, Minnesota, on September 15, 1983, two days after Ham's body was found.
Note: In November 1984 Gentry and fellow death row inmate Jewel McGee attempted to escape from the Ellis Unit by jumping a security fence. Correctional Officer Minnie Houston, armed with a shotgun, stopped the pair at the front gate and held them until assistance arrived. Gentry broke his ankle in the escape attempt.

Received at death row: March 5, 1984. *Time on death row:* 4,790 days (13.12 years).

Last meal: A bowl of butter beans, mashed potatoes, onions, tomatoes, biscuits, chocolate cake, and Dr Pepper with ice.

Last statement: "Thank you Lord for the past fourteen years that have allowed me to grow as a man. To JD's family, I am sorry for the suffering you have gone through the past fourteen years. I hope you can get some peace tonight. To my family, I am happy to be going home to Jesus. Sweet Jesus, here I come. Take me home. I am going your way."

Pronounced dead: 6:24 P.M.

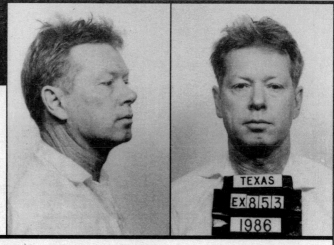

114

Benjamin H. Boyle

Executed:
April 21,
1997

Personal data: *Born:* July 22, 1943. *Race:* White. *Height:* 5'5". *Weight:* 192 pounds. *Education:* 10 years. *Prior occupation:* Truck driver. *County of conviction:* Potter. *Age at time of execution:* 53.

Sentenced to death for: Convicted in the October 1985 murder of 20-year-old Gail Lenore Smith, near Amarillo. Smith, who worked as a cocktail waitress in Fort Worth and often hitched rides with truckers, was raped and strangled to death with a necktie by Boyle, a driver for Jewett Scott Trucking, of Magnum, Oklahoma. Her nude body was found north of Amarillo, near the Canadian River bridge on Highway 287. Both her hands and feet had been bound by duct tape. Boyle's fingerprints were lifted from the adhesive side of some duct tape found in a trash can not far from the victim's body. Smith's mother told police that her daughter often hitchhiked and preferred to ride with truckers because she trusted them. She had accepted a ride with Boyle in Fort Worth on October 14. The truck was reportedly traveling to Canon City, Colorado, with a load of lumber when the murder occurred.

Received at death row: December 5, 1986. *Time on death row:* 3,790 days (10.38 years).

Last meal: A double-meat cheeseburger, french fries with ketchup, and Coke.

Last statement: None.

Pronounced dead: 6:21 P.M.

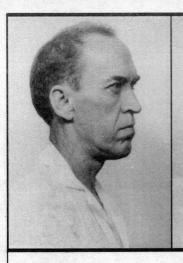

115

Ernest Orville Baldree

Executed: April 29, 1997

Personal data: *Born:* March 27, 1942. *Race:* White. *Height:* 5'9". *Weight:* 174 pounds. *Education:* 7 years. *Prior occupation:* Construction worker. *County of conviction:* Navarro. *Age at time of execution:* 55.

Sentenced to death for: Convicted in the August 1986 deaths of Homer and Nancy Howard at their residence in Coolidge. Baldree was last paroled to the care of a Coolidge man who was a friend of the Howards. He said that on August 20, 1986, the Howards had come to his home and convinced him to return with them so he could help Mr. Howard fix his fence. The bodies of the husband and wife were found seven days later. Mrs. Howard was found lying on the kitchen floor with knife and gunshot wounds. Her husband's body was found inside his pickup, parked in a field adjacent to their house trailer. He had been shot once in the head. Baldree fled in the victim's car, taking cash and jewelry worth approximately $1,500. He was arrested in Arlington on October 31, 1986.

Received at death row: December 10, 1986. *Time on death row:* 3,793 days (10.39 years).

Last meal: A double-meat cheeseburger, french fries, and a pack of cigarettes (prohibited by policy).

Last statement: None.

Pronounced dead: 6:25 P.M.

116

Terry Washington

Executed:
May 6,
1997

Personal data: *Born:* September 12, 1963. *Race:* Black. *Height:* 5'6". *Weight:* 150 pounds. *Education:* 9 years. *Prior occupation:* Dishwasher. *County of conviction:* Brazos. *Age at time of execution:* 33.

Sentenced to death for: Convicted in the January 1987 robbery-slaying of 29-year-old Beatrice Louise Huling, manager of Julie's Place restaurant at 607 Texas Avenue in College Station. Washington, a dishwasher at the restaurant, stabbed Huling eighty-five times after closing and then stole $628 from the restaurant safe and cash register. Witnesses reported seeing Washington with several $100 bills days after the murder. Police also discovered Huling's blood on the pants and boots Washington had worn to work the day of the murder. He was arrested at his aunt's home in Bryan on February 25, 1987.

Received at death row: September 15, 1987. *Time on death row:* 3,521 days (9.65 years).

Last meal: Steak, mashed potatoes, green beans, buttered rolls, chocolate ice cream, and punch.

Last statement: None.

Pronounced dead: 6:18 P.M.

117

Anthony Ray Westley

Executed: May 13, 1997

Personal data: *Born:* July 18, 1960. *Race:* Black. *Height:* 6'3". *Weight:* 225 pounds. *Education:* 8 years. *Prior occupation:* Laborer. *County of conviction:* Harris. *Age at time of execution:* 36.

Sentenced to death for: Convicted in the April 1984 robbery and murder of 39-year-old Chester Frank Hall, owner of Eileen's Bait and Tackle Shop on C. E. King Parkway in northeast Harris County. Westley and two accomplices were robbing a female clerk of approximately $75 from the cash register when Hall entered with a pistol. Shots were exchanged, with one fatally wounding accomplice Lee Edward Dunbar. He died at the scene. When Hall retreated from the store, Westley pursued him and shot him once in the back with a .22 caliber pistol after a struggle.

Received at death row: May 23, 1985. *Time on death row:* 4,373 days (11.98 years).

Last meal: Fried chicken, french fries, bread, and cigarettes (prohibited by policy).

Last statement: "I want you to know that I did not kill anyone. I love you all." [Inmate's words were not clear—he was choked up.]

Pronounced dead: 6:30 P.M.

118

Clifton Eugene Belyeu

Executed: May 16, 1997

Personal data: *Born:* June 30, 1958. *Race:* White. *Height:* 5'8". *Weight:* 165 pounds. *Education:* 7 years. *Prior occupation:* Painter. *County of conviction:* McLennan. *Age at time of execution:* 38.

Sentenced to death for: Convicted in the December 10, 1985, murder of 36-year-old Melodie Lundgren Bolton, of West, about fifteen miles north of Waco, during a robbery of her home.

Received at death row: September 3, 1986. *Time on death row:* 3,908 days (10.71 years).

Last meal: A cheeseburger, french fries, Coke, and a pack of cigarettes (prohibited by policy).

Last statement: See Appendix.

Pronounced dead: 6:22 P.M.

Richard G. Drinkard

Executed: May 19, 1997

TEXAS
EX846
1986

Personal data: *Born:* July 11, 1957. *Race:* White. *Height:* 5'11". *Weight:* 150 pounds. *Education:* 12 years. *Prior occupation:* Carpenter. *County of conviction:* Harris. *Age at time of execution:* 39.

Sentenced to death for: Convicted of capital murder in connection with the stabbing-bludgeoning slayings of three people in a Houston townhome in November 1985. Killed were Lou Ann Anthony, 44, owner of the townhome; her sister, LaDean Hendrix, 47; and Hendrix's friend, Jerry Mullens, 43. The three were stabbed and beaten with a claw hammer. Drinkard had been introduced to Anthony the day of the murder and had several drinks in her townhome that night. Drinkard returned to the townhome hours later, broke in by prying open a window and dismantling a deadbolt lock, and began beating the victims. He took $350 from the house. Police arrested Drinkard on November 20, 1985.

Received at death row: October 16, 1986. *Time on death row:* 3,868 days (10.60 years).

Last meal: A double cheeseburger, french fries, Coke, and strawberry ice cream.

Last statement: None.

Pronounced dead: 6:17 P.M.

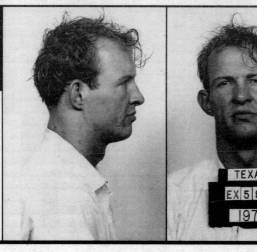

120

**Clarence
Allen
Lackey**

Executed:
May 20, 1997

Personal data: *Born:* August 3, 1954. *Race:* White. *Height:* 6'1". *Weight:* 190 pounds. *Education:* 9 years. *Prior occupation:* Laborer. *County of conviction:* Tom Green. *Age at time of execution:* 42.

Sentenced to death for: Convicted in the July 1977 abduction and slashing death of 20-year-old Diane Kumph in Lubbock. Kumph was raped and beaten and had her throat slashed by Lackey, who also burglarized her apartment. Her partially nude body was discovered beside a dirt road near Lackey's house outside Lubbock. Kumph's apartment door had been kicked open, and there were indications of a violent struggle inside her apartment. In September 1982, the Texas Court of Criminal Appeals ruled that a juror was improperly dismissed at Lackey's trial and reversed the case. He was tried a second time in Midland County in May 1983 and sentenced to death upon conviction.

Received at death row: April 18, 1978. *Time on death row:* 6,972 days (19.10 years).

Last meal: T-bone steak, salad, french fries, chocolate ice cream, and a pack of Camel cigarettes (prohibited by policy).

Last statement: "I would like to thank my Lord Jesus Christ for keeping me strong all these years. I would also like to thank my mother for standing by me all these years. I would also like to thank my pen pals Joe and Camille Nelling and Jo Ann for helping me stay strong all these years. I also thank my two lawyers, Rita and Brent, for fighting to keep me alive."

Pronounced dead: 6:17 P.M.

121

Bruce Edwin Callins

Executed: May 21, 1997

Personal data: *Born:* February 22, 1960. *Race:* Black. *Height:* 5'11". *Weight:* 190 pounds. *Education:* 10 years. *Prior occupation:* Cement finisher. *County of conviction:* Tarrant. *Age at time of execution:* 37.

Sentenced to death for: At approximately four P.M. on June 27, 1980, Callins, armed with a gun, entered a Dallas bar and announced he would "shoot anyone who held anything back." Callins apparently thought bar customer Allen Huckleberry was responding too slowly and shot him once in the neck. Callins was sentenced to die for the murder of Huckleberry, given two life sentences, and fined $20,000 for the aggravated robberies of George Torrez and Kathy Harmon.
Note: On April 15, 1985, Callins threw a caustic liquid in the face and eyes of TDCJ officer Deryl W. Robertson and cut Officer Charles B. Anderson with a handmade spear. He was sentenced to five years for aggravated assault.

Received at death row: July 5, 1982. *Time on death row:* 5,434 days (14.89 years).

Last meal: Steak, french fries, salad, pecan pie, and a pack of cigarettes (prohibited by policy).

Last statement: "I want to let all of my people know and everybody who is here and supported me that I love them and wish them all the best."

Pronounced dead: 6:29 P.M.

122

Larry Wayne White

Executed: May 22, 1997

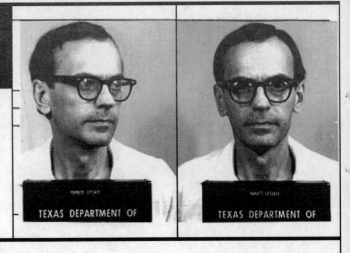

TEXAS DEPARTMENT OF

TEXAS DEPARTMENT OF

Personal data: *Born:* March 10, 1950. *Race:* White. *Height:* 5'8". *Weight:* 140 pounds. *Education:* 12 years. *Prior occupation:* Produce manager. *County of conviction:* Harris. *Age at time of execution:* 47.

Sentenced to death for: Convicted in the March 1977 robbery-slaying of Elizabeth St. John at the Airline Apartments in Houston. St. John (court records list her age as 72, while newspaper accounts list her age as 92) was strangled and stabbed in the back with a screwdriver. White, who at the time of the murder worked as a maintenance man at the apartment complex in the 4300 block of Airline, stole St. John's car and drove to Myrtle Beach, South Carolina, where he was arrested while burglarizing a restaurant.

Received at death row: August 6, 1979. *Time on death row:* 6,499 days (17.81 years).

Last meal: Liver and onions, cottage cheese, red tomatoes, and a single cigarette (prohibited by policy).

Last statement: "I would like to apologize for all of the hurt and pain and disappointment I caused to my family, the victim's family, and all my friends. I hope all the veterans and teenagers out there who have a drug problem will get help. I hope the Lord will forgive me of all of my sins. I thank Jack and Kathy for being with me. I hope those who support the death row inmates will continue to work and maybe we can get this resolved and do away with the death penalty. I hope that this is a lot better place where I am going."

Pronounced dead: 6:16 P.M.
Note: White was the first executed offender in Texas to be given a military burial. He was a veteran of the Vietnam War.

123

Robert Anthony Madden

Executed: May 28, 1997

Personal data: *Born:* September 27, 1963. *Race:* White. *Height:* 5'9". *Weight:* 138 pounds. *Education:* 12 years. *Prior occupation:* Cook. *County of conviction:* Leon. *Age at time of execution:* 33.

Sentenced to death for: Convicted in the September 1985 shooting-stabbing deaths of Herbert Elbert Megason, 56, and his son Don Gary Lynn Megason, 22. The bodies of the victims had been bound and placed in a small creek with brush piled on top of them. One man's throat was cut.

Received at death row: February 28, 1986. *Time on death row:* 4,107 days (11.25 years).

Last meal: Asked that final meal be provided to a homeless person.

Last statement: "Yes sir, I do. Well, here we are. I apologize for your loss and your pain but I didn't kill those people. Hopefully we will all learn something about ourselves and about each other, and we will learn enough to stop the circle of hate and vengeance and come to value what is really going on in this world. We can't look back. I forgive everyone for this process, which seems to be wrong. We all end up doing experiences which we create. That is all I have to say about that." [There were a couple of sentences that could not be understood.]

Pronounced dead: 6:42 P.M.

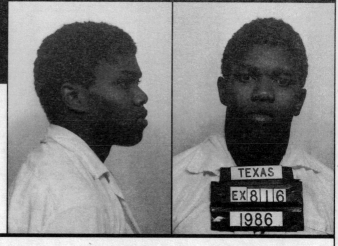

124

Patrick F. Rogers

Executed:
June 2,
1997

TEXAS
EX 8 1 6
1986

Personal data: *Born:* January 6, 1964. *Race:* Black. *Height:* 5'5". *Weight:* 150 pounds. *Education:* 10 years. *Prior occupation:* Waiter. *County of conviction:* Collin. *Age at time of execution:* 33.

Sentenced to death for: Convicted in the September 1985 shooting death of 23-year-old David Wilburn Roberts, a Paris, Texas, police officer. Rogers and codefendant Willis Deron Cooper had robbed a Paris store of approximately $685, when their car was spotted and stopped by Officer Roberts at the entrance of the Ramada Inn in Paris. Before Officer Roberts could get out of his patrol car, Rogers reportedly got out of his vehicle and fired shots through the patrol car windshield. He then stepped to the driver's side window and fired four to six more times through the window. Officer Roberts died at the scene. Rogers and Cooper were arrested after robbing a Paris woman of her car and wedding ring and kidnapping another man.
Codefendant: Willis Deron Cooper was convicted of aggravated robbery with a deadly weapon and sentenced to life in prison.

Received at death row: January 20, 1986. *Time on death row:* 4,151 days (11.37 years).

Last meal: A Coke.

Last statement: "Yes. I would like to praise Allah and I am praying to Allah. Allah is most gracious. I will ask Allah for forgiveness because he created me and he will forgive me. All for the brothers on the row stay strong. [Some words about Allah that were not intelligible] I love my family. My mother, I will see you sooner or later. Life goes on. Don't let these people break you. Keep true to nature. You do not have to act like them. Rise above it [garbled]. Praise Allah [garbled]."

Pronounced dead: 6:17 P.M.

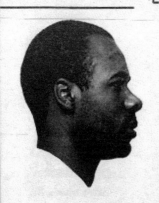

Kenneth Bernard Harris

Executed: June 3, 1997

1986 rape and sl[...] f 28-year-old

Personal data: *Born:* August 8, 1962. *Race:* Black. *Height:* 5'11". *Weight:* 184 pounds. *Education:* 11 years. *Prior occupation:* Truck driver. *County of conviction:* Harris. *Age at time of execution:* 34.

Sentenced to death for: Convicted in the July 1986 rape and slaying of 28-year-old Lisa Ann Stonestreet in Houston. Stonestreet was raped inside her apartment at 5402 Renwick, then strangled and drowned. Prosecutors contend Harris committed at least seven other rapes and robberies in Houston between December 1985 and July 1986.

Received at death row: May 13, 1988. *Time on death row:* 3,308 days (9.06 years).

Last meal: Barbecue, french fries, ice cream, punch, and cigarettes (prohibited by policy).

Last statement: "I would like to thank all of you for coming. I am sorry for all of the pain I have caused both the families—my family and yours. I would like for you to know that I am sorry for all the pain I caused for all these years. I have had time to understand the pain I have caused you. I am ready, Warden."

Pronounced dead: 6:17 P.M.

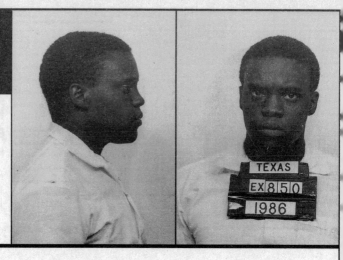

126

Dorsie Johnson Jr.

Executed:
June 4,
1997

TEXAS
EX 850
1986

Personal data: *Born:* March 10, 1967. *Race:* Black. *Height:* 5'2". *Weight:* 158 pounds. *Education:* 11 years. *Prior occupation:* Janitor. *County of conviction:* Scurry. *Age at time of execution:* 30.

Sentenced to death for: Convicted in the March 1986 shooting death of 53-year-old Jack Huddleston, a clerk at Allsup's convenience store in Snyder. Huddleston was shot once in the head with a .25 caliber pistol after being told to lie down on the floor during a robbery that netted $161.92.
Codefendant: Amanda Lynn Miles was convicted of aggravated robbery and sentenced to sixty years in prison.

Received at death row: November 20, 1986. *Time on death row:* 3,849 days (10.55 years).

Last meal: Fried chicken, french fries, chocolate cake, and Coke.

Last statement: "I would like to tell my family that I love them and always be strong and keep their heads up and keep faith in Jesus. That's it."

Pronounced dead: 6:18 P.M.
Note: Johnson was executed the same day as Davis Losada. (See entry 127, Davis Losada.)

**Davis
Losada**

Executed:
June 4,
1997

Personal data: *Born:* April 28, 1965. *Race:* Hispanic. *Height:* 5'9". *Weight:* 166 pounds. *Education:* 11 years. *Prior occupation:* Cook. *County of conviction:* Cameron. *Age at time of execution:* 32.

Sentenced to death for: Convicted along with three codefendants in the rape and murder of 15-year-old Olga Perales near San Benito. Perales was stabbed twice in the chest and abdomen and beaten around the head with a pipe. She had been raped repeatedly before her death.
Codefendants: Jesus Romero Jr. was convicted of capital murder, sentenced to death by lethal injection, and executed on May 20, 1992. (See entry 49, Jesus Romero Jr.) Jose F. Cardenas was convicted of murder and sentenced to life in prison. Rafael Layva Jr. was convicted of sexual assault, sentenced to twenty years, and released under mandatory supervision on July 1, 1996.

Received at death row: June 20, 1985. *Time on death row:* 4,367 days (11.96 years).

Last meal: Declined last meal.

Last statement: "If it matters to anyone, I didn't kill Olga. Brian, thank you for caring. Dee Dee, you have been a good sister to all of us. Ana and Chico, trust in God. I will always love you, Lynn. I will always love you. OK, Warden."

Pronounced dead: 7:30 P.M.
Note: Losada was executed the same day as Dorsie Johnson Jr. (See entry 126, Dorsie Johnson Jr.)

128

Earl Russell Behringer

Executed: June 11, 1997

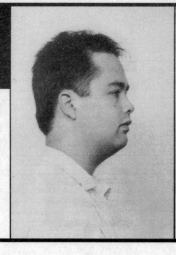 

Personal data: *Born:* January 3, 1964. *Race:* White. *Height:* 5'11". *Weight:* 186 pounds. *Education:* 14 years. *Prior occupation:* Student/sales. *County of conviction:* Tarrant. *Age at time of execution:* 33.

Sentenced to death for: Convicted in the September 1986 slayings of 22-year-old Daniel B. Meyer Jr. and his 21-year-old fiancée, Janet Louise Hancock. Meyer, a Texas A&M student, and Hancock, who attended the University of Texas at Arlington, were shot to death after Behringer and codefendant Lawrence Scott Rouse saw the couple parked in a field near Mansfield. Both were shot repeatedly in the head with a 9mm pistol police later recovered from Behringer. Meyer's wallet and Hancock's purse were taken. Rouse surrendered to police and confessed that Behringer had wanted to go to the area so he could harass parkers. *Codefendant:* Lawrence Scott Rouse was convicted of murder and sentenced to forty years in prison.

Received at death row: September 27, 1988. *Time on death row:* 3,179 days (8.71 years).

Last meal: Large portion of scrambled eggs, two tablespoons of picante sauce on the side, hash browns, two pieces of toast, gravy, two pieces of sausage, and grape juice.

Last statement: "It's a good day to die. I walked in here like a man and I am leaving here a man. I've had a good life. I have known the love of a good woman, my wife. I have a good family. My grandmother is the pillar of the community. I love and cherish my friends and family. Thank you for your love. To the Hancock family, I am sorry for the pain I caused you. If my death gives you any peace, so be it. I want my friends to know it is not the way to die, but I belong to Jesus Christ. I confess my sins. I have been baptized. I am going home with Him. I thank my friends for their support, and I thank the Dallas Cowboys for bringing me lots of joy these past years. Tell my wife and family I love them."

Pronounced dead: 6:17 P.M.

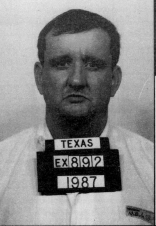

Personal data: *Born:* January 25, 1959. *Race:* White. *Height:* 5'11". *Weight:* 223 pounds. *Education:* 8 years. *Prior occupation:* Heavy equipment operator/carpenter. *County of conviction:* Hale. *Age at time of execution:* 38.

Sentenced to death for: Convicted in the November 1986 robbery-slaying of 50-year-old David Manrrique, a clerk at Allsup's convenience store in Hale Center. Manrrique was shot with a .22 caliber pistol during an early morning robbery that netted $60. Stoker also served a thirty-year sentence for delivery of methamphetamine. That sentence was assessed in Swisher County in August 1988.

Received at death row: December 7, 1987. *Time on death row:* 3,479 days (9.53 years).

Last meal: Two double-meat cheeseburgers, french fries, ice cream, and cigarettes (prohibited by policy).

Last statement: "I have a statement prepared that I have given to the chaplain that I want released to the media. I am ready, Warden." [Statement n/a.]

Pronounced dead: 6:15 P.M.

130

Eddie James Johnson

Executed:
June 17, 1997

Personal data: *Born:* July 31, 1952. *Race:* Black. *Height:* 6'2". *Weight:* 225 pounds. *Education:* 11 years. *Prior occupation:* Welder. *County of conviction:* Aransas. *Age at time of execution:* 44.

Sentenced to death for: Convicted in the September 1987 abduction and slaying of three people in Aransas County. Victims David Magee, Virginia Cadena, and Cadena's 10-year-old daughter, Elizabeth Galvan, were abducted from the Jackson Square Apartments in Aransas Pass and driven to a remote location near the intersection of FM 1069 and Johnson Road, where they were shot to death with a .25 caliber pistol. Magee's hands and feet were bound with telephone and electrical cords, as were Cadena's hands. Her young daughter died from four bullet wounds to the abdomen. Johnson, who once worked for the same company as Magee, had recently been fired from his job and reportedly blamed Magee for his termination. The victims' bloodstained car was found parked at a nursing home close to Johnson's residence. Police also found Johnson's fingerprints at Magee's apartment and on a can inside the car. A pair of blood-soaked blue jeans worn by Johnson was also recovered from a Dumpster near his home.

Received at death row: April 19, 1988. *Time on death row:* 3,346 days (9.17 years).

Last meal: A double-meat cheeseburger, french fries, and broccoli with cheese.

Last statement: "I would like to say to the Magee family and to the Cadena family that I was friends with David and Virginia and I did not commit this offense. I have tried to do something to compensate the families by writing a book. I would like for the proceeds to go to the Magee family and the Cadena family. There is someone who will be contacting them, or they can get in touch with my attorney. I would like to thank you for standing by me and Canney. My best to my sun, my butterfly. Good-bye sun, I love you."

Pronounced dead: 6:34 P.M.

131

Irineo Montoya

Executed:
June 18, 1997

Personal data: *Born:* June 3, 1967. *Race:* Hispanic. *Height:* 5'8". *Weight:* 140 pounds. *Education:* 5 years. *Prior occupation:* Laborer. *County of conviction:* Cameron. *Age at time of execution:* 30.

Sentenced to death for: Convicted in the November 1985 robbery and murder of 46-year-old John Edgar Kilheffer in Brownsville. Kilheffer, a resident of South Padre Island, was stabbed to death after offering Montoya and accomplice Juan Villavicencio a ride as they were hitchhiking. Kilheffer suffered twenty-one stab wounds to the neck, torso, and legs. His body was stripped of clothing and dumped in a grapefruit orchard, where it was discovered a week later. The victim's bloodstained 1984 Chevrolet Blazer was recovered by Mexican state police in Matamoros on Thanksgiving Day. Records indicate that Montoya was also suspected in the abduction, rape, and robbery of two Brownsville women. He reportedly told the court following his conviction for capital murder that he would have the prosecutors and the trial judge killed.
Codefendant: Juan Villavicencio was arrested and charged with capital murder December 3, 1985. It is unclear whether he was acquitted of the charge or won a dismissal.

Received at death row: October 20, 1986. *Time on death row:* 3,894 days (10.67 years).

Last meal: Fish, french fries, jalapeño peppers, carrots, and ice cream.

Last statement: "Good-bye. I wait for you in heaven. I will be waiting for you. I love my parents. I am at peace with God. Fight for the good."

Pronounced dead: 6:16 P.M.

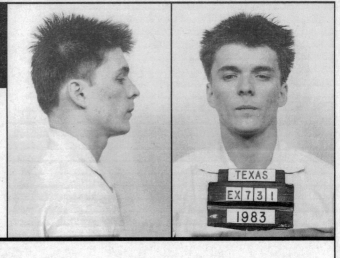

132

Robert Wallace West Jr.

Executed: July 29, 1997

Personal data: *Born:* December 12, 1961. *Race:* White. *Height:* 5'10". *Weight:* 139 pounds. *Education:* 8 years (GED). *Prior occupation:* Student. *County of conviction:* Harris. *Age at time of execution:* 35.

Sentenced to death for: Convicted in the slaying of 22-year-old DeAnn Klaus at the Memorial Park Hotel on Waugh Drive in Houston. Klaus, who lived and worked as a waitress at the hotel, was strangled with a belt and a pillowcase and then beaten and stabbed with a wooden club after West broke in to her room, stripped her of her clothes, and tied her up. West, who was also staying at the hotel, told police he killed the woman because he believed she was indirectly responsible for the death of one of his friends. Other guests of the hotel saw West leaving the woman's room covered with blood. He was arrested at the scene about thirty minutes after Klaus's body was found with the splintered piece of wood still embedded in her back.

Received at death row: February 3, 1983. *Time on death row:* 5,290 days (14.49 years).

Last meal: A cheeseburger, french fries, Coke, and Camel cigarettes (prohibited by policy).

Last statement: "I would like to apologize for all of the pain and suffering I put you all through. I hope this will give you closure now and later on down the line. Bob, I appreciate you coming. Stacy and Jess, I will wait for you."

Pronounced dead: 6:41 P.M.

133

James Carl Lee Davis

Executed: September 9, 1997

Personal data: *Born:* February 8, 1963. *Race:* Black. *Height:* 5'9". *Weight:* 156 pounds. *Education:* 8 years. *Prior occupation:* Roofer. *County of conviction:* Travis. *Age at time of execution:* 34.

Sentenced to death for: Convicted of beating to death three children—Even Johnson, 15, Tyron Johnson, 6, and Tom Johnson, 4—with a lead pipe during a burglary of their home. The Johnsons lived next door to Davis. Even Johnson was raped and sodomized.

Received at death row: March 22, 1985. *Time on death row:* 4,554 days (12.48 years).

Last meal: Steak and eggs (eggs over-easy), toast, punch, and a pack of Marlboro cigarettes (prohibited by policy).

Last statement: "All my friends in my heart I'm ready." [Officials could not understand him, but this is what it sounded like.]

Pronounced dead: 6:17 P.M.

134

**Jessel
Turner**

Executed:
September
22, 1997

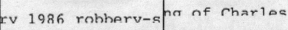
rv 1986 robbery-s | ng of Charles Hun

Personal data: *Born:* June 7, 1960. *Race:* Black. *Height:* 6'1". *Weight:* 180 pounds. *Education:* 11 years. *Prior occupation:* Truck driver. *County of conviction:* Harris. *Age at time of execution:* 37.

Sentenced to death for: Convicted in the February 1986 robbery-slaying of Charles Hunter, a Houston cab driver. Hunter was robbed and shot in the chest with a .22 caliber pistol after picking up Turner in Houston's Fifth Ward. Hunter's body was found in the street about a half mile from where he picked up Turner. Turner stole Hunter's cab and drove it to his apartment complex. The cab was found ransacked. Turner was arrested a short time later while driving another car near the murder scene. The murder weapon was found in the car Turner was driving.

Received at death row: November 12, 1988. *Time on death row:* 3,236 days (8.87 years).

Last meal: Declined last meal.

Last statement: "First I would like to give praise to God for the love and grace that He has allowed for all of this to come together. I would like to thank and ask blessings for all of the men who are in prison and have shared in my struggle and have allowed me to help them. I would like to thank my family for their blessings and for sharing my struggle and having been there for me and endured this with me. I would like to thank the chaplain and all the rest who have offered their prayers. I would also like to thank Mrs. Hunter's brother and family who have offered their forgiveness and all of their prayers. I pray that God's praise be upon all of you and that you will be touched by the grace of God. Till we meet again, may all of God's blessings be upon you."

Pronounced dead: 6:18 P.M.

Benjamin C. Stone

Executed: September 25, 1997

Personal data: *Born:* June 3, 1952. *Race:* White. *Height:* 6'0". *Weight:* 175 pounds. *Education:* 12 years. *Prior occupation:* Plumber. *County of conviction:* Nueces. *Age at time of execution:* 45.

Sentenced to death for: Convicted in the strangling death of his 34-year-old ex-wife, Patsy Lynn Stone, and his 12-year-old stepdaughter, Keith Lynn Van Coney, at their Corpus Christi home. Stone used his hands to strangle the two victims following a verbal and physical altercation with his ex-wife. The victims were also sexually assaulted by Stone. Stone was arrested the next day after he called 911 from a highway rest area and confessed to killing the two women.

Received at death row: April 25, 1996. *Time on death row:* 518 days (1.42 years).

Last meal: A Coke.

Last statement: None.

Pronounced dead: 6:16 P.M.

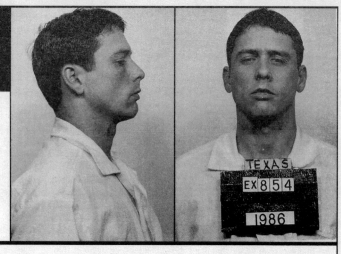

136

John William Cockrum

Executed: September 30, 1997

Personal data: *Born:* December 20, 1958. *Race:* White. *Height:* 5'9". *Weight:* 175 pounds. *Education:* 9 years. *Prior occupation:* Bricklayer. *County of conviction:* Bowie. *Age at time of execution:* 38.

Sentenced to death for: Convicted in the May 1986 death of 69-year-old Eva May near DeKalb. May was shot once in the head during a robbery of the L.A. May Grocery located approximately six miles east of DeKalb. Cockrum was arrested the next day. Codefendant Jerry Morgan reportedly led police to the .22 caliber pistol used in the shooting and later testified against Cockrum in exchange for a reduced charge.
Codefendant: Jerry Morgan was convicted of burglary of a habitation and sentenced to ninety-nine years in prison.

Received at death row: December 9, 1986. *Time on death row:* 3,948 days (10.82 years).

Last meal: A cheeseburger, onion rings, banana pudding, and iced tea.

Last statement: "I would like to apologize to the victim's family for all of the pain I have caused them. I would like to tell my family I love them and I hope to see them again soon. Lord Jesus, thank you for giving me the strength and the time in my life to find Jesus Christ and to be forgiven for all of my sins. Thank you for the changes in my life you have given me. The love and closeness of my family and my beautiful daughter. Thank you for using me."

Pronounced dead: 6:17 P.M.

Dwight Dwayne Adanandus

Executed: October 1, 1997

Personal data: *Born:* February 19, 1956. *Race:* Black. *Height:* 5'10". *Weight:* 148 pounds. *Education:* 11 years. *Prior occupation:* Auto mechanic. *County of conviction:* Bexar. *Age at time of execution:* 41.

Sentenced to death for: Convicted in the January 1988 shooting death of Vernon Hanan during a bank robbery in San Antonio. Hanan, vice president of W. F. Castello & Associates, was shot to death in the foyer of Continental Bank when he attempted to stop Adanandus from escaping with $10,000 stolen from a bank teller. Adanandus was apprehended four hours later after police and FBI SWAT teams were called to the neighborhood residence where he had fled.

Received at death row: May 23, 1989. *Time on death row:* 3,053 days (8.36 years).

Last meal: A cheeseburger, french fries, and iced tea.

Last statement: "Ms. Croft and Mr. Betthi, I don't know what to say to you, but I apologize for the pain I have caused you and your family over the years. I hope that you will accept my apology and that you will know that it is sincere. I hope this will allow you and your family to move on and I hope you will forgive me and I hope Mr. Hanan will forgive me for taking his life. Please accept my apology. I love you all. I am finished."

Pronounced dead: 6:16 P.M.

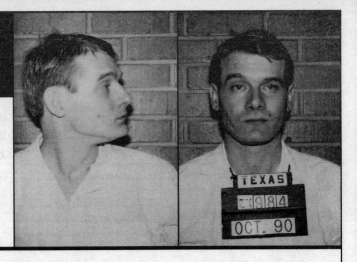

138

Ricky Lee Green

Executed: October 8, 1997

Personal data: *Born:* December 27, 1960. *Race:* White. *Height:* 5'8". *Weight:* 170 pounds. *Education:* 8 years. *Prior occupation:* Radiator repairman. *County of conviction:* Travis. *Age at time of execution:* 36.

Sentenced to death for: Convicted in the September 1986 sexual mutilation and murder of 28-year-old Steven Fefferman, an advertising executive with KXAS-TV of Fort Worth. Fefferman was castrated and stabbed repeatedly with a butcher knife at his home after meeting Green and engaging in sex with him on a beach in Fort Worth. After killing Fefferman, Green stole the victim's car. Green was charged with the killing in April 1989 after his wife went to police with information. Green later confessed to three sexual mutilation slayings in 1985. His wife, Sharon Green, was convicted and sentenced to nineteen years probation in one of the 1985 killings.

Received at death row: October 5, 1990. *Time on death row:* 2,560 days (7.01 years).

Last meal: Five scrambled eggs, four sausage patties, eight slices of toast, six slices of bacon, and four pints of milk.

Last statement: "I want to thank the Lord for giving me this opportunity to get to know him. He has shown me a lot and he has changed me in the past two months. I have been in prison eight and a half years and on death row for seven and I have not gotten into any trouble. I feel like I am not a threat to society anymore. I feel like my punishment is over, but my friends are now being punished. I thank the Lord for all he has done for me. I do want to tell the families that I am sorry but killing me is not going to solve nothing. I really do not believe that if Jesus were here tonight that he would execute me. Jesus is all about love. I want to thank all of my friends for supporting me and for being here for me. Thank all of my friends on the row. Thank you, Lord. I am finished."

Pronounced dead: 6:31 P.M.

139

Kenneth Ray Ransom

Executed: October 28, 1997

Personal data: *Born:* May 15, 1963. *Race:* Black. *Height:* 5'9". *Weight:* 169 pounds. *Education:* 12 years. *Prior occupation:* Plumber. *County of conviction:* Harris. *Age at time of execution:* 34.

Sentenced to death for: Convicted in the July 1983 stabbing death of 19-year-old Arnold Pequeno, an employee of the Malibu Grand Prix Race Track amusement center in Houston. Also slain were Anil Varughese, 18, a night manager; 22-year-old Roddy Harris; and Arnold Pequeno's 18-year-old brother, Joerene Pequeno. All four victims died of multiple stab wounds to the upper body, neck, and head.

Codefendant: Richard J. Wilkerson was convicted of capital murder in the stabbing death of Anil Varughese. Wilkerson had been fired from his job as a pit attendant at the raceway and amusement center located in the 6100 block of the Southwest Freeway about two weeks before the murders. Richard Wilkerson was sentenced to death and executed by lethal injection on August 31, 1993. (See entry 67, Richard J. Wilkerson.) James Edward Randall was convicted of capital murder and sentenced to life in prison.

Received at death row: September 13, 1984. *Time on death row:* 4,793 days (13.13 years).

Last meal: Declined last meal.

Last statement: "First and foremost I would like to tell the victims' families that I am sorry because I feel like I am guilty. I am sorry for the pain all of them have gone through during holidays and birthdays they are without their loved ones. I have said from the beginning and will say it again: I am innocent. I did not kill no one. I feel like this is the Lord's will that will be done. I love you all. You know it. Don't cry. Tell my brothers I love them. You all be strong."

Pronounced dead: 6:20 P.M.

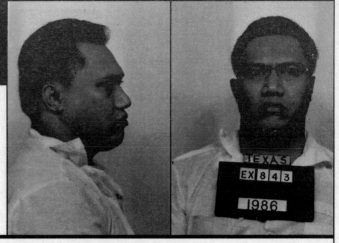

140

Aua Lauti

Executed: November 4, 1997

Personal data: *Born:* June 18, 1954. *Race:* Other. *Height:* 5'10". *Weight:* 225 pounds. *Education:* 11 years. *Prior occupation:* Landscaper. *County of conviction:* Harris. *Age at time of execution:* 43.

Sentenced to death for: Convicted of capital murder in the beating-strangulation death of his 9-year-old cousin, Tara Lauti, on December 19, 1985. Evidence showed that Lauti, despondent over a breakup with his girlfriend, kidnapped his cousin from her father's home and drove her to a field, where she was beaten, sexually assaulted, and strangled. Police said Lauti knocked the girl unconscious with his fist while abducting her from the home at 11015 Maple Rock in northeast Harris County and then twice more knocked her unconscious by hitting her on the head with a beer bottle and hitting her in the chest with his fist. She died of a skull fracture, strangulation, and a crushed right chest.

Received at death row: September 18, 1986. *Time on death row:* 4,065 days (11.14 years).

Last meal: A double-meat cheeseburger, french fries, and a soft drink.

Last statement: "I would like to say that I have spent eleven years living on death row and during that time I have made a lot of friends. I do not feel anger and hatred. I feel love and forgiveness. I would like to say that I have come to realize that I have been blessed by God with good friends. I have friends on the inside and I have friends on the outside who support me. They write to me. I do not know them, and they do not know me. I have a wonderful family who loves me and supports me and who forgives me, and that is the most important thing. I am glad I found God and am so happy for it. I love my family and I want them to know that. That is about all I have to say."

Pronounced dead: 6:32 P.M.

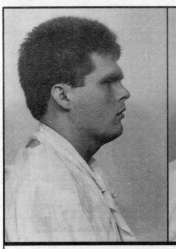

141

Aaron Lee Fuller

Executed: November 6, 1997

Personal data: *Born:* August 26, 1967. *Race:* White. *Height:* 5'11". *Weight:* 175 pounds. *Education:* 11 years. *Prior occupation:* Diesel mechanic. *County of conviction:* Dawson. *Age at time of execution:* 30.

Sentenced to death for: Convicted in the March 1989 robbery and murder of 68-year-old Loretta Stephens. In a statement to police, Fuller said he decided to burglarize Stephens's residence in Lubbock after seeing her sleeping in a recliner in the living room. After finding more than $500 cash in the house, Fuller said he stood over Stephens for about ten minutes and then started beating and choking her. He finally suffocated the woman with a pillow when he realized she had survived the beating. After tying Stephens's hands and feet with telephone cord and sexually assaulting her, Fuller placed the victim's body into the trunk of her car; later, accompanied by a friend, he drove to a spot eight miles north of Lamesa off Highway 87 and dumped it into a stand of weeds. Fuller and his friend then drove back to Lubbock, where they abandoned the stolen vehicle in a parking lot across from the bus station.
Codefendant: Juan Victor Gomez was reportedly charged with unauthorized use of a motor vehicle in connection with the case. Disposition of the case is unknown.

Received at death row: February 14, 1990. *Time on death row:* 2,282 days (7.73 years).

Last meal: Declined last meal.

Last statement: "Jesus the Lord is everything to me. I am nothing without him. Praise Jesus. Praise God."

Pronounced dead: 6:20 P.M.

142

Michael Eugene Sharp

Executed:
November
19, 1997

Personal data: *Born:* April 24, 1954. *Race:* White. *Height:* 5'11". *Weight:* 150 pounds. *Education:* 13 years. *Prior occupation:* Oil field worker. *County of conviction:* Crockett. *Age at time of execution:* 43.

Sentenced to death for: Convicted in the June 1982 abduction and stabbing death of 31-year-old Brenda Kay Broadway, of Kermit. Broadway and her two daughters, ages 8 and 15, were reportedly abducted from a car wash and driven to a remote location in Ector County, where they were sexually abused. Broadway and her 8-year-old daughter, Christie Michelle Elms, were then stabbed to death. Broadway's other daughter managed to escape during the stabbings. Naked and with her arms bound, she ran five miles through the desert before finding help at an oil rig. The bodies of the two victims were found buried in a shallow grave. Sharp was arrested five days after the bodies were found. In November 1982, Sharp was convicted of murder in Christie Elms's death and sentenced to life in prison. He was also a suspect in several other West Texas killings. In late November 1982, he led police to the grave of 18-year-old Blanca Guerrero of Odessa, who had been missing since May 17, 1982. Her body was found buried under a water tank in Andrews County.

Received at death row: June 6, 1983. *Time on death row:* 5,280 days (14.47 years).

Last meal: A small pizza, a dish of Italian spaghetti, marble cake, and punch.

Last statement: n/a.

Pronounced dead: 6:21 P.M.

143

Charlie Livingston

Executed: November 21, 1997

Personal data: *Born:* February 14, 1962. *Race:* Black. *Height:* 5'8". *Weight:* n/a. *Education:* 10 years. *Prior occupation:* Warehouseman. *County of conviction:* Harris. *Age at time of execution:* 35.

Sentenced to death for: Convicted in the robbery-murder of 38-year-old Janet Caldwell outside a grocery store in Houston. Livingston reportedly drove to the Weingarten's store at West Forty-third Street and waited until he saw a woman, alone, drive up to the store and park. When Caldwell went inside, Livingston crawled underneath her van and waited until she returned with an armload of groceries. He then crawled from underneath her van, pointed a 9mm pistol at her, and attempted to steal her purse. As the two struggled, Livingston shot Caldwell twice in the throat and fled with her purse. He was apprehended a short time later and identified by witnesses.

Received at death row: July 25, 1985. *Time on death row:* 4,502 days (12.33 years).

Last meal: Ribs smothered in onions and gravy, rice with butter, ice water, and Dr Pepper.

Last statement: "You all brought me here to be executed, not to make a speech. That's it."

Pronounced dead: 6:17 P.M.

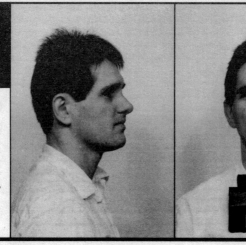

144

Michael Lee Lockhart

Executed: December 9, 1997

TEXAS
EX 9117
1988

Personal data: *Born:* September 30, 1960. *Race:* White. *Height:* 5'10". *Weight:* 165 pounds. *Education:* 11 years. *Prior occupation:* Laborer/truck driver. *County of conviction:* Bexar. *Age at time of execution:* 37.

Sentenced to death for: Convicted in the March 1988 shooting death of Beaumont police officer Douglas Hulsey Jr. The officer was shot to death while attempting to arrest Lockhart for driving a stolen vehicle.
Note: Lockhart had been tied to a string of robberies and thefts across the country and also faced capital murder charges in Florida and Indiana.

Received at death row: October 26, 1988. *Time on death row:* 3,331 days (9.13 years).

Last meal: A double-meat cheeseburger, french fries, and Coke.

Last statement: "A lot of people view what is happening here as evil, but I want you to know that I found love and compassion here. The people who work here, I thank them for the kindness they have shown me. And I deeply appreciate all that has been done for me by the people who work here. That's all, Warden. I'm ready."

Pronounced dead: 6:24 P.M.

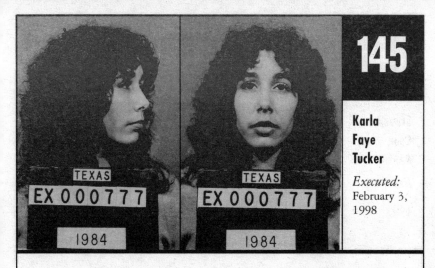

Karla Faye Tucker

Executed: February 3, 1998

TEXAS
EX 000777
1984

TEXAS
EX 000777
1984

Personal data: *Born:* November 18, 1959. *Race:* White. *Height:* 5'3". *Weight:* 121 pounds. *Education:* 7 years. *Prior occupation:* Office worker. *County of conviction:* Harris. *Age at time of execution:* 38.

Sentenced to death for: Convicted in the June 1983 pickax slaying of 27-year-old Jerry Lynn Dean at the victim's apartment on Watonga Drive in northeast Houston. Dean and his companion, 32-year-old Deborah Thornton, were hacked to death after Tucker and accomplice Daniel Ryan Garrett sneaked into the apartment, supposedly to steal some motorcycle parts. Tucker testified that she and Garrett confronted Dean in the bedroom and that Garrett started beating Dean on the head with a hammer. Tucker said she heard a "gurgling sound" coming from Dean and struck him in the back with a pickax she spotted in the room to stop him from making a sound. Tucker turned the pickax on Thornton when she was discovered beneath a blanket. The bodies of both victims had more than twenty stab or puncture wounds and the pickax was found embedded in Thornton's chest. Witnesses testified that Tucker later bragged about receiving gratification every time she hit her victims with the ax, a claim she later denied. She did admit to hating Dean because he had defaced photographs of her mother.
Codefendant: Daniel Ryan Garrett was convicted of capital murder and sentenced to death. He died of liver disease in June 1993.

Received at death row: December 18, 1984. *Time on death row:* 4,795 days (13.14 years).

Last meal: A banana, a peach, and a garden salad with ranch dressing.

Last statement: See Appendix.

Pronounced dead: 6:45 P.M.
Note: Tucker was the first woman executed in Texas since 1863. See Appendix for a statement from Allan B. Polunsky, chairman of the Texas Board of Criminal Justice, regarding Tucker's execution.

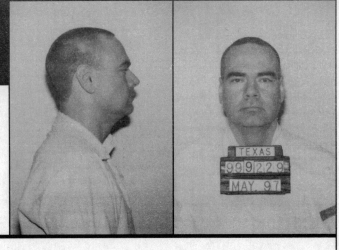

146

Steven Ceon Renfro

Executed: February 9, 1998

Personal data: *Born:* September 14, 1957. *Race:* White. *Height:* 6'1". *Weight:* 215 pounds. *Education:* n/a. *Prior occupation:* Laborer. *County of conviction:* Harrison. *Age at time of execution:* 40.

Sentenced to death for: Convicted in the August 1996 slaying of three people in Marshall during a shooting spree that also left a city police officer wounded. Killed were Renfro's common-law wife, Rhena Fultner, 36; his aunt, Rose Rutledge, 66; and an acquaintance, George Counts, 40. Renfro reportedly dressed in camouflage clothing and armed himself with assault weapons after claiming to have seen his common-law wife having sex with two unidentified men. He drove to the house he shared with his aunt at 614 N. Washington and shot Fultner once in the forehead. He then walked into his aunt's bedroom and shot her once in the head while she watched television in bed. Renfro shot Fultner a second time in the forehead when he found her still alive in the living room. He then went to Counts's trailer home at 1000 Calloway and fired a barrage of bullets into the structure when Counts refused his admittance. Counts's body was found just inside the door of the bullet-riddled trailer. Renfro said he killed Counts because he had once struck Fultner. Renfro then opened fire on the squad car of Marshall police officer Dominick Pondant and reserve officer George Gill as they responded to reports of shots being fired near the intersection of Main and Calloway streets. Pondant was hit by gunfire but managed to exit his vehicle and return fire, wounding Renfro in the arm and abdomen. At the hospital, Renfro reportedly told police, "I killed them all. I killed my whole family."

Received at death row: May 22, 1997. *Time on death row:* 263 days (0.72 year).

Last meal: A bacon, lettuce, and tomato sandwich with extra bacon; cherry pie; vanilla ice cream; and two cans of Dr Pepper.

Last statement: "I would like to tell the victims' families that I am sorry, very sorry. I am so sorry. Forgive me if you can. I know it's impossible, but try. Take my hand, Lord Jesus, I'm coming home."

Pronounced dead: 6:18 P.M.

Jerry Lee Hogue

Executed: March 11, 1998

Personal data: *Born:* September 26, 1950. *Race:* White. *Height:* 5'6". *Weight:* 170 pounds. *Education:* 10 years. *Prior occupation:* Auto repossessor. *County of conviction:* Tarrant. *Age at time of execution:* 47.

Sentenced to death for: Convicted of capital murder in the January 1979 death of 27-year-old Jayne Markham. Markham died in a house fire set by Hogue at 2412 Southcrest in Arlington. She had shared the rental house with her 8-year-old son and friends Mary Beth Crawford and Steve Renick. Hogue, who had lived in the same house a month before it was leased to the foursome in December 1978, apparently established some sort of amiable relationship with Markham and visited her the last two days of her life. While Markham, Crawford, and Hogue were eating breakfast on January 12, Hogue suddenly blurted out that he was a police officer and that he was arresting them for marijuana possession. Retrieving Renick's loaded pistol from a footlocker, Hogue later forced Crawford into an act of oral sodomy and then stabbed her in the stomach with a butcher knife. Markham was tied up and raped by Hogue prior to her death. Once Markham's son returned home from school and Renick returned from work, Hogue tied up or handcuffed the four inside the house and set it afire. All but Markham, whose hands and feet were tied behind her back with insulated wire, managed to escape. Hogue was arrested at a friend's home in Arlington on January 14.

Received at death row: June 6, 1980. *Time on death row:* 6,487 days (17.77 years).

Last meal: An old-fashioned cheeseburger, french fries with ketchup, chocolate cake, and two cans of Coke.

Last statement: "Mindy, I'm with you honey. I do not know why Mindy you are doing this but I will forgive you. You know he is a murderer. Why don't you support me? He will do it again. Mindy, you are lucky you are still alive. Give my love to my family. I love them. Mindy, you can stop this. OK. I'm ready."
Note: Mindy was a nickname for Mary Beth Crawford, who witnessed the execution.

Pronounced dead: 6:50 P.M.

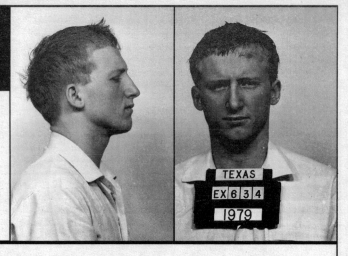

148

Joseph John Cannon

Executed: April 22, 1998

Personal data: *Born:* January 13, 1960. *Race:* White. *Height:* 6'1". *Weight:* 140 pounds. *Education:* None. *Prior occupation:* Laborer. *County of conviction:* Bexar. *Age at time of execution:* 38.

Sentenced to death for: Convicted of capital murder in the slaying of San Antonio attorney Anne C. Walsh. Walsh was shot seven times with a .22 caliber pistol after she had returned home for lunch. Walsh was the sister of Dan Carabin, Cannon's court-appointed attorney on a burglary of a habitation charge. Carabin and Walsh took an interest in Cannon's welfare following a burglary conviction, and he was permitted to live at the Walsh home while on probation. Cannon told police he found several guns in a bedroom on the day of the murder and "just went crazy." He said he attempted to sexually assault Walsh after killing her. Cannon was arrested after he was seen driving a 1977 Maverick belonging to Walsh's daughter. He had taken several firearms from the house and stolen two $250 in travelers checks and a few dollars from Walsh's purse.
Note: Cannon committed the murder when he was 17 years old.

Received at death row: May 9, 1979. *Time on death row:* 6,923 days (18.97 years).

Last meal: Fried chicken, barbecue ribs, baked potato, green salad with Italian dressing, chocolate cake or chocolate ice cream (or both), a thick chocolate shake or malt, and iced tea.

Last statement: [Inmate was crying; first words were unintelligible.] "I am really sorry. I love you all. I love you, God."
Note: The first attempt at lethal injection failed when a vein in Cannon's arm collapsed, requiring the needle to be removed. It took about fifteen minutes for officials to establish another injection.
Second last statement: "I am sorry for what I did to your mom. It isn't because I'm going to die. All my life I have been locked up. I could never forgive what I done. I am sorry for all of you. I love you all. Thank you for supporting me. I thank you for being kind to me when I was small. Thank you, God. All right."

Pronounced dead: 7:28 P.M.

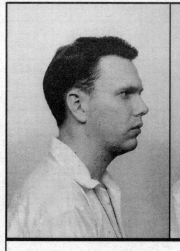

149

**Lesley
Lee
Gosch**

Executed:
April 24,
1998

Personal data: *Born:* July 8, 1955. *Race:* White. *Height:* 5'5". *Weight:* 140 pounds. *Education:* n/a. *Prior occupation:* n/a. *County of conviction:* Victoria. *Age at time of execution:* 42.

Sentenced to death for: Convicted of capital murder in the shooting death of 43-year-old Rebecca Smith Patton, of San Antonio, in September 1985. Patton, married to the president of Castle Hill National Bank in San Antonio, was shot seven times in the head with a .22 caliber pistol fitted with a silencer during an extortion attempt in her Alamo Heights neighborhood home by Gosch and accomplice John Lawrence Rogers. The men attempted to kidnap Patton in order to demand ransom from her family. Gosch was arrested on September 25, 1985, at his home. His trial was moved from Bexar County to Victoria County in a change of venue.
Codefendant: Rogers was convicted of extortion and sentenced to federal penitentiary.

Received at death row: September 15, 1986. *Time on death row:* 4,239 days (11.61 years).

Last meal: Declined last meal.

Last statement: None.

Pronounced dead: 6:38 P.M.

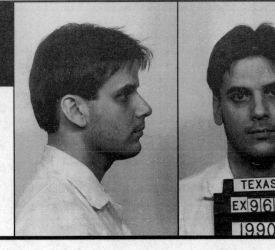

150

Frank Basil McFarland

Executed: April 29, 1998

TEXAS
EX963
1990

Personal data: *Born:* October 7, 1963. *Race:* White. *Height:* 5'10". *Weight:* 160 pounds. *Education:* 10 years. *Prior occupation:* Electrician. *County of conviction:* Tarrant. *Age at time of execution:* 34.

Sentenced to death for: Convicted in the February 1988 sexual assault and murder of 26-year-old Terri Lynn Hokanson, of Arlington. Hokanson, who worked as a shoe-shine girl at a Fort Worth bar, was found lying in the driveway of the First United Methodist Church in Hurst. Suffering from more than fifty stab wounds, Hokanson was alive when found and managed to tell police two men had raped and stabbed her. She died the next morning at a local hospital. Witnesses told police Hokanson was last seen with two men at a second Fort Worth bar the night of her disappearance. A knife and gold earring belonging to Hokanson were later found in McFarland's vehicle.
Codefendant: Alleged codefendant Ryan Michael Wilson was shot to death near Weatherford, in Parker County on March 11, 1988.

Received at death row: February 12, 1990. *Time on death row:* 2,998 days (8.21 years).

Last meal: Heaping portion of lettuce, a sliced tomato, a sliced cucumber, four celery stalks, four sticks of American or cheddar cheese, two bananas, and two cold half-pints of milk. He asked that all vegetables be washed prior to serving and asked that the cheese sticks be "clean."

Last statement: "I owe no apologies for a crime I did not commit. Those who lied and fabricated evidence against me will have to answer for what they have done. I know in my heart what I did and I call upon the spirit of my ancestors and all of my people and I swear to them, and now I am coming home."

Pronounced dead: 6:27 P.M.

Robert Anthony Carter

Executed: May 18, 1998

Personal data: *Born:* February 10, 1964. *Race:* Black. *Height:* 6'0". *Weight:* 156 pounds. *Education:* 10 years. *Prior occupation:* Laborer. *County of conviction:* Harris. *Age at time of execution:* 34.

Sentenced to death for: Convicted in the shooting death of Sylvia Reyes, 18, during a robbery. Reyes, manager of a Conoco service station in the 300 block of South Wayside in Houston, was shot once in the chest with a .38 caliber revolver as she attempted to stop Carter from taking $150 from the cash register. Reyes died at a Houston hospital about an hour after the shooting. During his capital murder trial, Carter was also implicated in the June 18, 1981, slaying of R. B. Scott, 63, during a robbery of a beauty supply store in Houston.

Received at death row: March 12, 1982. *Time on death row:* 5,911 days (16.19 years).

Last meal: A fried fish fillet, french fries, orange juice, and German chocolate cake.

Last statement: "I love all of you all. Thank you for caring so much about me. Keep the faith. I am going to a better place. I hope the victims' families will forgive me because I didn't mean to hurt no one or kill no one. I love you all."

Pronounced dead: 6:25 P.M.

152

**Pedro
Cruz
Muniz**

Executed:
May 18, 1998

Personal data: *Born:* September 25, 1956. *Race:* Hispanic. *Height:* 5'4". *Weight:* 152 pounds. *Education:* 10 years. *Prior occupation:* Laborer. *County of conviction:* Williamson. *Age at time of execution:* 41.

Sentenced to death for: Convicted in the December 1976 rape-murder of 19-year-old Janis Carol Bickham, a student at Southwestern University in Georgetown.

Received at death row: October 7, 1977. *Time on death row:* 7,528 days (20.62 years).

Last meal: Requested shrimp and salad (shrimp not available). Served a cheeseburger, french fries, and cola.

Last statement: "I know you can't hear me now but I know that it won't matter what I have to say. I want you to know that I did not kill your sister. If you want to know the truth and you deserve to know the truth, hire your own investigators. That is all I have to say."

Pronounced dead: 6:20 P.M.

153

Clifford Boggess

Executed: June 11, 1998

TEXAS
EX 887
1987

Personal data: *Born:* June 11, 1965. *Race:* White. *Height:* 6'2". *Weight:* 232 pounds. *Education:* 12 years. *Prior occupation:* Carpenter's helper. *County of conviction:* Clay. *Age at time of execution:* 33.

Sentenced to death for: Convicted in the murder-robbery of Moses Frank Collier, 86, owner of Collier Grocery and Produce Store in Saint Jo. Mr. Collier was beaten and stabbed to death. Boggess left the scene with approximately $700.

Received at death row: October 23, 1987. *Time on death row:* 3,884 days (10.64 years).

Last meal: Two double-meat cheeseburgers, salad, french fries with salt and ketchup, chocolate fudge brownies, cherry cake, a Pepsi, and iced tea.

Last statement: "I'd like to say that for the murders of Roy Hazelwood and Frank Collier, I'm sorry. For the pain it has caused you. To my friends, I'd like to say that I love you and I'm glad you've been a part of my life. Thank you. I'll miss you. Remember that today I'll be with Jesus in paradise. I'll see you again. Lord Jesus Christ, Son of Almighty God, mercy on me as a sinner, forgive me of my sins. I would like to offer up my death for the conversion of sinners on death row. Lord Jesus, into your hands I command my spirit."
Note: At the end of the last statement, Boggess began praying "for the conversion of sinners on death row."

Pronounced dead: 6:21 P.M.

154

Johnny Dean Pyles

Executed:
June 15,
1998

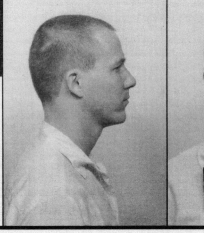

Personal data: *Born:* December 30, 1957. *Race:* White. *Height:* 5'6". *Weight:* 155 pounds. *Education:* 16 years. *Prior occupation:* Brick mason helper. *County of conviction:* Dallas. *Age at time of execution:* 40.

Sentenced to death for: Convicted in the June 20, 1982, shooting death of Dallas County sheriff's deputy Ray Edward Kovar, 34. Kovar was shot in the chest at close range with a .38 caliber revolver.

Received at death row: October 21, 1982. *Time on death row:* 5,716 days (15.66 years).

Last meal: Chicken-fried steak with gravy, potatoes, pineapple pie, and Coke.

Last statement: "I want to tell you folks there, I have a love in my heart for you. I hope you don't look for satisfaction or comfort or peace in my execution. Jesus Christ is my Lord and savior and I want him to be yours. I'm sorry for the pain and heartache I've caused your family. Too many years I've caused all my family problems and heartache. I'm sorry. I wanted to let you know that the Lord Jesus is my life and I just want to say I'm gonna fall asleep and I'll be in His presence shortly. I got reason to rejoice and I pray to see all of you there someday."

Pronounced dead: 6:24 P.M.

155

Leopoldo Narvaiz Jr.

Executed: June 26, 1998

Personal data: *Born:* March 13, 1968. *Race:* Hispanic. *Height:* 5'8". *Weight:* 155 pounds. *Education:* 9 years. *Prior occupation:* Stocker/laborer. *County of conviction:* Bexar. *Age at time of execution:* 30.

Sentenced to death for: Convicted in the April 1988 stabbing deaths of his ex-girlfriend and her two sisters and brother inside their San Antonio home. Stabbed repeatedly with butcher knives were Narvaiz's ex-girlfriend, Shannon Mann, 17; her two sisters, Jennifer Mann, 19, and Martha Mann, 15; and her brother, 11-year-old Ernest Mann Jr. The victims suffered more than one hundred wounds; some of the knife blades were broken and embedded in their bodies. Police responded to the victims' mobile home after Shannon placed a 911 emergency call and said her boyfriend was beating and killing them. Prosecutors charged that Narvaiz was angry over a spurned romance with Shannon and killed the siblings in a jealous rage.

Received at death row: November 22, 1988. *Time on death row:* 3,503 days (9.60 years).

Last meal: Declined last meal.

Last statement: None.

Pronounced dead: 6:29 P.M.

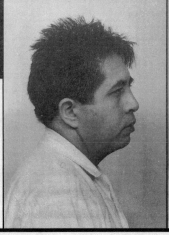
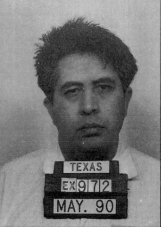

156

Genaro Camacho Jr.

Executed:
August 26,
1998

TEXAS
EX 9 7 2
MAY. 90

Personal data: *Born:* September 14, 1954. *Race:* Hispanic. *Height:* 5'7". *Weight:* 185 pounds. *Education:* 13 years. *Prior occupation:* Produce baker. *County of conviction:* Dallas. *Age at time of execution:* 43.

Sentenced to death for: Convicted in the May 1988 slaying of 24-year-old David L. Wilburn. Wilburn was shot in the back of the head after interrupting the kidnapping of two people from a home at 7917 Nassau Circle, in Dallas. Sam Wright, the 57-year-old owner of the home, told police that Camacho and two unnamed accomplices forced their way into the home and attempted to kidnap him along with 31-year-old Evellyn Banks and her 3-year-old son, Andre. Wright was able to escape the three intruders after they had shot Wilburn and called for police. Evellyn Banks, who was handcuffed, was taken from the home with her son and driven away in a car. Banks and her child reportedly were later killed by Comacho.
Codefendants: Two unnamed accomplices.

Received at death row: May 9, 1990. *Time on death row:* 3,031 days (8.30 years).

Last meal: Steak, baked potato, salad, and strawberry ice cream.

Last statement: "I love you all. We had a good service and I'll be with you. I'll be waiting for you in heaven. OK. Adios. That's all I have to say."

Pronounced dead: 7:49 P.M.

157

Delbert Boyd Teague Jr.

Executed: September 9, 1998

Personal data: *Born:* November 11, 1962. *Race:* White. *Height:* 5'8". *Weight:* 131 pounds. *Education:* 10 years. *Prior occupation:* Construction worker. *County of conviction:* Tarrant. *Age at time of execution:* 35.

Sentenced to death for: Convicted in the April 1985 robbery-slaying of 21-year-old Kevin Leroy Allen at a park near Fort Worth. Allen, a Fort Worth resident, was one of three men shot at Marion Sansom Park after Teague and accomplice Robin Scott Partine robbed Thomas Emmitt Cox, 22, and his date, an 18-year-old white female, at gunpoint. Cox had run over to the other two victims' vehicle to ask for help after Teague and Partine robbed the couple of about $80 and then started to leave the park overlooking Lake Worth with the woman. At that point, Teague pulled up behind the men in the stolen pickup he was driving and shot each in the head with a .22 caliber pistol. Allen died at a local hospital of two gunshot wounds to the head. David Suson, 32, and James Bell, 30, recovered from head and facial wounds. Following the shootings, Cox's date was kidnapped and sexually assaulted by Teague and Partine. The two were arrested the following day after the woman was able to leave a note asking for help in a service station restroom near Ramah, Louisiana.
Codefendant: Robin Scott Partine was convicted of aggravated sexual assault with threat of violence and sentenced to life in prison.

Received at death row: November 11, 1986. *Time on death row:* 4,320 days (11.84 years).

Last meal: Requested no last meal. At the last minute, he decided to eat a hamburger at his mother's request.

Last statement: "I have come here today to die, not make speeches. Today is a good day for dying. Est sularus oth mithas [my honor is my life]."

Pronounced dead: 6:24 P.M.

158

**David
Allen
Castillo**

Executed:
September
23, 1998

Personal data: *Born:* August 11, 1964. *Race:* Hispanic. *Height:* 5'6". *Weight:* 171 pounds. *Education:* 9 years. *Prior occupation:* Electrician. *County of conviction:* Hidalgo. *Age at time of execution:* 34.

Sentenced to death for: Convicted in the July 1983 stabbing of Clarencio Champion, 59, a cashier at the Party House liquor store in Mercedes. Castillo confronted Champion and demanded all of the cash in the register. When Champion resisted, Castillo attacked him with a long, solid knife, stabbing him in the chest and abdomen and slashing him across the face. Castillo took an undetermined amount of cash. Champion died a week later.

Received at death row: September 12, 1984. *Time on death row:* 5,124 days (14.04 years).

Last meal: Twenty-four soft-shell tacos, six enchiladas, six tostadas, two whole onions, five jalapeño peppers, two cheeseburgers, one chocolate shake, one quart of milk, and one pack of Marlboro cigarettes (prohibited by policy).

Last statement: "Keep it brief here. Just want to say, uh, family take care of yourselves. Uh, look at this as a learning experience. Everything happens for a reason. We all know what really happened. But there are some things you just can't fight. Little people always seem to get squashed. It happens. Even so, just got to take the good with the bad. There's no man that is free from all evil. Nor any man that is so evil to be worth nothing. But it's all part of life and my family take care of yourselves. Tell my wife I love her. I'll keep an eye on everybody, especially my nieces and nephews. I'm pretty good. I love y'all. Take care. I'm ready."

Pronounced dead: 6:23 P.M.

159

Javier Cruz

Executed:
October 1,
1998

TEXAS
999061
APR. 93

Personal data: *Born:* September 13, 1957. *Race:* Hispanic. *Height:* 5'7". *Weight:* 208 pounds. *Education:* 9 years. *Prior occupation:* Feed-store clerk. *County of conviction:* Bexar. *Age at time of execution:* 41.

Sentenced to death for: Convicted in the strangulation murders of Louis Menard Neal, 71, and James Michael Ryan, 69, at the victims' homes in San Antonio. Neal was gagged and his hands were bound behind his back with a sock before he was beaten with a hammer and strangled with a bathrobe belt. His decomposing body was found hanging by the neck from a towel rod inside his North Alamo Street apartment five days after the June 7, 1991, murder. Ryan's nude body was found inside his Mandalay Street residence the day after his July 14, 1991, murder. He was also strangled and his television and automobile were stolen. Cruz's accomplice later told police they sold the tires off Ryan's Cadillac to buy heroin. Cruz was arrested in the murders on October 22, 1991. *Codefendant:* Antonio Omero Ovalle agreed to testify against Cruz and plead guilty to murder, aggravated robbery, and attempted burglary in exchange for two life sentences.

Received at death row: June 7, 1991. *Time on death row:* 2,673 days (7.32 years).

Last meal: Venison steak, baked potato, beer, and Camel cigarettes (alcohol and tobacco prohibited by policy).

Last statement: [Written] "Thank you for setting me free. God bless you all. I love you Miguel. Take care of my Angel Leslie. Love, Javier Cruz."

Pronounced dead: 6:21 P.M.

160

Jonathan Wayne Nobles

Executed: October 7, 1998

Personal data: *Born:* August 27, 1961. *Race:* White. *Height:* 5'11". *Weight:* 202 pounds. *Education:* 8 years (GED). *Prior occupation:* Electrician/marketing. *County of conviction:* Travis. *Age at time of execution:* 37.

Sentenced to death for: Convicted in the September 1986 stabbing deaths of Mitzi Johnson-Nalley, 21, and Kelly Farquhar, 24, at their rented home in Austin. Nobles, who was employed by the Central Texas Crime Prevention Association of Round Rock at the time of the killings, broke in to the house at 5913 Sunshine Drive after consuming a combination of drugs and alcohol. Ronald Ross, Johnson-Nalley's 30-year-old date, was also stabbed in the assault but survived his wounds. Nobles, who wounded himself in the arm during the assault, was arrested at his home on September 19, 1986, and confessed to police the same day.

Received at death row: October 15, 1987. *Time on death row:* 4,010 days (10.99 years).

Last meal: Eucharist sacrament.

Last statement: See Appendix.

Pronounced dead: 6:25 P.M.

161

Kenneth Allen McDuff

Executed: November 17, 1998

Personal data: *Born:* March 21, 1946. *Race:* White. *Height:* 6'3". *Weight:* 255 pounds. *Education:* 9 years (GED). *Prior occupation:* Machine operator. *County of conviction:* Harris. *Age at time of execution:* 52.

Sentenced to death for: Convicted in the March 1992 abduction and murder of 22-year-old Melissa Ann Northrup. Northrup was working as a clerk at the Quic Pac convenience store, 4200 LaSalle in Waco, when she was abducted and driven from the location in her own vehicle, a 1977 Buick Regal. The car was found abandoned five days later near Seagoville, but it wasn't until April 26 that her body was found floating in a gravel pit about a mile from where the car was discovered. Her hands had been tied behind her back with shoelaces and a sock, and she had been strangled with a rope. Police were led to McDuff after his abandoned vehicle was found parked near the store. He had once worked with Northrup at the store and was arrested in Kansas City, Missouri, on May 4, 1992.
Note: McDuff had been convicted of murder with malice and given the death sentence on October 9, 1968. His sentence was commuted to life on August 29, 1972. He was paroled on December 6, 1990.

Received at death row: March 8, 1993. *Time on death row:* 2,080 days (5.70 years).

Last meal: Two 16-ounce T-bone steaks, five fried eggs, vegetables, french fries, coconut pie, and one Coke.

Last statement: "I'm ready to be released. Release me."

Pronounced dead: 6:26 P.M.

162

Daniel Lee Corwin

Executed: December 7, 1998

Personal data: *Born:* September 13, 1958. *Race:* White. *Height:* 5'9". *Weight:* 164 pounds. *Education:* 15 years. *Prior occupation:* Cabinet maker. *County of conviction:* Montgomery. *Age at time of execution:* 40.

Sentenced to death for: Convicted in the deaths of Mary Risinger, 36, of Huntsville; Alice Martin, 72, of Normangee; and Debra Lynn Ewing, 26, of Conroe. Risinger was stabbed to death on October 31, 1987, while washing her vehicle at a car wash on FM 2821 in Huntsville. She was stabbed in the neck while her 3-year-old daughter watched from inside the car. The young girl was not harmed. Martin was abducted while walking near her home on February 13, 1987. Her body was found the next day in a field in Robertson County. She had been raped, strangled, and stabbed. Ewing was abducted at gunpoint while working at the Vision Center in Huntsville on July 10, 1987. Her body was found two days later in an undeveloped subdivision in Montgomery County. Like Martin, Ewing had been raped, strangled, and stabbed.
Note: Corwin was the first person prosecuted under the state's serial killer statute.

Received at death row: February 13, 1987. *Time on death row:* 4,315 days (11.82 years).

Last meal: Steak, potatoes, peas, cake, and root beer.

Last statement: See Appendix.

Pronounced dead: 6:33 P.M.

163

Jeff Emery

Executed: December 8, 1998

Personal data: *Born:* June 25, 1959. *Race:* White. *Height:* 5'8". *Weight:* 160 pounds. *Education:* 8 years. *Prior occupation:* Air-conditioner repairman. *County of conviction:* Brazos. *Age at time of execution:* 39.

Sentenced to death for: Convicted in the October 1979 stabbing death of 19-year-old LaShan Muhlinghaus, a Texas A&M student, at her College Station apartment. Prosecutors said Emery hid in a closet and attacked Muhlinghaus when she walked in while he was burglarizing her apartment. After her death, Muhlinghaus was sexually assaulted and her lower body mutilated. The case went unsolved for four years until Emery's ex-wife, Debra, went to police in Milwaukee, Wisconsin. She later testified that her ex-husband came home the night of the murder covered with blood. Two of his friends testified that he admitted killing Muhlinghaus. When charged with Muhlinghaus's murder, Emery was being held in St. Paul, Minnesota, on three counts of murder.

Received at death row: October 12, 1979. *Time on death row:* 6,997 days (19.17 years).

Last meal: Two T-bone steaks, french fries, salad, cake, chocolate ice cream, coffee, and Coke.

Last statement: "I just want to tell Catharina I love you. Take care of yourself. That's all I have to say."

Pronounced dead: 6:24 P.M.

164

James Ronald Meanes

Executed: December 15, 1998

Personal data: *Born:* June 8, 1956. *Race:* Black. *Height:* 5'8". *Weight:* 145 pounds. *Education:* 12 years. *Prior occupation:* Welder. *County of conviction:* Harris. *Age at time of execution:* 42.

Sentenced to death for: Convicted of capital murder for the April 21, 1981, shooting death of Houston security guard Oliver Flores, 29, during a robbery of a Purolator Armored Inc. van containing more than $1 million. Carlos Santana was also convicted in the Purolator incident and given the death sentence. (See entry 55, Carlos Santana.)

Received at death row: August 13, 1981. *Time on death row:* 6,333 days (17.35 years).

Last meal: One bacon double cheeseburger, golden french fries, one tall strawberry milk shake, and six chocolate cookies.

Last statement: "As the ocean always returns to itself, love always returns to itself, so does consciousness, always returns to itself. And I do so with love on my lips. May God bless all mankind."

Pronounced dead: 6:36 P.M.

John Moody

Executed: January 5, 1999

Personal data: *Born:* October 17, 1952. *Race:* White. *Height:* 5'10". *Weight:* 175 pounds. *Education:* 12 years. *Prior occupation:* Landscaper. *County of conviction:* Taylor. *Age at time of execution:* 46.

Sentenced to death for: Convicted in the July 1988 robbery and murder of 77-year-old Maureen Louise Maulden in Abilene. Maulden was raped, beaten with a fireplace brush, and strangled with a telephone cord inside her home, at 881 Elmwood Drive. A bloody fingerprint found on the telephone led police to Moody's residence, where rings stolen from the house were recovered. Police said Moody had previously done yard work and odd jobs for Maulden.

Received at death row: March 6, 1989. *Time on death row:* 3,592 days (9.84 years).

Last meal: Two T-bone steaks, salad with French onion dressing, rolls, french fries with ketchup, five soft tacos, angel food cake, one pint of white chocolate-almond ice cream, and a six-pack of Pepsi.

Last statement: "I'd like to apologize and ask forgiveness for any pain and suffering I have inflicted upon all of you, including my family, all of you, I am very sorry. There is a point where a man wants to die in judgment. Though my judgment is merciful, I hope and pray that all those involved as well as the judgment upon y'all will one day be more merciful than mine. God bless you all. God speed, I love you. Remain strong, ask God to give mercy. I love you all too. I'm very sorry. I've got to go now, I love you."

Pronounced dead: 8:33 P.M.

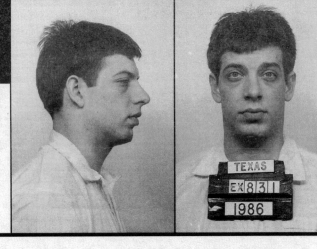

166

Troy Dale Farris

Executed:
January 13, 1999

TEXAS
EX 8311
1986

Personal data: *Born:* February 26, 1962. *Race:* White. *Height:* 6'0". *Weight:* 185 pounds. *Education:* 12 years. *Prior occupation:* Electrician/truck driver. *County of conviction:* Tarrant. *Age at time of execution:* 36.

Sentenced to death for: Convicted in the December 1983 shooting death of 28-year-old Clark Murell Rosenbaum Jr., a Tarrant County deputy sheriff. Rosenbaum was shot twice in the chest after he had driven up on Farris and codefendants Vance Nation and Charles Lowder during a drug buy on Old Decatur Road. Nation, who with Lowder had met Farris to buy three quarters of a pound of marijuana, told police that Farris shot Rosenbaum as the officer reached inside his car for the radio. As the officer fell and reached for his gun, Farris shot him a second time, Nation said. One of the .38 caliber bullets was stopped by Rosenbaum's bulletproof vest. The second bullet entered the deputy's shoulder and passed through his heart and lungs.
Codefendants: Charges against Lowder were dismissed and he was granted immunity from prosecution. File records indicate that a capital murder case against Nation is still pending.

Received at death row: June 3, 1986. *Time on death row:* 4,607 days (12.62 years).

Last meal: None.

Last statement: "First off, to the Rosenbaum family, to Cindy, to Scott, to everyone, I just want to say I have nothing but love for you and I mean that from the deepest part. I can only tell you that Clark did not die in vain. I don't mean to offend you by saying that. But what I mean by that is, through his death, he led this man to God. I have nothing but love for you. To my family, my soul beloved, you're so beautiful. For all your love and support is just miraculous. Everything that y'all have done. Be sure and tell T.D. he's in my heart. I send my love to Jay, to everyone. To Roger Burdge. I have nothing but love for all of you. Like they say in the song I guess, I just want to go out like Elijah, on fire with the spirit of God. I love you. I'm done."

Pronounced dead: 7:16 P.M.

167

Martin Sauceda Vega

Executed: January 26, 1999

Personal data: *Born:* October 17, 1946. *Race:* Hispanic. *Height:* 5'10". *Weight:* 165 pounds. *Education:* 3 years. *Prior occupation:* Laborer. *County of conviction:* Caldwell. *Age at time of execution:* 52.

Sentenced to death for: Convicted in the murder-for-hire killing of 36-year-old James William Mims. Vega told authorities that he and Mims's wife, Linda, plotted to kill Mims in order to collect approximately $250,000 in life insurance. Mims was beaten and shot seven times with a .22 caliber pistol. Vega went to authorities in Luling on January 2, 1988, and confessed his role in the murder. He later led police to an area where the murder weapon was found.

Received at death row: February 16, 1989. *Time on death row:* 3,631 days (9.95 years).

Last meal: T-bone steak, shrimp, and a Coke.

Last statement: See Appendix.

Pronounced dead: 6:22 P.M.

168

George Cordova

Executed: February 10, 1999

Personal data: *Born:* March 26, 1959. *Race:* Hispanic. *Height:* 5'8". *Weight:* 140 pounds. *Education:* 6 years (GED). *Prior occupation:* Laborer. *County of conviction:* Bexar. *Age at time of execution:* 39.

Sentenced to death for: On August 4, 1979, Cordova, Manuel Villanueva, and two unidentified males approached Jose "Joey" Hernandez, 19, and Hernandez's date, Cynthia West, as they sat in their car. Cordova asked Hernandez to take him to a station for gas. Hernandez refused because he noticed Villanueva had a knife. Cordova pulled Hernandez from his car and beat him on the head with a tire tool. Villanueva stabbed Hernandez in the neck. The other two men pulled West from the car and forced her into the woods and raped her, then Villanueva raped her. They ran to Hernandez's car and drove it away.
Codefendants: Mauel Villanueva was convicted of murder and sentenced to life in prison. The two other people involved in the incident were never identified.

Received at death row: March 4, 1982. *Time on death row:* 6,187 days (16.95 years).

Last meal: Declined last meal.

Last statement: "For the pain I have caused you, I am ashamed to even look at your faces. You are great people. To my brothers on death row. Mexico, Mexico." [Spoke in Spanish, not translated.]

Pronounced dead: 6:30 P.M.

169

Danny Lee Barber

Executed: February 11, 1999

Personal data: *Born:* May 8, 1955. *Race:* White. *Height:* 5'7". *Weight:* 140 pounds. *Education:* 12 years. *Prior occupation:* Roofer. *County of conviction:* Dallas. *Age at time of execution:* 43.

Sentenced to death for: Convicted in the October 8, 1979, slaying of Janice Louise Ingram at her home, in Balch Springs. Barber reportedly broke in to Ingram's home on Lake June Road and repeatedly struck her on the head and face with a piece of pipe when she surprised him. Ingram was also stabbed in the throat. Her leather purse, clock radio, and calculator were stolen from the home. Barber also served life sentences for three other murders, including the January 17, 1979, slaying of 48-year-old Mercedes Mendez, aka Mercy Mendez. The woman's body was dumped on a road in a wooded area near Mesquite after she had been beaten, sexually molested, and shot three times in the head. Barber was charged with the woman's murder on May 6, 1980, while being held in the Dallas County jail on other charges. He confessed to the murder the next day and later pleaded guilty to two other Dallas County murders committed on June 18, 1978, and April 21, 1980. Records indicate neither the victims nor the circumstances in those two cases.

Received at death row: October 31, 1980. *Time on death row:* 6,677 days (18.29 years).

Last meal: Two steaks, baked potato, chef salad, tea, and chocolate ice cream.

Last statement: "Hello, Ms. Ingram, it is good to see you. I said I could talk but I don't think I am gonna be able to. I heard one of your nieces had some angry words. I didn't have anything to do with the stay. I spent the last twenty years waiting to figure out what's going on. I pray that you get over it and that's the only thing I can think to say. I'm regretful for what I done. But I'm a different person from that time. If you could get to know me over the years, you could have seen it. I've got some people over here that believes that. I want to talk to my friends over here for a second. Well it's good to see you guys. Look after Mar Lynn for me. Like I said, I've called my mother already so she knows. Good-bye."

Pronounced dead: 6:26 P.M.

170

Andrew Cantu

Executed:
February 16,
1999

Personal data: *Born:* December 5, 1967. *Race:* Hispanic. *Height:* 5'7". *Weight:* 155 pounds. *Education:* 11 years. *Prior occupation:* Construction. *County of conviction:* Taylor. *Age at time of execution:* 31.

Sentenced to death for: Convicted in the stabbing deaths of three people inside an Abilene home in what authorities claim was a murder-for-hire scheme. Killed were Helen Summers, Mandell Eugene Summers, and Billy Mack Summers. All three were stabbed with a knife and then their home was set afire. Prosecutors charged that the three were killed for the promise of remuneration from codefendant Gregory Lynn Summers (see entry 377). Two other codefendants, Ramon Gonzales and Paul Flares, testified that Cantu stabbed the three victims. He later admitted the murders to family members and friends.
Codefendants: Cases are pending against Ramon Gonzales and Paul Flares.

Received at death row: June 6, 1991. *Time on death row:* 2,812 days (7.70 years).

Last meal: Pork baby-back ribs, hard-shell tacos, corn tortillas, french fries, salad with ranch dressing, red and green chili sauce, jalapeño peppers and tomatoes boiled with garlic and cumin, root beer, and chocolate ice cream.

Last statement: None.

Pronounced dead: 9:37 P.M.

171

Norman Evans Green

Executed: February 24, 1999

Personal data: *Born:* November 7, 1960. *Race:* Black. *Height:* 6'1". *Weight:* 160 pounds. *Education:* 14 years. *Prior occupation:* Hotel housekeeper. *County of conviction:* Bexar. *Age at time of execution:* 38.

Sentenced to death for: Convicted in the February 1985 shooting death of 19-year-old Timothy Adams during an attempted robbery of an electronics store in San Antonio. Green and accomplice Harold Bowens waited for the manager of Dyer Electronics, 9402 Perrin Beitel, to leave for lunch before entering the store to confront Adams, a clerk, with a .38 caliber pistol. When Adams was slow to follow instructions, Green fired four times, striking Adams in the arm, chest, and abdomen. He died twelve hours later. Witnesses identified Green and Bowens, who escaped from the scene empty-handed. Green reportedly surrendered to authorities on February 21, 1985.
Codefendant: Harold Bowens testified against Green and pleaded guilty to a lesser charge of murder in exchange for a life sentence.

Received at death row: September 27, 1985. *Time on death row:* 4,898 days (13.42 years).

Last meal: Barbecue ribs, pork chops, salad with French dressing, baked potato, Texas toast, and Coke.

Last statement: None.

Pronounced dead: 6:17 P.M.

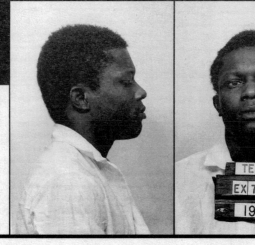

172

Charles Henry Rector

Executed: March 26, 1999

Personal data: *Born:* April 16, 1954. *Race:* Black. *Height:* 5'8". *Weight:* 160 pounds. *Education:* 8 years. *Prior occupation:* Paint and body repairman. *County of conviction:* Travis. *Age at time of execution:* 44.

Sentenced to death for: Convicted in the October 17, 1981, shooting, rape, and drowning death of Carolyn Kay Davis, 22. Her bruised and naked body was found in Town Lake (Austin). Rector was arrested the same night near the apartment complex where Davis lived. He was wearing the victim's blue jeans and carrying her rings and necklace.
Note: On March 28, 1986, Rector used a razor blade to inflict a four-inch laceration to his right wrist. On April 25, 1986, he attempted suicide by inflicting a large laceration to the right side of his neck and several lacerations to both arms. (Rector has a history of self-mutilation.) On October 25, 1983, Rector was stabbed by former death row inmate Jay Kelly Pinkerton (see entry 13, Jay Kelly Pinkerton) in the back and upper chest region with a homemade shank.

Received at death row: September 2, 1982. *Time on death row:* 6,049 days (16.57 years).

Last meal: Three beef enchiladas, three tacos, french fries, and one strawberry shake.

Last statement: See Appendix.

Pronounced dead: 6:22 P.M.

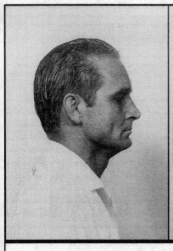

Robert Excell White

Executed: March 30, 1999

Personal data: *Born:* March 14, 1938. *Race:* White. *Height:* 6'1". *Weight:* 172 pounds. *Education:* 10 years. *Prior occupation:* Auto mechanic. *County of conviction:* Collin. *Age at time of execution:* 61.

Sentenced to death for: Convicted in the execution-style slaying of three men at the Hilltop Grocery, a rural country store near the communities of McKinney and Princeton. Killed were store owner Preston Broyles, 73, and store customers Gary Coker and Billy St. John, both 18 and residents of Princeton. All three were riddled with bullets from a .30 caliber machine gun stolen a day earlier from a Waco gun collector, who was found stabbed to death in his apartment. White and two accomplices left the store with $6 taken from the cash register and about $60 taken from the wallets of the victims. While White confessed to shooting all three men, he was tried and convicted only in Broyles's death. *Codefendants:* James Owen Livingston was convicted of capital murder and originally sentenced to death. The death sentence was commuted to life in April 1983. Gary Dale Livingston was convicted of murder (three) in May 1975 and sentenced to twenty years. He was discharged on July 28, 1984.

Received at death row: August 26, 1974. *Time on death row:* 8,982 days (24.61 years).

Last meal: Two hamburgers, french fries, and fried onion rings.

Last statement: "Send me back to my maker, Warden."

Pronounced dead: 6:17 P.M.

174

Aaron Christopher Foust

Executed: April 28, 1999

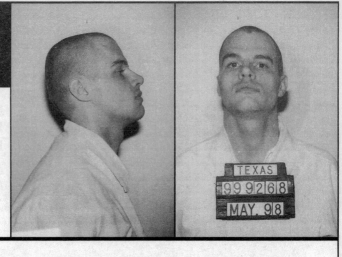

Personal data: *Born:* July 28, 1972. *Race:* White. *Height:* 6'0". *Weight:* 180 pounds. *Education:* n/a. *Prior occupation:* Laborer. *County of conviction:* Tarrant. *Age at time of execution:* 26.

Sentenced to death for: Convicted in the May 1997 robbery and murder of 43-year-old David S. Ward in Fort Worth. Stereo speaker wire was used to bind Ward's hands and feet before he was strangled inside his apartment, at 5624 Blue Ridge Court. Ward's credit cards were stolen and later used by Foust. Ward's BMW was also stolen. It was found on fire in Arlington two days after the murder. Before leaving the apartment, Foust and an accomplice sprayed words and letters to make the murder appear gang related.
Codefendant: Jamal Brown was charged with capital murder. Disposition is not immediately known.

Received at death row: May 19, 1998. *Time on death row:* 344 days (0.94 year).

Last meal: A cheeseburger, french fries, and Coke.

Last statement: "Adios, amigos. I'll see you on the other side. I'm ready when y'all are."

Pronounced dead: 6:22 P.M.

175

Jose
De La Cruz

Executed:
May 4, 1999

Personal data: *Born:* April 26, 1968. *Race:* Hispanic. *Height:* 5'9". *Weight:* 139 pounds. *Education:* 10 years. *Prior occupation:* Forklift operator/mechanic. *County of conviction:* Nueces. *Age at time of execution:* 31.

Sentenced to death for: Convicted in the June 1987 robbery-slaying of 24-year-old Domingo Rosas in Corpus Christi. De La Cruz, boyfriend of Rosas's cousin, stabbed the victim six times with a kitchen knife and broke his neck before robbing him of his driver's license and credit cards. The murder weapon was found in the car De La Cruz was driving the day after the murder, when he was arrested for public intoxication. De La Cruz was arrested and charged with capital murder June 3, 1987, when he attempted to withdraw money from Rosas's savings account at the Nueces National Bank by presenting Rosas's identification and forging his signature. Rosas was an epileptic who lived primarily off Social Security benefits due to a physical handicap. His body was found inside his apartment, at 4702 Old Brownsville Road, when family members complained he had not contacted them over a two-day period.

Received at death row: June 16, 1988. *Time on death row:* 3,974 days (10.89 years).

Last meal: Declined last meal.

Last statement: None.

Pronounced dead: 6:23 P.M.

176

Clydell Coleman

Executed: May 5, 1999

TEXAS
EX968
FEB. 90

Personal data: *Born:* October 1, 1936. *Race:* Black. *Height:* 6'1". *Weight:* 160 pounds. *Education:* 11 years. *Prior occupation:* Janitor. *County of conviction:* McLennan. *Age at time of execution:* 62.

Sentenced to death for: Convicted in the February 1989 robbery and murder of 87-year-old Leethisha Joe. Coleman and accomplice Yolanda Phillips entered Joe's home, at 706 Dawson, through the back door and confronted the victim. Coleman covered Joe's head with a blanket, hit her with a hammer, and then strangled her with her own stocking. Property stolen from the home included a television, clock radio, sheets, cooler, floor fan, and ladder. Phillips was arrested after her fingerprints were found inside the home. She then implicated Coleman in a statement to police.
Codefendant: Yolanda Phillips was convicted of burglary of a habitation and sentenced to thirty years in prison.

Received at death row: March 1, 1990. *Time on death row:* 3,352 days (9.18 years).

Last meal: Salmon croquettes, scrambled eggs, french fries, and biscuits.

Last statement: None.

Pronounced dead: 6:30 P.M.

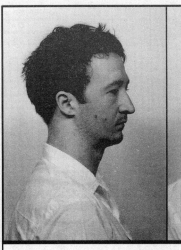

William Hamilton Little

Executed: June 1, 1999

Personal data: *Born:* October 25, 1960. *Race:* White. *Height:* 6'1". *Weight:* 191 pounds. *Education:* 9 years. *Prior occupation:* Roofer. *County of conviction:* Liberty. *Age at time of execution:* 38.

Sentenced to death for: Convicted in the stabbing death of 23-year-old Marilyn Peters at her rural Cleveland, Texas, home. Peters was raped, stabbed more than nineteen times with a kitchen knife, and then raped a second time after her death. Her nude body was found on the living room floor of her home in the Old Snake River Lake subdivision. Robbery was not a motive in the murder, since Peters was still wearing her jewelry and nearly $500 was found in her bedroom dresser. Authorities also found nearly two pounds of marijuana inside the residence. Little claimed he had become acquainted with the victim through her sale of marijuana to him. Bloodstained blue jeans and towels were found at Little's residence on Buckley Drive. He was arrested there on December 6, 1983.

Received at death row: April 15, 1985. *Time on death row:* 5,160 days (14.14 years).

Last meal: Fifteen slices of cheese, three fried eggs, three pieces of buttered toast, two hamburger patties with cheese, half tomato sliced, one onion slice, french fries with salad dressing, a half pound of crispy fried bacon, one quart of chocolate milk, and one pint of fresh strawberries.

Last statement: None.

Pronounced dead: 6:20 P.M.

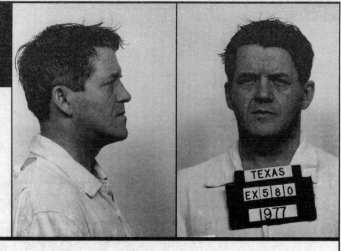

178

Joseph Stanley Faulder

Executed:
June 17, 1999

TEXAS
EX580
1977

Personal data: *Born:* October 19, 1937. *Race:* White. *Height:* 5'7". *Weight:* 171 pounds. *Education:* 10 years. *Prior occupation:* Auto mechanic. *County of conviction:* Gregg. *Age at time of execution:* 61.

Sentenced to death for: Convicted in the July 1975 beating-stabbing death of 75-year-old Inez Phillips at her Gladewater home. Faulder and accomplice Linda "Stormy" Summers (aka Linda "Stormy" McCann) broke into Phillips's home believing she had money hidden in a floor safe. When Faulder found no money in the safe, he stole other household valuables, including Phillips's wedding ring. She was bound and gagged with tape and beaten on the back of the head with a blackjack when she resisted. Faulder later stabbed the elderly widow in the chest with a knife. Phillips's maid found her body the morning of July 9 with the knife still embedded in her chest. Faulder, an acquaintance of Phillips's former employee, was charged in the murder in April 1977 while being held on unrelated charges in Colorado. The Texas Court of Criminal Appeals ruled Faulder's written confession inadmissible and reversed his first conviction. He was again convicted in 1981 and sentenced to death a second time. Records do not indicate that his accomplice was incarcerated.

Received at death row: December 9, 1977. *Time on death row:* 7,860 days (21.53 years).

Last meal: Declined last meal.

Last statement: None.

Pronounced dead: 6:18 P.M.

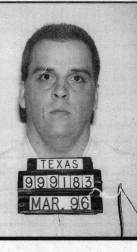

179

Charles Daniel Tuttle

Executed: July 1, 1999

Personal data: *Born:* June 26, 1964. *Race:* White. *Height:* 5'8". *Weight:* 212 pounds. *Education:* 10 years (GED). *Prior occupation:* Construction worker. *County of conviction:* Smith. *Age at time of execution:* 35.

Sentenced to death for: Convicted in the beating death of 42-year-old Cathy Harris, of Tyler. Harris was beaten to death with a hammer and her body placed in a closet in an effort to conceal the crime. Before fleeing, Tuttle took the victim's purse and a handgun from the residence off CR 1148. Tuttle had been staying with Harris a week prior to the killing but was told to leave for failing to pay his share of the bills. Tuttle was arrested four days later while visiting at a Beaumont hospital. He had Harris's .357 caliber revolver and two of her credit cards in his possession when arrested.

Received at death row: March 26, 1996. *Time on death row:* 1,192 days (3.27 years).

Last meal: Four fried eggs sunny-side up, four sausage patties, one chicken-fried steak patty, one bowl of white country gravy, five pieces of white toast, five tacos with meat and cheese only, four Dr Peppers with ice on the side, and five mint sticks.

Last statement: "To Cathy's family and friends that were unable to attend today, I am truly sorry. I hope my dropping my appeals has in some way begun your healing process. This is all that I am going to do to help you out in any way for the nightmare and pain that I have caused you. But I am truly sorry and I wish I could take back what I did, but I can't. I hope this heals you. To my family— I love you, when the tears flow let the smiles grow. Everything is all right. To my family, I love you. Warden, ATW."

Pronounced dead: 6:28 P.M.

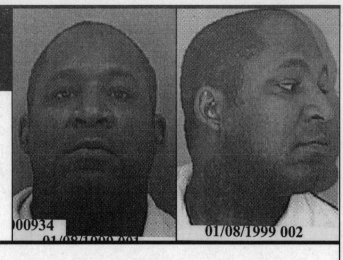

180

Tyrone Leroy Fuller

Executed: July 7, 1999

00934
01/08/1999 002

Personal data: *Born:* August 1, 1963. *Race:* Black. *Height:* 6'0". *Weight:* 212 pounds. *Education:* 11 years (GED). *Prior occupation:* Coach. *County of conviction:* Grayson. *Age at time of execution:* 35.

Sentenced to death for: Convicted in the January 1988 capital murder of 26-year-old Andrea Lea Duke, of Paris, Texas. Duke, a medical technologist working at McCuiston Hospital, was raped, tortured, and stabbed to death after Fuller and two accomplices broke in to her apartment at 1050 Thirty-fourth Street in Paris. Duke's car, jewelry, and credit cards were stolen. Her body was found on the front lawn of the apartment complex.
Codefendants: John Earl McGrew reportedly received a life sentence as part of a plea bargain. Charges against Kenneth Wayne Harmon are pending.

Received at death row: March 31, 1989. *Time on death row:* 3,750 days (10.27 years).

Last meal: One bacon, ham, and cheese omelet with diced onion and peppers; one cinnamon roll; three slices of toast; three milks; two orange juices; hot sauce, grape jelly, butter, salt, and pepper; and fruit.

Last statement: "To my family, I love you. Please do not mourn my death or my life. Continue to live as I want you to live. I hold no bitterness toward no one. Just remember the light. I'm gonna let this light shine. Let it shine. Let the light shine."

Pronounced dead: 6:20 P.M.

Ricky Don Blackmon

Executed: August 4, 1999

Personal data: *Born:* November 21, 1957. *Race:* White. *Height:* 6'1". *Weight:* 214 pounds. *Education:* n/a. *Prior occupation:* Cook. *County of conviction:* Shelby. *Age at time of execution:* 41.

Sentenced to death for: Convicted of capital murder in the robbery-stabbing death of Carl Joseph Rinkle, 26. Rinkle was slashed numerous times with a sword or machete and robbed.
Codefendant: Donna Mae Rogers was convicted of murder and sentenced to life in prison.

Received at death row: December 7, 1987. *Time on death row:* 4,258 days (11.67 years).

Last meal: No last meal was requested; only requested something to drink.

Last statement: None.

Pronounced dead: 6:22 P.M.

182

Charles Anthony Boyd

Executed: August 5, 1999

Personal data: *Born:* August 17, 1959. *Race:* Black. *Height:* 5'9". *Weight:* 148 pounds. *Education:* 12. *Prior occupation:* Janitor. *County of conviction:* Dallas. *Age at time of execution:* 39.

Sentenced to death for: Convicted of capital murder in the April 13, 1987, strangulation-drowning death of Mary Milligan. Milligan was found dead in her bathtub, and her 1984 Cadillac had been stolen.

Received at death row: December 3, 1987. *Time on death row:* 4,263 days (11.68 years).

Last meal: Declined last meal.

Last statement: "I want you all to know I did not do this crime. I wanted to wait for a thirty-day stay for a DNA test so you know who did the crime."

Pronounced dead: 6:22 P.M.

183

Kenneth Dunn

Executed: August 10, 1999

Personal data: *Born:* October 3, 1959. *Race:* Black. *Height:* 5'6". *Weight:* 130 pounds. *Education:* 9 years. *Prior occupation:* Laborer. *County of conviction:* Harris. *Age at time of execution:* 39.

Sentenced to death for: Convicted in the March 17, 1980, shooting death of bank teller Madeline Peters, 21, during a robbery at the Bank of Almeda. Dunn received the death penalty in November 1980, but the sentence was overturned because a court reporter lost part of the trial transcript.

Received at death row: December 19, 1980. *Time on death row:* 6,808 days (18.65 years).

Last meal: Beef fajitas, stir-fried beef, six cinnamon rolls, one pecan pie, one cherry pie, one diet cream soda, and three eggs.

Last statement: None.

Pronounced dead: 7:30 P.M.

184

James Otto Earheart

Executed:
August 11, 1999

TEXAS
EX9015
1988

Personal data: *Born:* April 29, 1943. *Race:* White. *Height:* 5'9". *Weight:* 258 pounds. *Education:* 7 years. *Prior occupation:* Sales/appliance repair. *County of conviction:* Lee. *Age at time of execution:* 56.

Sentenced to death for: Convicted in the May 1987 abduction and slaying of 9-year-old Kandy Janell Kirtland, of Bryan. Kirtland was abducted from her home at 3210 Deer Trail on May 12, 1987, after being dropped off by the school bus. Her parents found Kirtland's backpack on the front porch, the front door open, and the keys to the home on the kitchen stove. Her decomposed body was found on May 26, 1987, along a creek in the 2500 block of East Villa Maria Road. She had been shot once in the head after her hands had been tied behind her back with electrical cord. Earhart was arrested in Walker County's Stubblefield Lake Park the same day Kirtland's body was found. Police learned Earhart had gone to the Kirtland home on May 4, 1987, in response to a newspaper ad about a paint spray gun for sale. He returned the day Kirtland disappeared, asking a neighbor when the Kirtlands would be home.

Received at death row: May 27, 1988. *Time on death row:* 4,093 days (11.21 years).

Last meal: Steak, french fries, and one vanilla shake.

Last statement: None.

Pronounced dead: 6:24 P.M.

185

Joe Mario Trevino

Executed: August 18, 1999

Personal data: *Born:* July 25, 1962. *Race:* Hispanic. *Height:* 5'10". *Weight:* 165 pounds. *Education:* 12 years. *Prior occupation:* Paint and body work. *County of conviction:* Tarrant. *Age at time of execution:* 37.

Sentenced to death for: Convicted in the January 1983 rape-slaying of 80-year-old Blanche Miller at her home in Haltom City. Trevino broke in to Miller's home at 4901 Broadway through a kitchen window while she was away and killed her when she returned home. She was raped and then strangled to death. Trevino stole Miller's car after loading it with jewelry, a color television, stereo equipment, and other items from the house. Miller's car was recovered on Diamond Oaks Drive hours later and police discovered the stolen property at Trevino's residence at 5129 Jerri Lane.

Received at death row: July 10, 1984. *Time on death row:* 5,517 days (15.12 years).

Last meal: Fried chicken, watermelon, salad with Italian dressing, raw carrots, raw cucumbers, and a strawberry shake.

Last statement: None.

Pronounced dead: 6:25 P.M.

186

Raymond Jones

Executed: September 1, 1999

Personal data: *Born:* January 1, 1960. *Race:* Black. *Height:* 5'11". *Weight:* 150 pounds. *Education:* 8 years. *Prior occupation:* Laborer. *County of conviction:* Jefferson. *Age at time of execution:* 39.

Sentenced to death for: Convicted in the June 1988 robbery and murder of 51-year-old Su Van Dang at the victim's residence in Port Arthur. Dang was stabbed to death during a robbery of his home at 2348 Eighth Street. His body was found in a closet and had been partially burned in an attempt to destroy evidence.

Received at death row: December 20, 1989. *Time on death row:* 3,542 days (9.70 years).

Last meal: A double-meat cheeseburger, french fries, ice cream, and a soda.

Last statement: None.

Pronounced dead: 6:17 P.M.

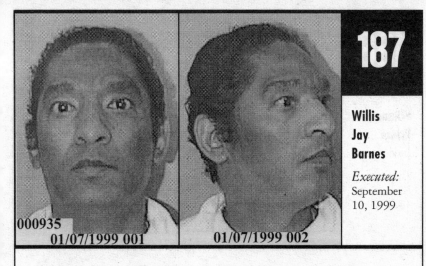

000935
01/07/1999 001

01/07/1999 002

187

Willis Jay Barnes

Executed: September 10, 1999

Personal data: *Born:* August 13, 1948. *Race:* Black. *Height:* 5'11". *Weight:* 153 pounds. *Education:* 11 years (GED). *Prior occupation:* Antique refinisher. *County of conviction:* Harris. *Age at time of execution:* 51.

Sentenced to death for: Convicted in the February 1988 strangulation death of 84-year-old Helen Greb. Barnes cut the telephone line to Greb's home before breaking in to the residence. Once inside, Barnes brutally beat and raped Greb before strangling her to death with his hands. An autopsy revealed that Greb suffered twenty broken ribs, a broken back, a crushed chest, and numerous lacerations. Police later traced two guns and a television set stolen from the residence to a fence who bought the items from Barnes.

Received at death row: April 3, 1989. *Time on death row:* 3,812 days (10.44 years).

Last meal: Three fried chicken breasts, three jalapeño peppers, five rolls, and a soda.

Last statement: "Yes. I would like to give love to my mother, sisters, and brothers and let them know that I am thinking of them right now and I want to thank God for giving me such a loving family. To the victim's family, I hope you find it in your heart to forgive me as I have forgiven you. I'm ready, Warden."

Pronounced dead: 6:19 P.M.

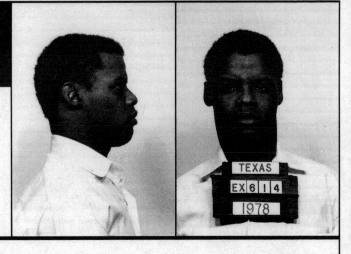

188

**William
Prince
Davis**

Executed:
September
14, 1999

TEXAS
EX 6 1 4
1978

Personal data: *Born:* April 24, 1957. *Race:* Black. *Height:* 5'7". *Weight:* 142 pounds. *Education:* 7 years. *Prior occupation:* Roofer. *County of conviction:* Harris. *Age at time of execution:* 42.

Sentenced to death for: Convicted in the June 1978 robbery-slaying of a man identified as the 60-year-old manager of the Red Wing Ice Cream Company in Houston. Records indicate the victim, identified only by the last name Lang, was receiving cash receipts from three drivers when Davis entered the company office with a pistol and shot Lang once. David fled with $712 and a shotgun taken from the office. He was later identified by the three company drivers and gave a written confession to police.

Received at death row: October 10, 1978. *Time on death row:* 7,644 days (20.94) years.

Last meal: Chicken-fried drumsticks, one bowl of chili, one bowl of cheese, five rolls, two bags of barbecue chips, a six-pack of Coke, one pack of Palmer cigarettes (prohibited by regulations), and one lighter (prohibited by regulations).

Last statement: See Appendix.

Pronounced dead: 6:19 P.M.

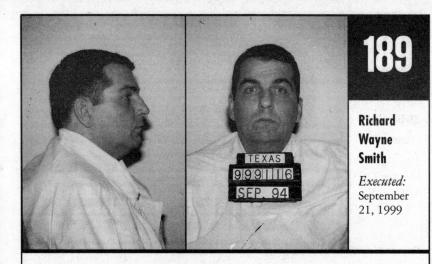

189

Richard Wayne Smith

Executed: September 21, 1999

Personal data: *Born:* January 12, 1956. *Race:* White. *Height:* 5'8". *Weight:* 246 pounds. *Education:* 14 years. *Prior occupation:* Electrician. *County of conviction:* Harris. *Age at time of execution:* 43.

Sentenced to death for: Convicted in the murder of Karen Birky, a Baytown convenience store clerk. Birky was working at the Stop-N-Go convenience store at 3312 Decker when Smith robbed her at gunpoint and attempted to abduct her in the stolen vehicle he was driving. When Birky refused to get into the vehicle, Smith shot her once in the neck, killing her. He was arrested a short time later with the pistol and stolen cash in his pockets.

Received at death row: September 2, 1994. *Time on death row:* 1,845 days (5.05 years).

Last meal: Three bacon, lettuce, and tomato sandwiches; french fries; one small bowl of pickles; one half onion; and one cup of iced tea.

Last statement: None.

Pronounced dead: 6:25 P.M.
Note: Smith dropped all appeals when he learned he was dying of liver failure.

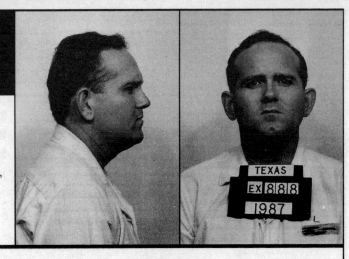

190

Alvin Crane

Executed:
October 12, 1999

TEXAS
EX 888
1987

Personal data: *Born:* May 6, 1958. *Race:* White. *Height:* 6'0". *Weight:* 204 pounds. *Education:* 8 years. *Prior occupation:* Oil field operator. *County of conviction:* Denton. *Age at time of execution:* 41.

Sentenced to death for: Convicted in the March 1987 shooting death of Melvin Kenneth Drum, an Ochiltree County deputy sheriff. Deputy Drum, responding to a disturbance call, was shot once in the face after stopping Crane's vehicle on the roadway. Crane exited his vehicle and shot Drum while he was still seated inside his patrol car. The officer died before he could be transported to a hospital. Crane was arrested for the killing on April 15, 1987.

Received at death row: November 12, 1987. *Time on death row:* 4,352 days (11.92 years).

Last meal: Fried chicken, mashed potatoes with gravy, corn on the cob, cauliflower, and chocolate cake.

Last statement: "I would like to say a little something. I just want to say I'm sorry to the family. I know I caused you a lot of pain and suffering and I hope that you will find some peace and comfort in this. That if there is any anger you can let it go. Not let it come between you and God. Sorry for causing everybody such trouble tonight, Bruce, Joe, y'all all treat me with respect. I appreciate it. I really do. I just want to tell my family, everybody I love and I want you to know that I love you, and that God loves you too. Everything is going to be just fine, just fine. I love y'all. That's it."

Pronounced dead: 6:23 P.M.

191

Jerry McFadden

Executed: October 14, 1999

Personal data: *Born:* March 21, 1948. *Race:* White. *Height:* 5'9". *Weight:* 208 pounds. *Education:* 7 years. *Prior occupation:* Telephone cable installer. *County of conviction:* Bell. *Age at time of execution:* 51.

Sentenced to death for: Convicted in the abduction, rape, and strangulation death of 18-year-old Suzanne Denise Harrison of Hawkins. Harrison and companions Gena Turner, 20, and Bryan Boone, 19, were abducted during an outing to Lake Hawkins. McFadden raped and sodomized Harrison and then strangled her with her panties. Her body was found atop Barnwell Mountain in Upshur County. The bodies of Turner and Boone were found five days later. Both had been shot to death, execution-style, with a .38 caliber pistol.
Note: On July 8, 1986, while being held in the Upshur County Jail, McFadden overpowered a male jailer and escaped in the car of a female jailer he took hostage. The hostage, eventually kept in an abandoned railroad boxcar in Big Sandy, escaped McFadden after twenty-eight hours. He was captured after three days of an extensive manhunt.

Received at death row: July 15, 1987. *Time on death row:* 4,474 days (12.26 years).

Last meal: BLT with pickles and onions, french fries, one pint of butter pecan ice cream, and Coke.

Last statement: None.

Pronounced dead: 6:16 P.M.

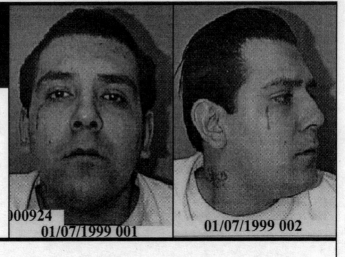

192

Domingo Cantu Jr.

Executed: October 28, 1999

000924
01/07/1999 001

01/07/1999 002

Personal data: *Born:* June 7, 1968. *Race:* Hispanic. *Height:* 5'8". *Weight:* 178 pounds. *Education:* n/a. *Prior occupation:* n/a. *County of conviction:* Dallas. *Age at time of execution:* 31.

Sentenced to death for: Convicted in the June 1988 sexual assault and slaying of 94-year-old Suda Eller Jones in Dallas. Cantu sexually assaulted the victim and then beat her head against a concrete sidewall outside a residence at 1139 North Madison. Jones died from multiple head injuries. Cantu was arrested after being spotted running from the scene. He later confessed to police.

Received at death row: December 1, 1988. *Time on death row:* 3,983 days (10.91 years).

Last meal: Fried chicken (twelve pieces white and dark meat), mashed potatoes with gravy, fourteen jalapeño peppers, orange juice, chocolate milk, buttermilk biscuits, and strawberry ice cream.

Last statement: "[In English] I love you. I will be waiting for you on the other side. Son be strong no matter what happens, know that God is looking over you. Jesus mercy, Jesus mercy, Jesus mercy! [In Spanish] Brother-in-law, take care of the family and let it be united. Yoli. [In German] My beautiful princess. You are all my heart and soul and I love you so much."

Pronounced dead: 6:23 P.M.

193

Desmond Jennings

Executed: November 16, 1999

Personal data: *Born:* October 4, 1971. *Race:* Black. *Height:* 5'6". *Weight:* 183 pounds. *Education:* 9 years. *Prior occupation:* Nurse's aid. *County of conviction:* Tarrant. *Age at time of execution:* 28.

Sentenced to death for: Convicted in the shooting deaths of Sylvester Walton, 44, and Wonda Matthews, 27, at a Fort Worth residence. Both Walton and Matthews were shot in the head with a .32 caliber pistol inside the residence at 2614 Langston. Walton's pockets were emptied by Jennings following the double murder. Police indicated that the killings were drug related.

Received at death row: August 22, 1995. *Time on death row:* 1,547 days (4.24 years).

Last meal: Declined last meal.

Last statement: None.

Pronounced dead: 6:22 P.M.
Note: Jennings refused to exit his cell at the Ellis Unit for transportation to the death house. A chemical agent was applied and a use-of-force team entered the cell and applied restraints.

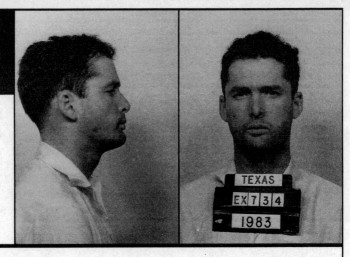

194

John Lamb

Executed:
November
17, 1999

TEXAS
EX 734
1983

Personal data: *Born:* July 24, 1957. *Race:* White. *Height:* 5'10". *Weight:* 145 pounds. *Education:* 11 years. *Prior occupation:* Laborer. *County of conviction:* Hunt. *Age at time of execution:* 42.

Sentenced to death for: Lamb admitted he shot Virginia businessman Jerry Harrison Chafin, 30, to steal his wallet, shaving kit, and car. Chafin was found dead by a cleaning woman the morning of November 6, 1982, two days after he had left Virginia for a new job in San Antonio. Lamb was arrested five days later near Perry, Florida, in Chafin's car. Lamb had been released on November 5, 1982, from a state prison in Searcy, Arkansas, hitchhiked to Greenville, and met Chafin later that day in the parking lot of a Greenville Motel. Lamb said the two men talked in Chafin's room for thirty minutes, and then he found Chafin's automatic pistol.

Received at death row: April 12, 1983. *Time on death row:* 6,063 days (16.61 years).

Last meal: Ten pieces of large deep-fried jumbo shrimp, two pieces of garlic bread, two pieces of fried chicken (dark meat), a tossed salad with thousand island dressing, and a chocolate milk shake.

Last statement: "I'm sorry, I wish I could bring them back. I'm done, let's do it."

Pronounced dead: 6:19 P.M.

TEXAS
EX 970
APR. 90

Jose Gutierrez

Executed: November 18, 1999

Personal data: *Born:* October 14, 1960. *Race:* Hispanic. *Height:* 5'4". *Weight:* 189 pounds. *Education:* 8 years. *Prior occupation:* Construction worker. *County of conviction:* Brazos. *Age at time of execution:* 39.

Sentenced to death for: Convicted in the September 1989 robbery and murder of 42-year-old Dorothy McNew, a College Station store clerk. McNew was working the counter at the Texas Coin Exchange, 404 University, when Gutierrez and his brother Jessie entered shortly after 10:00 A.M. When McNew saw one of the men pull a handgun from his coat, she attempted to flee into an office but was shot in the head. The Gutierrez brothers fled the store with gems and jewelry worth approximately $500,000. Both were traced to Houston, where they were arrested on September 1, 1989. Approximately $375,000 worth of the stolen merchandise was recovered.
Codefendant: Jessie Gutierrez was convicted of capital murder, sentenced to death, and executed by lethal injection on September 16, 1994. (See entry 80, Jessie Gutierrez.)

Received at death row: April 27, 1990. *Time on death row:* 3,492 days (9.57 years).

Last meal: Two double-meat cheeseburgers with all vegetables and bacon, french fries, two cans of Coke, five jalapeño peppers, five pieces of fried chicken (white and dark meat), three buttermilk biscuits, and a steak.

Last statement: "Mama Isabel told me to tell you hello. Holy, holy, holy! Lord God Almighty! Early in the morning our song shall rise to Thee. Holy, holy, holy, merciful and mighty! God in three persons, blessed Trinity. Holy, holy, holy! Merciful and mighty. All Thy works shall praise Thy name, in earth, and sky, and sea. Holy, holy, holy, merciful and mighty! God in three persons, blessed Trinity. Oh, our Father who art in heaven, holy, holy, holy be Thy name. Thy kingdom come, Thy will be done, on earth as it is in heaven. Give us this day our daily bread and forgive us our sins as we forgive our debtors. Lead us not into temptation, but deliver us from evil, for Thine is the kingdom and the power and the glory forever and ever. Now, Father, into thy hands I commit my spirit. Amen."

Pronounced dead: 6:22 P.M.

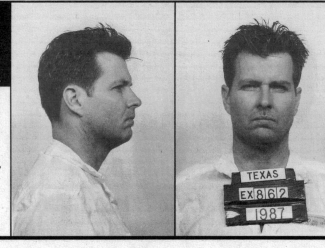

196

David Long

Executed:
December 8, 1999

TEXAS
EX862
1987

Personal data: *Born:* July 15, 1953. *Race:* White. *Height:* 5'9". *Weight:* 181 pounds. *Education:* 13 years. *Prior occupation:* Cable TV technician. *County of conviction:* Dallas. *Age at time of execution:* 46.

Sentenced to death for: Convicted in the hatchet slaying of three women in Lancaster, a Dallas suburb. Killed were Donna Sue Jester, 38; her blind cousin, Dalpha Lorene Jester, 64; and Laura Lee Owens, a 20-year-old drifter from Florida, who lived with the Jesters and Long in a house at 1010 Bayport. All were hacked to death with a hatchet by Long after he grew tired of hearing them argue. Long had lived at the house since September 19, 1986. He stole a purse, money, and a car from the residence after the killings. He was arrested about a month later in Austin.
Note: During his trial, Long, who called the triple homicide a "satanic" experience, said he would kill again if not given the death penalty. In a statement to police, Long also claims to have killed his former boss in Bayview in 1983 and a gas station attendant in San Bernardino, California, in 1978.

Received at death row: February 17, 1987. *Time on death row:* 4,677 days (12.81 years).

Last meal: Four bacon, lettuce, and tomato sandwiches; iced tea; and potato chips.

Last statement: "Ah, just ah sorry y'all. I think I've tried everything I could to get in touch with y'all to express how sorry I am. I, I never was right after that incident happened. I sent a letter to somebody, you know a letter outlining what I feel about everything. But anyway I just wanted, right after that to apologize to you. I'm real sorry for it. I was raised by the California Youth Authority, I can't really pinpoint where it started, what happened but I really believe that's just the bottom line, what happened to me was in California. I was in their reformatory schools and penitentiary, but, ah, they create monsters in there. That's it, I have nothing else to say. Thanks for coming, Jack."

Pronounced dead: 6:19 P.M.

James Beathard

Executed: December 9, 1999

Personal data: *Born:* February 23, 1957. *Race:* White. *Height:* 5'10". *Weight:* 197 pounds. *Education:* 15 years. *Prior occupation:* Motorcycle mechanic. *County of conviction:* Trinity. *Age at time of execution:* 42.

Sentenced to death for: Beathard, along with Gene Hathorn Jr., murdered Gene Hathorn Sr., 45; Linda Sue Hathorn, 35; and their son, Marcus, 14, in their Trinity County home. The pair ransacked the home and took VCRs, several guns, and a van to make it look like a robbery. Beathard's motive was the promise of renumeration ($12,500) from the estate, which was valued at $150,000. Only after the killings did Gene Hathorn Jr. discover that weeks before, his father had cut him out of his will.
Codefendant: Gene Hathorn Jr. was convicted of capital murder and sentenced to death.

Received at death row: March 5, 1985. *Time on death row:* 5,392 days (14.77 years).

Last meal: Fried catfish, fried chicken, french fries, onion rings, green salad, fresh carrots, and Coke.

Last statement: See Appendix.

Pronounced dead: 6:21 P.M.

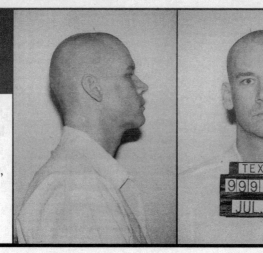

198

Robert Atworth

Executed: December 9, 1999

Personal data: *Born:* August 18, 1968. *Race:* White. *Height:* 6'1". *Weight:* 170 pounds. *Education:* 11 years (GED). *Prior occupation:* Laborer. *County of conviction:* Dallas. *Age at time of execution:* 31.

Sentenced to death for: Convicted in the April 1995 robbery and murder of 56-year-old Thomas Carlson in Richardson. Carlson's body was found between two trash dumpsters behind the President's Health Club at 110 W. Campbell Road. He had suffered multiple gunshot wounds to the head, torso, and groin area as well as knife wounds to the abdomen and chin. His wallet was missing and his right little finger, on which he had worn a ring, had been severed. Atworth was arrested the next day when he was caught burglarizing a residence in Garland. He was driving Carlson's car and had in his possession the 9mm murder weapon as well as the Manurhin .380 caliber pistol Carlson had carried for protection. Knives were also found in Atworth's pants pocket and boot.

Received at death row: July 18, 1996. *Time on death row:* 1,239 days (3.39 years).

Last meal: Grilled chicken, salad with ranch dressing, nachos and cheese with picante sauce, cookies, ice cream, and two root beers.

Last statement: "Well, first, my people, you guys have heard everything I needed to say today. I hope I said the right things. I hope you heard me. And I hope you go beyond here and do what you need to do, do the right thing. Strength in numbers. Look out for each other. You still got a chance with Shawn. Edwin, you know what you gotta do. You have my love. It's the right thing. And for everybody else, those people who have malice in their heart, allow ambitions to override what they know. Be right. Even though they just gotta do their job. For all of you with hatred in their veins, and think this is a sham. You've done nothing. I did this, I chose this, you've done nothing. Remember this, if all you know is hatred, if all you know is blood love, you'll never be satisfied. For everybody out there that is like that and knows nothing but negative, kiss my proud white Irish ass. I'm ready, Warden, send me home."

Pronounced dead: 6:21 P.M.

Sammie Felder Jr.

Executed:
December 15,
1999

Personal data: *Born:* August 23, 1945. *Race:* Black. *Height:* 6'0". *Weight:* 190 pounds. *Education:* 7 years. *Prior occupation:* Attendant. *County of conviction:* Harris. *Age at time of execution:* 54.

Sentenced to death for: Convicted in the February 1975 stabbing death of 42-year-old James Hanks, a paraplegic living at the Independent Life Style apartment complex in Houston. Hanks was reportedly stabbed with a pair of scissors and money was taken from his apartment in the 5100 block of South Willow. Felder was working as an attendant at the complex at the time. He was arrested by Idaho police for a traffic violation a month after the killing. Felder's 1976 conviction was overturned by the Fifth Circuit Court of Appeals because of an improperly admitted confession. He was again convicted in September 1986 and sentenced to death a second time.

Received at death row: June 19, 1976. *Time on death row:* 8,579 days (23.50 years).

Last meal: One pound of chitterlings, ten pieces of fried chicken (dark meat), ten pieces of bacon, one raw onion, fifteen pieces of fried shrimp, peach cobbler, and one pitcher of whole milk.

Last statement: "Like to tell my friends that I love them. Appreciate them being here to support me. Alison, I love you."

Pronounced dead: 6:15 P.M.

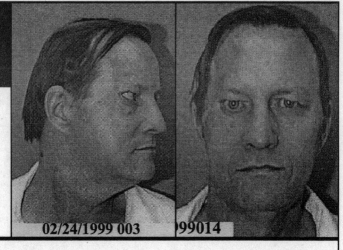

200

Earl Carl Heiselbetz Jr.

Executed: January 12, 2000

02/24/1999 003   99014

Personal data: *Born:* April 1, 1951. *Race:* White. *Height:* 6'2". *Weight:* 210 pounds. *Education:* 11 years. *Prior occupation:* Truck driver. *County of conviction:* Sabine. *Age at time of execution:* 48.

Sentenced to death for: Convicted in the abduction and murder of 27-year-old Rena Whitten Rogers and her 2-year-old daughter, Jacy. The two were taken from their home in Pineland and driven to Tyler County, where their skeletal remains were found in a barn on June 27, 1991. Both victims had been strangled. Heiselbetz lived next door to the victims and was unemployed at the time of the killing. Rena Rogers's husband reported a jar containing $8 in change, a .38 caliber pistol, and his wife's purse missing from the home. Police later found the victim's purse and the missing jar in a pond next to the home. Heiselbetz confessed after failing three polygraph tests.

Received at death row: November 22, 1991. *Time on death row:* 2,973 days (8.15 years).

Last meal: Two breaded pork chops, three scrambled eggs, french fries, and milk.

Last statement: "Love y'all, see you on the other side."

Pronounced dead: 6:19 P.M.

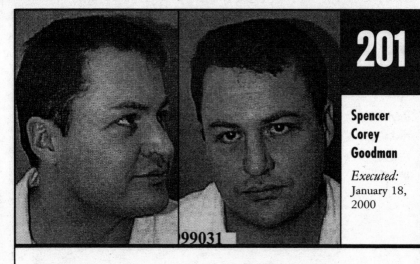

Spencer Corey Goodman

Executed: January 18, 2000

99031

Personal data: *Born:* October 28, 1968. *Race:* White. *Height:* 5'10". *Weight:* 200 pounds. *Education:* 12.5 years. *Prior occupation:* Restaurant manager. *County of conviction:* Fort Bend. *Age at time of execution:* 31.

Sentenced to death for: Convicted in the abduction and murder of 18-year-old Cecile Ham, wife of entertainment manager Bill Ham. Goodman approached Ham as she was getting into her car in the parking lot of a Walgreen's store at Dairy Ashford and Memorial in Houston. He knocked her unconscious, pushed her into her red Cadillac, and drove into Fort Bend County before stopping and breaking the woman's neck. Police tracked Ham's killer through his use of her credit cards in central Texas. Goodman, still driving Ham's car, was finally captured following a high-speed chase with police in Eagle County, Colorado, on August 7, 1991. He later confessed and directed authorities to where he had dumped Ham's body at a remote site near Pearsall in West Texas.

Received at death row: July 7, 1992. *Time on death row:* 2,751 days (7.54 years).

Last meal: A double cheeseburger; french fries topped with onions and cheese; a baked potato topped with sour cream, cheese, and butter; two fried pork chops; three beef enchiladas; and chocolate cake.

Last statement: "To my family, I love them. To Kami, I love you and will always be with you. That's it, Warden."

Pronounced dead: 6:22 P.M.

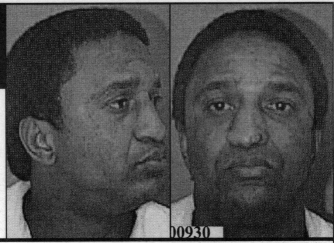

202

David Hicks

Executed:
January 20, 2000

00930

Personal data: *Born:* January 15, 1962. *Race:* Black. *Height:* 5'8". *Weight:* 148 pounds. *Education:* 11 years. *Prior occupation:* Laborer. *County of conviction:* Freestone. *Age at time of execution:* 38.

Sentenced to death for: Convicted in the April 1988 sexual assault and beating death of his 87-year-old grandmother, Ocolor Hegger, at her residence in Teague. Hegger suffered eight to ten blows to the head with a blunt instrument after being sexually assaulted. Hicks was seen at or near the scene of the crime, and prosecutors later discovered that his DNA matched semen found in the body of the victim. Hicks was was charged with capital murder following his arrest in August 1988 on an outstanding misdemeanor warrant for theft.

Received at death row: February 2, 1989. *Time on death row:* 4,004 days (10.97 years).

Last meal: Fish, fries, and soda.

Last statement: "Hey, how y'all doin' out there? I done lost my voice. Y'all be strong now. All right. I love all of y'all. Don, thanks, man. [To his wife, Gloria Hicks, a witness] I love you, Gloria, always baby. That's all I gotta say. Hey, don't y'all worry about me. OK?"

Pronounced dead: 7:29 P.M.

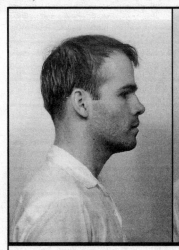

203

Larry Keith Robison

Executed: January 21, 2000

Personal data: *Born:* August 12, 1957. *Race:* White. *Height:* 6'0". *Weight:* 150 pounds. *Education:* 13 years. *Prior occupation:* Carpenter. *County of conviction:* Tarrant. *Age at time of execution:* 42.

Sentenced to death for: Convicted in the August 1982 stabbing-shooting death of 33-year-old Bruce M. Gardner, one of five people killed by Robison in two adjacent Lake Worth cottages. Robison, a former mental patient, also killed Georgia Ann Reed, 34; her son, Scott Reed, 11; her mother, Earline H. Barker, 55; and Rickey Lee Bryant, 31. Bryant, who shared his home with Robison and was portrayed by witnesses as Robison's lover, was decapitated and sexually mutilated. Robison fled in Gardner's car to Wichita, Kansas, following the mass murder.

Received at death row: September 9, 1983. *Time on death row:* 5,978 days (16.38 years).

Last meal: Declined last meal.

Last statement: None.

Pronounced dead: 6:16 P.M.

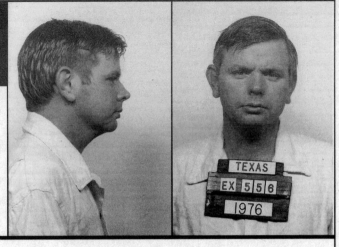

204

Billy George Hughes Jr.

Executed:
January 24,
2000

Personal data: *Born:* January 28, 1952. *Race:* White. *Height:* 5'10". *Weight:* 165 pounds. *Education:* 12 years. *Prior occupation:* Horseshoer. *County of conviction:* Matagorda. *Age at time of execution:* 47.

Sentenced to death for: Convicted of capital murder in the April 4, 1976, shooting death of state trooper Mark Frederick, of Bellville. Frederick was killed on Interstate 10 in Sealy as he walked toward Hughes's car to question him about a stolen credit card at a Brookshire motel.

Received at death row: September 17, 1976. *Time on death row:* 8,529 days (23.37 years).

Last meal: Two pieces of chicken-fried steak with white gravy, french fries, four pieces of white bread, peaches, and two Cokes.

Last statement: "I want to tell you all how much I love you all, how much I appreciate everything. I love you all and my family. I treasure every moment that I have had. I want the guys to know out there not to give up, not to give in, that I hope someday the madness in the system, something will come about, something will be resolved. I would gladly trade the last twenty-four years if it would bring back Mark Frederick. Give him back his life, give back my father his life, and my mother her health. All I ask is that I have one day and all the memories of you and my family and all the things that have happened. They are executing an innocent man because things did not happen as they say they happen and there's . . . The truth will come out someday. I am not the same person as I was twenty-four years ago. Who would have thought it would have taken twenty-four years to get to this moment? Don't give up, don't give in. If I am paying my debt to society, I am due a rebate and a refund, but I love you all and you all watch out for Mom and you all keep up, keep going. Thank you, Warden."

Pronounced dead: 6:18 P.M.

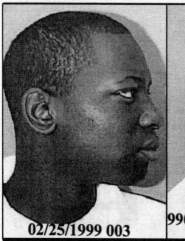

02/25/1999 003

99039
02/25/1999 003

205

Glen Charles McGinnis

Executed: January 25, 2000

Personal data: *Born:* January 11, 1973. *Race:* Black. *Height:* 6'0". *Weight:* 172 pounds. *Education:* 10 years. *Prior occupation:* Laborer. *County of conviction:* Montgomery. *Age at time of execution:* 27.

Sentenced to death for: Convicted in the robbery and murder of 30-year-old Leta Ann Wilkerson, of Conroe. Wilkerson was working as a clerk at Wilkins Cleaners & Laundry, 1200 South Frazier, when McGinnis walked in and shot her once in the head and three times in the back with a .25 caliber pistol he had taken from his aunt's apartment. McGinnis took $140 from the cash register and fled in Wilkerson's GMC Safari van. The van was recovered along Interstate 45 and McGinnis was arrested the following morning at his aunt's apartment. His thumbprint was found on the victim's wallet and $105 was recovered from his pants pocket. He was also serving a ten-year sentence for theft.

Received at death row: August 3, 1992. *Time on death row:* 2,731 days (7.48 years).

Last meal: A cheeseburger with lettuce, tomato, bacon, onion rings, and ketchup.

Last statement: None.

Pronounced dead: 6:17 P.M.

206

James Moreland

Executed: January 27, 2000

Personal data: *Born:* May 15, 1960. *Race:* White. *Height:* 5'7". *Weight:* 126 pounds. *Education:* 8 years. *Prior occupation:* Laborer. *County of conviction:* Henderson. *Age at time of execution:* 39.

Sentenced to death for: Convicted in the October 9, 1982, stabbing death of Clinton Corbet, 53. Moreland was also indicted in the death of John Royce Cravey, 41. A Dallas pathologist testified that the pair had been stabbed multiple times in the back. A court prosecutor said since the jury returned a death penalty punishment, Moreland would not be tried in Cravey's death.

Received at death row: June 17, 1983. *Time on death row:* 6,068 days (16.62 years).

Last meal: Three fried eggs over-easy, hash browns, several strips of bacon, toast (white bread), and orange juice.

Last statement: "Dad, I love you both. You've been the best. All of you, all of you have truly been the best. And ah, I believe I'm going home. I'm sorry, and I really mean that, it's not just words. My life is all I can give. I stole two lives and I know it was precious to y'all. That's the story of my whole life, that's what alcohol will do for you. Oh Jesus, Lord God, take me home. Precious Lord. Take me home, Lord. Take me home. Yes, sir. Take me home, oh Lord."

Pronounced dead: 6:21 P.M.

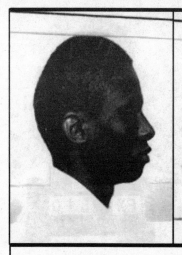

Cornelius Goss

Executed: February 23, 2000

Personal data: *Born:* May 24, 1961. *Race:* Black. *Height:* 5'9". *Weight:* 135 pounds. *Education:* 11 years. *Prior occupation:* Laborer. *County of conviction:* Dallas. *Age at time of execution:* 38.

Sentenced to death for: Convicted in the May 1987 beating death of Carl Leevy in Dallas. Goss broke in to Leevy's home at 10443 Heather Lane through a bedroom window and beat Leevy to death with a board. Goss then stole a $10 gold piece, a lady's bracelet, a camera, a necklace, a Rolex watch, and two men's rings. His fingerprints were found inside the home, and he later gave a voluntary statement to police.

Received at death row: August 25, 1988. *Time on death row:* 4,199 days (11.50 years).

Last meal: An apple, an orange, a banana, coconut, and peaches.

Last statement: "I'd like to apologize to the victim's family. Ah, no ah, I really can't say, I don't think I can say anything that will help, but I hope through your God, you can forgive me. I'm definitely not the person now that I was then. I was sick, afraid, and looking for love in all the wrong ways. I've caused you pain and grief beyond ever dreaming to cause someone of. I hope you will be able to forgive me. To my mother, I love you very much. Thanks, Jones."

Pronounced dead: 6:17 P.M.

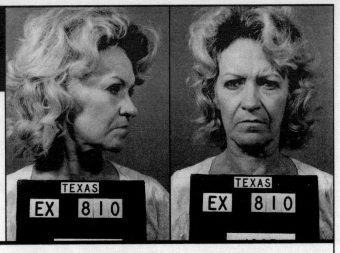

208

Betty Lou Beets

Executed: February 24, 2000

TEXAS EX 810

TEXAS EX 810

Personal data: *Born:* March 12, 1937. *Race:* White. *Height:* 5'2". *Weight:* 118 pounds. *Education:* 10 years. *Prior occupation:* Cashier/waitress. *County of conviction:* Henderson. *Age at time of execution:* 62.

Sentenced to death for: Convicted in the 1983 shooting death of her fifth husband, Jimmy Don Beets, at the couple's home near Gun Barrel City. Prosecutors said Beets killed her husband, a firefighter, to collect $100,000 in insurance and pension benefits. His body was found buried in a wishing well used as a flower garden at the home. Police also found the skeletal remains of Beets's fourth husband, Doyle Wayne Baker, buried under a storage shed at the home. Baker, who disappeared in 1981, had also been shot to death.
Note: The press dubbed Beets "the Black Widow."

Received at death row: October 14, 1985. *Time on death row:* 5,246 days (14.37 years).

Last meal: Declined last meal.

Last statement: None.

Pronounced dead: 6:18 P.M.

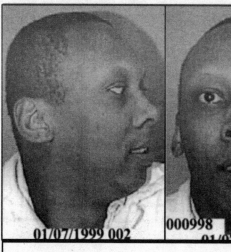

01/07/1999 002   000998   01/07/1999 001

209

Odell
Barnes Jr.

Executed:
March 1,
2000

Personal data: *Born:* March 22, 1968. *Race:* Black. *Height:* 6'2". *Weight:* 171 pounds. *Education:* 11 years. *Prior occupation:* Construction worker. *County of conviction:* Lubbock. *Age at time of execution:* 31.

Sentenced to death for: Convicted in the November 1989 robbery and murder of Helen Bass. Bass was killed inside her home at 1221 Harding. She was beaten with a lamp and rifle, stabbed in the neck, and then shot in the head. Her nude body was found on her bed, where she had been sexually assaulted prior to her death. Barnes stole a .32 caliber pistol and an undetermined amount of money from the home. He was later observed trying to sell the gun to different people.

Received at death row: May 20, 1991. *Time on death row:* 3,208 days (8.79) years.

Last meal: Justice, equality, and world peace.

Last statement: "I'd like to send great love to all my family members, my supporters, my attorneys. They have all supported me throughout this. I thank you for proving my innocence, although it has not been acknowledged by the courts. May you continue in the struggle and may you change all that's being done here today and in the past. Life has not been that good to me, but I believe that now, after meeting so many people who support me in this, that all things will come to an end, and may this be fruit of better judgments for the future. That's all I have to say."

Pronounced dead: 6:34 P.M.

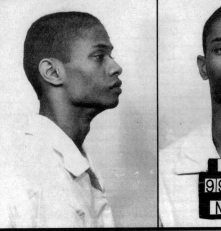

210

Ponchai Wilkerson

Executed:
March 14,
2000

TEXAS
9990111
NOV. 91

Personal data: *Born:* July 15, 1971. *Race:* Black. *Height:* 5'8". *Weight:* 140 pounds. *Education:* 11 years. *Prior occupation:* Laborer. *County of conviction:* Harris. *Age at time of execution:* 28.

Sentenced to death for: Convicted in the November 1990 robbery and shooting death of Chung Myong Yi, a Houston jewelry store clerk. Wilkerson reportedly watched codefendant Wilton Bethany buy pieces of jewelry at Royal Gold Wholesale, 9889 Harwin, and then returned with a pistol and shot Yi once in the head. Following his arrest, police found that Wilkerson had committed three additional burglaries and three auto thefts, and he had shot four other people in two separate drive-by shootings. Prosecutors also claimed that Wilkerson was a party to attempted capital murder when another store clerk was shot with a shotgun.
Note: On Thanksgiving Day 1998, Wilkerson and six other death row inmates cut through a recreation yard fence at the Ellis Unit and made it onto the roof. Wilkerson and five of the inmates were caught after guards started firing, but inmate Martin Gurule escaped, becoming the first inmate in sixty-four years to get out of death row. Gurule's body was found a week later in a creek not far from the prison; he had drowned. In 1999, Wilkerson and death row inmate Howard Guidry, 23, took a female prison guard, Jeanette Bledsoe, 57, hostage for nearly thirteen hours to demand better living conditions.

Received at death row: November 12, 1991. *Time on death row:* 3,045 days (8.34 years).

Last meal: Declined last meal.

Last statement: None.
Note: Wilkerson refused to leave his cell at the Ellis unit for transport to the death room. He was gassed before transport, refused to leave his holding cell near the death chamber, and was bound to the gurney with additional restraint bands. As the lethal drugs began to take effect, Wilkerson spit out a universal handcuff and leg restraint key he had been holding in his mouth. It was unknown how Wilkerson obtained the key.

Pronounced dead: 6:24 P.M.

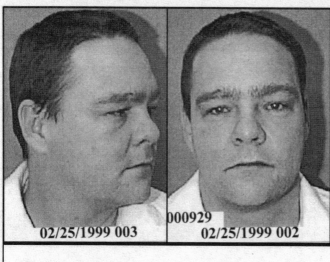

211

Timothy Gribble

Executed: March 15, 2000

02/25/1999 003

000929 02/25/1999 002

Personal data: *Born:* August 27, 1963. *Race:* White. *Height:* 5'10". *Weight:* 204 pounds. *Education:* 11 years. *Prior occupation:* Mechanic/roofer. *County of conviction:* Galveston. *Age at time of execution:* 36.

Sentenced to death for: Convicted in the September 1987 rape and strangulation of 36-year-old Elizabeth "Libby" Jones, of Clear Lake Shores. Gribble was working as a roofer at Jones's home, which was being remodeled at the time of the murder. He told police he returned to the home at 304 Queen Street several hours after work and raped Jones after she let him in to search for a billfold he claimed to have left behind. He said he later drove her to an isolated area near League City and strangled her with the sash from the robe she was wearing. Gribble was arrested on September 30, 1987, and led police to Jones's remains after confessing. Police found a cloth sash knotted around neck vertebrae at the site and later recovered Jones's purse from a nearby creek.

Received at death row: January 11, 1989. *Time on death row:* 4,081 days (11.18 years).

Last meal: Declined last meal.

Last statement: "OK, thank you. To the Weiss family, and ah I just want you to know from the bottom of my heart that I am truly sorry. I mean it, I'm not just saying it. Through the years of being in prison I have come to hear and respect our life. It was wrong what I did. I know you had to go through a lot of pain and I'm sorry. To the Jones family, the same is true, I am truly, truly sorry. I wanted to prepare a longer statement but time ran out. I had the chaplain write down a few words for my friends and for you, my family. I would like him to read them for me, and ah, just please find peace. [Chaplain Brazzil recites written statement, see Appendix.] No sir, I just want to pray a chant, do what you have to do."

Pronounced dead: 6:19 P.M.

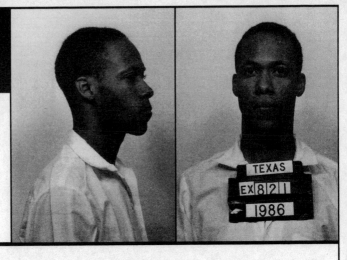

212

Tommy Ray Jackson

Executed: May 4, 2000

Personal data: *Born:* November 15, 1956. *Race:* Black. *Height:* 5'7". *Weight:* 120 pounds. *Education:* 14 years. *Prior occupation:* Computer technician. *County of conviction:* Williamson. *Age at time of execution:* 43.

Sentenced to death for: Convicted in the November 1983 abduction and shooting death of Rosalind Robison, a 24-year-old University of Texas student from Terre Haute, Indiana. Robison, an engineering student, was reportedly kidnapped from the UT campus in Austin and forced to withdraw money from an automatic teller machine. She was then driven to a rural location between Pflugerville and Round Rock and shot once in the head with a .25 caliber pistol. Her body was found a month later beneath a gravel pile. Jackson was arrested four days later outside an Austin grocery in the victim's car.

Received at death row: February 28, 1986. *Time on death row:* 5,179 days (14.19 years).

Last meal: Declined last meal.

Last statement: See Appendix.

Pronounced dead: 6:24 P.M.

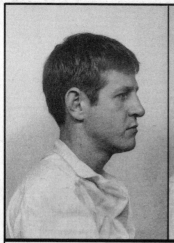

213

William Joseph Kitchens

Executed: May 9, 2000

Personal data: *Born:* April 26, 1963. *Race:* White. *Height:* 6'3". *Weight:* 185 pounds. *Education:* 8 years. *Prior occupation:* Painter. *County of conviction:* Taylor. *Age at time of execution:* 37.

Sentenced to death for: Convicted of capital murder in the death of Patricia Leann Webb near Abilene on May 17, 1986. Webb, who had met Kitchens at an Abilene bar on the day of her death, was raped and then driven to a secluded area eleven miles from Abilene, where she was severely beaten, strangled, and shot in the head with a .22 caliber pistol. Kitchens stole Webb's car along with her money, credit cards, and checkbook. Kitchens was arrested in his hometown of Blanchard, Oklahoma, on May 18 in possession of Webb's property.

Received at death row: September 2, 1986. *Time on death row:* 4,998 days (13.69 years).

Last meal: Six sunny-side-up eggs, eight pieces of pan sausage, six slices of toast with butter and grape jelly, crispy hash browns, milk, and orange juice.

Last statement: See Appendix.

Pronounced dead: 6:22 P.M.

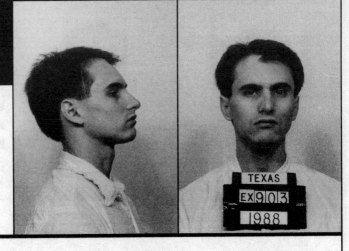

214

Michael Lee McBride

Executed: May 11, 2000

Personal data: *Born:* January 3, 1967. *Race:* White. *Height:* 5'4". *Weight:* 141 pounds. *Education:* 12 years. *Prior occupation:* Bar manager/bartender. *County of conviction:* Lubbock. *Age at time of execution:* 33.

Sentenced to death for: Convicted in the October 1985 shooting deaths of Christian Fisher and James Alan Holzler, both 18, in Lubbock. Fisher, McBride's ex-girlfriend, and her companion were shot to death with a .30 caliber rifle outside McBride's residence at 1903 Twenty-sixth Street. Witnesses said Fisher had gone to the residence to pick up some things and was killed by a volley of shots after challenging McBride to shoot. McBride then walked to the victim's car and shot Holzler, who was in the driver's seat, in the head and chest. Both died at the scene. McBride then turned the rifle on himself, shooting himself once in the head. Police found him lying on the ground and reaching for the rifle.

Received at death row: May 26, 1988. *Time on death row:* 4,368 days (11.97 years).

Last meal: Two chicken patties with Swiss cheese, a stuffed baked potato with jalapeño peppers and sour cream, and milk.

Last statement: "Thank you, um, I anticipated that I would try to memorize and recite beatitudes New Testament, more or less, Luke's beatitudes, I should say, and a, a chapter on love in First Corinthians chapter thirteen, ah, I pretty much knew that I would not be able to memorize so much. There was also a poem that went along with it and in anticipation of not being able to, um, fulfill that desire, I provided a written statement that will be made available to anybody that wants it, I believe. Isn't that correct? So, uh, I wanted you to hear me say that and I apologize and for any other grief I have caused you know, including the, ah, what you're about to witness now. It won't be very long. As soon as you realize that appear I am falling asleep. I would leave because I won't be here after that point. I will be dead at that point. It's irreversible. God bless all of you. Thank you." [See Appendix for written last words.]

Pronounced dead: 6:21 P.M.

215

James David Richardson

Executed: May 23, 2000

Personal data: *Born:* September 7, 1967. *Race:* Black. *Height:* 5'9". *Weight:* 170 pounds. *Education:* 11 years. *Prior occupation:* Construction worker. *County of conviction:* Navarro. *Age at time of execution:* 32.

Sentenced to death for: Convicted of capital murder in the shooting death of 35-year-old Gerald Abay during an armed robbery at Gusher Liquor Store in Angus on December 17, 1986. Richardson was with two other men, who had picked out some beer and were about to pay for it when Richardson pulled out a pistol and shot Abay in the throat and chest. Abay, of Corsicana, managed to fire several shots at the suspects and did hit Richardson in the left hand. Approximately $1,000 was taken from the liquor store cash register. Abay died about an hour after the shooting. Richardson was arested the next afternoon after evading authorities on foot.
Co-defendants: Michael James Ellison received a life sentence for murder. James McHenry received a life sentence for capital murder.

Received at death row: May 1, 1987. *Time on death row:* 4,771 days (13.07 years).

Last meal: Fresh fried chicken (no skin, five breasts and twenty wings), carrot cake, white coconut cake, and cheesecake with cherry topping.

Last statement: See Appendix.

Pronounced dead: 6:32 P.M.

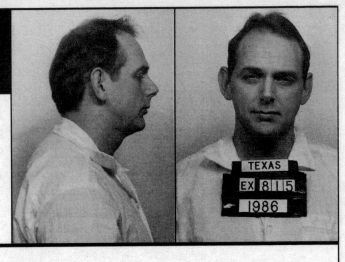

216

Richard Donald Foster

Executed:
May 24, 2000

Personal data: *Born:* August 16, 1952. *Race:* White. *Height:* 5'9". *Weight:* 195 pounds. *Education:* 11 years (GED). *Prior occupation:* Roofer/auto paint and body. *County of conviction:* Parker. *Age at time of execution:* 47.

Sentenced to death for: Convicted in the April 1984 shotgun slaying of Gary Michael Cox, owner of Cox's Feed and Farm Supply located two miles outside Springtown on SH 199. Cox was shot once in the back of the head during a robbery of his store that netted $250. Foster was apprehended on May 5, 1984, after holding seven employees of Citizen's National Bank in Breckenridge hostage for twelve hours. He was sentenced to four life terms on aggravated kidnapping charges in connection with the hostage incident. In August 1986, Foster, accompanied by a female inmate, escaped form the Stephens County Jail, where he was awaiting trial on the kidnapping charges. Police shot out the tires of the stolen vehicle he was driving and recaptured him near Possum Kingdom Lake on August 7. He was given a twenty-year sentence in Palo Pinto County in connection with the escape.

Received at death row: January 7, 1986. *Time on death row:* 5,251 days (14.39 years).

Last meal: Beef fajita, a blooming onion, fried chicken (white meat), jalapeño peppers, a large Caesar salad with blue cheese dressing, bread rolls with butter, vanilla ice cream, three bananas, a Coke, a pot of coffee, and a pack of cigarettes (prohibited by TDCJ regulations).

Last statement: "I have been crucified with Christ. It is no longer I who lives, but Christ who lives in me. So for the life for which I live now in the flesh, I live by faith in the Son of God who loved me and gave himself for me. I love you, Annie. You have been the best friend I have ever had in the world. I'll see you when you get there, OK? I am ready, Warden."

Pronounced dead: 6:23 P.M.

217

**James
Edward
Clayton**

Executed:
May 25,
2000

Personal data: *Born:* December 30, 1966. *Race:* Black. *Height:* 5'11". *Weight:* 188 pounds. *Education:* 14 years. *Prior occupation:* Clerical. *County of conviction:* Taylor. *Age at time of execution:* 33.

Sentenced to death for: Convicted in the September 1987 abduction and slaying of 27-year-old Lori M. Barrett, of Abilene. Barrett was reportedly abducted from her apartment at 1734 Avenue D after Clayton managed to break in through a bedroom window. Her body, tied at the hands with a telephone cord and wrapped in a blanket, was found on September 29, 1987, off the side of a rural road three miles north of the Jones-Taylor county line. She had been shot in the head, neck, and left shoulder with a .243 caliber rifle. Clayton was arrested on September 23, 1987, in connection with Barrett's disappearance.

Received at death row: November 14, 1988. *Time on death row:* 4,210 days (11.53 years).

Last meal: Three fried chicken breasts, fresh lettuce and cucumber salad with light vinegar salad dressing on the side, and a large pitcher of ice water.

Last statement: "I would like to take this time to, ah, to use this moment an example for Christ. I would like to follow his example and leave with peace in my heart and forgiveness. There is no anger in my heart about this entire situation. I just want to testify to all of y'all that I have loved you. I appreciate your concern and genuine love for me. God bless you. I love all of you all. Jesus is Lord."

Pronounced dead: 6:17 P.M.

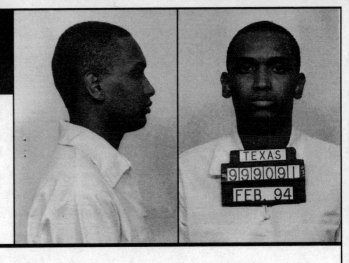

218

Robert Earl Carter

Executed:
May 31, 2000

TEXAS 999091 FEB. 94

Personal data: *Born:* March 7, 1966. *Race:* Black. *Height:* 5'9". *Weight:* 171 pounds. *Education:* 12 years. *Prior occupation:* Correctional officer. *County of conviction:* Burleson. *Age at time of execution:* 34.

Sentenced to death for: Convicted in the deaths of six people in Somerville. Killed were Bobbie Davis, 45; her daughter, Nicole Davis, 16; and her grandchildren, De'Nitra Davis, 9, Lea'Erin Davis, 5, and Brittany Davis, 6. Also killed was 4-year-old Jason Davis, who was stabbed to death as he cowered beneath a pillow at his grandmother's home. With the exception of Nicole, each victim died of multiple stab wounds. Nicole was killed by five gunshots to the head. Following the killings, the elder Davis's home was set afire in an effort to conceal the murders. Carter, who had recently been named in a paternity suit by Davis's daughter, attended funeral services for the victims wrapped in bandages for severe burns apparently suffered in the house fire.
Codefendant: Anthony Graves was convicted of capital murder and given the death penalty. He is awaiting an execution date.

Received at death row: February 23, 1994. *Time on death row:* 2,289 days (6.27 years).

Last meal: A double-meat cheeseburger and fries.

Last statement: "To the Davis family, I am sorry for all of the pain that I caused your family. It was me and me alone. Anthony Graves had nothing to do with it. I lied on him in court. My wife had nothing to do with it. Anthony Graves don't even know anything about it. My wife don't know anything about it. But I hope that you can find your peace and comfort in strength in Christ Jesus alone. Like I said, I am sorry for hurting your family. And it is a shame that it had to come to this. So I hope that you don't find peace, not in my death, but in Christ. 'Cause He is the only one that can give you the strength that you need. And to my family, I love you. Ah, you have been a blessing to me and I love you all and one day I will see y'all, so I hope y'all find y'all peace, comfort, and strength in Christ Jesus alone, because that's where it's at. Abul, behold your son, and Anitra, behold your mother. I love you. I am ready to go home and be with my Lord. I'm sorry for all the pain I've caused your family. It was me and me alone. Anthony Graves had nothing to do with it. I lied on him in court. I hope you will find peace and comfort with Christ Jesus. It's a shame it has come to this. I'm ready to go home with my Lord."

Pronounced dead: 6:20 P.M.

Thomas Wayne Mason

Executed: June 12, 2000

TEXAS 999035 JUL. 92

Personal data: *Born:* December 31, 1951. *Race:* White. *Height:* 6'1". *Weight:* 217 pounds. *Education:* 9 years. *Occupation:* Drywaller. *County of conviction:* Smith. *Age at time of execution:* 48.

Sentenced to death for: Convicted in the October 1991 shotgun slayings of his mother-in-law, 55-year-old Marsha Yvonne Brock, and her 80-year-old mother, Sybil Mares Dennis, at Brock's home in Whitehouse. Brock, a nurse, called 911 from her home at 113 Robinwood and screamed for help when Mason showed up brandishing a 12-gauge shotgun. Both victims were shot in the head at close range. The killings apparently stemmed from Mason's separation from Brock's daughter. Two months earlier, police had placed Brock's home under surveillance after she reported that Mason had threatened to burn it down.

Received at death row: July 14, 1992. *Time on death row:* 2,890 days (7.92 years).

Last meal: Declined last meal.

Last statement: See Appendix.

Pronounced dead: 6:24 P.M.

220

John Albert Burks

Executed:
June 14, 2000

Personal data: *Born:* January 18, 1956. *Race:* Black. *Height:* 5'6". *Weight:* 155 pounds. *Education:* 9 years. *Prior occupation:* Cement finisher. *County of conviction:* McLennan. *Age at time of execution:* 44.

Sentenced to death for: Convicted in the January 1989 murder of Jesse Contreras during the armed robbery of Jesse's Tortilla Factory at 1226 Webster in Waco. Contreras was shot in the mouth and chest with a .25 caliber pistol during the robbery. He died of his wounds at a Waco Hospital on February 16, 1989. *Codefendant:* Mark McConnell was convicted of robbery and burglary and given a forty-year sentence.

Received at death row: October 5, 1989. *Time on death row:* 3,905 days (10.70 years).

Last meal: Fried chicken (two thighs and wings), one pound of bacon, sixteen-ounce T-bone steak, Big Red, and coffee.

Last statement: "Hey, how are y'all doing? All right, it's going to be all right. There's some guys I didn't get a chance to visit with, ah I met when I first drove up here. Lester Byers, Chris Black, Alba, John Alba, and Rosales Rock. You know who you are. The Raiders are going all the way, y'all {mumbles}. Mo-B. Y'all pray for me. And it's going to be all right. That's it and it's time to roll up out of here. It's going down, let's get it over with. That's it."

Pronounced dead: 6:18 P.M.

221

**Paul
Selso
Nuncio**

Executed:
June 15,
2000

Personal data: *Born:* October 20, 1968. *Race:* Hispanic. *Height:* 5'4". *Weight:* 130 pounds. *Education:* n/a. *Prior occupation:* Clerk. *County of conviction:* Hale. *Age at time of execution:* 31.

Sentenced to death for: Convicted in the strangulation death of 61-year-old Pauline Crownover Farris in Plainview. Nuncio broke in to Farris's home at 708 Beech through the back door and beat the resident before sexually assaulting her and strangling her to death with his hands. He then stole several items from the home, including two television sets, a stereo, a VCR, several rings, and a watch. Nuncio was arrested five days later, after selling one of the stolen televisions. He told police he broke into Farris's home to steal items he could sell for money to buy drugs.

Received at death row: August 2, 1995. *Time on death row:* 1,779 days (4.87 years).

Last meal: Enchiladas, burritos, chocolate ice cream, and cantaloupe (whole, split in half).

Last statement: See Appendix.

Pronounced dead: 7:17 P.M.

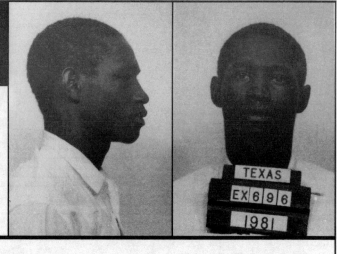

222

Gary
Lee
Graham

Executed:
June 22,
2000

Personal data: *Born:* September 5, 1960. *Race:* Black. *Height:* 5'10". *Weight:* 155 pounds. *Education:* 9 years. *Prior occupation:* Laborer. *County of conviction:* Harris. *Age at time of execution:* 39.

Sentenced to death for: Convicted in the May 1981 robbery and fatal shooting of 53-year-old Bobby Grant Lambert of Tucson, Arizona, outside a Houston supermarket. A witness testified Lambert was coming out of a Safeway store in the 8900 block of the North Freeway when Graham reached into Lambert's pockets and then shot Lambert with a pistol as they scuffled. Lambert, who staggered back into the store and died, was robbed only of change from a $100 bill, even though police found $6,000 in $100 bills on his body. Testimony showed Graham had been charged in ten separate robberies and suspected in two shootings, ten car thefts, and eight more robberies in Houston.

Received at death row: November 9, 1981. *Time on death row:* 6,800 days (18.63 years).

Last meal: Declined last meal.

Last statement: See Appendix.

Pronounced dead: 8:49 P.M.
Note: Graham's execution was postponed due to last-minute legal delays. The U.S. Supreme Court declined in a 5 to 4 vote to hear Graham's appeal, the Texas Court of Criminal Appeals denied an appeal, and Texas Federal District Judge James Nowlin rejected a civil lawsuit against the Texas Board of Pardons and Paroles by Graham's attorneys.

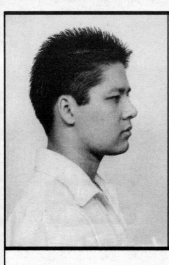

Jessy Carlos San Miguel

Executed: June 29, 2000

Personal data: *Born:* September 5, 1971. *Race:* Hispanic. *Height:* 5'7". *Weight:* 180 pounds. *Education:* 10 years. *Prior occupation:* Laborer. *County of conviction:* Dallas. *Age at time of execution:* 28.

Sentenced to death for: Convicted in the January 1991 robbery and murder of 28-year-old Michael John Phelan. Phelan was one of four people shot to death during the robbery of a Taco Bell restaurant in Irving. San Miguel and accomplice Jerome Mike Green, a part-time employee of the restaurant, forced Phelan, the restaurant manager, and employees Theresa Fraga, 16, who was several months pregnant, and her cousin, Frank Fraga, 23, into a walk-in freezer after taking an undisclosed amount of cash from the safe. Son Trang Nyugen, a friend of the Fragas, was also forced into the freezer. San Miguel shot all four at close range. He and Green were arrested while fleeing the scene. Jerome Mike Green was sentenced to fifty years for murder (three) and aggravated robbery with a deadly weapon (one).

Received at death row: September 21, 1991. *Time on death row:* 3,204 days (8.78 years).

Last meal: Pizza, ten quesadillas, five strips of open-flame grilled beef, five strips of stir-fried beef, chocolate peanut butter ice cream, sweet tea, double fudge chocolate cake, broccoli, and grapes.

Last statement: "Be strong, brother. Be strong, my brother. Be strong, Mom. It's going to be all right. I love all of you. Don't forget that. Ironic, isn't it? I'm a cross. Y'all take care of each other. I'll be watching over you. Thank you, Dana. Yes."

Pronounced dead: 6:19 P.M.

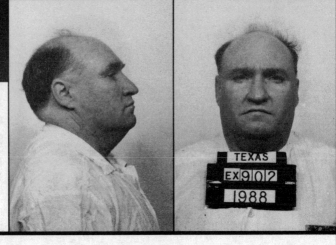

224

Orien Cecil Joiner

Executed:
July 12, 2000

Personal data: *Born:* October 27, 1949. *Race:* White. *Height:* 5'6". *Weight:* 199 pounds. *Education:* 12 years. *Prior occupation:* Truck driver. *County of conviction:* Lubbock. *Age at time of execution:* 50.

Sentenced to death for: Convicted in the December 1986 slayings of 26-year-old Carol Lynette Huckabee and 29-year-old Eva Marie DeForest, two Lubbock waitresses who shared an apartment. Both women were bound by duct tape inside their apartment and stabbed repeatedly. Huckabee, who reportedly was also raped, suffered multiple stab wounds to the chest, back, and face, and her throat was slashed. DeForest was beaten and stabbed forty-one times in the chest, and her throat was cut. A broken blade was found sticking out of her chest. Joiner lived next door to the women and was arrested after giving conflicting stories of how he found the murdered women.

Received at death row: May 26, 1988. *Time on death row:* 4,430 days (12.14 years).

Last meal: Hamburger steak (well done), brown gravy, grilled onions, french fries with ketchup, five pieces of butter-grilled Texas toast, iced tea with sugar, and hot honey buns with melted butter on the side.

Last statement: "Kathy, y'all take care and I bless all of you and I am glad I have had y'all in my life. As I have said from the very first thing, I am innocent of this crime and God knows I am innocent and the four people that was murdered know I am innocent and when I get to heaven I'll be hunting you and we'll talk. I feel sorry for the families that's had to suffer and my family and I have 'em all in my prayers. I love you all. Y'all take care and y'all look after Sheila and Shannon and them, call 'em and get the pictures to 'em and everything and, ah, again, like I said, I feel sorry for the families, but if it takes my death to make them happy, then I will bless them. I have no hard feelings toward anyone 'cause the Lord feels that it is my time to come home to Him, my work on earth is done and that, ah, like I said, I am just sorry for, but they will have to go through this one time again, 'cause sooner or later, whoever did this crime is going to be caught and they'll have to come down here and do this again and they will realize they witnessed an innocent man going to be with Jesus Christ.

Pronounced dead: 6:17 P.M.

225

Juan
Salvez
Soria

Executed:
July 26,
2000

Personal data: *Born:* May 15, 1967. *Race:* Hispanic. *Height:* 6'0". *Weight:* 163 pounds. *Education:* 9 years. *Prior occupation:* Auto body repairman. *County of conviction:* Tarrant. *Age at time of execution:* 33.

Sentenced to death for: Convicted in the June 1985 robbery-slaying of 17-year-old Allen E. Bolden of Arlington. Bolden was reported as a missing person when he failed to return home from the Fort Worth Boys' Club, where he worked as a lifeguard. Two days later, June 30, 1985, Soria was arrested along with a 14-year-old juvenile and codefendant Mike Lagunas when he was spotted driving Bolden's father's car near Del Rio. Police learned Bolden had been stabbed to death after agreeing to give Soria and Lagunas a ride from the Boys' Club in Fort Worth. Mike Lagunas received a forty-five-year sentence for aggravated kidnapping.

Received at death row: July 8, 1986. *Time on death row:* 5,132 days (14.06 years).

Last meal: Chicken, three pieces of fish, burgers, pizza, grapes, plums, a peach, apples, tangerines, doughnuts, walnuts, a chocolate candy bar, a bag of plain potato chips, picante sauce, a bottle of hot sauce, salad with ranch dressing, Coke, and Sprite.

Last statement: See Appendix.

Pronounced dead: 6:27 P.M.

226

Brian Keith Roberson

Executed:
August 9, 2000

Personal data: *Born:* October 8, 1963. *Race:* Black. *Height:* 5'11". *Weight:* 190 pounds. *Education:* 12 years. *Prior occupation:* Electrician. *County of conviction:* Dallas. *Age at time of execution:* 36.

Sentenced to death for: Convicted in the August 1986 stabbing death of 79-year-old James Louis Boots inside the victim's home in Dallas. Roberson, who lived next door, also killed Lillian Wallace Boots with a knife before burglarizing the home of assorted jewelry. Roberson was identified through fingerprints and later gave a voluntary statement to police.

Received at death row: October 22, 1987. *Time on death row:* 4,675 days (12.81 years).

Last meal: Two double-meat cheeseburgers all the way with mayonnaise and mustard, fries, fried chicken (well done), chocolate cake, onion rings, a pint of vanilla ice cream, and a six-pack of Sprite.

Last statement: "Since I have already said all I need to say to all my loved ones, I'm not going to say anything to y'all at this time. Y'all know I love you and y'all know where we're at. I will see y'all when you get there. So this is my statement. To all of the racist white folks in America that hate black folks and to all of the black folks in America that hate themselves: the infamous words of my famous legendary brother, Matt Turner, 'Y'all kiss my black ass.' Let's do it."

Pronounced dead: 6:17 P.M.

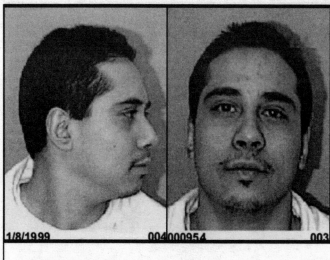

David Oliver Cruz

Executed: August 9, 2000

Personal data: *Born:* May 18, 1967. *Race:* Hispanic. *Height:* 5'4". *Weight:* 104 pounds. *Education:* 7 years. *Prior occupation:* Laborer. *County of conviction:* Bexar. *Age at time of execution:* 33.

Sentenced to death for: Convicted in the abduction, rape, and murder of 24-year-old Kelly Elizabeth Donovan, a senior airman stationed at Kelly Air Force Base in San Antonio. Donovan was abducted by Cruz and codefendant Jerry Daren Kemplin after she had left the base to take a walk. She was driven to an isolated area in the western part of the county, where she was sexually assaulted and then stabbed to death. Cruz and Kemplin told police they killed Donovan so she would not testify against them. Kemplin testified against Cruz in return for a sixty-five-year sentence for murder.

Received at death row: November 10, 1989. *Time on death row:* 3,925 days (10.75 years).

Last meal: Beef fajitas (spicy), beans and rice, flour tortillas, onions, tomatoes, an avocado, a banana split, and orange juice.

Last statement: "First of all, I want to apologize to the family of Kelly Elizabeth Donovan. I am sorry for what I did to her twelve years ago. I wish they could forgive me for what I did. I am sorry. I am sorry for hurting my family, for hurting my friends. Jesus forgive me. Take me home with you. I am ready. I love you all."

Pronounced dead: 6:50 P.M.

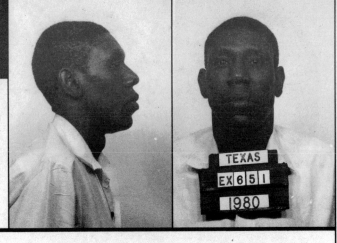

228

John Thomas Satterwhite

Executed:
August 16, 2000

Personal data: *Born:* December 29, 1946. *Race:* Black. *Height:* 5'6". *Weight:* 162 pounds. *Education:* 9 years. *Prior occupation:* Mechanic. *County of conviction:* Bexar. *Age at time of execution:* 53.

Sentenced to death for: Convicted in the March 1979 robbery-slaying of Mary Francis Davis, a clerk at the Lone Star Ice and Food Store in San Antonio. Davis was shot twice after she gave Satterwhite and Sharon Bell money from the cash register and store vault at gunpoint. The two robbers were arrested the next day when their car was stopped for speeding. The murder weapon was found in the glove compartment of the car. Sharon Bell received a twenty-year sentence for aggravated robbery with a deadly weapon and was paroled in 1986.

Received at death row: February 29, 1980. *Time on death row:* 7,474 days (20.48 years).

Last meal: A double-meat cheeseburger all the way with mustard and mayonnaise, french fries, three scrambled eggs, and a vanilla shake.

Last statement: None.

Pronounced dead: 6:29 P.M.
Note: Established IV in the right and left hands rather than the arms.

229

Richard Wayne Jones

Executed: August 22, 2000

Personal data: *Born:* April 9, 1960. *Race:* White. *Height:* 6'2". *Weight:* 184 pounds. *Education:* 12 years. *Prior occupation:* Construction worker. *County of conviction:* Tarrant. *Age at time of execution:* 40.

Sentenced to death for: Convicted in the February 1986 abduction and stabbing death of 27-year-old Tammy Livingston, of Hurst. Livingston was reported missing the day of the murder. Her body, which her killer had attempted to set afire after the stabbing, was found inside a residence in Fort Worth. Jones was arrested two days after the murder when he attempted to have his girlfriend cash a personal check stolen from Livingston.

Received at death row: August 31, 1987. *Time on death row:* 4,740 days (12.99 years).

Last meal: Two BLTs with cheese and mayonnaise, three deep-fried chicken breasts, french fries with ketchup, and a pitcher of strawberry milk shake.

Last statement: "I want the victim's family to know that I didn't commit this crime. I didn't kill your loved one. Sharon Wilson, y'all convicted an innocent man and you know it. There are some lawyers hired that is gonna prove that, and I hope you can live with it. To my family and loved ones, I love you. Thank you for supporting me. Y'all stay strong. Warden, take me home."

Pronounced dead: 6:19 P.M.

230

David Earl Gibbs

Executed: August 23, 2000

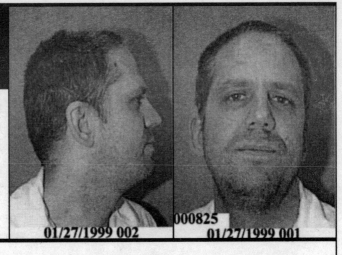

000825
01/27/1999 002   01/27/1999 001

Personal data: *Born:* March 17, 1961. *Race:* White. *Height:* 5'10". *Weight:* 166 pounds. *Education:* 10 years (GED). *Prior occupation:* Nursing assistant. *County of conviction:* Montgomery. *Age at time of execution:* 39.

Sentenced to death for: Convicted in the July 1985 slayings of Marietta Bryant and Carol Ackland. Gibbs reportedly burglarized their apartment, then cut their throats with a butcher knife. Gibbs, who reportedly worked as a maintenance man at the victims' apartment at the time of the murders, was arrested a month after the killings.

Received at death row: March 21, 1986. *Time on death row:* 5,269 days (14.44 years).

Last meal: Chef salad, any dressing except oil and vinegar, two bacon cheeseburgers all the way, cut the onions, deep-fried home fries with chili powder on top, a pitcher of fruit-flavored milk shake, two Scotch eggs (boiled and packed in a sausage roll, battered, deep-fried, and served with syrup), and a slice of pie.

Last statement: "Mr. Bryant, I have wronged you and your family and for that I am truly sorry. I forgive and I have been forgiven. Death is but a brief moment's slumber and a short journey home. I'll see you when you get there. I am done, Warden."

Pronounced dead: 6:18 P.M.

231

Jeffery
Henry
Caldwell

Executed:
August 30,
2000

Personal data: *Born:* March 1, 1963. *Race:* Black. *Height:* 6'2". *Weight:* 173 pounds. *Education:* 12 years. *Prior occupation:* Commercial printer. *County of conviction:* Dallas. *Age at time of execution:* 37.

Sentenced to death for: Convicted in the stabbing and beating death of his father, Henry; mother, Gwendolyn; and sister, Kimberly, at their Dallas home. All three victims were stabbed in the chest and beaten about the head with a hammer and another unknown blunt instrument. The bodies were taken from the home and placed inside the family motor home that was parked in the driveway. Caldwell's brother discovered the bodies when he noticed a foul odor coming from the mobile home. Caldwell was arrested the next day and gave a voluntary statement to police.

Received at death row: March 27, 1989. *Time on death row:* 4,174 days (11.44 years).

Last meal: Declined last meal.

Last statement: "I would like to extend my love to my family members and my relatives for all of the love and support you have showed me. I extend my special love to my daughter, who I love greatly. I hope that you forever remember me. I hope that you will always cherish the love and the strength that I have provided you. My love for you will remain with you within your heart and in part of your soul. As to all my brothers, I love you all with all of my heart. But during your time of departure from this earth plane you will have to face the judgment of God for the lack of love you have shown my aunt and my cousins. We were never brought up to be that way. As you know our parents brought us up to love one another no matter what. There was no love showed to my aunt or none of my cousins. I can forgive you all but you must ask forgiveness from God for how you have hurt our aunt and our family. I leave now at this moment to join my parents and my only sister, whose lives were not taken by me. To all the fellows on death row, I thank you for the love that you have shown me and for the strength that you provided me. You all keep your heads up. As for my attorneys, I thank you all for being there for me. As defense attorneys you have shown me a lot of strength. May my love touch each one of you all's souls as I leave this body."

Pronounced dead: 6:29 P.M.

232

Ricky Nolen McGinn

Executed: September 27, 2000

Personal data: *Born:* March 11, 1957. *Race:* White. *Height:* 5'9". *Weight:* 189 pounds. *Education:* 11 years. *Prior occupation:* Mechanic/carpenter. *County of conviction:* Brown. *Age at time of execution:* 43.

Sentenced to death for: Convicted in the rape and murder of his 12-year-old stepdaughter, Stephanie Rae Flanary. Flanary was sexually assaulted by McGinn and then beaten with the blunt side of an ax. Her body was found three days later in a culvert.

Received at death row: June 9, 1995. *Time on death row:* 1,937 days (5.31 years).

Last meal: Chicken-fried steak with white gravy, french fries with white gravy, salt, pepper, and sweet iced tea.

Last statement: "Robin you know this ain't right. Mama, Adam, Mike, Sonny, Michelle, y'all know I love you. Tell everybody I said hi and that I love them and I will see them on the other side. OK? And now I just pray that if there is anything against me that God takes it home. I don't want nobody to be mad at nobody. I don't want nobody to be bitter. Keep clean hearts and I will see y'all on the other side. OK? I love y'all, stay sweet. I love ya."

Pronounced dead: n/a

Note: Execution was delayed for DNA testing. Results were positive.

Jeffery Dillingham

Executed: November 1, 2000

Personal data: *Born:* March 6, 1973. *Race:* White. *Height:* 6'1". *Weight:* 205 pounds. *Education:* 12 years. *Prior occupation:* Video store manager. *County of conviction:* Tarrant. *Age at time of execution:* 27.

Sentenced to death for: Convicted in the March 1992 murder-for-hire of 40-year-old Caren Koslow, of Fort Worth. Koslow and her husband, Jack, were asleep in their residence when Dillingham and codefendant Brian Dennis Salter entered through a rear entrance and disarmed an alarm system with a code provided them by Kristi Koslow, the couple's daughter. The two intruders forced the couple to lie on the floor, beat them with a bar, and slashed their throats. The two stole Mr. Koslow's wallet, $200 in cash, and a wristwatch worth $1,600. Mrs. Koslow died at the scene, but Mr. Koslow survived to alert police. Statements revealed that the couple was attacked in return for $1 million promised by Kristi Koslow. Kristi Koslow was sentenced to life.

Received at death row: August 31, 1993. *Time on death row:* 2,619 days (7.18 years).

Last meal: One cheeseburger with cheddar, American, and mozzarella cheese—no mustard, mayo or onions—large french fries, a bowl of macaroni and cheese, lasagna, two slices of garlic bread, four ounces nacho cheese, three large cinnamon rolls, five scrambled eggs, and eight pints of chocolate milk.

Last statement: See Appendix.

Pronounced dead: 6:28 P.M.

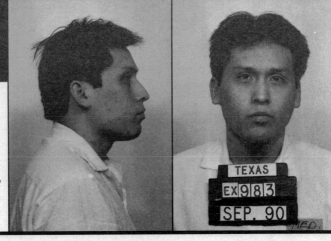

234

Miguel Angel Flores

Executed: November 9, 2000

Personal data: *Born:* June 7, 1969. *Race:* Hispanic. *Height:* 5'7". *Weight:* 165 pounds. *Education:* 12 years. *Prior occupation:* Laborer. *County of conviction:* Collin (change of venue from Hutchinson). *Age at time of execution:* 31.

Sentenced to death for: Convicted of capital murder for kidnapping, sexually assaulting, and killing a 20-year-old white female. Flores kidnapped the victim from a video store and took her to a remote area, where he sexually assaulted her. Flores drove the victim back to town in her car, eventually stabbing her to death. He left the victim in her car and fled the scene.

Received at death row: September 14, 1990. *Time on death row:* 3,709 days (10.16 years).

Last meal: Three beef enchiladas with onions, three cheese enchiladas with onions, Spanish rice, a bowl of jalapeño peppers, french fries, a cheeseburger all the way, bowl of mayonnaise, bowl of ketchup, bowl of pico de gallo, three Dr Peppers, pitchers of ice, banana split ice cream, and four quesadillas.

Last statement: "I want to thank my attorneys, Father Walsh . . . Sylvia, *te quiero mucho y a Consulado, te quiero decir muchas gracias por todo.* I want to say I am sorry and I say a prayer today for you so you can have peace and I hope that you can forgive me. God is waiting and God is waiting now."

Pronounced dead: 6:22 P.M.

Stacey Lamont Lawton

Executed: November 14, 2000

Personal data: *Born:* July 10, 1969. *Race:* Black. *Height:* 6'1". *Weight:* 180 pounds. *Education:* 10 years. *Prior occupation:* Carpenter. *County of conviction:* Smith. *Age at time of execution:* 31.

Sentenced to death for: Convicted in the December 1992 shotgun slaying of 44-year-old Dennis L. Price during a burglary in the victim's home west of Tyler. Price was shot in the chest when he confronted Lawton and two accomplices outside his home. He died at Tyler hospital fifteen minutes after arrival. Lawton and his accomplices fled in two stolen pickups, which were later abandoned. They then stole a third pickup and were apprehended following a high-speed chase. Karlos Renard Fields, one of the accomplices, received a life sentence for capital murder. The second accomplice was a 14-year-old juvenile.

Received at death row: July 23, 1993. *Time on death row:* 2,671 days (7.32 years).

Last meal: A jar of dill pickles.

Last statement: "I am saying, I want y'all to keep your heads up, hold on and stay strong for everybody. I mean ah, I don't want y'all to look at me like I am a killer or something man, cause I ain't no killer. I mean, I didn't, I didn't kill your father. I mean, I know how it look, but I didn't do it. You know what I am saying? You were out there with me, Tommy. I mean, you know man. [Mumbled] You know I always did want to say something to y'all. Right? I can't say that I done it because I didn't do it. I've got love for everybody. I am a Christian now. I'm saying I want everybody to keep their heads up and stay strong. I'm going to stay strong. I'll be seeing you, this is my last breath. Ricky, keep your head up baby. All y'all, Doreen, Melodee. I mean, I know y'all don't come down here. I just really don't know what y'all want me to say. I mean, I know, ah, I mean, I'm sorry anybody, ah, anybody got killed that night. It wasn't supposed to happen, but I didn't do it. I really didn't do it. I don't want y'all to go through life thinking that I did. You know what I am saying? I love everybody and I want y'all to stay strong. Right? It would take me an hour or a long time, man, but, ah, man, I don't want to hold y'all up, man, like that, ah. Y'all just keep your head up and stay strong, man. Give my love to everybody. I love y'all."

Pronounced dead: 6:22 P.M.

236

Tony Chambers

Executed: November 15, 2000

Personal data: *Born:* December 20, 1967. *Race:* Black. *Height:* 5'6". *Weight:* 125 pounds. *Education:* 10 years. *Prior occupation:* Laborer. *County of conviction:* Smith. *Age at time of execution:* 32.

Sentenced to death for: Convicted in the November 1990 abduction and murder of 11-year-old Carenthia Marie Bailey in Tyler. Bailey disappeared after attending a middle school basketball game. She was last seen leaving the school with Chambers. Police found her body off West Twenty-eighth Street. She had been sexually assaulted and strangled. Chambers initially called police and said he was responsible for Bailey's disappearance. He later denied involvement but made a written and verbal confession once Bailey's body was found.

Received at death row: September 6, 1991. *Time on death row:* 3,358 (9.20 years).

Last meal: Five chicken patties, ten slices of cheese, five hamburger buns with mustard on each side and two sliced pickles, two bags of Doritos, two Cokes, a pint of tin roof ice cream.

Last statement: "Mom, I just want y'all to know that I love you. No matter what in life, I want you to stay strong. Doreen, you have been a very special part of my life, too. I want you to keep doing what you are doing. Stay strong. Dad, I want you to stay strong."

Pronounced dead: 6:18 P.M.

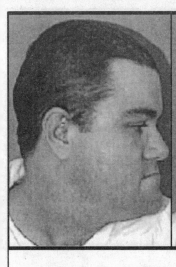

237

Garry Dean Miller

Executed: December 5, 2000

Personal data: *Born:* November 2, 1967. *Race:* White. *Height:* 5'11". *Weight:* 195 pounds. *Education:* 12 years. *Prior occupation:* Bartender/laborer. *County of conviction:* Jones. *Age at time of execution:* 33.

Sentenced to death for: Convicted in the November 1988 abduction, rape, and murder of 7-year-old April Marie Wilson, of Merkel. Wilson was spending the night at a residence Miller shared with another man and a female coworker of Wilson's mother. Miller told police he returned to the residence and found Wilson sleeping. He awoke the child and convinced her to go for a ride with him. He then drove to a remote area of Jones County, where he raped her, choked her, and bludgeoned her to death. Her body was found by two hunters the same day. Miller confessed to the murder while being questioned by police.

Received at death row: September 22, 1989. *Time on death row:* 4,092 days (11.21 years).

Last meal: Two grilled cheese sandwiches, french fries, ketchup, two boiled eggs, two cinnamon rolls with icing, two cans of grape juice, and coffee.

Last statement: "Maggie, I am sorry. I always wanted to tell you but I just didn't know how. I have been praying for y'all. I hope that y'all find the peace that y'all have been wanting. Lord, thank you for all my family, all my friends, and all my brothers on the row. Thank you for my spiritual family. Lord, be merciful with those who are actively involved with the taking of my life, forgive them as I am forgiving them. Be merciful to me, a sinner. Protect us Lord as we stay awake and watch over us as we sleep. As we wake may we keep watch with Christ and rest in His peace. All right, Warden. I am ready to go home."

Pronounced dead: n/a.

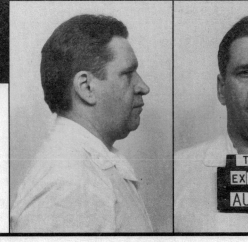

238

Daniel Joe Hittle

Executed: December 6, 2000

Personal data: *Born:* March 1, 1950. *Race:* White. *Height:* 5'7". *Weight:* 175 pounds. *Education:* 14 years. *Prior occupation:* Welder. *County of conviction:* Dallas. *Age at time of execution:* 50.

Sentenced to death for: Convicted in the November 1989 shooting death of Garland police officer Gerald Walker. Officer Walker was shot once in the chest with a .20-gauge shotgun after stopping Hittle's vehicle near the intersection of Saturn Road and Lexington Drive. Hittle's vehicle was later pursued by police and run off the road. Hittle fired at least two shots at officers before falling to the ground with his hands beneath him. After refusing orders to show his hands, Hittle was twice engaged by a police dog. Hittle then complied with police orders and was arrested.

Received at death row: August 16, 1990. *Time on death row:* 3,765 days (10.32 years).

Last meal: Relish tray with green olives, cheese, pickles, and celery; french fries with ketchup; two grilled cheese sandwiches, two cinnamon rolls, and a pitcher of milk.

Last statement: Transcriber could not translate and noted, "Spoke in an unknown language. Something like Snat Ajaib Singh Ji."

Pronounced dead: 6:20 P.M.

239

Claude Howard Jones

Executed: December 7, 2000

Personal data: *Born:* September 24, 1940. *Race:* White. *Height:* 5'8". *Weight:* 230 pounds. *Education:* 9 years (GED). *Prior occupation:* Electrician. *County of conviction:* San Jacinto. *Age at time of execution:* 60.

Sentenced to death for: Convicted in the November 1989 armed robbery and murder of 44-year-old Allen Hilzendager, owner of Zell's liquor store in Point Blank. Hilzendager was shot three times with a .357 Magnum as he turned to retrieve a bottle of liquor requested by Jones. Jones fled with $900 in cash taken from the register and joined at least one accomplice in a vehicle parked outside the store. Jones was arrested in Fort Myers, Florida, on December 2, 1989, after being charged with bank robbery and robbery there. Jones had served time on three previous occasions for assorted crimes, including robbery, assault, and murder. Cases were filed against accomplices Kerry Daniel Dixon Jr., and Timothy Mark Jordan.

Received at death row: August 10, 1990. *Time on death row:* 3,772 days (10.33 years).

Last meal: Eight soft fried eggs, bacon, sausage, a well-done T-bone steak, six slices of buttered toast with strawberry jelly, and a pitcher of cold milk.

Last statement: "To your family, ah, I hope that this can bring some closure to y'all. I am sorry for your loss and hey, I love all y'all. Let's go."

Pronounced dead: 6:42 P.M.

240

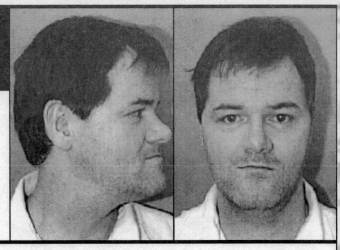

Jack Wade Clark

Executed: January 9, 2001

Personal data: *Born:* July 23, 1963. *Race:* White. *Height:* 5'4". *Weight:* 119 pounds. *Education:* 10 years. *Prior occupation:* Press operator. *County of conviction:* Lubbock. *Age at time of execution:* 37.

Sentenced to death for: Convicted in the October 1989 rape and murder of 23-year-old Melisa Ann Garcia, of Slaton. Garcia suffered two fatal stab wounds to the chest after she was taken to an isolated area and raped by Clark.

Received at death row: March 19, 1991. *Time on death row:* 3,584 days (9.82 years).

Last meal: A jar of Polish pickles (whole), a small wedge of cheddar cheese, salad (tossed) with Italian dressing, a cheeseburger with mayonnaise all the way, a large order of french fries with ketchup, a relish tray, and a pitcher of grape juice.

Last statement: "First, I would like to say to the family that I am sorry, and I do ask for forgiveness. There will be also a funeral mass at St. Thomas and I would like to invite all of those from the State and the family to be there if they would like to come. My last words will be: And He was the light that shineth in the hearts of all man from the foundations of the world. If we confess our sins He is just and true to forgive us of our sins and cleanse us from all unrighteousness. Peace and goodness."

Pronounced dead: n/a.

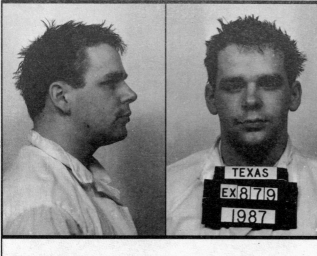

241

Alvin Urial Goodwin

Executed: January 18, 2001

Personal data: *Born:* December 27, 1963. *Race:* White. *Height:* 5'4". *Weight:* 190 pounds. *Education:* 10 years (GED). *Prior occupation:* Press operator/carpenter. *County of conviction:* Montgomery. *Age at time of execution:* 37.

Sentenced to death for: Convicted in the November 1986 abduction and shooting death of 20-year-old James Douglas Tillerson, of Conroe. Goodwin and accomplice Billy Dan Aitkens Jr. forced their way into Tillerson's mobile home and took a VCR, some videotapes, and a small amount of money while holding a gun on the victim. They then forced Tillerson into Aitkens's car and drove him to a wooded area, where he was shot in the arm and head with a .357 caliber pistol. His decomposing body was found there on January 17, 1987. Goodwin and Aitkens were arrested in Iowa and returned to Texas. Billy Dan Aitkens was sentenced to life for murder with a deadly weapon.

Received at death row: August 7, 1987. *Time on death row:* 4,913 days (13.46 years).

Last meal: T-bone steak, baked potato, salad, ice cream, and tea.

Last statement: Goodwin spoke in Irish, translating to "Good-bye."

Pronounced dead: 6:22 P.M.

242

Caruthers Alexander

Executed: January 29, 2001

Personal data: *Born:* September 7, 1948. *Race:* Black. *Height:* 5'10". *Weight:* 204 pounds. *Education:* 11 years. *Prior occupation:* Truck driver. *County of conviction:* Bexar. *Age at time of execution:* 52.

Sentenced to death for: Convicted of capital murder in the April 1981 rape-strangulation of Lori Bruch, who was attacked after leaving her job as a waitress at a club.

Received at death row: February 15, 1982. *Time on death row:* 6,923 days (18.97 years).

Last meal: Declined last meal.

Last statement: None.

Pronounced dead: n/a.

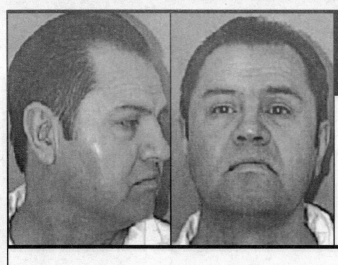

243

Adolph Gil Hernandez

Executed: February 8, 2001

Personal data: *Born:* September 1, 1950. *Race:* Hispanic. *Height:* 5'5". *Weight:* 175 pounds. *Education:* 7 years. *Prior occupation:* Barber. *County of conviction:* Lubbock. *Age at time of execution:* 50.

Sentenced to death for: Convicted in the murder and robbery of 69-year-old Elizabeth Alvarado, of Slaton. Alvarado was beaten to death with a baseball bat inside her home. Hernandez stole a purse from the home that contained $350 in cash. The victim's daughter confronted Hernandez as he attempted to flee the scene and managed to wrestle the bat from him and strike him with it. Hernandez was arrested at his Slaton residence after being found with bloodstains on his shirt, pants, and shoes.

Received at death row: June 27, 1990. *Time on death row:* 3,879 days (10.63 years).

Last meal: A double-meat cheeseburger with everything and jalapeño peppers, french fries with ketchup, three enchiladas, three tacos, banana pudding with real bananas, two Dr Peppers, an apple, and a Snickers bar.

Last statement: "I want to thank my family for their help and moral support and for their struggle. It would have been a lot harder without their love. So, I am just going home. I will see y'all one of these days. Just don't rush it. I will be there always. I'll always be watching over you. I love you. OK? Y'all be strong. God bless you. That is where I am going. I love y'all huh. I'll see y'all in Slayton, Texas. *Dios te mandas contigo mi espiritu.* [God, I command my spirit to go with you.] *Alabamos a Dios todos.* [We all praise God.] *Amen Cuida mi familia.* [Take care of my family.] I love you. That's it Warden."

Pronounced dead: n/a.

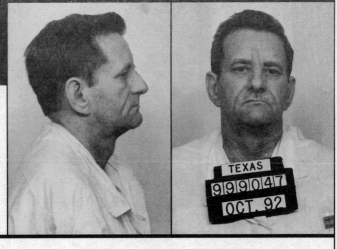

244

Dennis Thurl Dowthitt

Executed: March 7, 2001

TEXAS
999047
OCT. 92

Personal data: *Born:* June 20, 1945. *Race:* White. *Height:* 5'10". *Weight:* 155 pounds. *Education:* 10 years (GED). *Prior occupation:* Auto sales. *County of conviction:* Montgomery. *Age at time of execution:* 55.

Sentenced to death for: Convicted in connection with the deaths of sisters Grace Purnhagen, 16, and Tiffany Purnhagen, 9, in south Montgomery County. The bodies of the two girls were found along a pipeline. Grace's throat had been slashed and she had been assaulted with a beer bottle. Tiffany had been strangled with a rope. Grace's former boyfriend, Delton Dowthitt, then age 16, confessed to killing both girls following his arrest in Louisiana four days later. He later recanted, saying he killed Tiffany at the order of his father, who he said had actually killed and sexually assaulted Grace. Delton led police to where his father had disposed of the knife. Police also found a bloody bottle and rope at Dowthitt's auto sales business in Humble.

Received at death row: October 30, 1992. *Time on death row:* 3,050 days (8.36 years).

Last meal: Twelve fried eggs over easy, a loaf of bread, a bowl of salad dressing, french fries, and three cartons of milk.

Last statement: "I am so sorry for what y'all had to go through. I am so sorry for what all of you had to go through. I can't imagine losing two children. If I was y'all, I would have killed me. You know? I am really so sorry about it, I really am. I got to go sister, I love you. Y'all take care and God bless you. Gracie was beautiful and Tiffany was beautiful. You had some lovely girls and I am sorry. I don't know what to say. All right, Warden, let's do it."

Pronounced dead: 6:18 P.M.

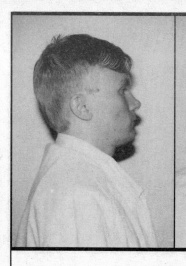

**Jason
Eric
Massey**

Executed:
April 3, 2001

Personal data: *Born:* January 7, 1973. *Race:* White. *Height:* 5'10". *Weight:* 156 pounds. *Education:* 8 years. *Prior occupation:* Roofer. *County of conviction:* Ellis. *Age at time of execution:* 28.

Sentenced to death for: Convicted in the July 1993 murders of James Brian King, 14, and Christina Benjamin, 13. The bodies of King, who was shot in the head, and Benjamin were found two days later.

Received at death row: October 14, 1994. *Time on death row:* 2,363 days (6.47 years).

Last meal: Three fried chicken quarters, fried squash, fried eggplant, mashed potatoes, snap beans, boiled cabbage, three corn on the cobs with butter, spinach, broccoli with cheese, a pint of caramel pecan fudge or tin roof ice cream, and a pitcher of sweet tea.

Last statement: See Appendix.

Pronounced dead: n/a.

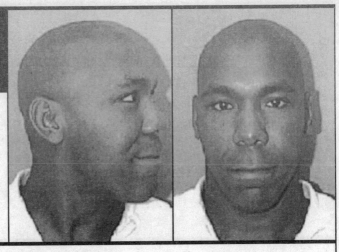

246

David Lee Goff

Executed: April 25, 2001

Personal data: *Born:* January 9, 1969. *Race:* Black. *Height:* 5'9". *Weight:* 151 pounds. *Education:* 8 years (GED). *Prior occupation:* Laborer. *County of conviction:* Tarrant. *Age at time of execution:* 32.

Sentenced to death for: Convicted in the September 1990 murder of 34-year-old Michael N. McGuire. McGuire was shot to death during an attempted robbery. The victim was reportedly kidnapped upon leaving a drug rehab center in Forth Worth and was shot after being handcuffed and drugged. Goff had previously served time for attempted capital murder with a deadly weapon. *Codefendant:* Craig Edward Ford had his capital murder case dismissed and was granted immunity.

Received at death row: December 27, 1991. *Time on death row:* 3,407 days (9.33 years).

Last meal: Declined last meal.

Last statement: "I want to give all the praise to God and glory and thank him for all that he done for me. With this let all debts be paid that I owed—real or imagined. The slate is wiped clean, all marks erased other than that there is no justice. That's not justice. Praise the Lord. Glory to Jesus Christ. Praise the Lord God."

Pronounced dead: 6:20 P.M.

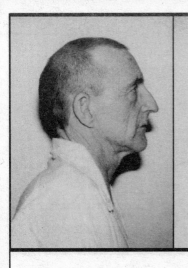
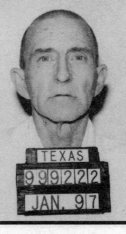

247

John L. Wheat

Executed: June 13, 2001

Personal data: *Born:* May 22, 1944. *Race:* White. *Height:* 5'9". *Weight:* 150 pounds. *Education:* 11 years. *Prior occupation:* Welder/mechanic. *County of conviction:* Tarrant. *Age at time of execution:* 57.

Sentenced to death for: Convicted in the July 1995 murder of infant Lacey Anderson during a shooting rampage at a Fort Worth apartment complex. Lacey, age 20 months, was one of six people shot by Wheat—three fatally—after Wheat argued with the victim's mother over claims that he had sexually fondled Lacey's 6-year-old sister, Ashley Ochoa, the previous day. Ashley and her 8-year-old brother, Edwardo Ochoa, were also fatally shot in the head by Wheat with a .45 caliber pistol. Wheat chased the victim's mother, Angela Anderson, into an apartment and shot her three times as she tried to hide in a bedroom closet. He then went to Anderson's apartment and shot each of her children in a rear bedroom. After shooting the children, Wheat took a carbine and fired into the apartment of Jessie Cranfill, the complex's 33-year-old security guard, wounding him in the back and leg. Wheat wounded another tenant and fired at Fort Worth police as they arrived at the scene. Officer Angela Jay was struck several times as she entered the complex. As other officers converged on Wheat, he put down his weapons and surrendered.

Received at death row: March 11, 1997. *Time on death row:* 1,555 days (4.26 years).

Last meal: Liver and onions, mashed potatoes and gravy, and whole milk (no 1 percent or 2 percent).

Last statement: "I deeply regret what happened. I did not intentionally or know-ingly harm anyone. That's it and *didmau* [Vietnamese for 'let's get out of here']."

Pronounced dead: 6:19 P.M.

248

Miguel A. Richardson

Executed: June 26, 2001

TEXAS
EX 6 9 1
1981

Personal data: *Born:* July 7, 1954. *Race:* Black. *Height:* 5'10". *Weight:* 170 pounds. *Education:* 14 years. *Prior occupation:* Laborer. *County of conviction:* Bexar. *Age at time of execution:* 46.

Sentenced to death for: Convicted in the March 1979 slaying and robbery of John G. Ebbert, one of two security guards shot to death at a Holiday Inn motel in San Antonio. Ebbert and the second victim were investigating a complaint from a motel guest when they found Richardson attempting to break into a room. As they were escorting Richardson to the front office, a gun in his waistband fell to the floor. He grabbed the gun and held the guards at gunpoint. Richardson handcuffed one of the guards, took their money, and then shot them both. He was arrested in June 1980 in Denver, Colorado. Three women identified as prostitutes were with Richardson at the time of the killings and testified during Richardson's trial.

Received at death row: September 24, 1981. *Time on death row:* 7,215 days (19.77 years).

Last meal: Birthday cake (chocolate) with "2/23/90" written on top, seven pink candles, a coconut, kiwi juice, pineapple juice, a mango, grapes (any kind), lettuce, cottage cheese and peaches, a banana, a delicious apple, chef salad (without meat) with thousand island dressing, fruit salad, and cheese and tomato slices.

Last statement: See Appendix.

Pronounced dead: 6:28 P.M.

249

James Joseph Wilkens Jr.

Executed: July 11, 2001

Personal data: *Born:* July 29, 1961. *Race:* White. *Height:* 5'5". *Weight:* 165 pounds. *Education:* 10 years (GED). *Prior occupation:* Cook. *County of conviction:* Smith. *Age at time of execution:* 39.

Sentenced to death for: Convicted in the December 1986 shooting deaths of 28-year-old Richard Allan Wood and 4-year-old Larry Wayne McMillan Jr., in Tyler. The two victims, along with Sandra Darlene Williams, the 20-year-old mother of Larry McMillan, returned to their residence to find Wilkens inside their trailer with a .22 caliber rifle. Wilkens, Williams's former boyfriend, shot Wood as he entered the trailer and then shot the boy as he sat on a couch. Wilkens chased Williams from the trailer and and shot her in the hip as she ran for help. She made it to the home of a neighbor, who called police. Williams, who was two months pregnant at the time of the shooting, survived her wound and identified Wilkens as the assailant.

Received at death row: February 19, 1988. *Time on death row:* 4,891 days (13.40 years).

Last meal: Six eggs scrambled, hash browns with onions, two sausage patties, biscuits with butter, two pints of strawberry cheesecake yogurt, two pitchers of sweet milk, and a pint of strawberry ice cream.

Last statement: See Appendix.

Pronounced dead: 6:23 P.M.

250

Mack Oran Hill

Executed: August 8, 2001

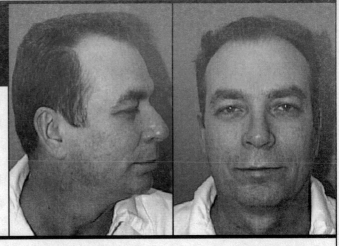

Personal data: *Born:* August 12, 1953. *Race:* White. *Height:* 6'0". *Weight:* 160 pounds. *Education:* 7 years. *Prior occupation:* Paint and body. *County of conviction:* Lubbock. *Age at time of execution:* 47.

Sentenced to death for: Convicted in the March 1987 robbery and murder of 43-year-old Donald Franklin Johnson. Johnson's body was found wrapped in plastic inside a fifty-five-gallon drum that had been filled with concrete and submerged in Amon Carter Lake in Montague County. The drum was found by a game warden five months after Johnson's disappearance. An autopsy revealed that Johnson had been shot once in the head with a .25 caliber pistol. Johnson and Hill had previously been partners in several unsuccessful business ventures. Following Johnson's disappearance, Hill was seen in possession of his truck and camper trailer. Hill was also involved in the theft of equipment from Johnson's paint and body shop in Lubbock and the sale of the equipment in flea markets.

Received at death row: January 25, 1990. *Time on death row:* 4,213 days (11.54 years).

Last meal: A Mexican dish with all the fixings.

Last statement: "First, I would like to tell my family that I love them. I will be waiting on them. I am fine. I hope that everyone gets some closure from this. I am innocent. Lubbock County officials believe I am guilty. I am not. Travis Ware has the burden on him to prove that he did not commit felonies. He needs to be stopped or he is going to do it time and time again. The power is invested in you as a public official to do your job. That's all, Warden. I love y'all."

Pronounced dead: 6:22 P.M.

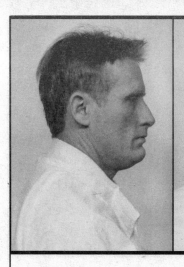

251

Jeffery Carlton Doughtie

Executed: August 16, 2001

Personal data: *Born:* October 3, 1961. *Race:* White. *Height:* 5'10". *Weight:* 177 pounds. *Education:* 9 years. *Prior occupation:* Laborer. *County of conviction:* Nueces. *Age at time of execution:* 39.

Sentenced to death for: Convicted in the August 1993 robbery and murders of Corpus Christi store owners Jerry Lee Dean, 80, and his 76-year-old wife, Sylvia. The Deans owned Golden Antiques and had known Doughtie for a number of years. On the day of the murders, Doughtie was refused a $30 loan from the couple to buy drugs. He soon returned to the store with a metal bar and beat the couple to death. Doughtie stole a number of rings, including Mrs. Dean's wedding ring, and money from the store before fleeing.

Received at death row: June 10, 1994. *Time on death row:* 2,624 days (7.19 years).

Last meal: Eight soft fried eggs (wants yellow runny), a big bowl of grits, five biscuits with bowl of butter, five pieces of bacon fried hard and crisp, two sausage patties, a pitcher of chocolate milk, two pints of vanilla Blue Bell, and two bananas.

Last statement: "For almost nine years I have thought about the death penalty, whether it is right or wrong, and I don't have any answers. But I don't think the world will be a better or safer place without me. If you had wanted to punish me you would have killed me the day after, instead of killing me now. You are not hurting me now. I have had time to get ready, to tell my family good-bye, to get my life where it needed to be. It started with a needle and it is ending with a needle. Carl, you have been a good friend, man. I am going to look for you. You go back and tell your daughter I love her. Tell her I came in here like a man and I will leave like a man. It's been good, dude. Thank you, Shorty. I appreciate you. I came in like a man and I will leave like a man. I will be with you. I will be with you every time you take a shower. If you leave crying you don't do me justice. If you don't see peace in my eyes you don't see me. I will be the first one you see when you cross over. They got these numbers that I called today. Calling my family. That is it. Ready, Warden."

Pronounced dead: 6:32 P.M.

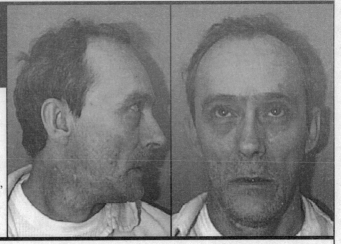

252

James Roy Knox

Executed: September 18, 2001

Personal data: *Born:* July 12, 1951. *Race:* White. *Height:* 5'11". *Weight:* 131 pounds. *Education:* 8 years. *Prior occupation:* Drywall finisher. *County of conviction:* Galveston. *Age at time of execution:* 50.

Sentenced to death for: Convicted in the November 1982 robbery-slaying of Joseph Sanchez, 39, the owner of Joe's Pharmacy in Galveston. Ronald Dya, who worked with Sanchez, told authorities Knox walked up to the store counter with a gun in his hand and demanded drugs. Sanchez was shot through the heart when he told Knox he had no drugs. Knox then demanded drugs from Dya, who gave him four bottles of Demerol worth $80. Knox also escaped with an undetermined amount of cash.

Received at death row: March 11, 1986. *Time on death row:* 5,670 days (15.53 years).

Last meal: A Western omelet, fried potatoes, sliced tomato, pan sausage, three biscuits, a big bowl of white gravy, a pitcher of vanilla milk shake, and a half cantaloupe.

Last statement: None.

Pronounced dead: 6:28 P.M.

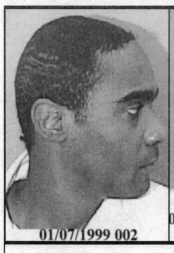

253

Gerald Lee Mitchell

Executed: October 22, 2001

01/07/1999 002

000838

01/07/1999 001

Personal data: *Born:* December 27, 1967. *Race:* Black. *Height:* 5'11". *Weight:* 168 pounds. *Education:* 10 years. *Prior occupation:* Carpenter. *County of conviction:* Harris. *Age at time of execution:* 33.

Sentenced to death for: Convicted in the June 1985 robbery-slaying of 20-year-old Charles Marino in Houston. Marino and his brother-in-law, Kenneth Fleming, went to the Acres Home area of Houston to buy some marijuana and met Mitchell in a city park. He offered to sell them the drug but then pulled a sawed-off shotgun on them and eventually forced them to drive to a vacant house. After taking $25 and car keys from Marino, he shot them both with a 12-gauge shotgun from a distance of ten feet. Fleming survived. Mitchell was arrested in Corpus Christi seven days after the shooting. He was also convicted in the shooting death of Hector Manguia, who was shot the same day as Marino and Fleming when he refused to give Mitchell a necklace.

Received at death row: July 24, 1986. *Time on death row:* 5,569 days (15.26 years).

Last meal: A bag of Jolly Rancher candy (assorted flavors).

Last statement: "Yes, sir. Where's Mr. Marino's mother? Did you get my letter? Just wanted to let you know, I sincerely meant everything I wrote. I am sorry for the pain. I am sorry for the life I took from you. I ask God for forgiveness and I ask you for the same. I know it maybe hard, but I'm sorry for what I did. To my family, I love each and every one of you. Be strong. Know my love is always with you . . . always. I know I am going home to be with the Lord. Shed tears of happiness for me. I love each and every one of you. Keep on living. Betty, you have been wonderful. You guided me to the Lord. You have been like a mother to me. Sean, Rusty, Jenny, Marsha, God bless each and every one of y'all. Jesus, I confess you as my Lord and savior. I know when I die, I'll have life in heaven and life eternal everlasting. I am ready for that mansion that you promised me. Take care. It's all right Sean, it's all right. I'm going to a better place."

Pronounced dead: 6:25 P.M.

254

Jeffery Eugene Tucker

Executed: November 14, 2001

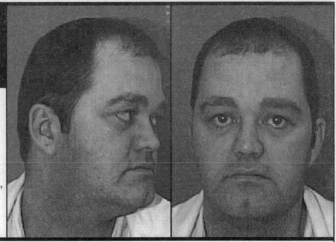

Personal data: *Born:* January 1, 1960. *Race:* White. *Height:* 6'4". *Weight:* 237 pounds. *Education:* 10 years (GED). *Prior occupation:* Truck driver. *County of conviction:* Parker. *Age at time of execution:* 41.

Sentenced to death for: Convicted in the July 1988 robbery and murder of 65-year-old Wilton B. Humphreys of Granbury. Tucker, using the alias J. D. Travis, answered a newspaper ad Humphreys had placed in an attempt to sell his pickup truck and trailer. After test-driving the vehicle, Tucker told Humphreys he would buy the pickup and trailer and pay the $18,000 in cash. Humphreys said he would accompany Tucker to the bank so he could deposit the money once the paperwork was completed. Once at the bank, Tucker pulled a pistol and told Humphreys he was stealing the truck and trailer. Tucker drove out of town and shot Humphreys when he refused to get out of the truck. Tucker was arrested in Santa Rosa, New Mexico, three days later, after he robbed a service station of $800.

Received at death row: October 18, 1989. *Time on death row:* 4,410 days (12.08 years).

Last meal: Six pieces of fried chicken, potato salad with mustard, macaroni and cheese, eight cinnamon rolls, a pint of vanilla ice cream, a pitcher of milk, and ketchup.

Last statement: "I'd like to tell the Humphreys family, I am sorry for the pain and suffering that I have caused you. I never intended for your husband and father to be killed, it was just an accident. I sincerely regret any pain and sorrow. I realize that my actions have caused this death and a lot of pain and grief. I pray that Jesus will give you peace. I just ask that my death bring you peace and solace. If my death brings you that, then I will gladly give it. I know that I leave this world for the crime that I committed. To my friends, Jack and Irene Wilcox. Bless you both, you've been my rock. Irene, you have been like a mother and Jack, you have been like a father. To my lawyers, Danalyn and Robert Owen, you are not just my lawyers but you are my friends. I know you weren't happy when I stopped my appeals, but you know the reason why. Thank you for understanding. Have a happy heart knowing I leave this world in peace. Father Walsh, you have helped me so much to come to a knowledge of the Lord. I would never have understood that without you. You give me patience and diligence. Someday I will see you there. I'll be there waiting for you but don't be in a hurry. You have a lot of work left to do. Just know that I'll be watching over you. I love you all and thank you for being a part of my life. [Recites the Lord's Prayer.]"

Pronounced dead: n/a.

255

Emerson Edward Rudd

Executed: November 15, 2001

Personal data: *Born:* August 9, 1970. *Race:* Black. *Height:* 5'8". *Weight:* 145 pounds. *Education:* 11 years. *Prior occupation:* Laborer. *County of conviction:* Dallas. *Age at time of execution:* 31.

Sentenced to death for: Convicted in the September 1988 shooting of 23-year-old Steve Morgan during the robbery of Captain D's Seafood restaurant in Dallas. Rudd and three accomplices entered the restaurant and demanded money at gunpoint. Morgan, manager of the restaurant, was shot once in the abdomen after handing over money from the cash register to the bandits. He died at a Dallas hospital early the next morning. Rudd and his accomplices were arrested two days later, when their getaway car was spotted by police. An employee who witnessed the shooting of Morgan positively identified Rudd as the killer. Approximately $800 was taken from the restaurant in the robbery.

Received at death row: April 13, 1989. *Time on death row:* 4,599 days (12.60 years).

Last meal: Declined last meal.

Last statement: "OK. I guess I'll address the Morgan family. Mrs. Morgan, the sister from the trial. Thirteen or fourteen years ago, I had a non-caring attitude at the time. I'm sorry for shooting your son down at that particular robbery. Politicians say that this brings closure. But my death doesn't bring your son back—it doesn't bring closure. I wish that I could do more, but I can't. I hope this brings you peace. Ursula, Manon, and Irene, I love y'all—take it easy. They've gotta do this thing. I'm still warm from the pepper gas. I love you. I'm ready to go. Call my mom and tell her that this particular process is over. Tell all the brothers to keep their heads up, eyes toward the sky."

Pronounced dead: 6:26 P.M.

256

Vincent Edward Cooks

Executed: December 12, 2001

01/07/1999 004

000927
01/07/1999 003

Personal data: *Born:* July 26, 1964. *Race:* Black. *Height:* 6'0". *Weight:* 318 pounds. *Education:* 9 years. *Prior occupation:* Electrician/carpenter. *County of conviction:* Dallas. *Age at time of execution:* 37.

Sentenced to death for: Convicted in the February 1988 shooting death of Dallas police officer Gary D. McCarthy outside a Dallas supermarket. McCarthy was working off-duty security for Brancato's Supermarket and had just returned to the store from the bank with employee Mark DeCardenas when Cooks approached and demanded the money DeCardenas carried. DeCardenas told police Cooks grabbed a money bundle amounting to $10,000 and then shot McCarthy before fleeing. McCarthy later died at Parkland Memorial Hospital. The following day, police arrested Tracy Dewayne Stallworth as a suspect in the robbery and slaying. Stallworth named Cooks and Tony Ray Harvey as accomplices. A witness later picked out Cooks from a police lineup and identified him as the slayer of Officer McCarthy. Stallworth and another accomplice were sentenced to twenty years for theft and robbery.

Received at death row: December 22, 1988. *Time on death row:* 4,738 days (12.98 years).

Last meal: Twelve pieces of chicken (thighs and drumsticks), two double-meat cheeseburgers on toasted buns, one large plate of french fries with ketchup, two large onions cut in slices, two large tomatoes cut in slices, six sweet pickles, salad dressing, five jalapeño peppers, pecan cobbler with extra crust, and milk.

Last statement: See Appendix.

Pronounced dead: n/a.

257

Michael Patrick Moore

Executed: January 9, 2002

Personal data: *Born:* September 16, 1961. *Race:* White. *Height:* 5'9". *Weight:* 160 pounds. *Education:* 8 years. *Prior occupation:* Painter. *County of conviction:* Coryell. *Age at time of execution:* 40.

Sentenced to death for: Convicted in the stabbing death of Christa E. Bentley during the burglary of her home.

Received at death row: November 4, 1994. *Time on death row:* 2,623 days (7.19 years).

Last meal: Lasagna, a pitcher of whole milk, corn, and chocolate cake.

Last statement: "I'll start by saying I love all of you. I will be waiting for your arrival, don't disappoint me by not showing up. I will be there with the give of Christ. We'll all be there. I promise I'll go up smiling. I am sorry. If I could think of a word in the vocabulary stronger, you need to hear something stronger, you deserve it. I'm sorry, I can't take back what I have done. I have asked Christ for forgiveness, and I ask that you forgive me. And I understand your feelings. God bless all of you. I will be waiting for your arrival. Do not disappoint me by not showing up. God bless everybody."

Pronounced dead: n/a.

258

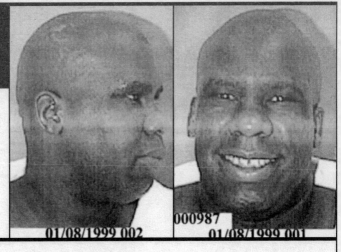

01/08/1999 002

000987   01/08/1999 001

Jermarr Carlos Arnold

Executed: January 16, 2002

Personal data: *Born:* September 29, 1958. *Race:* Black. *Height:* 6'1". *Weight:* 230 pounds. *Education:* 12 years. *Prior occupation:* Construction worker. *County of conviction:* Nueces. *Age at time of execution:* 43.

Sentenced to death for: Convicted in the July 1983 robbery and murder of 21-year-old Christine Marie Sanchez, of Corpus Christi. Sanchez was working alone at Greenberg's Jewelry Store when Arnold entered with a pistol and demanded jewelry from a display case. Arnold told Texas Rangers in 1988 that he wrestled a .357 Magnum pistol away from Sanchez after she pulled it from a drawer, then he shot her in the head as they struggled. Arnold left the store with numerous pieces of jewelry and fled to California, where he was later arrested in Los Angeles for bank robbery.

Received at death row: December 20, 1990. *Time on death row:* 4,045 days (11.08 years).

Last meal: Declined last meal.

Last statement: "Yes sir, members of Mrs. Sanchez's family, I don't know who you are, and other people present. As I said, I'm taking responsibility for the death of your daughter in 1983. I'm deeply sorry for the loss of your loved one. I am a human being also. I know how it feels, I've been there. I cannot explain and can't give you answers. I can give you one thing, and I'm going to give that today. I'm giving a life for a life. I pray you will have no ill will or animosity. You have the right to see this, I am glad you are here. All I can do is ask the Lord for forgiveness. I am not saying this to be facetious. I am giving my life. I hope you find comfort in my execution. As for me, I am happy, that is why you see me smiling. I am glad I am leaving this world. I am going to a better place. I have made peace with God; I am born again. Thank you for being here. I'm sorry. I hope you get over any malice or hatred you feel. Because it yields sorrow and suffering. I take responsibility for the loss of your daughter. I can't give answers. I hope you can find peace in the days to come. God bless all of you. Thank you all for being here. [Begins singing 'Amazing Grace.']"

Pronounced dead: 6:26 P.M.

259

Windell Broussard

Executed: January 30, 2002

TEXAS
999064

Personal data: *Born:* March 5, 1960. *Race:* Black. *Height:* 5'8". *Weight:* 117 pounds. *Education:* 7 years. *Prior occupation:* Farmer. *County of conviction:* Jefferson. *Age at time of execution:* 41.

Sentenced to death for: Convicted in the slaying of 28-year-old Dianna Fay Broussard and her son, Corey Harris, 10, outside their home in Port Arthur. Both victims were found in the front yard suffering from stab wounds. 8-year-old Toccara Harris was found inside the home with similar wounds but survived to identify Broussard as the assailant.

Received at death row: July 2, 1993. *Time on death row:* 3,134 days (8.59 years).

Last meal: Smothered chicken and rice, pinto beans with salt pork, corn, homemade rolls, pecan pie, and a pitcher of root beer.

Last statement: "Yes, Warden. I just want to let everyone know that this here is a tragedy. What happened to Diana, Corey, and what is happening to me . . . it is a tragedy. That is all, Warden."

Pronounced dead: n/a.

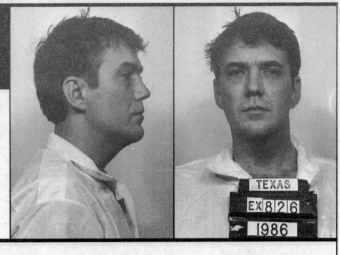

260

Randall Wayne Hafdahl Sr.

Executed: January 31, 2002

TEXAS
EX826
1986

Personal data: *Born:* June 1, 1953. *Race:* White. *Height:* 6'4". *Weight:* 196 pounds. *Education:* 10 years. *Prior occupation:* Painter/mechanic. *County of conviction:* Randall. *Age at time of execution:* 48.

Sentenced to death for: Convicted in the November 1985 shooting death of 42-year-old James D. Mitchell Jr., an off-duty Amarillo police officer. Mitchell was shot when he stopped to render aid after witnessing a one-car accident involving Hafdahl and two others. A witness told police that after the officer was shot, one of the men ran to the trunk of the wrecked car and grabbed what appeared to be a bag of marijuana from the trunk. Hafdahl and Shawn David Terry were sighted near the murder scene and arrested. The third man, Daniel Louis Helgran, was later arrested in Clovis, New Mexico. Terry told police he witnessed Hafdahl shoot the officer. Neither Helgran nor Terry stood trial.

Received at death row: April 8, 1986. *Time on death row:* 5,777 days (15,83 years).

Last meal: Chef salad with ranch dressing, double-meat cheeseburger all the way, french fries with ketchup, and chocolate cake.

Last statement: See Appendix.

Pronounced dead: 6:48 P.M.
Note: IV was placed in the right hand and right leg instead of the right and left arms.

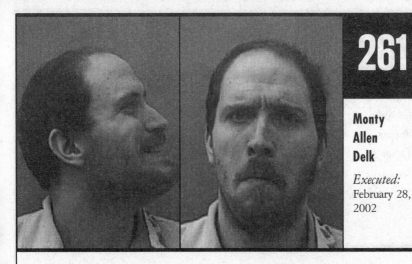

Monty Allen Delk

Executed: February 28, 2002

Personal data: *Born:* February 24, 1967. *Race:* White. *Height:* 5'11". *Weight:* 220 pounds. *Education:* 13 years. *Prior occupation:* Assistant restaurant manager. *County of conviction:* Anderson. *Age at time of execution:* 35.

Sentenced to death for: Convicted in the November 1986 shooting death and robbery of Gene Olan Allen II, of Grapeland. Allen was shot in the head with a shotgun and his body dumped in a ditch near Crockett after accompanying Delk on a test-drive of his wife's car, which the couple was selling. Delk stole the Z28 Camaro and Allen's wallet. He was arrested in Winnfield, Louisiana, on December 2, 1986. Delk is also suspected in the 1985 killing of William W. Richardson, a 19-year-old San Benito, Texas, man who was attending school in Orange County, Florida.

Received at death row: May 11, 1988. *Time on death row:* 5,041 days (13.81 years).

Last meal: Declined last meal.

Last statement: "I've got one thing to say, get your warden off this gurney and shut up. You are not in America. This is the island of Barbados. I am the warden of this unit. People are seeing you do this."

Pronounced dead: 7:53 P.M.
Note: Delk's head was secured to the gurney by an ace bandage.

262

Gerald Wayne Tigner Jr.

Executed: March 7, 2002

Personal data: *Born:* December 27, 1972. *Race:* Black. *Height:* 6'0". *Weight:* 210 pounds. *Education:* 9 years. *Prior occupation:* Laborer. *County of conviction:* McLennan. *Age at time of execution:* 29.

Sentenced to death for: Convicted in the shooting deaths of James Williams and Michael Watkins in Waco. The two victims were shot down in the street following an argument over money.

Received at death row: May 24, 1994. *Time on death row:* 2,844 days (7.79 years).

Last meal: Fried chicken, french fries, ketchup, two cheeseburgers all the way, a bag of potato chips, apple cobbler, white cake with white icing, a pitcher of lemonade, and a pitcher of Sprite.

Last statement: "Yes. My last statement. I was wrongfully convicted of this crime against Michael Watkins and James Williams on Tenth Street on August 31, 1993. I got convicted on a false confession because I never admitted to it, but my lawyer did not put this out to the jury. I did not kill those drug dealers. I send love to my family and friends, my east side family and friends. I am being real with the real. That's all that counts in my heart. I will see you later. That's it."

Pronounced dead: 6:21 P.M.

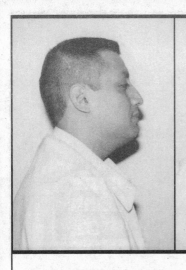

263

Jose Santellan Sr.

Executed: April 10, 2002

Personal data: *Born:* March 8, 1962. *Race:* Hispanic. *Height:* 5'10". *Weight:* 189 pounds. *Education:* 10 years. *Prior occupation:* Shipping and receiving, laborer. *County of conviction:* Kerr. *Age at time of execution:* 40.

Sentenced to death for: On August 22, 1993, Santellan was at a local hospital in Fredericksburg, Gillespie County, Texas. His girlfriend, Yolanda Garza, was in the parking lot and Santellan shot her with a .25 caliber handgun. He was observed putting Garza into his vehicle and driving off after threatening a witness. The subject drove on Interstate 10 to the Hill County Motel in Camp Wood, Texas, where he rented a room for two days. Police officers arrived shortly after midnight on August 24 and found Santellan inside the motel room with the body of the victim. He had drunk a twelve-pack of beer and taken an unknown number of pills that were in the victim's purse.

Received at death row: March 14, 1995. *Time on death row:* 2,584 days (7.08 years).

Last meal: Twelve pieces of fried chicken, mashed potatoes with brown gravy, two rolls with butter, two Pepsis, a pint of strawberry ice cream, and a pint of vanilla ice cream.

Last statement: "First of all, I would like to apologize to the Guajardo family even though they are not present. I loved Yolanda a lot. I hope and pray they can forgive me for all the pain. To my family, stay strong. Tom, Orlando, Celia, stay strong. Michael, thank you for your friendship. Thank you for the support you have given me. I thank all of you and I love all of you. To the guys on death row, stay strong and I hope to see you someday. Bye bye, I love you guys, don't worry about me. It's going to be all right."

Pronounced dead: 6:26 P.M.

264

William Kendrick Burns

Executed: April 11, 2002

Personal data: *Born:* July 4, 1958. *Race:* Black. *Height:* 5'7". *Weight:* 145 pounds. *Education:* 12 years. *Prior occupation:* Laborer. *County of conviction:* Bowie. *Age at time of execution:* 43.

Sentenced to death for: Convicted in the March 1981 murder of Johnny Lynn Hamlett, 18, who was killed while working the night shift at a wood preserving plant in Texarkana. Hamlett was shot fourteen times and robbed of $110. *Codefendant:* Victor Renay Burns received a life sentence for murder with a deadly weapon.

Received at death row: October 12, 1981. *Time on death row:* 7,486 days (20.51 years).

Last meal: Declined last meal.

Last statement: "I just want to tell my mom that I am sorry that I caused her so much pain and my family and stuff. I love them and I hurt for the fact that they are going to be hurting. I really hate that. And that I'm hoping they are going to be OK. That's it."

Pronounced dead: 6:21 P.M.

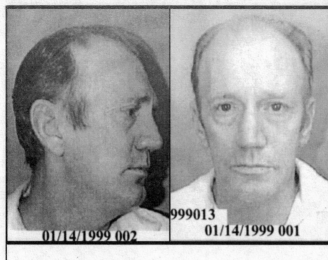

265

Gerald Dewight Casey

Executed: April 18, 2002

999013
01/14/1999 001
01/14/1999 002

Personal data: *Born:* January 15, 1955. *Race:* White. *Height:* 5'9". *Weight:* 140 pounds. *Education:* 11 years (GED). *Prior occupation:* Iron worker. *County of conviction:* Montgomery. *Age at time of execution:* 47.

Sentenced to death for: Convicted in the July 1989 robbery and murder of 29-year-old Sonya Lynn Howell. Howell was beaten over the head with a telephone receiver and then shot nine times with a .22 caliber pistol. Her home outside New Caney was then robbed of a gun collection belonging to her boyfriend, and several other items. Stolen jewelry and money from the victim's residence were later found in a motel room shared by Casey and codefendant Carla Smith in Humble. Police also recovered a pair of bloody jeans from Casey's vehicle. Some of the stolen guns were located in a wooded area in Harris County.
Codefendant: Carla Smith agreed to testify for the state in exchange for a ten-year sentence for theft.

Received at death row: November 15, 1991. *Time on death row:* 3,807 days (10.43 years).

Last meal: Three drumsticks, three thighs (fried), a quart of coleslaw, tea or juice, vanilla ice cream, and a Dr Pepper.

Last statement: None.

Pronounced dead: 6:18 P.M.

266

Rodolfo Hernandez

Executed:
May 9,
2002

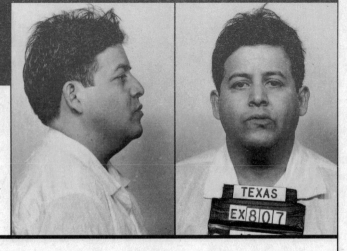

TEXAS
EX807

Personal data: *Born:* November 18, 1949. *Race:* Hispanic. *Height:* 5'8". *Weight:* 181 pounds. *Education:* 7 years. *Prior occupation:* Musician. *County of conviction:* Comal. *Age at time of execution:* 52.

Sentenced to death for: Convicted in the March 1985 shooting death of 20-year-old Victor Cerran, a Mexican national, in New Braunfels. Cerran and four other Mexican nationals reportedly agreed to pay $150 each for Hernandez and another man to drive them to Denton. They were instead taken to a residence in New Braunfels and shot with .22 caliber and .25 caliber weapons. Cerran suffered four wounds and was pronounced dead on arrival at a local hospital. The other four victims survived multiple gunshot wounds and later identified Hernandez and Jesse Garibay Jr., as the men who shot and robbed them. Jesse Garibay received a four-year sentence for theft of property.

Received at death row: September 30, 1985. *Time on death row:* 6,065 days (16.62 years).

Last meal: Two double-meat cheeseburgers all the way, a large order of french fries, three beef tacos, guacamole salad, salt, and two fried chicken breasts.

Last statement: "Yes, sir. I want to give thanks to Father Walsh, my spiritual adviser, and Mr. Whiteside and Irene Wilcox and her husband, Jack, and Richard Lopez for being there for me through all of this. I don't see O'Brien. Oh, there he is. Thanks to everybody. Everybody will be all right, because y'all are going where I am going. Remember what I said, I want to see you all where I'm going. I want to give thanks. God, come and do your will. I'm ready Warden."

Pronounced dead: 6:23 P.M.

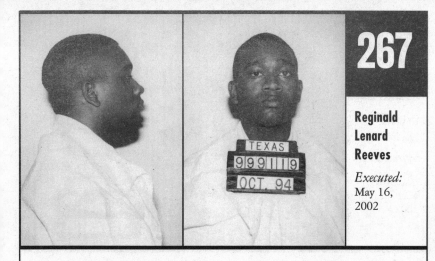

267

Reginald Lenard Reeves

Executed: May 16, 2002

Personal data: *Born:* April 21, 1974. *Race:* Black. *Height:* 5'5". *Weight:* 140 pounds. *Education:* 11 years. *Prior occupation:* Factory worker. *County of conviction:* Red River. *Age at time of execution:* 28.

Sentenced to death for: Convicted in the September 1993 rape-strangulation murder of 14-year-old Jenny Lynn Weeks, a runaway from a group home in Paris, Texas. Weeks met Reeves and his accomplice after fleeing the Willow Creek group home with another girl four days prior to her murder. After being raped and strangled, Weeks's body was dumped in a vacant house in Clarksville.

Received at death row: October 7, 1994. *Time on death row:* 2,778 days (7.61 years).

Last meal: Four pieces of fried chicken, two Cokes.

Last statement: "I pray that we all may learn to love and forgive so that we can have peace in the world. It is with loving and forgiveness and living to learn to love and loving to live that we can learn the power of forgiveness and learn to live as brothers and sisters on this earth. Until then, this will continue to happen—capital punishment; and if we don't forgive, sooner or later we will all self-destruct. You need to open up your heart and let God in. I apologize for taking the life of your daughter and I know how much pain you must be in because I saw my family today. And although my pain is not as deep as yours, I am very sorry. Today, this does not bring you peace because this is not really the way. We should forgive and love and I do apologize with all my heart and soul and I love you and I know your spirit and God dwells within us and we are all one big family of humanity; we must all learn to love and live together. I will see you on the other side. Thank you for your hospitality."

Pronounced dead: 6:22 P.M.

268

Ronford Lee Styron Jr.

Executed: May 22, 2002

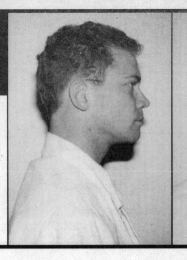 

TEXAS
999124
OCT. 94

Personal data: *Born:* September 23, 1969. *Race:* White. *Height:* 5'8". *Weight:* 180 pounds. *Education:* 11 years. *Prior occupation:* Laborer. *County of conviction:* Liberty. *Age at time of execution:* 32.

Sentenced to death for: Convicted in the October 1993 beating death of his 11-month-old son, Lee Hollace Styron. The young boy was taken to Liberty Baptist Hospital with a swollen face and several broken ribs after being beaten by his father. He died two days later. Doctors later discovered that young Lee had previously suffered at least ten broken bones. Styron told police he suspected Lee was not his biological offspring and took his anger out on him.

Received at death row: October 28, 1994. *Time on death row:* 2,763 days (7.57 years).

Last meal: A Mexican platter with all the works, two Cokes, pickles, olives, and cookies and cream ice cream.

Last statement: "Yes sir, thank you. I love y'all and I want y'all to know that. Y'all always told me not to worry about myself. I worry more about you all because I know where I am going. I want to see you there, so get your heart right. You know I love you and care for you. I am going to go with my little boy and play with him. Y'all take care and I love y'all. I love y'all. Chaplain Wilcox, Roger, Robin, Sarah, Grandma. I love you. Y'all be careful. Lord Jesus, I see your spirit, it's OK. I love you."

Pronounced dead: 6:20 P.M.

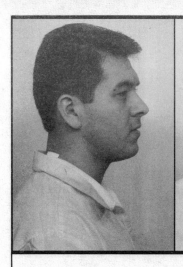

269

Johnny
Joe
Martinez

Executed:
May 22,
2002

Personal data: *Born:* November 20, 1972. *Race:* Hispanic. *Height:* 5'6". *Weight:* 174 pounds. *Education:* 11 years. *Prior occupation:* Direct care tech. *County of conviction:* Nueces. *Age at time of execution:* 29.

Sentenced to death for: Convicted in the robbery and murder of 20-year-old Clay Peterson in Corpus Christi. Peterson was working as a clerk at a 7-Eleven convenience store when he was robbed by Martinez and stabbed eight times. The robbery and murder were captured on videotape by a store camera. Martinez was apprehended a short time later at the Sandy Shores Motel, where he had placed a call to police to confess.

Received at death row: January 28, 1994. *Time on death row:* 3,036 days (8.32 years).

Last meal: Declined last meal.

Last statement: "First of all, I want to say that I want to apologize to Clay Peterson's father. I am sorry. And I want to thank you for everything you tried to do; it meant a lot to me. I want to thank David Dow; you have been great to me and I know that I am fixing to die—but not for my mistakes. My trial lawyers—they are the ones that are killing me. I love my family and I know where I am going. You all take care—Celina, David—and tell Mama I love her, too. I didn't call her 'cause I just couldn't. I am going to heaven and I'll see you there. Tom Crouch, and everybody, I love you. Chiara, thank you for everyhing. Fred, Rachel, Daniel, Oralia—thank you for being there for me. I will be there with you all in spirit. David Dow, you have been great. Mary Moreno, from the Corpus Christi *Caller-Times,* thank you for what you wrote. You have been sincere and I wanted to talk to you, but they wouldn't let me. David Dow, let them know what happened. I am fine; I am happy; I will see you on the other side."

Pronounced dead: 6:20 P.M.

270

Napoleon Beazley

Executed: May 28, 2002

Personal data: *Born:* August 5, 1976. *Race:* Black. *Height:* n/a. *Weight:* n/a. *Education:* 12 years. *Prior occupation:* Laborer. *County of conviction:* Smith. *Age at time of execution:* 25.

Sentenced to death for: Convicted in the carjacking and murder of 63-year-old John E. Luttig, of Tyler. Luttig, driving a 1987 Mercedes Benz, had pulled into the driveway of his home when he was approached by Beazley and shot in the head with a .45 caliber pistol. Beazley and two accomplices, who had followed Luttig home, fled in his vehicle. Beazley was 17 years old at the time of the offense.
Codefendants: Donald Coleman and Cedric Coleman were charged with capital murder and aggravated robbery.

Received at death row: March 21, 1995. *Time on death row:* 2,625 days (7.19 years).

Last meal: Declined last meal.

Last statement: See Appendix.

Pronounced dead: 6:17 P.M.

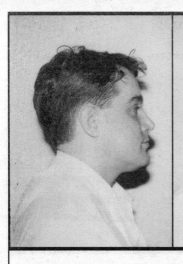

271

Stanley Allison Baker Jr.

Executed: May 30, 2002

Personal data: *Born:* December 30, 1966. *Race:* White. *Height:* 5'9". *Weight:* 200 pounds. *Education:* 14 years. *Prior occupation:* Receiving. *County of conviction:* Brazos. *Age at time of execution:* 35.

Sentenced to death for: Convicted in the September 1994 robbery and murder of Wayne John Walters, a clerk at the Adult Video store in College Station. Baker shot Walters, 44, once in the head with a shotgun before clearing the register of its cash. He then fled the store in the victim's pickup truck. The truck was later spotted in Bastrop by a Department of Public Safety trooper, who arrested Baker. Baker had a cut lip from the recoil of the shotgun and blood on his shirt. He confessed to the robbery and the murder following his arrest. Between $40 and $50 were reported missing from the register.

Received at death row: August 1, 1995. *Time on death row:* 2,494 days (6.83 years).

Last meal: Two ten-ounce rib-eye steaks, one pound of turkey breast (sliced thin), twelve strips of bacon, two large hamburgers with mayonnaise, onion, lettuce, two large baked potatoes with butter, sour cream, cheese, and chives, four slices of cheese or a half pound of grated cheddar, chef salad with blue cheese dressing, two corn on the cobs, a pint of mint chocolate chip ice cream, and four Vanilla Cokes or Mr. Pibb.

Last statement: "Well, I don't have anything to say. I am just sorry about what I did to Mr. Peters. That's all."

Pronounced dead: 6:19 P.M.

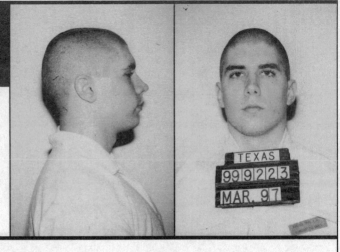

272

Daniel E. Reneau

Executed: June 13, 2002

Personal data: *Born:* April 15, 1975. *Race:* White. *Height:* 5'10". *Weight:* 170 pounds. *Education:* 11 years. *Prior occupation:* Nurse's aide. *County of conviction:* Kerr. *Age at time of execution:* 27.

Sentenced to death for: Convicted in the January 1996 robbery and murder of service station attendant Kris Lee Keeran in Kerrville. Keeran, 31, was working at the Goldstar Texaco service station when Reneau pulled a .22 caliber pistol and shot him once in the face. Reneau fled with the store safe, a cash box, and a VCR containing a security tape. The safe and cash box contained approximately $11,350 in cash and checks. Reneau and accomplice Jeffery Wood were arrested the next day and confessed to the crime. Police recovered the murder weapon, the store safe, and the charred remains of the security tape the two had attempted to destroy. Charges were pending against Jeffery Wood.

Received at death row: March 21, 1997. *Time on death row:* 1,910 days (5.23 years).

Last meal: One tray of french fries with salt and ketchup, one tray of nachos with cheese and sliced jalapeño peppers, a cheeseburger—with everything—and mustard, and a pitcher of sweet tea.

Last statement: None.

Pronounced dead: 6:15 P.M.

273

Robert O. Coulson

Executed: June 25, 2002

Personal data: *Born:* March 11, 1968. *Race:* White. *Height:* 5'11". *Weight:* 176 pounds. *Education:* 14 years. *Prior occupation:* Sales. *County of conviction:* Harris. *Age at time of execution:* 34.

Sentenced to death for: Convicted in the November 1992 murders of Robin and Robert Wentworth, two of five family members Coulson killed for inheritance. Coulson plotted over a four-month period to kill his parents for their estate and eventually decided to include his two sisters and brother-in-law as victims. Coulson went to his parents' home and lured each family member into separate rooms, where he bound each with plastic flex cuffs and suffocated them by placing plastic bags over their heads and securing the bags with tape. He then doused the bodies and house with gasoline and ignited a fire in an effort to cover his crime. An accomplice, Jared Lee Althaus, later confessed and led police to Coulson.

Received at death row: August 31, 1994. *Time on death row:* 2,855 days (7.82 years).

Last meal: Declined last meal.

Last statement: "I'm innocent. I had nothing to do with my family's murders. I want to thank everyone who has supported me. I hope they continue to fight. You know who you are. That's all. Thank you, Warden."

Pronounced dead: 6:23 P.M.

274

Jeffrey Lynn Williams

Executed: June 26, 2002

Personal data: *Born:* October 15, 1971. *Race:* Black. *Height:* 5'9". *Weight:* 191 pounds. *Education:* 9 years. *Prior occupation:* Cook. *County of conviction:* Harris. *Age at time of execution:* 30.

Sentenced to death for: Convicted in the October 1994 rape and strangulation of Barbara Jackson Pullins inside her Houston apartment. Williams forced his way in to Pullins's apartment at knifepoint, forced her to disrobe, and raped her. He then tried to suffocate her by placing a plastic bag over her head. When that failed, he strangled her with a telephone cord. After burning her body with a cigarette to make sure she was dead, Williams attempted to set her body afire by igniting a roll of paper towels. He then moved to a bedroom, where he found the victim's 9-year-old daughter. She was raped and beaten but survived to identify Williams. Williams took several items from the apartment and drove off in Pullins's car.

Received at death row: n/a.

Last meal: Six pieces of fried chicken, french fries, six rolls, tin roof ice cream, strawberry soda, and chocolate cake.

Last statement: "The Lord is my shepherd, I shall not want. He maketh me lie down in green pastures; He leadeth me beside the still waters; He restoreth my soul. He leadeth me in the paths of righteousness for His name's sake. Yea, though I walk through the valley of the shadow of death, I will fear no evil; for Thou art with me. Thy rod and Thy staff, they comfort me. Thou preparest a table before me, in the presence of mine enemies. He anointeth my head with oil; my cup runneth over. Surely goodness and mercy shall follow me all the days of my life, and I will dwell in the House of the Lord forever. Amen. Amen."

Pronounced dead: 6:17 P.M.

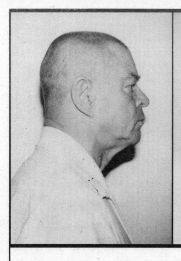

275

Richard William Kutzner

Executed: August 7, 2002

Personal data: *Born:* November 17, 1942. *Race:* White. *Height:* 5'9". *Weight:* 180 pounds. *Education:* 12 years. *Prior occupation:* Gardener. *County of conviction:* Harris. *Age at time of execution:* 59.

Sentenced to death for: Convicted in the January 1996 robbery and murder of Houston businesswoman Reta Sheron Van Huss. Kutzner went to Huss's place of business and strangled her with a plastic tie wrap after binding her feet and wrists with the same plastic material. He fled after stealing money and two money orders from the business. One of the money orders was later traced back to Kutzner.

Received at death row: April 29, 1997. *Time on death row:* 1,926 days (5.28 years).

Last meal: Declined last meal.

Last statement: "Well, yes, sir. Rebecca, I understand that you wanted this day to come; you got what you wanted. I didn't kill your mother. The two guys that worked for me killed your mother and they are still out there. If Mr. McDougal had allowed the DNA evidence, I would be exonerated. Mr. Tolson, I understand you are out there. If there is any justice in this world, please use this to keep other people from being where I'm at. Warden, this is murder just as surely as the people that killed Rebecca's mother. Send me home."

Pronounced dead: 6:33 P.M.

276

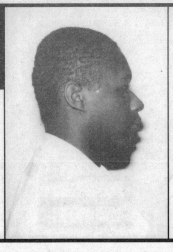

T. J. Jones

Executed:
August 8, 2002

Personal data: *Born:* November 1, 1976. *Race:* Black. *Height:* n/a. *Weight:* n/a. *Education:* 8 years. *Prior occupation:* Fast-food cook. *County of conviction:* Gregg. *Age at time of execution:* 25.

Sentenced to death for: Convicted in the February 1994 robbery and murder of 75-year-old Willard Lewis Davis of Longview. Jones and three accomplices pulled Davis from his vehicle as he was backing out of the driveway of his home in order to rob him. When Davis resisted, Jones shot him once in the head with a .357 Magnum pistol. Leaving his body in the roadway, the four men fled in Davis's vehicle. They were arrested a short time later, after wrecking the car. All gave written confessions to police.

Received at death row: December 16, 1994. *Time on death row:* 2,792 days (7.65 years).

Last meal: A triple-meat cheeseburger with everything (bun fried), french fries with ketchup, four pieces of chicken (two legs, two thighs), and a fried pork chop sandwich.

Last statement: "I would like to say to the family, I regret the pain I've put you through and I hope you can get over it someday. Mom and Dad, I love you. Take care. I'm ready."

Pronounced dead: 6:18 P.M.

277

Javier Suarez Medina

Executed: August 14, 2002

Personal data: *Born:* June 17, 1969. *Race:* Hispanic. *Height:* 5'7". *Weight:* 121 pounds. *Education:* 10 years. *Prior occupation:* Food service worker. *County of conviction:* Dallas. *Age at time of execution:* 33.

Sentenced to death for: Convicted in the December 1988 robbery and slaying of 43-year-old Lawrence Cadena, a Dallas narcotics officer. Cadena, a seventeen-year veteran of the Dallas Police Department, had arranged to meet Medina, his accomplice, Fernando Fernandez, 17, and three unnamed suspects in the parking lot of a Stop N Go store to make a drug purchase as part of an undercover investigation. After Medina had given a bag of cocaine to Cadena, he opened the passenger door of the car and shot the officer seven times. After Cadena was shot, Fernandez allegedly attempted to rob the officer of the cocaine and his money. Both Medina and Fernandez were shot by an assisting officer and arrested at the scene.

Received at death row: July 27, 1989. *Time on death row:* 4,766 days (13.06 years).

Last meal: Declined last meal.

Last statement: See Appendix.

Pronounced dead: 6:23 P.M.

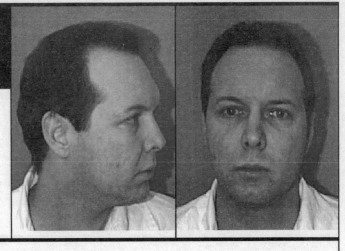

278

Gary Wayne Etheridge

Executed: August 20, 2002

Personal data: *Born:* January 3, 1964. *Race:* White. *Height:* 5'10". *Weight:* 165 pounds. *Education:* 9 years (GED). *Prior occupation:* Maintenance worker. *County of conviction:* Brazoria. *Age at time of execution:* 38.

Sentenced to death for: Convicted in the February 1990 murder of 15-year-old Christi Chauvierre. Chauvierre was sexually abused and stabbed to death when Etheridge went to her Brazoria County home looking for money to buy drugs. The victim's mother, Gail Chauvierre, was also stabbed numerous times in the attack, but she survived. Etheridge had once worked for Gail Chauvierre, who managed a condominium complex near Surfside.

Received at death row: November 9, 1990. *Time on death row:* 4,302 days (11.79 years).

Last meal: Nachos with cheese and peppers, crispy french fries, a cheeseburger, a fried chicken patty, a cinnamon roll, cheese, ketchup, and pickles (on the side).

Last statement: "Yes, sir. To the victim's family, I'm sorry for what was taken from you. I hope you find peace. To my sweet Claudia, I love you. Stay strong, keep building, and be careful. Be careful. I love you. I'm through."

Pronounced dead: 6:22 P.M.

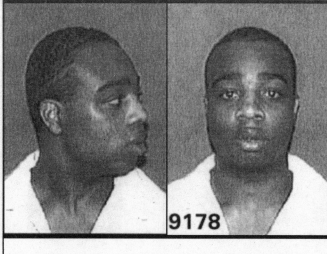

279

Toronto Markkey Patterson

Executed: August 28, 2002

Personal data: *Born:* October 17, 1977. *Race:* Black. *Height:* 6'2". *Weight:* 174 pounds. *Education:* 10 years. *Prior occupation:* Laborer. *County of conviction:* Dallas. *Age at time of execution:* 24.

Sentenced to death for: Convicted in the June 1995 shooting death of 3-year-old Ollie Brown at her home in Dallas. The young girl was shot and killed along with her mother, Kimberly Brewer, and 6-year-old sister, Jennifer Brewer, inside their home. All were shot with a 9mm pistol. Before fleeing, Patterson stole three wheel rims valued at $2,000 from Kimberly Brewer's car. He was arrested the following day and gave a written confession to police.

Received at death row: January 11, 1996. *Time on death row:* 2,421 days (6.63 years).

Last meal: Six pieces of fried chicken, four jalapeño peppers, four buttered buttermilk biscuits, chef salad with bacon bits, black olives, ham, and Italian dressing, six Sprites, and white cake with white icing.

Last statement: "I am sorry for the pain, sorry for what I caused my friends, family, and loved ones. I feel a great deal of responsibility and guilt for all this crime. I should be punished for the crime, but I do not think I should die for a crime I did not commit. I am sorry, but nothing can bring Kim, Ollie, and Gigi back. But I pray my death brings peace for my family that may unite the family. I ask for your forgiveness and that you will all forgive me. I have no animosity; I am at peace and invite you all to my funeral. We are still family. I love you all, Mama, Aunt Deidra, family, and everybody. I love you. I am ready, Warden."

Pronounced dead: 6:20 P.M.

280

Tony Lee Walker

Executed: September 10, 2002

Personal data: *Born:* April 15, 1966. *Race:* Black. *Height:* 5'9". *Weight:* 235 pounds. *Education:* 9 years. *Prior occupation:* Welder. *County of conviction:* Morris. *Age at time of execution:* 36.

Sentenced to death for: Convicted in the May 1992 beating deaths of 82-year-old Willie Simmons and his wife, Virginia Simmons, 66, inside their Dangerfield home. Walker told police he had been smoking crack cocaine the night of the killings and went to the Simmons home to rob the couple so he could buy more cocaine. Allowed inside by Mrs. Simmons, Walker, an acquaintance of the couple, pulled a club from the back of his pants and beat them to death. Virginia Simmons was also raped. Walker fled with Mr. Simmons's wallet, which contained $95. He was arrested when his bloodstained clothes were found in the woods behind his house.

Received at death row: November 19, 1993. *Time on death row:* 3,217 days (8.81 years).

Last meal: French fries, fives pieces of fried chicken, and three Dr Peppers.

Last statement: "I would like to say good-bye to a good friend of mine in Switzerland, Diego. I appreciate all the help and support he gave me through the years. A friend of mine in England, Wildflower: I love you and will never forget you. And to my family. That's all." [*Written*] "I wish to tell the family how sorry I am about what I done. I know that nothing I say will bring Mr. and Mr. Bo Simmons back. I ask that if Linda and Gary and their family can find it in their hearts to forgive me, but if not, I will understand. I am truly sorry."

Pronounced dead: 6:16 P.M.

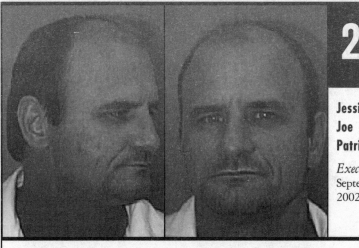

281

**Jessie
Joe
Patrick**

Executed:
September 17,
2002

Personal data: *Born:* February 23, 1958. *Race:* White. *Height:* 5'11". *Weight:* 154 pounds. *Education:* 10 years (GED). *Prior occupation:* Landscaper. *County of conviction:* Dallas. *Age at time of execution:* 44.

Sentenced to death for: Convicted in the July 1989 murder of 80-year-old Nina Rutherford Redd. Redd was killed inside her home in Dallas. She had been sexually assaulted before her throat was cut with a knife. Patrick was a neighbor of Redd's. He broke in to Redd's home through a bathroom window and ransacked the home following the killing. A blood-soaked sock was later found at Patrick's residence. The weave of the sock matched a blood impression at the scene.

Received at death row: June 14, 1990. *Time on death row:* 4,478 days (12.27 years).

Last meal: Declined last meal.

Last statement: None.

Pronounced dead: 6:17 P.M.

282

Ron Scott Shamburger

Executed: September 18, 2002

Personal data: *Born:* November 11, 1971. *Race:* White. *Height:* 5'9". *Weight:* 173 pounds. *Education:* 16 years. *Prior occupation:* Cashier/laborer. *County of conviction:* Brazos. *Age at time of execution:* 30.

Sentenced to death for: Convicted in the September 1994 shooting death of Lori A. Baker, 20, during the burglary of her home in College Station. Shamburger, a senior medical student at Texas A&M, who knew the victim from school, entered Baker's house in an attempt to steal money. He shot Baker in the head with a 9mm pistol when she awoke to find him in her bedroom. Shamburger then kidnapped Baker's roommate Victoria Kohlar when she returned home by placing her in the trunk of a car after binding her hands with duct tape. Shamburger drove only a few blocks from the house before abandoning Kohlar in the unlocked trunk. Shamburger returned to the home and, after probing Baker's head wound with a knife in an effort to retrieve the bullet, poured gasoline on her body and set it afire. Shamburger later walked into the College Station Police Station and surrendered, emptying the bullets from his pistol onto the floor.

Received at death row: October 31, 1995. *Time on death row:* 2,514 days (6.89 years).

Last meal: Nachos with chili and cheese; a bowl of sliced jalapeño peppers; a bowl of picante sauce; two large onions, sliced and grilled; tacos with fresh tomatoes, lettuce, and cheese, and toasted corn tortilla shells.

Last statement: See Appendix.

Pronounced dead: 6:17 P.M.

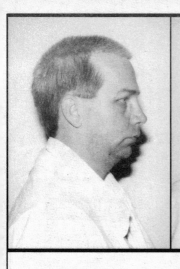

283

Rex Warren Mays

Executed: September 24, 2002

Personal data: *Born:* January 21, 1960. *Race:* White. *Height:* 5'7". *Weight:* 176 pounds. *Education:* n/a. *Prior occupation:* n/a. *County of conviction:* Harris. *Age at time of execution:* 42.

Sentenced to death for: Convicted in the July 1992 stabbing deaths of Kynara Lorin Carreiro and her playmate Kristin Michelle Wiley inside Wiley's Houston home. The girls, ages 7 and 10, were alone in the home when Mays, a neighbor of the Wileys, entered and attacked them with a knife. Both girls were stabbed numerous times in the neck and face. Following the deadly assault, Mays returned home, changed clothes, and met sheriff deputies as a concerned neighbor when they arrived to investigate the murders. Mays ultimately gave authorities a written confession, noting that he was distraught over having lost his job the same day of the killing.

Received at death row: November 17, 1995. *Time on death row:* 2,503 days (6.86 years).

Last meal: Six scrambled eggs with shredded cheese, gravy (cream), hash browns, pan sausage, orange juice, and milk.

Last statement: See Appendix.

Pronounced dead: 6:19 P.M.

284

Calvin Eugene King

Executed: September 25, 2002

Personal data: *Born:* October 31, 1953. *Race:* Black. *Height:* 6'2". *Weight:* 200 pounds. *Education:* 9 years. *Prior occupation:* Landscaper. *County of conviction:* Jefferson. *Age at time of execution:* 48.

Sentenced to death for: Convicted in the February 1994 stabbing death of Billy Wayne Ezell in Beaumont. Records indicate that Ezell was lured to the Cedar Sands Motel in connection with a drug deal. King stabbed Ezell to death with a knife and robbed him of an unspecified amount of cash.

Received at death row: June 28, 1995. *Time on death row:* 2,646 days (7.25 years).

Last meal: Half a fried chicken cooked in garlic powder, red pepper, french fries, a Dr Pepper, and hot sauce.

Last statement: "I want to say God forgives as I forgive. God is the greatest. Thank you."

Pronounced dead: 6:20 P.M.

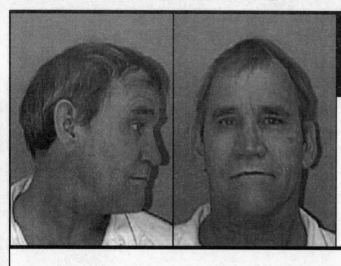

285

James Rexford Powell

Executed: October 1, 2002

Personal data: *Born:* August 23, 1946. *Race:* White. *Height:* 5'8". *Weight:* 160 pounds. *Education:* n/a. *Prior occupation:* Electrician. *County of conviction:* Newton. *Age at time of execution:* 56.

Sentenced to death for: Convicted in the October 1990 abduction and murder of 10-year-old Falyssa Van Winkle. Van Winkle was abducted from Larry's Antique Mall in Beaumont and driven to an area near Orange, where she was sexually assaulted and then strangled with a piece of rope. Powell's vehicle was spotted in the area during the offense, and he was arrested for the murder on October 11, 1990.

Received at death row: June 10, 1991. *Time on death row:* 4,131 days (11.32 years).

Last meal: A pot of coffee.

Last statement: "I am ready for the final blessing."

Pronounced dead: 6:17 P.M.

286

Craig Neil Ogan

Executed:
November 19, 2002

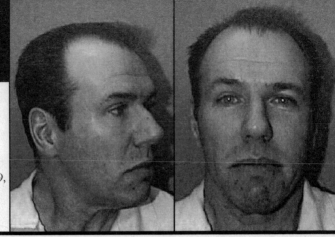

Personal data: *Born:* December 18, 1954. *Race:* White. *Height:* 5'10". *Weight:* 190 pounds. *Education:* 15 years. *Prior occupation:* Informant/laborer. *County of conviction:* Harris. Age at time of execution: 47.

Sentenced to death for: Convicted in the December 1989 murder of Houston police officer James C. Boswell. Officer Boswell and his partner were working a minor traffic violation on South Main Street across from the Astromotor Inn when Ogan approached the officers and demanded their attention. Ogan said he was an informant for the Drug Enforcement Agency and needed their help. Boswell told Ogan they would help him as soon as they finished with the traffic violator. Ogan, however, demanded immediate attention. Relenting due to Ogan's persistence, Boswell began to unlock the rear door of the patrol car. As he did, Ogan shot the officer once in the left temple. Ogan attempted to flee on foot but was shot once in the lower back by Boswell's partner. At the time of his arrest, Ogan, who had worked as a DEA informant since January 1988, had a sawed-off shotgun, two pistols, and several knives in his apartment. He also had a human target on the walls with numerous bullet holes in the head.

Received at death row: July 11, 1990. *Time on death row:* 4,514 days (12.37 years).

Last meal: Declined last meal.

Last statement: See Appendix.

Pronounced dead: 6:20 P.M.

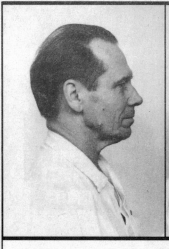

287

William Wesley Chappell

Executed: November 20, 2002

Personal data: *Born:* September 26, 1936. *Race:* White. *Height:* 5'8". *Weight:* 148 pounds. *Education:* 11 years (GED). *Prior occupation:* Analyst engineer. *County of conviction:* Tarrant. *Age at time of execution:* 66.

Sentenced to death for: Convicted in the May 1988 retaliation killing of Martha Lindsay, 50, and her daughter, Alexandra Heath, in Fort Worth. Lindsey and Heath were the grandmother and aunt of a 3-year-old girl Chappell was charged with molesting in 1984. He was convicted of the offense in 1987, and while the case was on appeal, he killed Lindsey and Heath, allegedly to remove them as witnesses. Both victims were shot in the face with a 9mm pistol. Also shot was the victim's grandfather, Elbert Sitton, 71. Although wounded six times, Sitton survived to give police a description of the assailant, who entered his home wearing dark clothes and a ski mask. Chappell had allegedly attempted to burn the victim's house down in January 1988 and had threatened to have his former wife killed for testifying against him.

Received at death row: January 23, 1990. *Time on death row:* 4,684 days (12.83 years).

Last meal: "Whatever is served in the main chow hall."

Last statement: See Appendix.

Pronounced dead: 6:17 P.M.

288

Leonard Uresti Rojas

Executed:
December 4, 2002

TEXAS
999194
JUN. 96

Personal data: *Born:* June 16, 1950. *Race:* Hispanic. *Height:* 5'10". *Weight:* 190 pounds. *Education:* 11 years. *Prior occupation:* Carpenter. *County of conviction:* Johnson. *Age at time of execution:* 52.

Sentenced to death for: Convicted in the shooting deaths of his 34-year-old common-law wife, JoAnn Reed, and his 43-year-old brother, David Rojas, in Alvarado. Rojas shot Reed between the eyes with a .32 caliber revolver after she told him she wanted to move out of their mobile home because she had found a new boyfriend. He then walked to the bathroom and called out to his brother, who was shot three times in the chest when he opened the door. Returning to the bedroom where he had shot Reed, Rojas tied a plastic bag around her head when he found she was still breathing. She then suffocated. Rojas turned himself in to Dallas County authorities the following day.

Received at death row: June 7, 1996. *Time on death row:* 2,371 days (6.50 years).

Last meal: A whole fried chicken (extra crispy), salad with thousand island dressing, French toast, two Diet Cokes, one apple pie, and french fries.

Last statement: None.

Pronounced dead: 6:17 P.M.

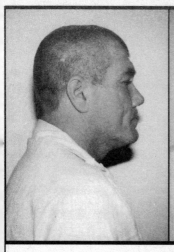

289

**James
Paul
Collier**

Executed:
December 11,
2002

Personal data: *Born:* January 7, 1947. *Race:* White. *Height:* 5'11". *Weight:* 170 pounds. *Education:* 7 years. *Prior occupation:* Carpenter. *County of conviction:* Wichita. *Age at time of execution:* 55.

Sentenced to death for: Convicted in the March 1995 shooting deaths of Gwendolyn Joy Reed, 51, and Timmy Reed, 32. Both victims were shot repeatedly with a .30-30 rifle inside a residence in Wichita Falls. Nine days following the shootings, Collier fled to New Mexico, where he was arrested. He reportedly went to the residence to kidnap or murder his 12-year-old daughter.

Received at death row: May 3, 1996. *Time on death row:* 2,413 days (6.61 years).

Last meal: Ten jumbo shrimp with cocktail sauce, baked potato, french fries, ketchup, butter, T-bone steak, a chocolate malt, one gallon of vanilla ice cream, and three cans of Big Red.

Last statement: "The only thing I want to say is that I appreciate the hospitality that you guys have shown me and the respect; and the last meal was really good. That is about it. Thank you guys for being there and giving me a little bit of spiritual guidance and support."

Pronounced dead: 6:15 P.M.

290

Samuel Clark Gallamore

Executed: January 14, 2003

Personal data: *Born:* February 15, 1971. *Race:* White. *Height:* 6'2". *Weight:* 165 pounds. *Education:* 8 years. *Prior occupation:* Sculptor. *County of conviction:* Comal (change of venue from Kerr). *Age at time of execution:* 31.

Sentenced to death for: Convicted in the March 1992 murders of Clayton Kenney, 83; his wife, Juliana, 74; and Mrs. Kenney's daughter, Adrienne Arnot, 44, at their country home east of Kerrville. The victims were all beaten and stabbed after Gallamore and accomplice James John Steiner forced their way inside. After killing the occupants, the intruders fled with cash and several valuables, including silver servings, a rare spoon collection, and brass and porcelain figurines. Gallamore confessed that he and Steiner had been shooting crack cocaine and decided to rob the Kenneys for more dope. Steiner had once cared for Mrs. Kenney at an area nursing home.

Received at death row: February 14, 1994. *Time on death row:* 3,256 days (8.92 years).

Last meal: Declined last meal.

Last statement: [Written] "There are many things I would like to say, but none more important than how I feel toward Mr. and Mrs. Kenney, and Ms. Arnott. I would like to apologize and say I'm sorry but words seem so hollow and cheap. Their death should not have happened, but it did. I'm so sorry that all of this took place. Now I have devastated my family as well, but my heart has grown in the last few minutes because I was forgiven by the family of Mr. and Mrs. Kenney, and Ms. Arnott. Thank You. You have given me more hope than I have had in a long time. If I could change things I would, not for my sake but for all those who have loved me over the years, and for those who have forgiven me. Thank you for all that you have given me."

Pronounced dead: 6:14 P.M.

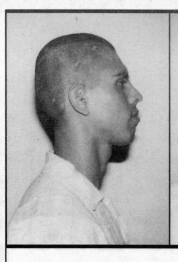

291

John
Richard
Baltazar

Executed:
January 15,
2003

Personal data: *Born:* May 9, 1972. *Race:* Hispanic. *Height:* 5'11". *Weight:* 155 pounds. *Education:* 9 years. *Prior occupation:* Laborer. *County of conviction:* Nueces. *Age at time of execution:* 30.

Sentenced to death for: On September 17, 1997, Baltazar and one codefendant kicked in the front door of a Corpus Christi home and began shooting. A 5-year-old Hispanic female was struck and killed by two bullets. Another female and a male in the residence were struck by bullets but survived the wounds.

Received at death row: March 13, 1998. *Time on death row:* 1,769 days (4.85 years).

Last meal: Cool Whip and cherries.

Last statement: None.

Pronounced dead: 6:16 P.M.

292

Robert Andrew Lookingbill

Executed: January 22, 2003

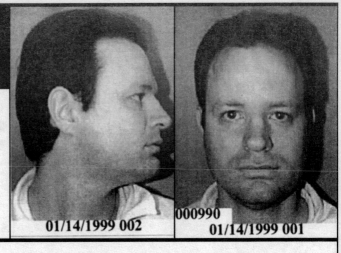

01/14/1999 002

000990
01/14/1999 001

Personal data: *Born:* July 22, 1965. *Race:* White. *Height:* 5'11". *Weight:* 165 pounds. *Education:* 11 years. *Prior occupation:* Construction worker. *County of conviction:* Hidalgo. *Age at time of execution:* 37.

Sentenced to death for: Convicted in the December 1989 beating death of his 70-year-old grandmother, Adeline Waunita Dannenberg, of San Juan, Texas. Lookingbill was living with his grandmother and grandfather, 77-year-old Lorenz K. Dannenberg, at their home when he beat them with a metal bar weighing more than twenty pounds. Following the attack, Lookingbill stole $568 from his grandmother's purse. She died at a hospital ten days later from head injuries. Mr. Dannenberg survived the attack but suffered brain damage. Lookingbill confessed after blood was found on his shoes and pants. He said he wanted to take his grandparents' money so he could buy cocaine.

Received at death row: February 21, 1991. *Time on death row:* 4,353 days (11.93 years).

Last meal: Fried chicken, french fries, iced tea, apple pie, jalapeño peppers, garlic bread, and vanilla ice cream.

Last statement: "I would like to thank all my loved ones that are standing over there for all the kindness and support you have shown me over the years. Be strong. Do not hate, but learn from this experience. Just because it happens, do not think that God doesn't care. He will be with you. I will be there with all of you. I love you all and appreciate all of you. You won't be forgotten and there are a lot of people out there that love you. It has been a blessing to know all of you. This is not easy for any of us. Don't be upset about my situation, because I am not. I am still faithful and I am still strong. Just give my love to everyone out there. Don't forget me and burn a candle for me when you can. I love you all."

Pronounced dead: 6:18 P.M.

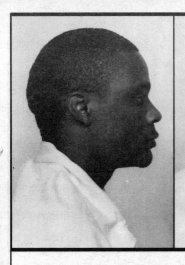

Alva Curry

Executed: January 28, 2003

TEXAS

999080

Personal data: *Born:* March 22, 1969. *Race:* Black. *Height:* 5'7". *Weight:* 152 pounds. *Education:* 9 years. *Prior occupation:* Laborer. *County of conviction:* Travis. *Age at time of execution:* 33.

Sentenced to death for: Convicted in the October 1991 robbery and murder of David Vela, a clerk at a Texaco convenience store in Austin. Vela, 20, was shot five times, execution-style, after Curry and accomplice Mark Davis broke the store window and demanded money at gunpoint. Police arrested the two after viewing a videotape of the incident captured by a hidden camera. Curry was also convicted of killing Brendon Proske, 23, a clerk at a Payless convenience store in Austin, one week after the Vela murder. Mark Davis received a life sentence.

Received at death row: November 3, 1993. *Time on death row:* 3,373 days (9.24 years).

Last meal: Chicken-fried steak with country gravy, hot buttered corn, mashed potatoes with country gravy, hot buttered rolls, hot apple pie, a bowl of vanilla ice cream, and tea.

Last statement: "I pray with the help of God that you will forgive me for the pain I caused your family. I am truly sorry. I wish I could take it back, but I just pray and ask that you forgive me."

Pronounced dead: 8:09 P.M.

294

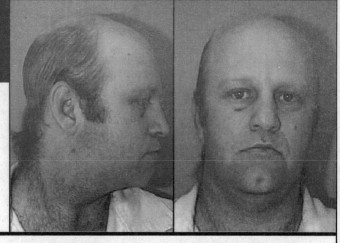

Richard Eugene Dinkins

Executed:
January 29, 2003

Personal data: *Born:* September 29, 1962. *Race:* White. *Height:* 5'6". *Weight:* 126 pounds. *Education:* 12 years. *Prior occupation:* Machinist. *County of conviction:* Jefferson. *Age at time of execution:* 40.

Sentenced to death for: Convicted in the September 1990 murders of two women inside a Beaumont business. Killed were Katherine Thompson, the 46-year-old owner of Therapeutic Massage, and customer Shelly Cutler, 32. Dinkins shot both women in the head with a .357 Magnum pistol following an argument he had with Thompson concerning bad checks he had written to the business. Thompson, who also suffered a chest wound, died at a hospital shortly after the shooting. Cutler, a registered nurse, died the next morning. Dinkins's name was found in an appointment book at the business. He confessed to the murder after police found blood on his pants and the murder weapon in his truck.

Received at death row: February 26, 1992. *Time on death row:* 3,990 days (10.93 years).

Last meal: Liver and onions, two double-meat hamburgers with bacon and mayonnaise, two orders of french fries, vanilla ice cream, two Dr Peppers, salad with ranch dressing, and M&M's.

Last statement: [Written] "To the families of Ms. Thompson and Ms. Cutler. I am sorry for what happened and that it was because of me that they are gone. If there were any way I could change things and bring them back I would. But I can't. Because of what I caused to happen many people were affected and I am very sorry that I did. I have made my peace with God and I pray that soon everyone will be able to have closure in their hearts and lives. To my family and friends, I love you and someday we will all be together again."

Pronounced dead: 6:18 P.M.

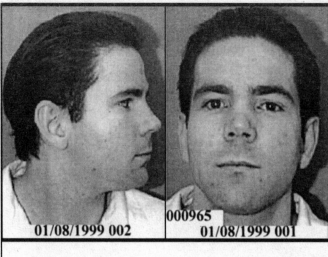

295

Granville Riddle

Executed: January 30, 2003

01/08/1999 002

000965 01/08/1999 001

Personal data: *Born:* June 17, 1969. *Race:* White. *Height:* 5'8". *Weight:* 166 pounds. *Education:* 8 years. *Prior occupation:* Electrician's helper. *County of conviction:* Potter. *Age at time of execution:* 33.

Sentenced to death for: Convicted in the October 1988 murder of 39-year-old Ronnie Hood Bennett of Amarillo. Riddle broke in to Bennett's home and beat the victim to death with a tire tool. Bennett's wallet and pickup truck were stolen from the residence. The pickup was found burned the next day in a ravine outside Borger. Riddle was arrested five days after the murder, following a statement to police from the man who drove Riddle to Bennett's residence. The man, 18, was initially charged with murder in the case. Those charges were apparently dropped. Riddle escaped from the Potter County Jail February 24, 1989, and was recaptured twenty miles north of Amarillo three days later.

Received at death row: February 21, 1990. *Time on death row:* 4,726 days (12.95 years).

Last meal: Steak, baked potato, cherry cheesecake, salad with blue cheese dressing, rolls, Coke, coffee, strawberries, and oranges.

Last statement: "I would just . . . [speaking in French] I love all of you. I love you Lundy, Levi, my dad. I have no grudges against anyone, or any of the things that have gone wrong. I would like to say to the world, I have always been a nice person. I have never been mean-hearted or cruel. I wish everybody well."

Pronounced dead: 6:17 P.M.

296

John William Elliott

Executed: February 4, 2003

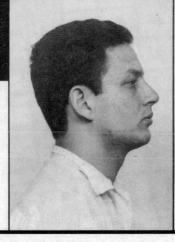

Personal data: *Born:* March 25, 1960. *Race:* Hispanic. *Height:* 5'11". *Weight:* 160 pounds. *Education:* 9 years (GED). *Prior occupation:* Carpenter. *County of conviction:* Travis. *Age at time of execution:* 42.

Sentenced to death for: Convicted in the June 1986 rape-beating death of 19-year-old Joyce Munguia in East Austin. Police said Munguia was raped and then beaten to death with a motorcycle chain under an overpass in East Austin. An autopsy showed that Munguia was hit sixteen times in the head and eight times on the face with the chrome-plated chain.
Codefendants: Ricky Elizondo pleaded guilty to sexual assault and was sentenced to ten years in prison. Pete Ramirez was convicted of sexual assault and given a fifteen-year sentence.

Received at death row: January 20, 1987. *Time on death row:* 5,859 days (16.05 years).

Last meal: One cup of hot tea (from tea bags) and six chocolate chip cookies.

Last statement: None.

Pronounced dead: 7:09 P.M.

297

Henry Earl Dunn Jr.

Executed: February 6, 2003

Personal data: *Born:* July 29, 1974. *Race:* Black. *Height:* 5'7". *Weight:* 145 pounds. *Education:* 10 years. *Prior occupation:* Cook/janitor. *County of conviction:* Smith. *Age at time of execution:* 28.

Sentenced to death for: Convicted in the November 1993 abduction and murder of 23-year-old Nicholus West. Dunn and two codefendants abducted West from Bergfeld Park in Tyler and drove him to an area known as Clay Hill. After making him strip, Dunn and his accomplices took West's money and wallet and marched him to an area where he was shot repeatedly with .357 caliber pistols. An autopsy revealed that West, a medical records clerk, suffered nine to fifteen bullet wounds.
Codefendant: Donald Aldrich was convicted of capital murder and executed on October 12, 2004 (see entry 329, Donald Loren Aldrich). David Ray McMillan received a life sentence for aggravated robbery and aggravated kidnapping.

Received at death row: October 11, 1995. *Time on death row:* 2,675 days (7.33 years).

Last meal: A cheeseburger with extra cheese, pickles, onion, lettuce, and salad dressing, a tray of french fries, a bottle of ketchup, twenty-five breaded fried shrimp, four cans of pineapple juice, two banana splits, a bottle of Hershey's syrup, and a jar of apple butter jam.

Last statement: See Appendix.

Pronounced dead: 6:15 P.M.

298

Richard Head Williams

Executed: February 25, 2003

Personal data: *Born:* July 19, 1969. *Race:* Black. *Height:* 6'0". *Weight:* 208 pounds. *Education:* 10 years. *Prior occupation:* Laborer. *County of conviction:* Harris. *Age at time of execution:* 33.

Sentenced to death for: On March 24, 2001, Williams carried out a contract killing of a 44-year-old black female in Houston's Third Ward. The victim was stabbed repeatedly in the chest and throat with an eight-inch steak knife; her body was left in the middle of the street. Bruce and Michelle Gilmore reportedly paid Williams $400 to commit the murder. In all, Williams was to receive $12,000 from the two accomplices.

Received at death row: January 7, 1998. *Time on death row:* 1,875 days (5.14 years).

Last meal: Two chili cheese dogs, two cheeseburgers, two orders of onion rings with French dressing, turkey salad, french fries, chocolate cake, apple pie, butter pecan ice cream, egg rolls, a peach, three Dr Peppers, jalapeño peppers, ketchup, and mayonnaise.

Last statement: See Appendix.

Pronounced dead: 6:19 P.M.

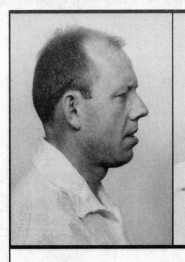

299

Bobby Glen Cook

Executed: March 11, 2003

Personal data: *Born:* December 3, 1961. *Race:* White. *Height:* 5'6". *Weight:* 148 pounds. *Education:* 9 years. *Prior occupation:* n/a. *County of conviction:* Anderson. *Age at time of execution:* 41.

Sentenced to death for: Convicted in the February 1993 robbery and murder of 42-year-old Edwin Earl Holder of Buffalo, Texas. Holder was reported missing when he failed to return from a fishing trip on the Trinity River. His body was found inside a sleeping bag in the bed of his pickup, which was partially submerged in the river. He had been shot six times in the head while camping overnight near the river. Cook and two codefendants sank Holder's boat and stole his outboard motor and two lanterns. Cook also took Holder's wallet, which contained about $25. No information is available concerning the codefendants.

Received at death row: April 26, 1994. *Time on death row:* 3,241 days (8.88 years).

Last meal: A double-meat cheeseburger, jalapeño peppers and trimmings on the side, a vanilla malt, french fries, onion rings, ketchup, picante sauce (hot), vanilla ice cream, two Cokes, two Dr Peppers, and a chicken-fried steak sandwich with cheese, pickles, lettuce, tomatoes, and salad dressing.

Last statement: "I would like to say to the victim's family, if this goes on record, that I know they have gotten grief and I know with this execution, it will not be any relief to them. That with my death, it will just remind them of their loved one, Mr. Holder. I would like to say to them, please forgive me for what happened; it was self defense. . . . And I was never able to get up on the stand to tell them. I know this is wrong. I am going home to the Lord."

Pronounced dead: 6:20 P.M.

300

**Keith
Bernard
Clay**

Executed:
March 20,
2003

Personal data: *Born:* February 18, 1968. *Race:* Black. *Height:* 5'9". *Weight:* 180 pounds. *Education:* 12 years. *Prior occupation:* Laborer. *County of conviction:* Harris. *Age at time of execution:* 35.

Sentenced to death for: On January 4, 1994, Clay murdered a male store clerk during the robbery of a Houston convenience store. The victim was severely beaten and repeatedly shot by Clay.

Received at death row: September 10, 1997. *Time on death row:* 2,017 days (5.53 years).

Last meal: Four pieces of fried chicken, mashed potatoes, two pints of ice cream, a bacon cheeseburger, and two Vanilla Cokes.

Last statement: "I would like to say first and foremost to the Lord God Almighty that I am sorry and forgive me of every single solitary sin I have committed these thirty-five years I have lived upon this earth. To the Varghese family, I would ask that you forgive me because I know you have suffered a great loss and I am truly, truly sorry. I know what you have suffered, but please grant me your forgiveness. I am truly sorry, and there is not a day that I have not prayed for you. And to my Mom, I love you. I am going to see the Lord. The Lord is my shepherd. Let everyone know that I love them; this is not good-bye. I will see you later."

Pronounced dead: 6:23 P.M.

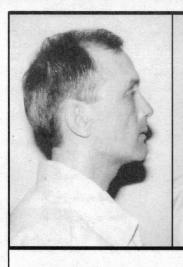

301

James Blake Colburn

Executed: March 26, 2003

Personal data: *Born:* February 19, 1960. *Race:* White. *Height:* 5'6". *Weight:* 141 pounds. *Education:* 9 years. *Prior occupation:* Laborer. *County of conviction:* Montgomery. *Age at time of execution:* 43.

Sentenced to death for: Convicted in the June 1994 murder of 55-year-old Peggy Murphy. Colburn reportedly lured Murphy to his apartment, where he attempted to rape her. When she resisted, Colburn stabbed her several times with a kitchen knife and strangled her. Following the killing, Colburn went to a neighboring apartment and asked its residents to notify the sheriff's department. Arrest records indicate that Colburn told authorities he killed the woman because he wanted to return to prison.

Received at death row: November 1, 1995. *Time on death row:* 2,702 days (7.40 years).

Last meal: Tortillas, tacos, burritos, Spanish rice, cheese dip with chips, six Cokes, and chocolate cake.

Last statement: "The statement that I would like to make is, none of this should have happened and now that I'm dying, there is nothing left to worry about. I know it was a mistake. I have no one to blame but myself. It's no big deal about choosing right from wrong. I pray that everyone involved overlooks the stupidity. Everybody has problems and I won't be a part of the problem anymore. I can quit worrying now; it was all a mistake. That's all I want to say."

Pronounced dead: 6:21 P.M.

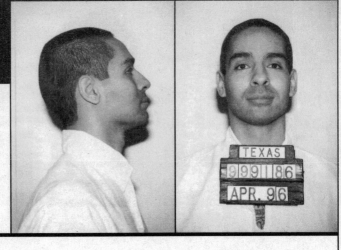

302

John Chavez

Executed:
April 22,
2003

Personal data: *Born:* April 27, 1968. *Race:* Hispanic. *Height:* 5'8". *Weight:* 143 pounds. *Education:* 8 years. *Prior occupation:* Painter. *County of conviction:* Dallas. *Age at time of execution:* 34.

Sentenced to death for: Convicted in the July 1995 robbery and murder of 40-year-old Jose Morales in Dallas. Morales was at a phone booth when Chavez approached him and exchanged words with him. Chavez then pulled a gun and shot Morales in the chest. Before fleeing, Chavez stole Morales's wallet from his pants pocket. Morales died at Parkland Memorial Hospital.

Received at death row: April 11, 1996. *Time on death row:* 2,567 days (7.03 years).

Last meal: Declined last meal.

Last statement: "To the media, I would like for you to tell all the victims and their loved ones that I am truly, truly sorry for taking their loved ones' lives. And I hope they will find it in their heart to forgive me for what I did to them. I am a different person now, but that does not change the fact of the bad things I have committed. God can give you the same peace he gave me and you can be in his hands. And to my beautiful family, be strong. Remember what I said, 'God is the Way, the Truth, and the Life.' OK, Warden."

Pronounced dead: 6:18 P.M.

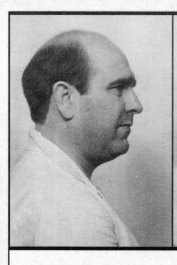

303

Roger Dale Vaughn

Executed: May 6, 2003

Personal data: *Born:* October 11, 1954. *Race:* White. *Height:* 6'1". *Weight:* 243 pounds. *Education:* 10 years (GED). *Prior occupation:* Electrician. *County of conviction:* Wilbarger. *Age at time of execution:* 48.

Sentenced to death for: Convicted in the October 1991 strangulation murder of 66-year-old Dora Leveille Watkins at her home in Vernon. Watkins was sexually assaulted and then strangled with a piece of cloth after Vaughn broke into her residence. Checks and rings were taken from the home, and Vaughn's fingerprints were later found on the woman's wallet. Vaughn was an escapee from the Lubbock County Jail at the time of the murder. He escaped after being charged with forgery and robbery in a separate incident. On the same day of the murder, Vaughn also burglarized the home of his aunt, who lived four blocks from Watkins.

Received at death row: May 28, 1992. *Time on death row:* 3,995 days (10.95 years).

Last meal: Baked potato, a double-meat cheeseburger (with everything), salad, butter pecan ice cream, and a Coke.

Last statement: None. The chaplain read the 103rd Psalm of David.

Pronounced dead: 6:26 P.M.

304

Bruce Charles Jacobs

Executed:
May 15, 2003

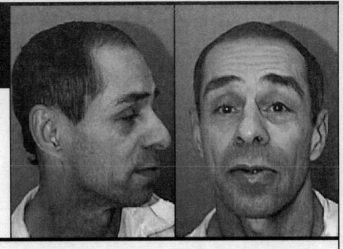

Personal data: *Born:* October 13, 1946. *Race:* White. *Height:* 5'2". *Weight:* 138 pounds. *Education:* 10 years. *Prior occupation:* Laborer. *County of conviction:* Dallas. *Age at time of execution:* 56.

Sentenced to death for: Convicted in the July 1986 stabbing death of 16-year-old Conrad Harris at the teenager's home in Dallas. Harris was stabbed repeatedly in his bedroom after Jacobs broke in to the residence early in the morning. Harris's father and stepmother heard him screaming and found Jacobs standing over the boy with a knife in his hand. Jacobs pointed the knife at the couple and then ran out the back door. Jacobs's fingerprints were found on a butter knife in the house and police found a pair of bloodstained blue jeans at his residence following his arrest. The Harrises reported $100 missing from the home. The victim's step-mother told police that Jacobs came to the house the day before the murder and tried to force his way in through the back door. He ran off after she managed to close it and lock it.

Received at death row: July 20, 1987. *Time on death row:* 5,778 days (15.83 years).

Last meal: A whole fried chicken, twelve buttered bread slices, fried onion rings and okra, a six-pack of RC Cola, a large bag of Fritos, salt and pepper, and two tomatoes.

Last statement: See Appendix.

Pronounced dead: 6:17 P.M.

305

Kia Levoy Johnson

Executed: June 11, 2003

Personal data: *Born:* December 23, 1964. *Race:* Black. *Height:* 6'2". *Weight:* 160 pounds. *Education:* 12 years. *Prior occupation:* Cook. *County of conviction:* Bexar. *Age at time of execution:* 38.

Sentenced to death for: Convicted in the October 1993 robbery and murder of 32-year-old William Matthew Rains, a night manager of a Stop N Go convenience store in San Antonio. Rains was shot in the abdomen with a .32 caliber pistol in a robbery that netted $23 from the store cash register. The robbery and shooting were captured on videotape by a store surveillance camera.

Received at death row: March 14, 1995. *Time on death row:* 3,011 days (8.25 years).

Last meal: Four breasts of fried chicken, one order of onion rings, fried shrimp, one order of french fries, fried catfish, a double-meat cheeseburger with grilled onions, two strawberry fruit juices, and pecan pie.

Last statement: "Tell Mama I love her and tell the kids I love them, too. I'll see you all."

Pronounced dead: 6:18 P.M.

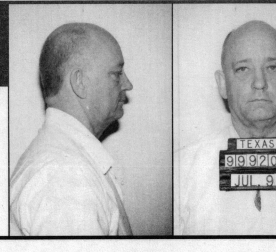

306

Hilton Lewis Crawford

Executed:
July 2, 2003

Personal data: *Born:* March 14, 1939. *Race:* White. *Height:* 5'11". *Weight:* 208 pounds. *Education:* 15 years. *Prior occupation:* Police officer/security guard. *County of conviction:* Montgomery. *Age at time of execution:* 64.

Sentenced to death for: Convicted in the September 1995 abduction and murder of 12-year-old McKay Everett, the son of a family friend, who had affectionately referred to his killer as "Uncle Hilty." Crawford kidnapped the boy from his Conroe home after luring his parents away to a meeting of Amway distributors. Crawford locked the boy in the trunk of his car and drove him to Louisiana. Meanwhile, Crawford's codefendant, Irene Flores, placed a ransom call to Everett's parents, demanding $500,000 for his safe return. Near Whiskey Bay, Louisiana, Crawford drove to a remote area and shot Everett twice with a .45 caliber pistol after striking him on the head with a blunt object. Arrested at his Conroe home three days following the abduction, Crawford admitted kidnapping Everett but would not tell authorities the boy's whereabouts or whether he was still alive. Later, Crawford described the area where Everett's body was found. Crawford claims he concocted the kidnapping to bail himself out of financial difficulties. He said he did not strike Everett but that a man he identified as R. L. Remington actually killed the boy. R. L. Remington's identity has not been verified.

Received at death row: July 25, 1996. *Time on death row:* 2,533 days (6.94 years).

Last meal: Twelve beef ribs, three enchiladas, chicken-fried steak with cream gravy, a crisp bacon sandwich, a bowl of ketchup, a loaf of bread, any kind of cobbler, three Cokes, three root beers, french fries, and onion rings.

Last statement: See Appendix.

Pronounced dead: 6:19 P.M.

307

Christopher Black Sr.

Executed: July 9, 2003

Personal data: *Born:* August 2, 1959. *Race:* Black. *Height:* 6'0". *Weight:* 240 pounds. *Education:* 12 years. *Prior occupation:* n/a. *County of conviction:* Bell. *Age at time of execution:* 43.

Sentenced to death for: Black fatally shot his 36-year-old wife, his 5-month-old daughter, and his 17-month-old granddaughter. He shot and killed all three of the victims with a 9mm pistol. After he shot all three, he called 911; when the officers arrived, he was holding his deceased daughter in his arms.

Received at death row: August 11, 1998. *Time on death row:* 1,793 days (4.91 years).

Last meal: A steak (medium-well), fried chicken (wings and thighs), french fries with mushroom gravy, mixed steamed vegetables, chocolate fudge cake, peach cobbler, sweet tea, bread, and chief [sic] salad with Italian dressing.

Last statement: None.

Pronounced dead: 6:19 P.M.

308

Cedric Lamont Ransom

Executed: July 23, 2003

Personal data: *Born:* August 18, 1973. *Race:* Black. *Height:* 5'8" *Weight:* 160 pounds. *Education:* 9 years. *Prior occupation:* Laborer. *County of conviction:* Tarrant. *Age at time of execution:* 29.

Sentenced to death for: Convicted in the December 1991 robbery and shooting death of 42-year-old Herbert P. Primm Jr., of Arlington. Primm, an optometrist, was shot to death in the driveway of his home after opening the trunk of his car to show three TEC-9 assault pistols to Nathan Clark, an accomplice in the murder. Primm held a federal firearms license and sold guns out of his home. When Primm opened his trunk to show the guns, Clark and three accomplices, including Ransom, pulled weapons and stole Primm's guns. After Primm told the robbers to "just take them," Ransom bent him over the hood of the car and shot him once in the head with a .44 Magnum. He was arrested three days later in connection with a separate murder case in Fort Worth. Cases were pending against the three accomplices.

Received at death row: January 11, 1993. *Time on death row:* 3,845 days (10.53 years).

Last meal: Declined last meal.

Last statement: "I just want to address Katrina and Rebecca. You have been beautiful to me. Without you in my life, I would not have been able to make it like this. Probably, I would have put up a good fight; you have calmed me. I love you. I respect you. Big brother, you put up the best fight you could and I love you. That is it."

Pronounced dead: 6:21 P.M.

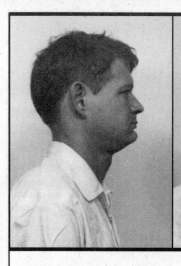

309

Allen Wayne Janecka

Executed: July 24, 2003

Personal data: *Born:* November 3, 1949. *Race:* White. *Height:* 6'0". *Weight:* 165 pounds. *Education:* 12 years. *Prior occupation:* Laborer. *County of conviction:* Harris. *Age at time of execution:* 53.

Sentenced to death for: Convicted in the July 1979 murder-for-hire killing of 14-month-old Kevin Wanstrath at his parents' home in Houston. The infant was shot to death in his crib after his parents, John, 35, and Diana, 36, were slain by Janecka. Janecka was hired to commit the murders by Markum Duff-Smith, Diana Wanstrath's brother. Duff-Smith plotted the killings of his sister and her family to collect their estate. All were shot with a .22 caliber pistol. Janecka was charged with the murders on November 23, 1980. He was also the accused triggerman in the contract killing of Duff-Smith's wealthy adoptive mother, Gertrude Duff-Smith Zabolio, in Houston on October 15, 1975. Her son reportedly had her killed so he could collect his inheritance. Markum Duff-Smith was executed for his involvement in the crime June 29, 1993. (See entry 60, Markum Duff-Smith).

Received at death row: June 8, 1981. *Time on death row:* 8,081 days (22.14 years).

Last meal: Chicken-fried steak with gravy, french fries with ketchup, salad, blue cheese dressing (or what's available), iced tea with lemon, two sodas, and rolls with butter.

Last statement: "First of all, I want to say God bless everyone here today. For many years I have done things my way, which caused a lot of pain to me, my family, and many others. Today I have come to realize that for peace and happiness, one has to do things God's way. I want to thank my family for their support. I love you. I am taking you with me. You all stay strong. I love you. I also want to say thanks to the chaplains who I have met through the years and who have brought me a long way. And I cherish you as my family and at this time . . . oh, Ken, my little son, I am coming to see you. Oh Lord, into your hands I commit my spirit. Thy will be done."

Pronounced dead: 6:21 P.M.

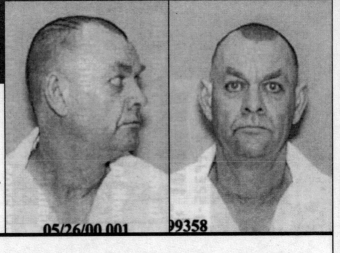

310

Larry Allen Hayes

Executed: September 10, 2003

05/26/00 001   99358

Personal data: *Born:* November 23, 1948. *Race:* White. *Height:* 5'9". *Weight:* 198 pounds. *Education:* 12 years. *Prior occupation:* Laborer. *County of conviction:* Montgomery. *Age at time of execution:* 54.

Sentenced to death for: On July 15, 1999, in Conroe, Hayes fatally shot his wife, 46. He used a .44 caliber pistol to shoot her eight times in the head. He left the scene of the incident and went to a convenience store. There he shot an 18-year-old black female two times in the head and took her car.

Received at death row: May 26, 2000. *Time on death row:* 1,202 days (3.29 years).

Last meal: Two double cheeseburgers, french fries, onion rings, ketchup, coleslaw, two Diet Cokes, a quart of milk, a pint of rocky road ice cream, fried okra, extra salad dressing, tomato, and onion.

Last statement: "I would like for Rosalyn's family and loved ones and my wife, Mary's, family to know that I am genuinely sorry for what I did. I would like you to reach down in your hearts and forgive me. There is no excuse for what I did. Rosalyn's mother asked me at the trial, Why? and I do not have a good reason for it. Please forgive me. As for my friends and family here—thanks for sticking with me and know that I love you and will take part of you with me. I would like to thank one of the arresting officers that I would have killed if I could have. He gave me CPR, saved my life, and gave me a chance to get my life right. I know I will see Mary and Rosalyn tonight. I love you all."

Pronounced dead: 6:29 P.M.
Note: The lethal dose was administered to the right hand, not the right arm.

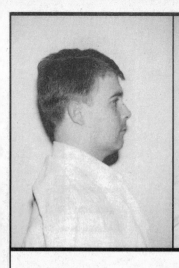 

Robert L. Henry

Executed: November 20, 2003

Personal data: *Born:* September 26, 1962. *Race:* White. *Height:* 5'8". *Weight:* 184 pounds. *Education:* 14 years. *Prior occupation:* Sales/data entry. *County of conviction:* San Patricio. *Age at time of execution:* 41.

Sentenced to death for: Convicted in the September 1993 killing of Carol Lea Arnold, 57, and her 83-year-old mother, Hazel V. Rumohr, at their home in Portland, Texas. Henry, who was known by the victims, told police he repeatedly stabbed each with a knife after smoking marijuana. Their bodies were found inside their residence two days later. Henry later turned himself in to police in Corpus Christi and confessed.

Received at death row: November 15, 1994. *Time on death row:* 3,292 days (9.02 years).

Last meal: Declined last meal.

Last statement: None.

Pronounced dead: 6:19 P.M.

312

Richard Charles Duncan

Executed: December 3, 2003

Personal data: *Born:* May 19, 1942. *Race:* White. *Height:* 6'1". *Weight:* 170 pounds. *Education:* 12 years. *Prior occupation:* Government contractor. *County of conviction:* Harris. *Age at time of execution:* 61.

Sentenced to death for: Convicted in the October 1987 murders of John Abner High, 71, and Ruth Brown High, 73, the parents of his homosexual lover. Mr. High was beaten on the head with a blunt instrument and his wife was smothered. Duncan killed the couple in hopes of getting half their $500,000 estate from their son. After killing the couple, Duncan turned on a portable cooker in the house in an attempt to cause an explosion. The case remained unsolved until a witness came forward after seven years.

Received at death row: July 12, 1995. *Time on death row:* 3,066 days (8.40 years).

Last meal: Fried chicken (three chicken breasts) well done, french fries, lettuce, tomato, berry cobbler, and Coke.

Last statement: "I did have, but now I see my family here and everything—all I want to say is I love you all so much. I am innocent. I love you all so much. You are beautiful. OK Warden, I am through."

Pronounced dead: 6:21 P.M.
Note: The lethal dose was administered to the right hand, not the right arm.

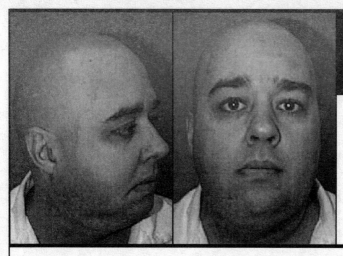

313

Ivan Murphy Jr.

Executed: December 4, 2003

Personal data: *Born:* January 10, 1965. *Race:* White. *Height:* 5'8". *Weight:* 185 pounds. *Education:* 12 years. *Prior occupation:* Mechanic. *County of conviction:* Grayson. *Age at time of execution:* 38.

Sentenced to death for: Convicted in the January 1989 beating death and robbery of 80-year-old Lula Mae Denning in Denison. Denning was beaten to death inside her home by Murphy and an accomplice. Jewelry, including a wedding ring valued at $7,000, was taken from the residence. Murphy's prints were found in the home. He was arrested in Hugo, Oklahoma, on January 20, 1989. *Codefendant:* Douglas Wayne Stoff received life for murder with a deadly weapon.

Received at death row: January 24, 1991. *Time on death row:* 4,697 days (12.87 years).

Last meal: Four pieces of fried white-meat chicken, five pieces of deep-fried fish, four deep-fried pork chops, extra-large order of deep-fried french fries, large order of deep-fried onion rings, ketchup, tartar sauce, one pint Blue Bell Moollennium Crunch ice cream, and two quarts of chocolate milk.

Last statement: "Yes sir, I do. I would like to thank everybody for coming out tonight and celebrating life. This is a celebration of life, not death. Through Jesus Christ, we have victory over death. I would like to thank the Holy Father and Pope John Paul for their angelic blessings and all the prayers and support. And thanks to Father [name unknown] and Guido Todeschini for your love and support. I want to thank everybody around the world and Father, let Your will be done. I am going to keep this statement short. I love you all. I am ready, Warden."

Pronounced dead: 6:24 P.M.
Note: The lethal dose was administered to the hands, not the arms.

314

Ynobe Matthews

Executed: January 6, 2004

Personal data: *Born:* March 14, 1976. *Race:* Black. *Height:* 5'9". *Weight:* 288 pounds. *Education:* 11 years. *Prior occupation:* Cook, carpenter, laborer. *County of conviction:* Brazos. *Age at time of execution:* 27.

Sentenced to death for: On May 28, 2000, in College Station, Matthews kidnapped and sexually assaulted a 21-year-old white female. He then strangled the victim with his hands, killing her. Matthews also set the building on fire before leaving the scene.

Received at death row: June 19, 2001. *Time on death row:* 931 days (2.55 years).

Last meal: Three pieces of fried chicken, a pork chop, two pieces of fried fish, strawberry ice cream, a six-pack of Coke, and a pack of cigarettes (Newport).

Last statement: None.

Pronounced dead: 6:18 P.M.

315

Kenneth Eugene Bruce

Executed: January 14, 2004

Personal data: *Born:* October 21, 1971. *Race:* Black. *Height:* 5'7". *Weight:* 151 pounds. *Education:* 11 years. *Prior occupation:* Delivery man. *County of conviction:* Collin. *Age at time of execution:* 32.

Sentenced to death for: Convicted in the December 1990 robbery and murder of 54-year-old Helen Elizabeth Ayers, of Prosper. Bruce and three accomplices went to Ayers's home complaining of car trouble. Invited inside by Ayers's husband, Robert, 58, the men pulled guns and robbed the couple of money and jewelry. The two were then forced into their bedroom; each was shot twice. Mrs. Ayers died of leg and head wounds. Her husband survived wounds to the back and shoulder.
Codefendants: Eric Lynn Moore received a death sentence for capital murder. Anthony Quinn Bruce received life for capital murder. The third accomplice's disposition is unknown.

Received at death row: February 28, 1992. *Time on death row:* 4,338 days (11.88 years).

Last meal: A double-meat cheeseburger, with lettuce, tomato, mayonnaise, french fries, orange juice, and pecan pie.

Last statement: "Yes sir. I would like to thank God for all the blessings he has given me. And I pray that through His mercy, He will allow me into His grace. And to the family of Ms. Ayers, I would like to apologize for all the pain and suffering and that God gives you closure. And I pray that He blesses you. And to my family, know that I love every single one of you and pray that God gives you peace and strength. I may not be with you in the physical, but by grace, my heart will be with you all and I know God loves every one of you all."

Pronounced dead: 6:29 P.M.

316

Kevin Lee Zimmerman

Executed:
January 21, 2004

Personal data: *Born:* May 17, 1961. *Race:* White. *Height:* 5'10". *Weight:* 135 pounds. *Education:* 6 years. *Prior occupation:* Tankerman. *County of conviction:* Jefferson. *Age at time of execution:* 42.

Sentenced to death for: Convicted in the October 1987 stabbing death of 33-year-old Leslie Gilbert Hooks Jr. at a Beaumont motel. Hooks, a resident of Suisun City, California, was stabbed with a knife inside a room at a Motel 6. His body was found the next morning by a maid. Evidence, including the murder weapon, was later located and linked to Zimmerman. He was arrested on October 28, 1987.

Received at death row: June 19, 1990. *Time on death row:* 4,964 days (13.60 years).

Last meal: A double-meat cheeseburger, with lettuce, tomatoes, onions, salad dressing, ketchup, half a plate of french fries, almost burnt with ketchup, two pints of milk, and chocolate cake with lots of icing.

Last statement: "Yes. Connie, Nanny, Bea, Kathy, and Richard, I love you all and I thank you all very much for supporting me with your love. In the name of Jesus, I am sorry for the pain I caused you all. I am sorry. Gilbert didn't deserve to die and I want you all to know I am sorry. I pray that the good Lord will give you all peace. OK."

Pronounced dead: 6:19 P.M.

317

Billy Frank Vickers

Executed: January 28, 2004

Personal data: *Born:* July 30, 1945. *Race:* White. *Height:* 5'7". *Weight:* 191 pounds. *Education:* 6 years (GED). *Prior occupation:* Car salesman. *County of conviction:* Lamar. *Age at time of execution:* 58.

Sentenced to death for: Convicted in the March 1993 killing of 50-year-old Phillip Kinslow during an attempted robbery outside the victim's Arthur City home. Kinslow, owner of Arthur City Superette, was carrying a money bag inside his truck when he arrived home from work. As he opened his driveway gate, he was shot three times from behind. Although wounded, Kinslow fired back, striking Vickers three times. Kinslow got back into his truck and drove to his home, where he collapsed. He later died at a local hospital.
Codefendants: Tommy Perkins received life for capital murder. Jason Paul Martin received twenty-five years for robbery with threats.

Received at death row: January 4, 1994. *Time on death row:* 3,676 days (10.07 years).

Last meal: Four eggs, an extra onion and cheese omelet, a bowl of chili, four thick slices of fried bologna, four pieces of dry toast, jelly, one chopped onion (stir fry it), four slices of cheese, pan-fried potatoes, bowl of gravy, sliced tomato, hot coffee, black walnut or vanilla ice cream, cigar and light (sub-camels).

Last statement: See Appendix.

Pronounced dead: 6:21 P.M.

318

Edward Lewis Lagrone

Executed: February 11, 2004

Personal data: *Born:* March 3, 1957. *Race:* Black. *Height:* 5'10". *Weight:* 206 pounds. *Education:* 10 years (GED). *Prior occupation:* Cook. *County of conviction:* Tarrant. *Age at time of execution:* 46.

Sentenced to death for: Convicted in connection with the May 1991 shotgun slayings of three people. Killed were Shakiesha Lloyd, 10, Zenobia Anderson, 87, and Caroline Lloyd, 80. The two elder victims were the aunts of Dempsey Lloyd, Shakiesha's father, who was also shot but survived. Dempsey told police that Lagrone shot him as he opened the door to his home. Lagrone then went through the house, shooting the other three victims. Records indicate the young girl may have been pregnant by Lagrone.

Received at death row: December 7, 1993. *Time on death row:* 3,718 days (10.19 years).

Last meal: Five pieces of fried chicken and two Cokes or Dr Peppers.

Last statement: "Yes. I just want to say I am not sad today or bitter with anybody. Like I've said from day one, I did not go in there and kill them—but I am no better than those that did. Jesus is Lord."

Pronounced dead: 6:18 P.M.

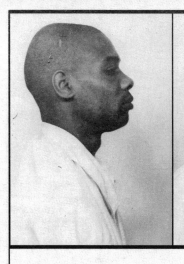

319

Bobby Ray Hopkins

Executed: February 12, 2004

Personal data: *Born:* February 23, 1967. *Race:* Black. *Height:* 5'8". *Weight:* 139 pounds. *Education:* 11 years. *Prior occupation:* Bull rider. *County of conviction:* Johnson. *Age at time of execution:* 36.

Sentenced to death for: Convicted in the July 1993 stabbing deaths of Jennifer Weston, 19, and her cousin, Sandi Marbut, 18. The two were stabbed inside the residence they shared in Grandview. Days prior to the murders, Marbut had accused Hopkins of stealing money from a purse in the home and told him not to return. When arrested four days later, Hopkins was found to have deep cuts on his hands.

Received at death row: June 1, 1994. *Time on death row:* 3,543 days (9.71 years).

Last meal: Declined last meal.

Last statement: None.

Pronounced dead: 8:19 P.M.

320

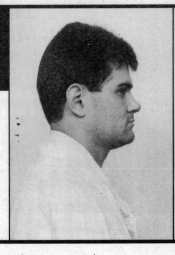

Cameron Todd Willingham

Executed: February 17, 2004

TEXAS
999041
AUG. 92

Personal data: *Born:* January 9, 1968. *Race:* White. *Height:* 5'9". *Weight:* 177 pounds. *Education:* 10 years. *Prior occupation:* Auto mechanic. *County of conviction:* Navarro. *Age at time of execution:* 36.

Sentenced to death for: Convicted in the December 1991 deaths of his three young children in a house fire. Killed in the fire in Corsicana were Amber Louis Kuykendall, 2, and twins Karmon Diane Willingham, 1, and Kameron Marie Willingham, 1. The defendant told authorities the fire started when he and the children were asleep. An investigation, however, revealed the fire was intentionally set with a flammable liquid.

Received at death row: August 21, 1992. *Time on death row:* 4,197 days (11.50 years).

Last meal: Three barbecue pork ribs, two full orders of onion rings, fried okra, three beef enchiladas with cheese, and two slices of lemon cream pie.

Last statement: "Yeah. The only statement I want to make is that I am an innocent man—convicted of a crime I did not commit. I have been persecuted for twelve years for something I did not do. From God's dust I came and to dust I will return—so the earth shall become my throne. I gotta go, road dog. I love you Gabby." [Remaining portion of statement omitted due to profanity.]

Pronounced dead: 6:20 P.M.

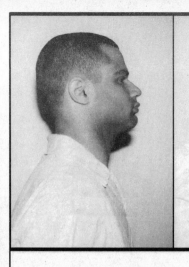

321

Marcus B. Cotton

Executed: March 3, 2004

Personal data: *Born:* September 28, 1974. *Race:* Black. *Height:* 5'6". *Weight:* 147 pounds. *Education:* 9 years. *Prior occupation:* Laborer. *County of conviction:* Harris. *Age at time of execution:* 29.

Sentenced to death for: Convicted in the September 1996 shooting death of a white male Fort Bend County assistant district attorney outside the Jewish Community Center in Houston. Cotton and accomplice Lawrence Watson, both armed with pistols, were riding bicycles through the community center parking lot when Watson spotted another male exiting his vehicle. Watson approached this male, put a .38 caliber pistol to his head, and robbed him of his cash. Meanwhile, Cotton saw the assistant district attorney outside the center and demanded money from him after pulling a .380 semiautomatic pistol. The victim told Cotton he had no money but that he had valuables in his car. As Cotton put him in the backseat of the Mustang, the other robbery victim, who had gone driving around to the front of the community center to call police, again drove into the parking lot and began blowing his car horn and blinking his lights in an effort to ward off the robbers. Cotton reportedly ordered Watson to shoot the man blowing the horn and then fired two shots into the assistant district attorney's head. As the robbers attempted to flee on their bicycles, the man in the other vehicle gave chase in his car and struck Cotton, who with Watson managed to escape on foot by jumping a fence. Following his arrest, Watson implicated Cotton, telling police Cotton killed the assistant district attorney because he had seen the gold badge the victim carried with him as a member of the district attorney's office. The badge was found lying at the victim's feet inside the car. Witnesses also told police that Cotton later bragged about "shooting the law" after seeing the badge.

Received at death row: February 4, 1998. *Time on death row:* 2,219 days (6.08 years).

Last meal: Chicken-fried steak with cream gravy, one serving of macaroni and cheese, one serving of fried okra, one slice of cheesecake with whipped cream and sprinkled pecans, one slice pecan pie, and apple juice.

Last statement: "Yes, Warden, I do. Well Mom, sometimes it works out like this. Love life; live long. When you are dealing with reality, real is not always what you want it to be. Take care of yourselves. I love you. Tell my kids I love them. God is real. He is fixing to find out some deep things that are real. Bounce back, baby. You know what I'm saying. You all take care of yourselves. That is it."

Pronounced dead: 6:13 P.M.

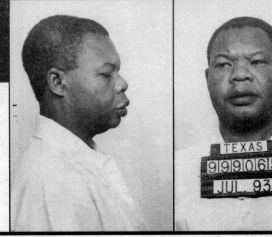

322

Kelsey Patterson

Executed: May 18, 2004

Personal data: *Born:* March 24, 1954. *Race:* Black. *Height:* 5'10". *Weight:* n/a. *Education:* n/a. *Prior occupation:* n/a. *County of conviction:* Anderson. *Age at time of execution:* 50.

Sentenced to death for: Convicted in the September 1992 killings of Louis Oates, the 63-year-old owner of Oates Oil Co. in Palestine, Texas, and business secretary Dorothy Harris, 41. Oates was standing on the loading dock of his business when Patterson walked up behind him and shot him with a .38 caliber pistol. Patterson walked away after the shooting but returned to shoot Harris in the head when she came out and began screaming. Patterson then walked a short distance to a friend's house, put down the gun, and took off his clothes. He was standing naked in the street when arrested. A motive in the murders was unclear, but a friend of Oates told police Patterson and the victim had once argued over who was a better football player, Patterson or Oates's son.

Received at death row: July 7, 1993. *Time on death row:* 3,968 days (10.87 years).

Last meal: Declined last meal.

Last statement: "Statement to what? State what? I am not guilty of the charge of capital murder. Steal me and my family's money. My truth will always be my truth. There is no kin and no friend; no fear what you do to me. No kin to you undertaker. Murderer. [Portion of statement omitted due to profanity.] Get my money. Give me my rights. Give me my rights. Give me my rights. Give me my life back."

Pronounced dead: 6:20 P.M.

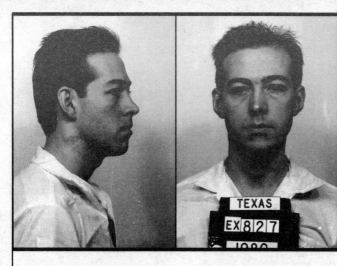

323

David
Ray
Harris

Executed:
June 30,
2004

TEXAS
EX827

Personal data: *Born:* October 19, 1960. *Race:* White. *Height:* 5'10". *Weight:* 160 pounds. *Education:* 9 years (GED). *Prior occupation:* Apprentice bricklayer. *County of conviction:* Jefferson. *Age at time of execution:* 43.

Sentenced to death for: Convicted in the September 1985 shooting death of 30-year-old Mark Mays, finance manager for a Beaumont car dealership. Mays was shot five times in the parking lot of his apartment complex when he attempted to stop Harris from kidnapping his 26-year-old girlfriend, Roxanne Lockard. Mays and Lockard were sleeping inside Mays's Towne Oaks apartment when Harris entered with a .38 caliber pistol and abducted Lockard after forcing Mays into a bathroom. Mays freed himself, grabbed a 9mm pistol, and followed Harris to the parking lot, where a shootout ensued. Both men fired shots. Harris was hit in the neck and arm, while Mays suffered wounds to both shoulders, the chin, and the chest. Harris, who bandaged his own wounds, was arrested four days after the shooting when police suspected him of drunk driving. Lockard escaped during the shootout unharmed.

Received at death row: April 30, 1986. *Time on death row:* 6,636 days (18.18 years).

Last meal: A double bacon cheeseburger, lettuce, onion, mayonnaise and tomato, onion rings, fries, a barbecue beef sandwich, with fries and coleslaw, two pieces of coffee cake, tea with lemon, one pitcher of lemonade, one and a half pints of milk.

Last statement: "Yes I do. Sir, in honor of a true American hero, Let's roll. Lord Jesus receive my spirit."

Pronounced dead: 6:48 P.M.

324

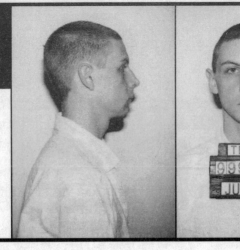

Jasen Shane Busby

Executed:
August 25, 2004

Personal data: *Born:* November 21, 1975. *Race:* White. *Height:* 5'7". *Weight:* 130 pounds. *Education:* 11 years. *Prior occupation:* Laborer. *County of conviction:* Cherokee. *Age at time of execution:* 28.

Sentenced to death for: Convicted in the April 1995 shooting deaths of two teenagers inside a mobile home near Jacksonville. Killed were 18-year-old Tenille Hamilton Thompson and 16-year-old Brandy Gray. A companion, 18-year-old Christopher Kelley, was shot in the neck by Busby but survived his wound to identify his assailant. Busby, another teen, and the three victims traveled to Tyler together in Kelley's truck the afternoon of the murder and ended up at the mobile home in the community of Antioch, west of Jacksonville, later that night. After they all smoked marijuana, Busby walked outside and picked up an automatic assault rifle he had stolen from his parents's home in Tyler. When Kelley opened the door to the mobile home to walk outside, Busby shot him in the neck. Busby then walked in and shot Gray as she begged for her life. He then turned the rifle on Thompson as she huddled screaming in a corner, shooting her in the head. Busby took money from Kelley's billfold and fled in Kelley's truck to Jacksonville, throwing the rifle out along the way. He was arrested there and led police to the murder weapon. Busby said he shot the three only because he was high on drugs.

Received at death row: August 1, 1996. *Time on death row:* 2,946 days (8.07 years).

Last meal: Cherries, strawberries, peaches, two milks with chocolate syrup, plain M&M's, french fries, ketchup, two fried chicken breasts, two jalapeños, three or four barbecue ribs, catfish, tartar sauce, and a six-ounce (cooked medium) steak.

Last statement: See Appendix.

Pronounced dead: 6:14 P.M.

325

James Vernon Allridge III

Executed: August 26, 2004

Personal data: *Born:* November 14, 1962. *Race:* Black. *Height:* 6'2". *Weight:* 153 pounds. *Education:* 12 years. *Prior occupation:* Custom furniture builder. *County of conviction:* Tarrant. *Age at time of execution:* 41.

Sentenced to death for: Shot and killed Brian Clenbennen, a convenience store clerk, at a Circle K store in Fort Worth. Allridge robbed the store of approximately $300.

Received at death row: June 9, 1987. *Time on death row:* 6,288 days (17.23 years).

Last meal: A double-meat bacon cheeseburger with lettuce, tomatoes, salad dressing, shoestring or crinkle-cut french fries with ketchup, banana pudding or banana pudding ice cream, and watermelon or white seedless grapes.

Last statement: "Yeah. I want to thank my family and friends; my family for all loving me and giving me so much love. I am sorry, I really am. You, Brian's sister, thanks for your love—it meant a lot. Shane—I hope he finds peace. I am sorry I destroyed you all's life. Thank you for forgiving me. To the moon and back—I love you all."

Pronounced dead: 6:22 P.M.

326

Andrew Flores

Executed:
September 21, 2004

Personal data: *Born:* August 9, 1972. *Race:* Hispanic. *Height:* 6'2". *Weight:* 163 pounds. *Education:* 10 years. *Prior occupation:* Restaurant worker. *County of conviction:* Bexar. *Age at time of execution:* 32.

Sentenced to death for: Convicted in the July 1993 robbery and murder of convenience store clerk Juan Gabriel Moreno, 23, in San Antonio. Moreno was working the counter at a Stop N Go when Flores and an accomplice entered and demanded cash from the register and Moreno's car keys. Moreno gave the robbers $44 from the register, but asked them to take his car. He then kneeled down on the floor, where he was shot in the head. Flores retrieved Moreno's keys but couldn't get the car started. He and his accomplice fled on foot with the money. Disposition of the case involving the codefendant, Joseph Fritz, is not known.

Received at death row: May 25, 1994. *Time on death row:* 3,772 days (10.33 years).

Last meal: Four barbecue beef ribs, one beef steak, skinless mashed potatoes, pinto beans, ten flour tortillas, two Big Red sodas, three orange sodas, a pint of vanilla ice cream, two chalupas, three tamales, salad with thousand island dressing, barbecue chicken, fried chicken, beef fajitas, and chicken fajitas.

Last statement: "Yes sir. Today I go home to the Lord. But first, I have to say something. I am real sorry. I took your family member's life and I shouldn't have. I hope that you can move on. I am just sorry. I don't know what else to say. I can't bring anyone back. I would if I could. I hope you will be fine. I won't ask for your forgiveness. God will be my judge. To my family and friends, I love you all. You all take care and somebody find Void. Be strong and I will see you all, hopefully not soon. Keep your head up. That is all I have to say."

Pronounced dead: 6:20 P.M.

327

Edward Green III

Executed: October 5, 2004

TEXAS
999073
OCT. 93

Personal data: *Born:* March 5, 1974. *Race:* Black. *Height:* 5'7". *Weight:* 154 pounds. *Education:* 9 years. *Prior occupation:* Laborer. *County of conviction:* Harris. *Age at time of execution:* 30.

Sentenced to death for: Convicted in the August 1992 shooting deaths of Edward Perry Haden and Helen O'Sullivan in Houston. Green and codefendant Jimmy Lee Daniels spotted the victims stopped at a traffic light and decided to rob them for "weed" money. Green jumped from the car Daniels was driving and pointed a gun at Haden, who was seated on the passenger side of the car driven by O'Sullivan. When Haden failed to react quickly to Green's threats, Green fired three times through the window, striking Haden twice and O'Sullivan once. Disposition of the case involving Jimmy Lee Daniels is not known.

Received at death row: October 8, 1993. *Time on death row:* 4,015 days (10.99 years).

Last meal: Two chicken-fried steaks, fried chicken strips, fried shrimp, curly fries, one-half gallon of grape juice, pint of caramel pecan fudge ice cream, ketchup, and a pack of bubble gum.

Last statement: "Yes I do. To my family, to my friends, and people who have accepted me for being the person that I am. To the Sullivan and Hayden families, I do not come here with the intention to make myself out to be a person that I am not. I never claimed to be the best person. I am not the best father, the best son, or the best friend in the world. I did the best I could with what I had. I come with no hate in my heart or bitterness. To my family and to you people, I can only apologize for all the pain I caused you. May God forgive us on this day. I am ready when you are."

Pronounced dead: 8:21 P.M.

328

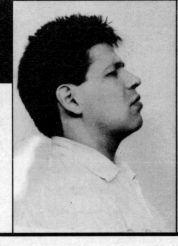

Peter J. Miniel
aka Peter Hernandez

Executed:
October 6, 2004

Personal data: *Born:* June 23, 1962. *Race:* Hispanic. *Height:* 5'7". *Weight:* 190 pounds. *Education:* 9 years. *Prior occupation:* Construction worker. *County of conviction:* Harris. *Age at time of execution:* 42.

Sentenced to death for: Convicted in the May 1986 slaying and robbery of 20-year-old Paul Manier at Manier's North Harris County apartment. Miniel and codefendant James Warren Russell reportedly met Manier's roommate in Galveston and returned to the apartment to drink beer and smoke marijuana. When Manier's roommate fell asleep, Miniel and Russell attacked the victim, striking him in the head with a heavy beer mug, stabbing him thirty-nine times in the head and back with knives, and beating him about the head with an automobile shock absorber. Miniel and Russell then stole the victim's wallet, which contained $20, and a stereo system from the apartment. They then reportedly cleaned up and went out for hamburgers. Russell, who fled to Brookshire following the murder, testified against Miniel in exchange for a fifty-year prison sentence.

Received at death row: November 9, 1988. *Time on death row:* 5,810 days (15.92 years).

Last meal: Twenty beef tacos, cheese, jalapeño peppers, twenty beef enchiladas, cheese, two double cheeseburgers with onions, pizza with jalapeños and salt on the side, half of a chocolate cake, half of a vanilla cake, four pints of ice cream (cookies and cream, dulce de leche, and caramel pecan fudge), a small fruitcake, fried chicken, spaghetti with salt, two Cokes, orange juice, two root beers, and two Pepsis.

Last statement: "Into your hands oh Lord, I commence my spirit. Amen."

Pronounced dead: 6:22 P.M.

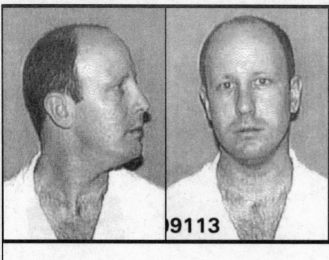

329

Donald Loren Aldrich

Executed: October 12, 2004

9113

Personal data: *Born:* November 6, 1964. *Race:* White. *Height:* 5'8". *Weight:* 190 pounds. *Education:* 10 years (GED). *Prior occupation:* Baker. *County of conviction:* Smith. *Age at time of execution:* 39.

Sentenced to death for: Convicted in the November 1993 murder of 23-year-old Nicholus West in Tyler. Following his arrest, Aldrich told police he and two accomplices abducted West from a Tyler park and robbed him because they believed him to be a homosexual. West's half-naked, bullet-riddled body was found in a clay pit about ten miles outside Tyler. Aldrich and his codefendants were said to have been involved in earlier drive-by shootings, robberies, burglaries, carjackings, arson, and gay bashing.
Codefendant: Henry Earl Dunn was executed on February 6, 2003. (See entry 297, Henry Earl Dunn Jr.)

Received at death row: August 10, 1994. *Time on death row:* 3,716 days (10.18 years).

Last meal: Chef salad, French dressing, fried chicken breasts and legs, french fries, a cheeseburger, chocolate cake, deviled eggs, and biscuits with white gravy.

Last statement: "Yes sir, I would. To the West family, I would just like to apologize for your loss. I hope that you can forgive me. To my family and loved ones and friends, I thank all of you all for your support and I am sorry for the pain and hurt I have caused you. I love you all and I will see you on the other side. OK, Warden."

Pronounced dead: 6:18 P.M.

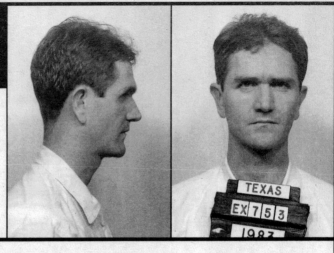

330

Ricky Eugene Morrow

Executed: October 20, 2004

Personal data: *Born:* May 29, 1951. *Race:* White. *Height:* 5'10". *Weight:* 145 pounds. *Education:* 10 years. *Prior occupation:* Welder. *County of conviction:* Dallas. *Age at time of execution:* 53.

Sentenced to death for: Convicted in the January 1982 robbery at gunpoint of the Metropolitan Savings and Loan Association in the Hillside Village Shopping Center. The robbery netted approximately $5,000. Morrow received fifty years concurrent for the attempted capital murder of an FBI agent who was attempting to arrest him.

Received at death row: December 8, 1983. *Time on death row:* 7,622 days (20.88 years).

Last meal: Cheeseburger, french fries, onion rings, and iced tea.

Last statement: "Yes, I do. I want to say first that I love you Pam. I love you, Ann, Jenny, Carla, Fran, Mom, and Dad. What a blessing, what a blessing you have been in my life. And I am so sorry you are going through what you are now. But we are both headed to a better place. Thank you, baby girl—love you people. Sister, Blackie, Dixie, Rusty, Andy, Buster, Milo—we got so many—Grace and Sonny man. I love you all. You have a treat coming to you. Thank you for having been there for me—and our father and mother. Give them a hug and give them my love. I am ready, Warden."

Pronounced dead: 6:32 P.M.

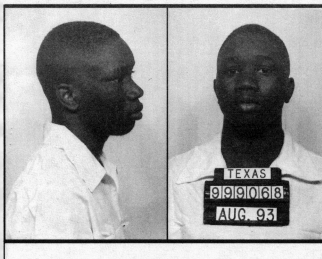

331

Dominique Jerome Green

Executed: October 26, 2004

Personal data: *Born:* May 13, 1974. *Race:* Black. *Height:* n/a. *Weight:* n/a. *Education:* 12 years. *Prior occupation:* n/a. *County of conviction:* Harris. *Age at time of execution:* 30.

Sentenced to death for: Convicted in the robbery and shooting death of Andrew Lastrapes. Green and two codefendants were riding around committing robberies when they spotted Lastrapes in the parking lot of a convenience store. Green and accomplice Michael Neal approached Lastrapes and demanded his wallet. When Lastrapes refused to hand it over, Green shot him in the chest with a 9mm pistol. Green ripped off Lastrapes's pants pocket to get to his wallet, which contained $50. During the punishment phase of the Green trial, nine other people testified to being robbed by him and his codefendant.
Codefendant: Michael Neal received a sentence of forty years for aggravated robbery.

Received at death row: August 17, 1993. *Time on death row:* 4,088 days (11.20 years).

Last meal: Declined last meal.

Last statement: See Appendix.

Pronounced dead: 7:59 P.M.

332

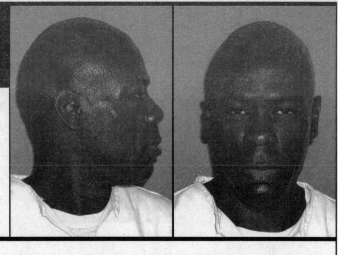

Lorenzo Morris

Executed:
November 2, 2004

Personal data: *Born:* September 25, 1952. *Race:* Black. *Height:* 5'9". *Weight:* 164 pounds. *Education:* 10 years (GED). *Prior occupation:* Laborer. *County of conviction:* Harris. *Age at time of execution:* 52.

Sentenced to death for: Convicted in the August 1990 murder of 71-year-old Jesse Fields. Morris and an accomplice broke into Fields's Houston home and stabbed him with a butcher knife before demanding money. In an effort to defend himself, Fields grabbed a hammer but was struck repeatedly with it after Morris took it away from him. Fields was in a coma for eight months before he died. Morris was charged with the killing following his arrest for the March 1991 robbery of a washateria, where a clerk was shot twice.
Codefendant: Ricky Darnell Henson received a life sentence for aggravated robbery.

Received at death row: August 3, 1992. *Time on death row:* 4,474 days (12.26 years).

Last meal: Fried chicken and fish with French bread and hot peppers, apple pie with butter pecan ice cream, two Sprites or Big Red sodas, and a pack of Camel cigarettes and matches.

Last statement: None.

Pronounced dead: 6:13 P.M.

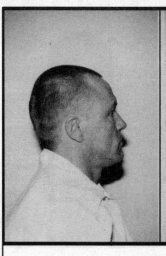

333

Robert Brice Morrow

Executed: November 4, 2004

Personal data: *Born:* June 3, 1957. *Race:* White. *Height:* 5'11". *Weight:* 175 pounds. *Education:* GED. *Prior occupation:* Roughneck. *County of conviction:* Liberty. *Age at time of execution:* 47.

Sentenced to death for: On April 3, 1996, in Liberty, Morrow abducted and murdered a 21-year-old white female. The victim was home on spring break from college when she left her parents' home at approximately 8:30 P.M. to wash her father's car at a nearby car wash. The young woman had planned to drive the car to Houston the following day for a date. Her body was found floating in the Trinity River the day after her disappearance. She had been beaten and her throat was slashed. Hair and blood samples taken from Morrow matched those taken from the car Allison drove. A jury took just thirteen minutes to sentence Morrow to death following his capital murder conviction.

Received at death row: November 18, 1997. *Time on death row:* 2,543 days (6.97 years).

Last meal: Ten pieces of crispy fried chicken (leg quarters), two double-meat cheeseburgers, with a side order of sliced onions, pickles and tomatoes, mayonnaise, ketchup on the side, salt and pepper, lettuce if possible, three deep-fried pork chops, breaded, trimmed, and well done, one small chef salad with chopped ham and thousand island dressing, one large order of french fries cooked with onions, five big buttermilk biscuits with butter, four jalapeño peppers, two Sprites, two Cokes (regular), one pint of rocky road ice cream (substitute for a banana split), and one bowl of peach cobbler or apple pie.

Last statement: "Yes I do. Mike and Ms. Allison, I would like to tell you that I am responsible and I am sorry for what I did and the pain I caused you all. I love you, Earline, and all of my friends that stood by me. I feel blessed to have had you all. Stay strong and take care of them kids. Set me free, Warden. Father, accept me."

Pronounced dead: 6:35 P.M.

334

Demarco Markeith McCullum

Executed: November 9, 2004

Personal data: *Born:* October 2, 1974. *Race:* Black. *Height:* n/a. *Weight:* n/a. *Education:* 12 years. *Prior occupation:* Unemployed. *County of conviction:* Harris. *Age at time of execution:* 30.

Sentenced to death for: Convicted in the July 1994 abduction and murder of 29-year-old Michael Burzinski. McCullum and three codefendants accosted and then abducted Burzinski in the Montrose area of Houston, forcing him to drive to an ATM, where $400 was withdrawn from his account. The accomplices then drove Burzinski in his car to an isolated area, where he was shot once in the back of the head while he pleaded for his life. The four then drove Burzinski's car a short distance away and set it afire. McCullum later confessed the killing to police. Charges and disposition of the cases against the three accomplices is unknown.

Received at death row: January 26, 1996. *Time on death row:* 3,210 days (8.79 years).

Last meal: A big cheeseburger, a lot of french fries, three Cokes, apple pie, and five mint sticks.

Last statement: "I do. I just wanted to say to all of those that have supported me over the years that I appreciate it and I love you. And I just want to tell my mom that I love her and I will see her in heaven."

Pronounced dead: 6:17 P.M.

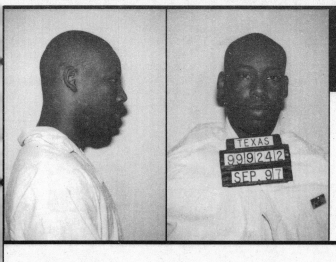

Frederick Patrick McWilliams

Executed: November 10, 2004

Personal data: *Born:* December 1, 1973. *Race:* Black. *Height:* 5'7". *Weight:* 201 pounds. *Education:* 11 years. *Prior occupation:* Warehouse worker. *County of conviction:* Harris. *Age at time of execution:* 30.

Sentenced to death for: On September 28, 1996, in Houston, McWilliams murdered a Hispanic male during a robbery. McWilliams and his accomplices were driving around Houston looking for a car to steal for use in robberies when they happened upon the victim asleep inside his parked car. Shaking the victim from his sleep, McWilliams and his accomplices attempted to put him into the trunk of his car. When he resisted, McWilliams shot him once in the head at point-blank range. The killing occurred in the midst of a crime spree by McWilliams and accomplices in Waller and Harris counties.

Received at death row: October 1, 1997. *Time on death row:* 2,597 days (7.12 years).

Last meal: Six fried chicken breasts, ketchup, deep-fried french fries, six-layer lasagna (ground chicken, beef, cheese, minced tomatoes, noodles, and sautéed onions), six egg rolls, shrimp fried rice, soy sauce, six chimichangas, melted cheese, salsa, six lemonades with extra sugar, six slices of turkey, liver and gizzard dressing, dirty rice, and cranberry sauce.

Last statement: "Yes. Well here we are again, folks, in the catacombs of justice. You know there is a lot I wanted to say—a lot I thought I'd say—but there is not a whole lot to say. There are people that will be mad thinking I try to seek freedom from this, but as long as I see, freedom belongs to me and I'll keep on keeping on. The shackles and chains that just might hold my body can't hold my mind, but will kill me otherwise. I love you Mama, and Misty and Annette, Brenda and Anthony—and all my friends and everybody that supported me. I leave my love here; I am never going to stop loving you. My love is going to stay here."

Pronounced dead: 6:18 P.M.

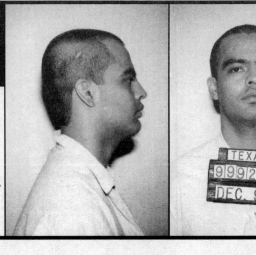

336

Anthony Guy Fuentes

Executed: November 17, 2004

Personal data: *Born:* November 5, 1974. *Race:* Hispanic. *Height:* 5'9". *Weight:* 140 pounds. *Education:* 12 years. *Prior occupation:* Mover. *County of conviction:* Harris. *Age at time of execution:* 30.

Sentenced to death for: Convicted in the February 1994 shooting death of Robert Tate during a Houston convenience store robbery. Tate, who lived in the neighborhood of the convenience store robbed by Fuentes and three accomplices, was shot twice in the chest with a 9mm pistol as he tried to stop the robbers as they fled to a getaway car.

Received at death row: December 18, 1996. *Time on death row:* 2,891 days (7.92 years).

Last meal: Fried chicken with biscuits and jalapeño peppers, steak, french fries, ice water, Coke, fajita tacos, pizza, and a hamburger.

Last statement: "Yes sir. Sorry that I have to put my family through this. All of you know I got my peace. And I hope you find peace. And to the family, the truth will come out and I hope you find peace. I got my peace. I hope everybody has their peace. I am tired. I am going to be in your heart. I love you all. To everybody else, the truth will be known. It didn't come out in time to save my life. It is wrong to put the families through this. But when it comes out, I hope it stops this. It is wrong for the prosecutors to lie and make witnesses say what they need them to say. The truth has always been there. I just hope everybody has their peace. Today I get mine. I love you all."

Pronounced dead: 6:17 P.M.

James Porter

Executed: January 4, 2005

Personal data: *Born:* August 15, 1971. *Race:* White. *Height:* 5'9". *Weight:* 131 pounds. *Education:* 7 years. *Prior occupation:* Carpenter, laborer. *County of conviction:* Bowie. *Age at time of execution:* 33.

Sentenced to death for: On May 28, 2000, Porter, an offender serving time for murder with a deadly weapon, entered a dayroom of the Telford Unit in Bowie County. He fatally assaulted an adult Hispanic male offender with a rock inside a pillowcase, a homemade knife, and his boots.

Received at death row: March 14, 2001. *Time on death row:* 1,392 days (3.81 years).

Last meal: Two thighs and two breasts of fried chicken (extra crispy), french fries, onion rings, fried okra, five slices of buttered garlic toast, one bowl of country gravy, a couple slices of onion, pickles, jalapeño peppers, ketchup, mustard, sliced tomato, one pot of thick coffee, and a banana split.

Last statement: "Yes sir, I do. I would like to apologize to the family of the victim. I am sorry for the pain I have caused you. I know it is a great loss and I want to apologize. I am sorry. And to my family, I love you and I will see you all in heaven. OK."

Pronounced dead: 6:12 P.M.

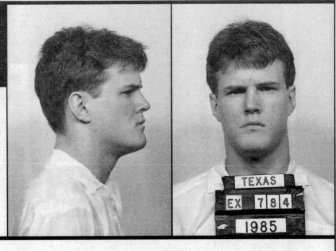

338

Troy Albert Kunkle

Executed: January 25, 2005

Personal data: *Born:* May 27, 1966. *Race:* White. *Height:* 6'1". *Weight:* 163 pounds. *Education:* 11 years. *Prior occupation:* Student. *County of conviction:* Nueces. *Age at time of execution:* 38.

Sentenced to death for: Convicted in the August 1984 abduction, robbery, and shooting death of Steven Wayne Horton, 31, in Corpus Christi. After driving from San Antonio and visiting the beach in Corpus Christi, Kunkle and three codefendants drove around town looking for someone to rob. They saw Horton walking and induced him into the car by offering him a ride home. Once Horton was in the car, codefendant Russell Stanley put a gun to the victim's head and demanded his wallet. When Horton refused, Kunkle told Stanley to kill him, but Stanley said it wasn't necessary. Kunkle then took the .22 caliber pistol from Stanley and told accomplice Aaron Adkins to drive behind a nearby skating rink, where he shot Horton once in the back of the head. Accomplice Lora Lee Zaiontz, Kunkle's girlfriend, then pushed Horton's body from the car and took his wallet, which contained $13. After the killing, Kunkle reportedly said, "another day, another death, another sorrow, another breath." Later, he reportedly said the murder was "beautiful." *Codefendants:* Lora Lee Zaiontz received life for capital murder. Aaron Adkins and Russell Stanley each received thirty years for murder.

Received at death row: March 2, 1985. *Time on death row:* 7,269 days (19.92 years).

Last meal: Fried chicken, cauliflower, chicken-fried steak, french fries, ketchup, hamburger with cheese and onions, cinnamon rolls, apple pie, and milk.

Last statement: See Appendix.

Pronounced dead: 8:12 P.M.

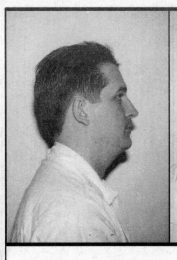

**Dennis
Bagwell**

Executed:
February 17,
2005

Personal data: *Born:* December 27, 1963. *Race:* White. *Height:* 5'11". *Weight:* 160 pounds. *Education:* 9 years. *Prior occupation:* Salesman. *County of conviction:* Atascosa. *Age at time of execution:* 41.

Sentenced to death for: Convicted in the September 1995 deaths of his mother, Leona Boone, 47; his half sister, Libby Best, 24; her 4-year-old daughter, Reba Best; and 14-year-old Tassy Boone, granddaughter of Ronald Boone, Leona's husband. Ronald Boone found all four victims upon returning home from work. Leona and Tassy had been beaten and strangled so violently their necks were broken. Tassy had also been sexually assaulted. Libby had been shot twice in the head, and Reba's skull was crushed with a hammer and a metal exercise bar. Records indicate that Bagwell had gone to his mother's home to borrow money and killed the four when she refused his request.

Received at death row: November 13, 1996. *Time on death row:* 3,018 days (8.27 years).

Last meal: Steak (cooked medium-rare) with A1 sauce, fried chicken (three breasts and three thighs), barbecue ribs, large french fries, large onion rings, one pound of fried bacon, a dozen scrambled eggs with onions, fried taters with onions, sliced tomatoes, salad with ranch dressing, ketchup, milk and coffee, salt and pepper, two hamburgers with everything, peach pie or peach cobbler, and iced tea with real sugar.

Last statement: "Yes sir, can you hear me? To you, Irene, thank you. I love you all. All right, Warden, I'm ready."

Pronounced dead: 6:19 P.M.

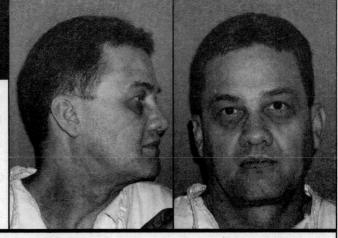

340

George Anderson Hopper

Executed: March 8, 2005

Personal data: *Born:* October 6, 1955. *Race:* White. *Height:* 5'9". *Weight:* 183 pounds. *Education:* 12 years. *Prior occupation:* Auto body repair. *County of conviction:* Dallas. *Age at time of execution:* 49.

Sentenced to death for: Convicted in the October 1983 murder of Rozanne Gailiunas, 33, at her Richardson home. Hopper, who allegedly was paid $1,500 to kill Gailiunas for another man, forced his way into her home at gunpoint and attempted to sexually assault the woman after forcing her to remove her clothes and binding her to a bed. He then began to strangle Gailiunas with a rope but used his gun to shoot her twice through a pillow when she managed to free one of her hands and struggle with him. Hopper was arrested for the murder in December 1988 and confessed to the crime in February 1989. It was unclear whether the man identified as the solicitor of the murder was charged.

Received at death row: July 23, 1992. *Time on death row:* 4,611 days (12.63 years).

Last meal: Six eggs over-easy, ten biscuits, twelve pieces of bacon, a bowl of grits, a bowl of thick milk white gravy, strawberry preserves, french fries, fried chicken, and chocolate meringue pie.

Last statement: "I want to apologize to you, and I am sorry. I have made a lot of mistakes in my life. The things I did changed so many lives. I can't take it back; it was an atrocity. I am sorry. I beg your forgiveness; I know I am not worthy of it. I love you, Mom and Dad, and all my family. Thank you for everything. Jesus, thank you for your love and saving grace. Thank you for shedding your blood on Calvary for me. Thank you, Jesus, for the love you have shown me."

Pronounced dead: 6:22 P.M.

341

Douglas Alan Roberts

Executed: April 20, 2005

Personal data: *Born:* July 8, 1962. *Race:* White. *Height:* 5'10". *Weight:* 215 pounds. *Education:* 12 years. *Prior occupation:* Machinist. *County of conviction:* Kendall. *Age at time of execution:* 42.

Sentenced to death for: Convicted in the May 1996 kidnapping, robbery, and murder of 40-year-old Jerry Velez. Velez was abducted in his car at knifepoint outside his San Antonio apartment complex and forced to drive out of the city on Interstate 10. In Kendall County, Roberts instructed Velez to turn onto a road and stop the car. When Roberts demanded Velez's shirt, the victim allegedly lunged at Roberts, who stabbed Velez seven times. In fleeing the scene in the victim's car, Roberts ran over Velez's body. Roberts drove to Austin and called 911 from a pay phone, saying he had killed a man. He was arrested by a responding officer.

Received at death row: January 22, 1997. *Time on death row:* 3,010 days (8.25 years).

Last meal: Three Southern fried chicken breasts, tomato, lettuce, cheese, picante sauce, jalapeño peppers, two BLTs on wheat, lightly grilled with garlic butter, three beef and cheese enchiladas, twelve green olives, Italian ketchup, butter beans and cabbage seasoned with ham bone, seasoned ground beef, six corn tortillas, onions, fried onion rings, french fries, four deviled eggs, broccoli with cheese sauce, and two grilled barbecue pork chops.

Last statement: "Yes sir, Warden. OK, I've been hanging around this popsicle stand way too long. Before I leave, I want to tell you all—when I die, bury me deep, lay two speakers at my feet, put some headphones on my head, and rock and roll me when I'm dead. I'll see you in heaven someday. That's all, Warden."

Pronounced dead: 6:21 P.M.

342

Lonnie Wayne Pursley

Executed: May 3, 2005

Personal data: *Born:* September 17, 1961. *Race:* White. *Height:* 5'8". *Weight:* 229 pounds. *Education:* 9 years. *Prior occupation:* Cook, laborer. *County of conviction:* Polk. *Age at time of execution:* 43.

Sentenced to death for: On March 29, 1997, Pursley and a codefendant murdered Robert Earl Cook, 47, inside the Deer County subdivision in Livingston. They took the victim into a wooded area, where they beat him to death and robbed him.

Received at death row: January 20, 1999. *Time on death row:* 2,295 days (6.29 years).

Last meal: A cheeseburger, four fried pork chops (well done), one piece of cheesecake, french fries (extra ketchup), two dinner rolls, and iced tea with sugar.

Last statement: "Yes. I would like to address the victim's family. I received your poem and I am very grateful for your forgiveness. I still want to ask for it anyway. I have Jesus in my heart and I am sorry for any pain I caused you all. Thank you for your forgiveness. I am sorry. Ashlee, Pam—I am going to miss you all. I love you all. Give everybody my love. Give everybody my love, OK? Mother, James, Justin, Corey, Brent, grandbabies, and Daddy—I love you, Pam. I love you, Ashlee, Pammy, and Irene. I will see you all on the other side. Couple friends on death row who have helped me: Shy Town and Crazy Jay, I love you all and for all your support. Uncle Ray too. I am saved and I am going home, OK? You all stay strong. You all stay strong. That is all."

Pronounced dead: 6:23 P.M.

343

Bryan Eric Wolfe

Executed: May 18, 2005

Personal data: *Born:* June 7, 1960. *Race:* Black. *Height:* 5'8". *Weight:* 162 pounds. *Education:* 12 years. *Prior occupation:* Food service worker. *County of conviction:* Jefferson. *Age at time of execution:* 44.

Sentenced to death for: Convicted in the February 1992 robbery and murder of 84-year-old Bertha Lemell at her home in Beaumont. Lemell was stabbed twenty-six times with a knife inside her home. Wolfe cut himself during the attack, trailing blood out the front door to the driveway. A bloody knife was found at the defendant's home and police discovered blood inside Wolfe's car after he had driven it

Received at death row: November 2, 1993. *Time on death row:* 4,215 days (11.55 years).

Last meal: Fried chicken legs, fried pork chops, barbecue ribs, french fries, peach cobbler, and a banana.

Last statement: "Yes, sir. To Edie, Tom, and Carma—I love all you all. I appreciate all your support. I love you, Margherita, Father Guido, and Father Angelo. I appreciate your spiritual support and all those that were in prayer for me. I will be OK. I am at peace with all of this and I won't have to wake up in prison anymore. I love you all. I totally surrender to the Lord. I am ready, Warden."

Pronounced dead: 6:31 P.M.

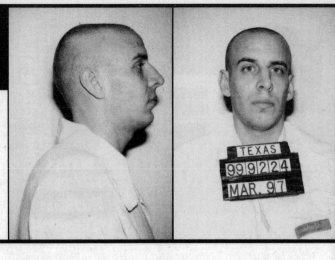

344

Richard Cartwright

Executed:
May 19, 2005

Personal data: *Born:* February 11, 1974. *Race:* White. *Height:* 6'2". *Weight:* 175 pounds. *Education:* 12 years. *Prior occupation:* Mechanic/laborer. *County of conviction:* Nueces. *Age at time of execution:* 31.

Sentenced to death for: Convicted in the August 1996 robbery and murder of 37-year-old Nick Moraida in Corpus Christi. Cartwright and two codefendants lured Moraida to a remote gulf-side park and robbed him of his wallet, watch, and money. Codefendant Kelly Overstreet then cut Moraida's throat and Cartwright shot him in the back with a .38 caliber pistol. Moraida's body washed up on the beach in the 100 block of Ocean Way the following day. The robbery netted the three accomplices between $60 and $200, money they all used to buy drugs.
Codefendant: Kelly Overstreet was sentenced to fifty years in prison.

Received at death row: March 21, 1997. *Time on death row:* 2,981 days (8.17 years).

Last meal: Fried chicken, a cheeseburger, onion rings, french fries, bacon, sausage, cheesecake, and cinnamon rolls.

Last statement: "Yes, I do. I just want to thank all my friends and family who gave me support these past eight years. I want to apologize to the victim's family for the pain I caused them. And to everyone at the Polunsky Unit, just keep your heads up and stay strong."

Pronounced dead: 6:16 P.M.

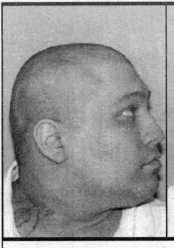

Alexander Martinez

Executed: June 7, 2005

Personal data: *Born:* June 16, 1976. *Race:* Hispanic. *Height:* 5'1". *Weight:* 227 pounds. *Education:* 8 years. *Prior occupation:* Fast-food worker. *County of conviction:* Harris. *Age at time of execution:* 28.

Sentenced to death for: On August 12, 2001, in Houston, Martinez sexually assaulted and stabbed a 45-year-old white female, resulting in her death. In addition, Martinez took $150 from the victim.

Received at death row: January 7, 2003. *Time on death row:* 882 days (2.42 years).

Last meal: A double-meat cheeseburger with everything, six scrambled eggs (slightly cooked), mashed potatoes with gravy, well-done bacon, tall glass of orange juice, one fried steak, a fried pork chop, fried onion rings, one bowl of well-done, thin-sliced french fries, three pieces of quarter-leg fried chicken, and a bowl of shredded cheese.

Last statement: "Yes. The victim's family is not here so I won't address them. I want to thank my family and friends for everything. My wife, Ailsa, my sister-in-law, Laura—thank you for being here for me. I love you. And thanks for the friends at the Polunsky Unit that helped me get through this that didn't agree with my decision—and still gave me their friendship. I thank them. Warden."

Pronounced dead: 6:18 P.M.

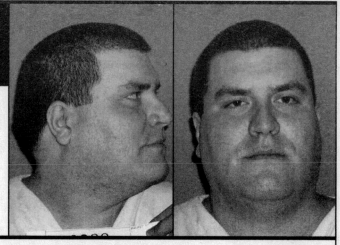

346

David Martinez

Executed:
July 28, 2005

Personal data: *Born:* April 24, 1976. *Race:* Hispanic. *Height:* 5'10". *Weight:* 224 pounds. *Education:* 11 years. *Prior occupation:* n/a. *County of conviction:* Travis. *Age at time of execution:* 29.

Sentenced to death for: On July 22, 1997, Martinez murdered a 24-year-old white female. The victim's body was found on a bike trail in a park in Austin. The victim had been sexually assaulted and strangled, and her throat had been cut with a pocketknife.

Received at death row: December 10, 1998. *Time on death row:* 2,422 days (6.64 years).

Last meal: Declined last meal.

Last statement: "Only the sky and the green grass goes on forever and today is a good day to die."

Pronounced dead: 6:17 P.M.

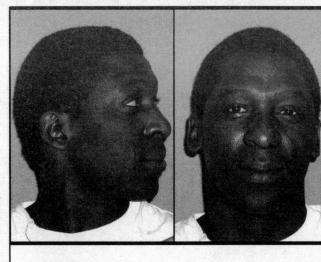

Gary Lynn Sterling

Executed: September 10, 2005

Personal data: *Born:* July 25, 1967. *Race:* Black. *Height:* 6'1". *Weight:* 176 pounds. *Education:* 12 years. *Prior occupation:* Farm worker. *County of conviction:* Navarro. *Age at time of execution:* 38.

Sentenced to death for: Convicted in the May 1988 robbery and murder of 72-year-old John Wesley Carty. Carty and 52-year-old Deloris June Smith were abducted from Carty's home, driven to an isolated area of Navarro County, and killed. Carty suffered blows to the head with a bumper jack. A car, television, shotgun, and lantern were stolen from Carty's house. Sterling confessed to the murders and led authorities to the bodies of Carty and Smith. Later, Sterling also admitted his involvement in the May 17, 1988, murders of William Manuel Porter, 72, and Leroy Porter, 70, in Hill County.

Received at death row: February 9, 1989. *Time on death row:* 6,057 days (16.59 years).

Last meal: Chicken-fried steak, mashed potatoes, french fries, fried chicken, pecan pie, sweet tea, and a vanilla shake.

Last statement: "I would like the chaplain to say a prayer, not only for me but for the victim's family. For them being misled, I am sorry. That is all I have to say."

Pronounced dead: 6:16 P.M.

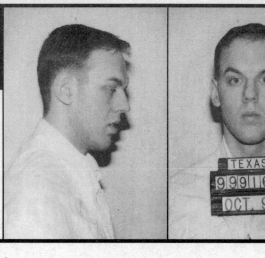

348

Robert Alan Shields Jr.

Executed:
August 23, 2005

Personal data: *Born:* January 23, 1975. *Race:* White. *Height:* 5'10". *Weight:* 171 pounds. *Education:* 12 years. *Prior occupation:* Sales. *County of conviction:* Galveston. *Age at time of execution:* 30.

Sentenced to death for: Convicted in the murder of Paula Stiner, 27, during the burglary of her Friendswood home. Stiner, who had lived in the home only three months, was beaten with a hammer and repeatedly stabbed after being confronted by Shields upon her return from work. Shields had entered the home earlier in the day but waited inside for several hours so he could also steal the owner's car upon her return from work. Shields attacked Stiner first with a hammer and then with a knife, inflicting twenty-eight cut and stab wounds. Before fleeing in Stiner's car, Shields stole credit cards from her purse and used one at Willowbrook Mall only an hour and a half after the killing. He was arrested three days later while driving the victim's car in the Woodlands.

Received at death row: October 20, 1995. *Time on death row:* 3,595 days (9.85 years).

Last meal: Fajitas with flour tortillas, shredded cheddar and mozzarella cheeses, diced tomatoes, diced onions, sour cream, pico de gallo, bacon, breakfast sausage, onion rings, french fries, barbecue sauce, and picante sauce.

Last statement: None.

Pronounced dead: 6:15 P.M.

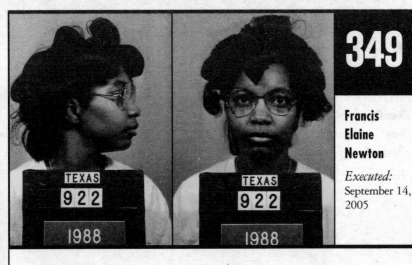

349

Francis Elaine Newton

Executed: September 14, 2005

Personal data: *Born:* April 12, 1965. *Race:* Black. *Height:* 5'3". *Weight:* 128 pounds. *Education:* 12 years. *Prior occupation:* Accounting. *County of conviction:* Harris. *Age at time of execution:* 40.

Sentenced to death for: Convicted in the April 1987 slaying of her husband and children for insurance money. Killed were her husband, Adrian, 23; her son, Alton, 7; and her daughter, Farrah, 21 months. All were shot to death with a .25 caliber pistol that belonged to Newton's boyfriend. Newton and her husband had separated about a month prior to the killings. In March 1987, Newton had taken out $50,000 life insurance policies on Adrian, Farrah, and herself. A policy already existed on Alton's life. Newton admitted taking a gun with her to her husband's apartment on the night of the killings, but she said she took it for protection and that her family members were alive when she left. Newton filed insurance claims on April 21, 1987, and was arrested and charged with capital murder the next day.

Received at death row: November 17, 1988. *Time on death row:* 6,145 days (16.84 years).

Last meal: Declined last meal.

Last statement: None.

Pronounced dead: 6:17 P.M.

350

Ronald Ray Howard

Executed: October 6, 2005

Personal data: *Born:* July 22, 1973. *Race:* Black. *Height:* 5'11". *Weight:* 168 pounds. *Education:* 7 years. *Prior occupation:* Food service worker. *County of conviction:* Travis (change of venue from Jackson). *Age at time of execution:* 32.

Sentenced to death for: Convicted in the April 1992 shooting death of Texas Department of Public Safety trooper Bill Davidson, 43. Davidson was shot through the neck after stopping Howard in a stolen vehicle on U.S. 59 approximately five miles south of Edna in Jackson County. Howard fled in the stolen 1986 GMC Jimmy to Victoria, where he was pursued and arrested after he lost control of the vehicle and struck a house. He was arrested in possession of a loaded 9mm pistol, the same weapon used to shoot Trooper Davidson. Davidson died from his wounds three days after the shooting. At the scene, he told witnesses he had been shot by a lone black male.

Received at death row: August 25, 1993. *Time on death row:* 4,425 days (12.12 years).

Last meal: Declined last meal.

Last statement: "Yes sir, I do. To the victim's family, I hope it helps a little. I do not know how, but I hope it helps. I love you all, all of you. You know I love you. Thank you for bringing my children back to my life. Thank you. I love you all. I love you all very much. Thank you very much." [Statement amended January 9, 2006.]

Pronounced dead: 6:24 P.M.

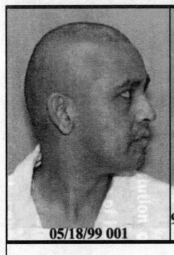

351

Luis Ramirez

Executed: October 20, 2005

999309

05/18/99 001   05/18/99 000

Personal data: *Born:* July 19, 1963. *Race:* Hispanic. *Height:* 5'5". *Weight:* 148 pounds. *Education:* 12 years. *Prior occupation:* Carpenter, laborer. *County of conviction:* Tom Green. *Age at time of execution:* 42.

Sentenced to death for: On April 4, 1999, in San Angelo, codefendant Edward Bell fatally shot a Hispanic male. The victim was lured to a secluded area in San Angelo, under the pretext of fixing a washing machine. (The victim fixed appliances in his spare time.) He was handcuffed and walked to a shallow grave, which had been previously dug, and fatally shot. Ramirez had hired the codefendant to carry out the shooting.

Received at death row: May 18, 1999. *Time on death row:* 2,347 days (6.43 years).

Last meal: Declined last meal.

Last statement: "Yes I do. I would like to address you first. I did not kill your loved one, but I hope that one day you find out who did. I wish I could tell you the reason why, or give some kind of solace; you lost someone you love very much. The same as my family and friends are going to lose in a few minutes. I am sure he died unjustly, just like I am. I did not murder him; I did not have anything to do with his death. And to you my family and friends, I love you dearly. Even though I die, that love for you will never die. Into your hands, Lord, I commit my spirit. Thank you. Thank you all."

Pronounced dead: 6:12 P.M.

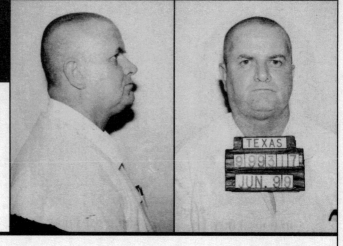

352

Melvin Wayne White

Executed: November 3, 2005

Personal data: *Born:* January 25, 1950. *Race:* White. *Height:* 5'9". *Weight:* 205 pounds. *Education:* 9 years. *Prior occupation:* Mechanic, laborer. *County of conviction:* Pecos. *Age at time of execution:* 55.

Sentenced to death for: On August 4, 1997, White kidnapped a 9-year-old white female in Ozona during the nighttime hours. He then took her to a roadside park outside city limits and attempted to have sexual intercourse with her. The victim resisted, but he taped her hands behind her back with black electrical tape and continued to sexually assault her. During this time, a vehicle pulled up behind him and he left the location. He then took the victim to another location, hit her several times on the head with a tire tool, and left the scene. Authorities were given the location of the body by White. The victim was found dead with her hands tied behind her back.

Received at death row: June 21, 1999. *Time on death row:* 2,327 days (6.38 years).

Last meal: Four-egg Spanish omelets with gravy and hash browns with jalapeño peppers. On the side, six slices of buttered toast, one gallon of homogenized milk, sliced peppers, onion rings, pitcher of ice, gravy, french fries, sliced bread, peach cobbler and vanilla ice cream, one double-meat cheeseburger with mayonnaise and everything, two Cokes, one fried chicken quarter, one fried pork chop with gravy, six slices of bread.

Last statement: See Appendix.

Pronounced dead: 6:21 P.M.

353

Charles Daniel Thacker

Executed: November 9, 2005

Personal data: *Born:* September 18, 1968. *Race:* White. *Height:* 5'8". *Weight:* 172 pounds. *Education:* 8 years (GED). *Prior occupation:* Maintenance. *County of conviction:* Harris. *Age at time of execution:* 37.

Sentenced to death for: Convicted in the April 1993 murder of 26-year-old Karen G. Crawford in Houston. Crawford was strangled during an attempted rape at her mailbox in the commons area of her apartment complex in northwest Houston.

Received at death row: June 3, 1994. *Time on death row:* 4,177 days (11.44 years).

Last meal: Two double-meat cheeseburgers with everything, big batch of fries with ketchup and onion rings, six strips of fajita meat with flour tortillas, two Mountain Dews, two Cokes, two Dr Peppers, guacamole with tortilla chips, four slices of pepperoni pizza, chocolate chip cookie, two slices of double chocolate cake, and two pints of ice cream (cookies and cream or anything with chocolate).

Last statement: "Jack and Irene, I love you guys. Tell my family I love them. I am sorry for the things I have done. I know God will forgive me. Keep track of Danielle for me. I will miss you guys. I love you. I guess that's all."

Pronounced dead: 6:32 P.M.

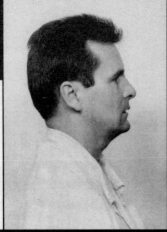

354

Robert Dale Rowell

Executed:
November 15, 2005

Personal data: *Born:* April 8, 1955. *Race:* White. *Height:* 5'8". *Weight:* 168 pounds. *Education:* 9 years. *Prior occupation:* Laborer. *County of conviction:* Harris. *Age at time of execution:* 50.

Sentenced to death for: On May 10, 1993, in Houston, Rowell entered a crack house in an attempt to rob Irving Wright of drugs and money. Rowell started shooting with a .25 caliber pistol, striking three victims and killing Wright and Mata. Perez was shot in the left arm and leg and paralyzed. Rowell then robbed Wright of an unknown amount of money and fled the scene by car.

Received at death row: June 6, 1994. *Time on death row:* 4,180 days (11.45 years).

Last meal: Tea.

Last statement: "Yes, sir. I would like to apologize to the victim's family and all the grief I have caused them. I would like to say I love the girls next to them. Praise the Lord. Let's go, Warden. That's it."

Pronounced dead: 6:24 P.M.

355

Shannon Charles Thomas

Executed: November 16, 2005

Personal data: *Born:* July 27, 1971. *Race:* Black. *Height:* 5'9". *Weight:* 250 pounds. *Education:* 13 years. *Prior occupation:* Machinist. *County of conviction:* Harris. *Age at time of execution:* 34.

Sentenced to death for: Convicted in the December 1993 murder of three people, including two children, at a Baytown residence. Killed inside their home were Roberto Rios and his two children, Victor Roberto Rios, 11, and Maria Elda Isbell Rios, 10. Thomas and codefendant Keith Clay went to the Rios home to rob him of marijuana and money he had from selling small amounts of drugs. Known as "Vato Man," Roberto was shot and stabbed to death; then Thomas went upstairs and shot his children, execution-style, so there would be no witnesses. Thomas later told friends and associates what he had done.

Received at death row: December 4, 1996. *Time on death row:* 3,269 days (8.96 years).

Last meal: Declined last meal.

Last statement: "Yes. Man, I just want you to know how much I love them. I want you to be strong and get through this time. Do not fall back. Keep going forward. Don't let this hinder you. Let everybody know I love them: [Several names listed], Kevin—as well as everyone else in the family. Tell them that I love them and stay strong. This is kind of hard to put words together; I am nervous and it is hard to put my thoughts together. Sometimes you don't know what to say; I hope these words give you comfort. I don't know what to say. I want you to know I love you. Just stay strong and don't give up. Let everybody know I love them . . . and love is unconditional, as Mama has always told us. I may be gone in the flesh, but I am always with you in spirit. I love you."

Pronounced dead: 6:52 P.M.

356

Marion Butler Dudley

Executed: January 25, 2006

Personal data: *Born:* May 13, 1972. *Race:* Black. *Height:* 5'6". *Weight:* 149 pounds. *Education:* 10 years. *Prior occupation:* Laborer. *County of conviction:* Harris. *Age at time of execution:* 33.

Sentenced to death for: Convicted in the June 1992 murders of three people shot during a drug buy at a Houston residence. Killed were Jose Tovar, Jessica Quinones, and Frank Farias. Dudley and two accomplices had gone to the home of Jose and Rachel Tovar to buy three kilograms of cocaine, when they decided to rob them of their drugs and money. Three other people were also shot by the conspirators, two of whom survived head wounds to identify Dudley as one of their attackers.
Codefendant: Arthur Brown was convicted of capital murder and sentenced to death.

Received at death row: February 10, 1995. *Time on death row:* 4,002 days (10.96 years).

Last meal: Declined last meal.

Last statement: None.

Pronounced dead: 6:16 P.M.

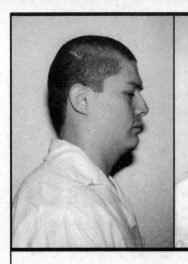

357

Jaime Elizalde Jr.

Executed:
January 31,
2006

Personal data: *Born:* December 12, 1971. *Race:* Hispanic. *Height:* 5'6". *Weight:* 115 pounds. *Education:* 8 years (GED). *Prior occupation:* Welder. *County of conviction:* Harris. *Age at time of execution:* 34.

Sentenced to death for: Convicted in the November 1994 shooting deaths of Juan Saenz Guajardo and Marcos Sanchez Vasquez in Houston. Elizalde and his father, Jaime Elizalde Sr., reportedly got into a confrontation with the two victims inside a Houston lounge, with the elder Elizalde convincing them to follow him outside. As the two men walked out the door, the junior Elizalde pulled a gun from his waistband and shot them to death.

Received at death row: June 12, 1997. *Time on death row:* 3,155 days (8.64 years).

Last meal: Fried chicken, onion rings, two milk shakes, french fries, peach cobbler, and orange juice.

Last statement: "Yes, sir. Darling Kerstin, these last few years have been blessed having you in my life. And to all my friends that have been out there, thank you for your friendship and support and all you have done for me. The guys back there waiting, keep the faith and stay strong and put your faith in the Lord. Many times in life we take the wrong road and there are consequences for everything. Mistakes are made, but with God all things are possible. So put your faith and trust in Him. We talk about a reprieve or stay from the Supreme Court, but the real Supreme Court you must face it up there and not down here. Keep your heads up and stay strong. I love you all. That is it. Stay strong. Thank you."

Pronounced dead: 6:17 P.M.

358

TEXAS
999293
JAN. 99

Robert James Neville Jr.

Executed: February 8, 2006

Personal data: *Born:* October 5, 1974. *Race:* White. *Height:* 6'0". *Weight:* 140 pounds. *Education:* 11 years. *Prior occupation:* Laborer. *County of conviction:* Tarrant. *Age at time of execution:* 31.

Sentenced to death for: On February 15, 1998, in Arlington, Neville and codefendant Michael Wayne Hall kidnapped a 19-year old white female and took her to a remote area, where they shot her seven times with a .22 caliber pistol. Neville and Hall knew the victim from work. The subjects fled the scene and attempted to flee the country, but they were stopped at the border.

Received at death row: January 5, 1999. *Time on death row:* 2,591 days (7.10 years).

Last meal: Chicken-fried steak, mashed potatoes with gravy, fried okra, bread and butter, sweet tea, chocolate cake with icing, mixed fresh vegetables, and doughnuts.

Last statement: "Yes. Ms. Carolyn Barker, and Tina, I would like to apologize to you all. To Amy's sister, and everybody else here. I love you all. I hope you can find it in yourselves to forgive me and I hope all this here will kinda settle your pain and I hope the Lord will give you comfort and peace. And I just want you to know I am very sorry for what I have done. And if I see Amy on the other side, I will tell her how much you love and miss her and we will have a lot to talk about. Mom, Dad, and Charlotte—I am sorry for putting you through all this pain and stuff. I did talk to Brandon and I think I got a little stuff stopped. I love you all and I will see you on the other side. OK."

Pronounced dead: 6:19 P.M.

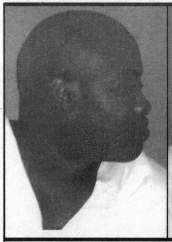

359

Clyde Smith Jr.

Executed: February 15, 2006

Personal data: *Born:* August 31, 1973. *Race:* Black. *Height:* 6'0". *Weight:* 191 pounds. *Education:* 9 years (GED). *Prior occupation:* Security. *County of conviction:* Harris. *Age at time of execution:* 32.

Sentenced to death for: Convicted in the February 1992 murder of Yellow Cab driver David Jacobs in Houston. Jacobs picked up Smith at the Hyatt Regency and was told to drive to a deserted area, where he was shot three times in the head. Smith is also charged with the March 1992 killing of United Cab driver Victor Bilton in Houston.

Received at death row: January 14, 1993. *Time on death row:* 4,780 days (13.10 years).

Last meal: A cheeseburger.

Last statement: "Yes. I want to thank you all for being here and for your love and support. And thanks for the efforts, Peter and Lorrell. I love you all. Celina, I love you. I'm done."

Pronounced dead: 6:17 P.M.

360

Tommie Hughes

Executed: March 15, 2006

Personal data: *Born:* August 15, 1974. *Race:* Black. *Height:* 5'7". *Weight:* 195 pounds. *Education:* 12 years. *Prior occupation:* Laborer. *County of conviction:* Dallas. *Age at time of execution:* 31.

Sentenced to death for: While Hughes was attempting to rob a black female's vehicle, he shot and killed her with a firearm.

Received at death row: June 18, 1998. *Time on death row:* 2,827 days (7.75 years).

Last meal: Six pieces of fried chicken with hot sauce, six jalapeño peppers, extra-large french fries with ketchup and salt, two Sprites, two cigarettes (menthol preferred), and four buttered rolls or biscuits.

Last statement: "I love my family. You all stay strong. Watch over each other. Stay strong. I love you. I love you. It's my hour. It's my hour. I love you. Stay strong."

Pronounced dead: 6:23 P.M.

361

Robert Salazar Jr.

Executed:
March 22,
2006

Personal data: *Born:* October 24, 1978. *Race:* Hispanic. *Height:* 5'7". *Weight:* 190 pounds. *Education:* 9 years. *Prior occupation:* Laborer. *County of conviction:* Lubbock. *Age at time of execution:* 27.

Sentenced to death for: On April 23, 1997, in Lubbock, Salazar fatally injured a 2-year-old Hispanic female, whom he was babysitting. He inflicted wounds consisting of a fractured skull, a bruised heart, fractured ribs, and ruptured intestines. After injuring the victim, Salazar placed her in her crib and left the residence. The victim's mother arrived from work, finding the child in her crib and Salazar absent. The victim was pronounced dead at a local hospital.

Received at death row: April 28, 1999. *Time on death row:* 2,520 days (6.90 years).

Last meal: Twelve tamales (no onions), six brownies, refried beans with chorizo, two Rolo candies, six hard-shell tacos with lettuce, three Big Red sodas, ketchup, hot sauce, six jalapeño peppers, tomatoes, cheese, and extra ground beef.

Last statement: "Yes. Yes, I do. Do I just talk to the front? OK. To everybody on both sides of that wall—I want you to know I love you. I am sorry that the child had to lose her life, but I should not have to be here. Tell my family I love them all and I will see them in heaven. Come home when you can. I am done. Love you all."

Pronounced dead: 6:20 P.M.

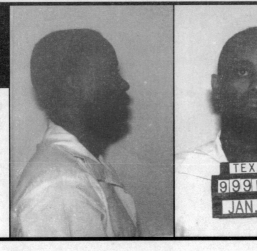

362

Kevin Christopher Kincy

Executed: March 29, 2006

Personal data: *Born:* January 31, 1968. *Race:* Black. *Height:* 5'10". *Weight:* 140 pounds. *Education:* 12 years. *Prior occupation:* Roughneck. *County of conviction:* Harris. *Age at time of execution:* 38.

Sentenced to death for: Convicted in the March 1993 robbery and murder of Jerome Samuel Harville in Houston. Kincy and his cousin and codefendant Charlotte Marie Kincy went to Harville's home with the intent to rob him. Harville, an Exxon employee, let the two inside because he knew Charlotte. Once inside, Kincy pulled a .25 caliber revolver and shot Harville in the head. He and Charlotte then loaded up Harville's car with several items from the home, including stereo equipment, furniture, and a 9mm pistol, and fled. Kincy later bragged to friends about the murder and showed off the stolen pistol. He was finally arrested after leading police on a high-speed chase from Orange, Texas, to Sulpher, Louisiana.
Codefendant: Charlotte Kincy received forty years for aggravated robbery.

Received at death row: January 1, 1996. *Time on death row:* 3,740 days (10.25 years).

Last meal: Declined last meal.

Last statement: "Yes. I would like to thank all my friends and supporters. Anne West, who I love and respect. Gabrielle Uhl from Germany, and so many countless other friends. And of course my family, my mother and father, brothers and sisters, nieces and nephews, my wife Barbara, and my children—Nadia, Amenia, Kira, and Noemi. I love my children. I love my family. That's it."

Pronounced dead: 6:26 P.M.

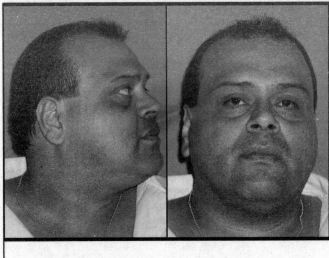

Jackie Barron Wilson

Executed: May 4, 2006

Personal data: *Born:* February 12, 1967. *Race:* White. *Height:* 5'8". *Weight:* 265 pounds. *Education:* 12 years. *Prior occupation:* Bricklayer. *County of conviction:* Dallas. *Age at time of execution:* 39.

Sentenced to death for: Convicted in the November 1988 abduction and murder of 5-year-old Lottie Margaret Rhodes of Arlington. As the child slept, Wilson broke in to her bedroom through a window and abducted her. He later sexually assaulted the child, then suffocated her. He threw the body into a ditch in north Grand Prairie and then drove over her body with his vehicle. Wilson's fingerprints were later lifted from the outside and inside of the child's bedroom window. Wilson was identified as a friend of the Rhodes family's live-in babysitter.

Received at death row: November 21, 1989. *Time on death row:* 6,008 days (16.46 years).

Last meal: A cheeseburger, onion rings, beef enchilada, tea, Coke, a whole onion, a whole tomato, and lemon pie.

Last statement: "May I speak to my family? Honey, I love you. Be strong and take care of yourselves. Thanks for being there. Take care of yourself. Ms. Irene, thank you for everything you have done. Chaplain Hart, thank you for helping me. Gary, thank you. Maria, Maria, I love you, baby. Thank you for being there for me and all these people here will find the one who did this damn crime. I am going home to be with God. Thank you. Thank you, Warden."

Pronounced dead: 6:20 P.M.

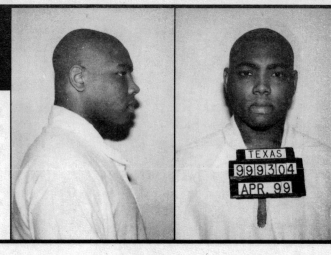

364

Jermaine Herron

Executed:
May 17,
2006

Personal data: *Born:* January 13, 1979. *Race:* Black. *Height:* 5'11". *Weight:* 220 pounds. *Education:* 10 years. *Prior occupation:* Ranch helper, painter, laborer. *County of conviction:* Refugio. *Age at time of execution:* 27.

Sentenced to death for: On June 25, 1997, Herron murdered a 15-year-old white male and his mother in their home. A sawed-off shotgun and a 9mm pistol were used in the murders. The home had been burglarized and set on fire. An extreme amount of property was taken from the residence, including a 1997 pickup truck, guns, ammunition, sports equipment, and sports clothes.

Received at death row: April 29, 1999. *Time on death row:* 2,575 days (7.05 years).

Last meal: Sirloin steak, Worcestershire sauce (spicy), a bacon cheeseburger with ten slices of bacon, onion rings and fries with cheese, French dressing, a Butterfinger Blizzard with caramel, pecan pie, vanilla ice cream, and peach cobbler.

Last statement: "Yes, sir. To Mr. Jerry Nutt, I just hope this brings some kind of peace to your family. I wish I could bring them back, but I can't. I hope my death brings peace; don't hang on to the hate. Momma, stay strong. Lord forgive me for my sins because here I come. Let's go, Warden."

Pronounced dead: 7:25 P.M.

365

Jesus Ledesma Aguilar

Executed:
May 24, 2006

Personal data: *Born:* November 28, 1963. *Race:* Hispanic. *Height:* 5'9". *Weight:* 185 pounds. *Education:* 11 years. *Prior occupation:* Bricklayer. *County of conviction:* Cameron. *Age at time of execution:* 42.

Sentenced to death for: Convicted in the June 1995 shooting deaths of Leonardo Chavez and his wife, Annette Esparza Chavez, at a trailer home in Harlingen. Both victims were shot execution-style with a .22 caliber weapon. Police said Leonardo was pistol-whipped prior to being shot in the back of the head. Annette was shot through the neck. During the shooting, the couple's 22-month-old son slept on a bed while their 9-year-old son hid beneath a table. Neither was harmed. Police said the shooting was drug related, with reports of Annette making frequent trips to Mississippi and returning with large amounts of cash.
Codefendant: Christopher Quiroz received life for capital murder.

Received at death row: May 13, 1996. *Time on death row:* 3,663 days (10.04 years).

Last meal: A full meal of enchiladas.

Last statement: "Yes, sir. I would like to say to my family, I am all right. [In Spanish] Where are you Leo; are you there Leo? Don't lie, man. Be happy. Are you happy? Are you all happy?"

Pronounced dead: 6:32 P.M.

366

Timothy Tyler Titsworth

Executed: June 6, 2006

Personal data: *Born:* March 8, 1972. *Race:* White. *Height:* 5'9". *Weight:* 204 pounds. *Education:* 8 years. *Prior occupation:* Roofer. *County of conviction:* Randall. *Age at time of execution:* 34.

Sentenced to death for: Convicted in the July 1993 robbery and murder of 26-year-old Christine Marie Sossaman, his live-in girlfriend. Sossaman was attacked with an ax inside the trailer the two shared in Amarillo. Titsworth told police he left the trailer to buy crack cocaine after the two argued the night of the murder. He said he was high on cocaine when he returned to the trailer, took an ax from the closet, and struck Sossaman as she slept. Titsworth stole the victim's credit cards and car. He returned to the trailer on different occasions following the killing to steal additional property and sell it for crack cocaine.

Received at death row: November 2, 1993. *Time on death row:* 4,599 days (12.60 years).

Last meal: Beef fajitas with jalapeño peppers, rib-eye steak, baked potato, beef enchiladas with cheese, and six Mountain Dews.

Last statement: "Yes, your honor. I know you people are here to find closure for the things that you have done or that I have done. There are no words to describe the pain and suffering that you have gone through all these years; that is something that I cannot take back from you all. I hope that Megan, if she is here present today, knows that today I hope you get peace and joy. I am sorry that it has taken fourteen years to get closure. If it would have brought closure or brought her back, I would have done this years ago, I promise, I promise. My family all knows the sincerity in my heart when I say these words to you. I didn't mean to inflict the pain and suffering on your family. I pray that she is safe in heaven. I pray that you find closure and strength. My family prays for you and everybody, if these words can ever touch your heart, I am sorry, I am truly sorry. Y'all take care. I love y'all. Pastor, tell Megan I am sorry."

Pronounced dead: 7:25 P.M.

367

Lamont Reese

Executed:
May 24, 2006

TEXAS
999374
JANUARY 2001

Personal data: *Born:* October 16, 1977. *Race:* Black. Height: 5'10". *Weight:* 207 pounds. *Education:* 10 years. *Prior occupation:* Laborer. *County of conviction:* Tarrant. *Age at time of execution:* 28.

Sentenced to death for: On March 1, 1999, in Fort Worth, Reese shot and killed a 17-year-old black male, a 25-year-old black male, and a 26-year-old black male with a handgun. Also injured were a 13-year-old black male and a 24-year-old black male.

Received at death row: January 18, 2001. Time on death row: 1,952 days (5.35 years).

Last meal: Beef or chicken fajitas with cheese and sour cream, jalapeño peppers, beef and cheese enchiladas, salsa, a bacon cheeseburger, with the works and jalapeño peppers, pizza with jalapeño peppers and everything, chicken salad, ranch dressing, and jalapeño peppers, soft beef tacos with salsa, fried chicken with ketchup and hot sauce.

Last statement: "Yeah. Mama, I just want you to know I love you. I want all of you to know I love you all. I am at peace; we know what it is. We know the truth. Stay out of crime; there is no point in it. I am at peace. We know the truth and I know it. I have some peace. I am glad it didn't take that long—no ten or twenty years. I am at peace. And I want everyone to know I did not walk to this, because this is straight up murder. I just want everybody to know I didn't walk to this. The reason is because it's murder. I am not going to play a part in my own murder. No one should have to do that. I love you all. I do not know all of your names. And I don't know how you feel about me. And whether you believe it or not, I did not kill them. I just want you all to have peace; you know what I'm saying. There is no point in that. It is neither here nor there. You have to move past it. It is time to move on. You know what I'm saying. I want each one of my loved ones to move on. I am glad it didn't last long. I am glad it didn't last long. I am at peace. I am at peace to the fullest. The people that did this—they know. I am not here to point fingers. God will let them know. If this is what it takes, just do what you got to do to get past it. What it takes. I am ready, Warden. Love you all. Let my son know I love him."

Pronounced dead: 6:27 P.M.

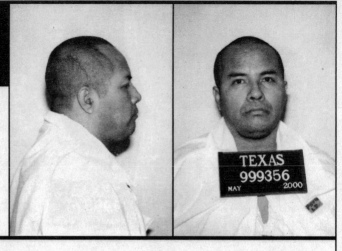

368

Angel Maturino Resendiz

Executed: June 27, 2006

TEXAS
999356
MAY   2000

Personal data: *Born:* August 1, 1960. *Race:* Hispanic. *Height:* 5'6". *Weight:* 190 pounds. *Education:* 7 years. *Prior occupation:* Laborer. *County of conviction:* Harris. *Age at time of execution:* 45.

Sentenced to death for: On the night of December 17, 1998, in Houston, Resendiz killed an adult Hispanic female by beating her to death with a statuette from her home. Resendiz had broken in to the victim's house through an open door. He took the victim's cash and fled the scene in her jeep. Resendiz is believed to have committed a series of murders throughout Texas and other states. He was a Mexican national.

Received at death row: May 24, 2000. *Time on death row:* 2,225 days (6.10 years).

Last meal: Declined last meal.

Last statement: "Yes, sir. I want to ask if it is in your heart to forgive me. You don't have to. I know I allowed the devil to rule my life. I just ask you to forgive me and ask the Lord to forgive me for allowing the devil to deceive me. I thank God for having patience with me. I don't deserve to cause you pain. You did not deserve this. I deserve what I am getting."

Pronounced dead: 8:05 P.M.

369

Sean Derrick O'Brien

Executed: July 11, 2006

Personal data: *Born:* April 5, 1975. *Race:* Black. *Height:* 5'8". *Weight:* 177 pounds. *Education:* 9 years. *Prior occupation:* Laborer. *County of conviction:* Harris. *Age at time of execution:* 31.

Sentenced to death for: Convicted in the June 1993 kidnapping, sexual assault, and strangling of Elizabeth Pena, 16, and Jennifer Ertman, 15. The two teens had taken a shortcut home when they were attacked by O'Brien and five other members of the Black and White gang. Raped repeatedly by the gang members, each was then beaten and strangled; their bodies were left in the woods. O'Brien confessed to strangling Ertman with a belt after she was sexually assaulted.
Codefendants: Peter Cantu, Raul Villareal, Efrain Perez, and Joe Medellin all were sentenced to death for the murders.

Received at death row: November 18, 1994. *Time on death row:* 4,253 days (11.65 years).

Last meal: Declined last meal.

Last statement: "I do. I am sorry. I have always been sorry. It is the worst mistake that I ever made in my whole life. Not because I am here, but because of what I did and I hurt a lot of people—you, and my family. I am sorry; I have always been sorry. I am sorry. You look after each other. I love you all. Be there for one another. All right. But I am sorry, very sorry. I love you too. All right."

Pronounced dead: 6:19 P.M.

370

Mauriceo M. Brown

Executed: July 19, 2006

Personal data: *Born:* July 3, 1975. *Race:* Black. *Height:* 6'1". *Weight:* 159 pounds. *Education:* 10 years. *Prior occupation:* Telemarketing. *County of conviction:* Bexar. *Age at time of execution:* 31.

Sentenced to death for: Convicted in the August 1996 attempted robbery and murder of 25-year-old Michael T. Lahood Jr., in San Antonio. Lahood was standing near his vehicle on a San Antonio street when he was approached by Brown and three accomplices. Brown pulled a pistol and demanded Lahood's money and car keys. When Lahood refused to comply, Brown shot him once in the face. Brown was a known member of the Crips street gang at the time of the killing.
Codefendants: Kenneth Foster was sentenced to death. The dispositions of the two other codefendants is unknown.

Received at death row: July 1, 1997. *Time on death row:* 3,305 days (9.05 years).

Last meal: Fifteen enchiladas, heavy with cheese and onions, onion rings or fries, eight pieces of fried chicken, eight pieces of barbecue chicken, eight whole peppers, ten hard-shell tacos with plenty of meat, cheese, onions and sauce, four double-meat, double-cheese, double-bacon burgers, T-bone steak with A1 sauce, and a pan of peach cobbler.

Last statement: "Yes, I do. To the victim's family, I am sorry you lost a brother, loved one, and friend. To my family, I love you all. Keep your heads up and know I will be in a better place. And you all look after Aleda and make sure she is a part of this family. I appreciate you all and love you. I apologize that you lost a loved one this way. God bless you all. OK, Warden."

Pronounced dead: 6:47 P.M.

Robert James Anderson

Executed: July 20, 2006

Personal data: *Born:* May 29, 1966. *Race:* White. *Height:* 6'2". *Weight:* 149 pounds. *Education:* 12 years. *Prior occupation:* Security officer. *County of conviction:* Potter. *Age at time of execution:* 40.

Sentenced to death for: Convicted in the June 1992 kidnapping and murder of 5-year-old Audra Reeves of Amarillo. In a written confession, Anderson told police he kidnapped Reeves in front of his home as she returned from playing with other children at San Jacinto Park. He took her inside, where he attempted to rape her. Unsuccessful in his sexual assault, Anderson beat, stabbed, and drowned the young girl. He placed her body in a Styrofoam ice chest and carried it in a grocery cart to a garbage Dumpster behind a residence. The ice chest containing the girl's nude body was found in the dumpster by the homeowner. Anderson said he kidnapped and killed the girl after arguing with his wife about infidelity.

Received at death row: December 27, 1993. *Time on death row:* 4,588 days (12.57 years).

Last meal: Lasagna, mashed potatoes with gravy, lemonade, tea, beets, green beans, fried okra, two pints of mint chocolate chip ice cream, and a fruit pie.

Last statement: "Yes, I would like to make a short brief one, please. To Audra's grandmother, I am sorry for the pain I have caused you for the last fifteen years and your family. I have regretted this for a long time. I am sorry. I only ask that you remember the Lord because He remembers us and He forgives us if we ask Him. I am sorry. And to my family, and my loved ones—I am sorry for the pain for all those years and for putting you through all the things we had to go through. I ask the Lord to bless you all. Tammy, Irene, Betty, Dan, Judy—I love you all. And Jack, thank you. Warden . . ."

Pronounced dead: 6:19 P.M.

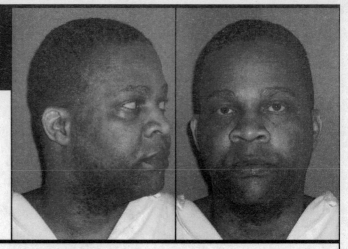

372

William E. Wyatt Jr.

Executed: August 3, 2006

Personal data: *Born:* December 20, 1964. *Race:* Black. *Height:* 6'1". *Weight:* 250 pounds. *Education:* 12 years. *Prior occupation:* Correctional officer. *County of conviction:* Bowie. *Age at time of execution:* 41.

Sentenced to death for: Wyatt sexually assaulted and smothered to death a black male child under the age of six. At the time of the offense, Wyatt worked as an officer at the Bowie County Corrections Center in Texarkana.

Received at death row: February 19, 1998. *Time on death row:* 3,087 (8.46 years).

Last meal: Declined last meal.

Last statement: "Yes, I do. I would like to say to my two brother-in-laws and the rest of my family that I would like to thank you for supporting me through all of this. I went home to be with my Father and I went home as a trooper. I would like to say to Damien's family I did not murder your son. I did not do it. I just want you to know that—I did not murder Damien and would ask for all of your forgiveness and I will see all of you soon. I love you guys. I love you guys. That's it."

Pronounced dead: 6:20 P.M.

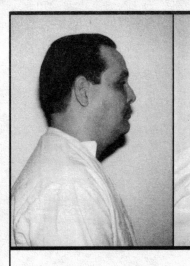 

373

Richard Hinojosa

Executed: August 17, 2006

Personal data: *Born:* November 17, 1961. *Race:* Hispanic. *Height:* 5'10". *Weight:* 224 pounds. *Education:* 5 years. *Prior occupation:* Construction worker. *County of conviction:* Bexar. *Age at time of execution:* 44.

Sentenced to death for: On May 10, 1994, in San Antonio Hinojosa kidnapped, robbed, sexually assaulted, and murdered a 19-year-old white female. The victim found Hinojosa burglarizing her residence. She was driven in her own car to an isolated location, where she was robbed, sexually assaulted, and stabbed to death with what is believed to have been a screwdriver. DNA testing linked Hinojosa to the killing.

Received at death row: December 9, 1997. *Time on death row:* 3,173 days (8.69 years).

Last meal: Chef salad with ranch dressing, french fries, onion rings, twelve pieces of fried chicken, five jalapeño nachos with chili cheese, four fried eggs over-easy, six Cokes, six Big Reds, and ketchup.

Last statement: "Yes sir, to my family and children, I love you very much. Dianne, Virginia, Toby, and Irene, I love all of you. I apologize for not being the man you wanted me to be. I am going to be free; I am going to heaven. Please be strong and I love you all. To the Wright family, I pray for you; please find peace in your heart. I know you may hate me for whatever reason; the Lord says hate no one. I hope you find peace in your heart. I know my words cannot help you; I truly mean what I say. God Bless you all. I love you Dianne, Mary, Virginia. Kick the tires and light the fire, I am going home to see my son and my mom. I love you and God bless you."

Pronounced dead: 6:19 P.M.

374

Justin Fuller

Executed:
August 24, 2006

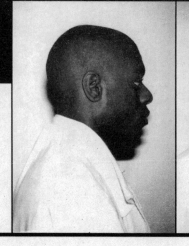

Personal data: *Born:* August 29, 1978. *Race:* White. *Height:* 6'0". *Weight:* 165 pounds. *Education:* 12 years. *Prior occupation:* Laborer. *County of conviction:* Smith. *Age at time of execution:* 27.

Sentenced to death for: On April 21, 1997, Fuller abducted, robbed, and murdered a 22-year-old white male near Tyler. The victim was bound and blindfolded inside his Tyler apartment and driven to his bank, where $300 was withdrawn from his account using his ATM card. The victim was then driven to Lake Tyler and shot three times with a .22 caliber weapon.

Received at death row: April 29, 1998. *Time on death row:* 3,039 days (8.33 years).

Last meal: Declined last meal.

Last statement: "Yes I do. I would like to tell my family thank you for your support, and my friends. And let everyone know that you must stay strong for each other. Take care of yourselves. That's it, Warden."

Pronounced dead: 6:18 P.M.

375

Derrick Frazier

Executed: August 31, 2006

Personal data: *Born:* April 28, 1977. *Race:* Black. *Height:* 5'10". *Weight:* 176 pounds. *Education:* 9 years. *Prior occupation:* n/a. *County of conviction:* Refugio. *Age at time of execution:* 29.

Sentenced to death for: On June 26, 1997, Frazier and one codefendant burglarized a private residence. Then they took the property and went next door to a residence where a white female was alone with her son. The victim offered them a ride into town and when she went out to start her vehicle, Frazier followed her. When she went back into the house, he shot her in the face with a 9-millimeter handgun. He then shot her again in the back of the head. The codefendant shot the son one time in the head and three more times in the chest and abdominal area with a 9mm handgun. Frazier and the codefendant then took the vehicle and fled the scene.

Received at death row: October 9, 1998. *Time on death row:* 2,883 days (7.90 years).

Last meal: Declined last meal.

Last statement: "Yes, I do. Debbie, my baby, I love you; do you know I love you. You are my life. You are my wife—always stay strong. Stay strong everybody. I am innocent. I am being punished for a crime I did not commit. I have professed my innocence for nine years, and I continue to say I am innocent. Let my people know I love them. We must continue on. Do not give up the fight; do not give up hope for a better future. Because we can make it happen. I love you, I love my son, and I love my daughter. Bruno, Chuckie, Juanita, Ray—I love you, all of you. Stay strong, baby. I love you forever."

Pronounced dead: 6:18 P.M.

376

Farley Charles Matchett

Executed: September 12, 2006

TEXAS 999060 APR. 93

Personal data: *Born:* November 19, 1962. *Race:* Black. *Height:* 6'1". *Weight:* 166 pounds. *Education:* 12 years. *Prior occupation:* Truck driver. *County of conviction:* Harris. *Age at time of execution:* 43.

Sentenced to death for: Convicted in the July 1991 robbery and murder of Uries Anderson at the victim's home in Houston. Anderson was stabbed with a knife and struck in the head with a hammer. Matchett reportedly robbed the home of money so he could buy crack cocaine. Matchett is accused of committing capital murder in Huntsville, where he was then living, a day prior to the Anderson murder.

Received at death row: April 30, 1993. *Time on death row:* 4,883 days (13.39 years).

Last meal: Four olives with seeds, and a bottle of wild berry water.

Last statement: "To my family and my mother and my three precious daughters, I love you all. And to my brother and sister for standing with me throughout this situation. Stay strong and know that I'm in a better place. I ask for forgiveness. And to the victim's family, find peace and cancellation with my death and move on. Our Lord Jesus Christ, I commend myself to you. I am ready."

Pronounced dead: 6:16 P.M.

Gregory Lynn Summers

Executed: October 25, 2006

Personal data: *Born:* March 14, 1958. *Race:* White. *Height:* 5'10". *Weight:* 140 pounds. *Education:* 11 years (GED). *Prior occupation:* General contractor. *County of conviction:* Denton (change of venue from Taylor). *Age at time of execution:* 48.

Sentenced to death for: Convicted in a murder-for-hire scheme to kill three people, including Summers's stepfather, Mandell Eugene Summers. Also killed were Helen Summers and Bill Mack Summers. All were stabbed to death inside their Abilene home, which was later set afire. Summers reportedly promised to pay codefendant Andrew Cantu $10,000 for killing his family members. Cantu was convicted of capital murder and sentenced to death. Two codefendants testified against him.

Received at death row: September 26, 1991. *Time on death row:* 5,508 days (15.09 years).

Last meal: Salad with Italian or ranch dressing, sweet iced tea, onion rings, and chili dogs.

Last statement: Offender declined to make a last statement.

Pronounced dead: 9:16 P.M.

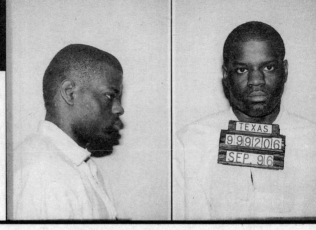

378

Donell Jackson

Executed: November 1, 2006

Personal data: *Born:* December 11, 1972. *Race:* Black. *Height*: n/a. *Weight*: n/a. *Education:* 8 years. *Prior occupation:* Laborer. *County of conviction:* Harris. *Age at time of execution:* 33.

Sentenced to death for: Convicted in the August 1993 murder-for-hire shooting death of Mario Stubblefield in Houston. Jackson was hired by codefendant Darryl Scott to kill Stubblefield in exchange for $200 in cash. Scott reportedly wanted Stubblefield killed because the victim was scheduled to testify against Scott in a separate aggravated assault case. Jackson was identified by an eyewitness as the triggerman in the Stubblefield shooting. Following the murder, Jackson was involved in an aggravated robbery during which he shot a high school friend and stole money from him.

Received at death row: September 27, 1996. *Time on death row:* 3,687 days (10.10 years).

Last meal: Peach cobbler, barbecue ribs, banana split ice cream, freedom fries, onion rings, root beer soda, two double-meat bacon burgers.

Last statement: "To my family, first and foremost—I love you all. The calmness that I was telling you about, I still have it. You are Mario's uncle, correct? I just wanted you to know that I wronged your family. I received nothing, I was not paid. I took his life for the love of a friend. I love you all. I just want you to know that. I know he does, I feel it. I'm all right. Make sure Momma knows, all right. Jermaine, I love you too man. All right, Warden."

Pronounced dead: 6:21 P.M.

379

Willie Marcel Shannon

Executed:
November 8, 2006

Personal data: *Born:* June 12, 1973. *Race:* Black. *Height:* 5'10". *Weight:* 150 pounds. *Education:* 10 years. *Prior occupation:* Laborer. *County of conviction:* Harris. *Age at time of execution:* 33.

Sentenced to death for: Convicted in the murder of Benjamin Garza outside a Houston shopping center. Garza was in his car outside the shopping center in southwest Houston, waiting for his wife and children, when Shannon entered the passenger side. After a brief struggle, Shannon shot Garza in the head, kicked him out of the vehicle, and drove off. Shannon was arrested later in Beaumont after being spotted driving the stolen car. Police said Shannon had raped a maid at a nearby motel just ten minutes before he killed Garza.

Received at death row: December 15, 1993. *Time on death row:* 4,711 days (12.91 years).

Last meal: None.

Last statement: "All praises be to God. I would like to say to the Garza family, see my smile, it is not from happiness. I took a father, it wasn't my fault, it was an accident. God knows the truth. If my life could bring your father back, then let it be. Don't take my smile for disrespect. If I see your father I will ask him forgiveness. I told the judge the truth it was an accident. I'll smile and I am not sad. If my life could make you happy, be free. I'll say when I see him I'm sorry. I have no anger nor fear. Mom have no fear. Mommy I will be home when I get there."

Pronounced dead: 6:24 P.M.

380

Carlos Granados

Executed:
January 10, 2007

Personal data: *Born:* September 18, 1970. *Race:* Hispanic. *Height:* 5'3". *Weight:* 172 pounds. *Education:* 11 years. *Prior occupation:* Laborer. *County of conviction:* Williamson. *Age at time of execution:* 36.

Sentenced to death for: On September 13, 1998, in Georgetown, Granados went to his girlfriend's residence and an argument ensued. Granados used a long kitchen knife and stabbed his girlfriend, Katherine Jiminez, who then required hospitalization. Granados killed the girlfriend's 3-year-old child, Anthony O'Brien Jiminez, with a large kitchen knife. On September 14, 1998, the police officers were alerted due to a welfare concern for the 3-year-old child and his mother, because their family had not seen them for a full day. When police officers arrived they were unable to get a response to their knocking and calling at the door. Officers called the residence, but the telephone was never answered. Upon entering the apartment after the door was broken down, they found the mother on the floor with several knife wounds. They then observed the child, Anthony, lying on the floor. Granados entered the room through an open hallway and began shouting at the officers, "Shoot me, just shoot me." The officers observed that Granados had gaping wounds to his throat, both wrists, and inside both elbows. Grenados continued to beg the officers to shoot him.

Received at death row: May 6, 1999. *Time on death row:* 2,806 days (7.69 years).

Last meal: Fried chicken, pizza, soda.

Last statement: "Yes. Love you mom, love you Pop, love you Sara, and Amanda. Um, Cathy, you know I never meant to hurt you. I gave you everything and that's what made me so angry. But I didn't mean to hurt you. I am sorry. That's it."

Pronounced dead: 6:21 P.M.

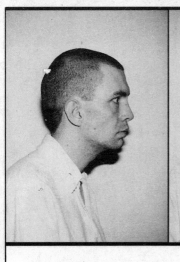

381

Jonathan Bryant Moore

Executed: January 17, 2007

Personal data: *Born:* April 4, 1974. *Race:* White. *Height:* 6'0". *Weight:* 145 pounds. *Education:* 12 years. *Prior occupation:* Telemarketer. *County of conviction:* Bexar. *Age at time of execution:* 32.

Sentenced to death for: Convicted in the January 1995 shooting death of San Antonio police officer Fabian Dominguez, 29. Moore and two codefendants had earlier burglarized the home of William Braden on Country Flower and returned to steal more items when Officer Dominguez spotted the three in the driveway and tried to stop them by pulling his weapon and ordering them out of their car. As Dominguez approached the car, Moore brushed his gun away and shot him in the face with a .25 caliber pistol he had pulled as the officer approached. Moore then grabbed the officer's pistol, which had fallen into the front seat of the suspects' car and shot Dominguez three more times in the head at close range as he lay helpless on the ground. Police later arrested Moore after a chase. He gave a full confession.

Received at death row: January 7, 1997. *Time on death row:* 3,662 days (10.03 years).

Last meal: Kraft Cheese & Macaroni, beef-flavored Rice-A-Roni.

Last statement: "Jennifer, where are you at? I'm sorry, I did not know the man but for a few seconds before I shot him. It was done out of fear, stupidity, and immaturity. It wasn't until I got locked up and saw the newspaper. I saw his face and his smile and I knew he was a good man. I am sorry for all your family and my disrespect—he deserved better. Sorry Gus. I hope all the best for you and your daughters. I hope you have happiness from here on out. Quit the heroin and methadone. I love you dad, Devin, and Walt. We're done, Warden."

Pronounced dead: 6:21 P.M.

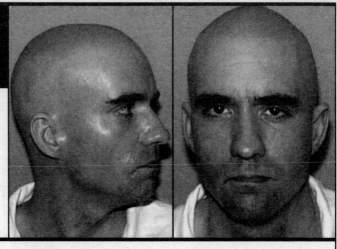

382

Christopher Jay Swift

Executed: January 30, 2007

Personal data: *Born:* February 12, 1975. *Race:* White. Height: 5'9". *Weight:* 150 pounds. *Education:* 8 years. *Prior occupation:* Laborer. *County of conviction:* Harris. *Age at time of execution:* 33.

Sentenced to death for: On April 29, 2003 in Denton County, Texas, Swift killed his wife, Amy Sabeh-Swift, a 29-year-old white female, by strangling her with his hands and striking her in the face with his fist approximately five times while Swift's 5-year-old son watched. Swift also killed his mother-in-law, Sandra Stevens Sabah, 61, by strangling her with his hands.

Received at death row: April 11, 2003. *Time on death row:* 1,390 (3.81 years).

Last meal: Steak (cooked medium well) with A1 sauce, bacon bits, one baked potato with sour cream, two slices of apple pie, one large roll, two Cokes, and one cup of coffee.

Last statement: None.

Pronounced dead: 6:20 P.M.

James Lewis Jackson

Executed: February 7, 2007

Personal data: *Born:* June 13, 1959. *Race:* Black. *Height:* 6'3". *Weight:* 204 pounds. *Education:* 12 years. *Prior occupation:* Gardener. *County of conviction:* Harris. *Age at time of execution:* 47.

Sentenced to death for: Jackson murdered Ericka Shauntae Mayes and Sonceria Messia Mayes, his two stepdaughters, at their home in Houston in April 1997. Upset that the girl's mother planned to divorce him, Jackson asked each of his stepdaughters how they felt about the impending split. When one of the girls said she didn't care one way or the other, Jackson choked her to death with his arm. He asked the same question of the other girl when she returned home to the apartment, and also choked her to death even though she told him she loved him and wanted him to stay in her life. Jackson placed both girls in their beds and then strangled their mother, Sharon Jackson, when she returned home and spurned his advances and attempts at reconciliation.

Received at death row: June 17, 1998. *Time on death row:* 3,157 days (8.65 years).

Last meal: : Fried chicken dark meat, fried okra, french fries, salad with blue cheese, four hardboiled eggs with cheese, two regular Cokes, one pint of butter pecan ice cream, and two honey buns.

Last statement: "You know, once upon a time diamonds were priceless. I never knew until I ran across my own. I just want Eve to know that. One of these days I'm going to return and get that for myself. Thank you to my family, I love you. Each and every one of you. This is not the end, but the beginning of a new chapter for you and I together forever. I love you all. Remember what I told you, Brad. Ms. Irene, God bless you, I love you. See you on the other side. Warden, murder me. Sodom and Gomorrah which is Harris County."

Pronounced dead: 6:18 P.M.

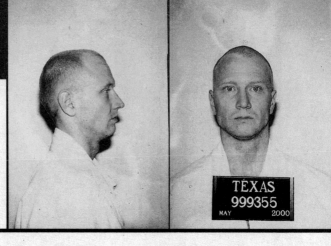

384

Newton Anderson

Executed: February 22, 2007

TEXAS
999355
MAY 2000

Personal data: *Born:* August 8, 1976. *Race:* White. Height: 5'10". *Weight:* 163 pounds. *Education:* 8 years. *Prior occupation:* Laborer. *County of conviction:* Smith. *Age at time of execution:* 30.

Sentenced to death for: On March 4, 1999, during the night in Tyler, Anderson burglarized a private residence. Anderson was caught in the act when the owners came home. Anderson shot Frank Cobb, the 60-year-old white male victim, in the upper torso with the victim's 410 shotgun, killing the victim. Anderson then tied up Bertha Cobb, the 65-year-old white female, bound her with duct tape, strangled her, and shot her one time with the shotgun. Anderson took approximately $100 in cash, clothes, and electronic equipment and fled the scene by car.

Received at death row: May 15, 2000. *Time on death row:* 2,474 days (6.79 years).

Last meal: Boiled eggs, pork chops, fried okra, pickles, potato salad, sliced onions, jalapeño peppers, tacos, fried chicken, cabbage, tomatoes, french fries, bacon, Sprite, baked potatoes, and sour cream.

Last statement: "Yes, for all of those that want this to happen, I hope that you get what you want and it makes you feel better and that it gives you some kind of relief. I don't know what else to say. For those that I have hurt, I hope after a while it gets better. I love you, I love you. I am sorry. That's it, good-bye. I love you Irene, I love you sis."

Pronounced dead: 6:17 P.M.

385

Donald Miller

Executed: February 27, 2007

Personal data: *Born:* June 12, 1962. *Race:* White. *Height:* 6'0". *Weight:* 155 pounds. *Education:* 11 years. *Prior occupation:* Painter (industrial). *County of conviction:* Harris. *Age at time of execution:* 44.

Sentenced to death for: Miller was indicted, tried, and convicted for murdering Michael Dennis Mozingo, 29, while committing or attempting to commit aggravated robbery. Also killed during the spree was Kenneth White, 19. The bodies of Mozingo and White were found by a passerby along a road near Lake Houston. Both had been shot in the head.

Received at death row: December 4, 1982. *Time on death row:* 8,851 days (24.25 years).

Last meal: One piece of fried chicken, one BLT sandwich, sweet iced tea, two enchiladas, ketchup, and a cinnamon roll.

Last statement: None.

Pronounced dead: 6:16 P.M.

386

Robert Martinez Perez

Executed: March 6, 2007

Personal data: *Born:* June 29, 1958. *Race:* Hispanic. Height: 5'5". *Weight:* 165 pounds. *Education:* 8 years. *Prior occupation:* Laborer. *County of conviction:* Harris. *Age at time of execution:* 33.

Sentenced to death for: On April 17, 1994, in San Antonio, Texas, Perez and two codefendants fatally shot Jose Travieso and James Robert Rivasat, two adult Hispanic males, numerous times with a .380 caliber pistol, a 9mm pistol, and a .38 caliber pistol. The shooting was a result of an internal power struggle within the Mexican mafia.

Received at death row: July 29, 1999. *Time on death row:* 2,777 days (7.61 years).

Last meal: Five pieces of fried chicken, one double-beef hamburger with cheese and onion, onion rings, three cheese and onion enchiladas, one onion, french fries, two Cokes, hot sauce, pico de gallo, and jalapeño pepper.

Last statement: "Yes, sir. Ernest, Christopher, Ochente, Mary, and Jennifer tell all the kids I love them and never forget. Tell Bobby, Mr. Bear will be dancing for them. Tell Bear not to feel bad. My love always, I love you all. Stay strong Mary, take care of them. I love you too. I am ready, Warden."

Pronounced dead: 6:17 P.M.

387

Joseph
Bennard
Nichols

Executed:
March 7,
2007

Personal data: *Born:* September 8, 1961. *Race:* Black. *Height:* n/a. *Weight:* 165 pounds. *Education:* 11 years. *Prior occupation:* Laborer. *County of conviction:* Harris. *Age at time of execution:* 45.

Sentenced to death for: Nichols was convicted and sentenced to death in the October 13, 1980, killing of Claude Schaffer Jr. during a Houston delicatessen robbery. His accomplice, Willie Ray Williams, was also sentenced to death for the robbery and executed (see entry 89). Lawyers for Nichols claimed that Williams went back inside after the robbery was completed and shot Schaffer.

Received at death row: March 12, 1982. *Time on death row:* 9,126 days (24.99 years).

Last meal: None.

Last statement: Profanity directed toward staff.

Pronounced dead: 6:19 P.M.
Note: Officers carried offender to gurney.

388

Charles Anthony Nealy

Executed: March 20, 2007

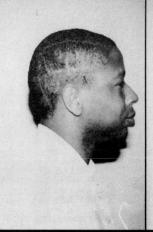 

Personal data: *Born:* March 23, 1964. *Race:* Black. Height: 6'0". *Weight:* 180 pounds. *Education:* 10 years. *Prior occupation:* n/a. *County of conviction:* Dallas. *Age at time of execution:* 42.

Sentenced to death for: On August 29, 1997 in Dallas, Nealy murdered Jiten Bhakta, a 25-year-old Asian male clerk while robbing a convenience store. Nealy shot the victim, resulting in his death, then fled the scene on foot with approximately $4,000. Nealy was later identified by a witness and the witness said Nealy had admitted to the murder.

Received at death row: December 10, 1998. *Time on death row:* 3,022 days (8.28 years).

Last meal: None.

Last statement: "Ya'll know I love you; you too, Warden. You have been a good friend. You are a good investigator. Doug, I thank you for coming from Michigan. Chris and David, I love you. Thank them for their support, Doug. Debra, James, I'm not crying so you don't cry. Don't be sad for me. I'm going to be with God, Allah, and Momma. I'm gonna ask Dad why didn't give you away at your wedding. Randy Greer, my little brother, I'll be watching you, stay out of trouble. All my nieces and nephews, I love you all. Sammie, Vincent, and Yolanda, I will be watching over you all.

The reason it took them so long is because they couldn't find a vein. You know how I hate needles—I used to stay in the doctor's office. Tell the guys on death row that I'm not wearing a diaper. I can't think of anything else. You all stay strong. Now you can put this all aside. Don't bury me in the prison cemetery. Bury me right beside Momma. Don't bury me to the left of Dad, bury me on the right side of Mom.

Kim Schaeffer, you are a evil woman. You broke the law. The judges and courts helped you and you didn't have all the facts. When you look at the video, you know you can't see anyone. You overplayed your hand looking for something against me and to cover it up the State is killing me. I'm not mad or bitter though. I'm sad that you are stuck here and have to go through all of this. I am going somewhere better. My time is up. Let me get ready to make my transition. Doug, don't forget Marcy."

Pronounced dead: 7:20 P.M.

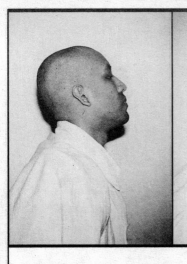

389

Vincent Gutierrez

Executed: March 28, 2007

Personal data: *Born:* October 1, 1978. *Race:* Hispanic. *Height:* 5'6". *Weight:* 142 pounds. *Education:* 8 years. *Prior occupation:* Never worked. *County of conviction:* Bexar. *Age at time of execution:* 28.

Sentenced to death for: On March 11, 1997, Gutierrez and and two codefendants murdered Jose Cabo, a 40-year-old Hispanic male during a carjacking.

Received at death row: March 15, 1998. *Time on death row:* 3,300 days (9.04 years).

Last meal: Five cheese enchiladas, two jalapeño peppers, two carne guisada tacos, one pint of butter pecan ice cream, one onion, one tomato, one bunch of grapes, one banana milk shake/strawberry milk.

Last statement: "I do. I would like to tell everybody that I'm sorry about the situation that happened. My bad—everybody is here because of what happened. I'd like to thank everybody that's been here through the years. The little kids overseas—they really changed me. Sister Doris, Mom, brothers, sister, Dad; I love ya'll. My brother . . . where's my stunt double when you need one? My Lord is my life and savior, nothing shall I fear."

Pronounced dead: 6:23 P.M.

390

Ray Lee Pippin

Executed:
March 29, 2007

Personal data: *Born:* March 30, 1955. *Race:* White. Height: 5'11". *Weight:* 235 pounds. *Education:* 12 years. *Prior occupation:* AC/heating tech. *County of conviction:* Harris. *Age at time of execution:* 51.

Sentenced to death for: Convicted in the kidnapping and shooting deaths of Elmer Buitrago and Fabio Buitrago in Houston. Pippin was part of a Columbian-linked organization that moved millions of dollars in drug sale proceeds across the border. When $1.6 million turned up missing, Pippin and four codefendants kidnapped the Buitragos and two other men and took them to a warehouse where Pippin ran an air-conditioning repair service. There, Elmer and Fabio Buitrago were shot, along with a third man, Javier Riasco. The fourth man, Jair Salas, escaped after being beaten. Fabio Buitrago died at the warehouse. Elmer managed to run to a neighboring apartment complex before collapsing in the courtyard. He died fourteen hours later at a hospital.

Received at death row: November 3, 1995. *Time on death row:* 4,164 days (11.41 years).

Last meal: None.

Last statement: "Yes, sir. I charge the people of the jury, trial judge, the prosecutor that cheated to get this conviction. I charge each and every one of you with the murder of an innocent man. All the way to the CCA, Federal Court, 5th Circuit and Supreme Court. You will answer to your maker when God has found out that you executed an innocent man. May God have mercy on you. My love to my son, my daughter, Nancy, Cathy, Randy, and my future grandchildren. I ask for forgiveness for all of the poison that I brought into the U.S., the country I love. Please forgive me for my sins. If my murder makes it easier for everyone else let the forgiveness please be a part of the healing. Go ahead, Warden, murder me. Jesus, take me home."

Pronounced dead: 6:42 P.M.

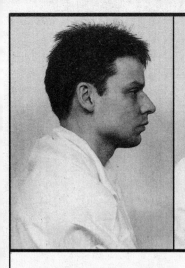

391

James Lee Clark

Executed: April 11, 2007

Personal data: *Born:* May 13, 1968. *Race:* White. *Height:* 5'9". *Weight:* 157 pounds. *Education:* 9 years. *Prior occupation:* Plumber's helper. *County of conviction:* Denton. *Age at time of execution:* 38.

Sentenced to death for: Convicted in the June 1993 robbery, rape, and murder of 17-year-old Car Crews. Crews was shot to death after being sexually assaulted.

Received at death row: May 4, 1994. *Time on death row:* 4,725 days (12.95 years).

Last meal: None.

Last statement: "Uh, I don't know, um, I don't know what to say. I don't know. [Pauses] I didn't know anybody was there. Howdy."

Pronounced dead: 6:17 P.M.

Note: The last statements appear as recorded by the Texas Department of Criminal Justice. Since no sound recordings are made, it is not possible to check the accuracy of the statements as transcribed by the TDCJ personnel.

3. Ronald Clark O'Bryan: [Written] What is about to transpire in a few moments is wrong! However, we as human beings do make mistakes and errors. This execution is one of these wrongs. Yet it doesn't mean our whole system of justice is wrong. Therefore, I would forgive all who have taken part in any way in my death. Also, to anyone I have offended in anyway during my 39 years, I pray and ask your forgiveness, just as I forgive anyone whose offended me in anyway. And, I pray and ask God's forgiveness for all of us respectively as human beings. To my loved ones, I extended my undieing [*sic*] love. To those close to me, know in your hearts I love you one and all. God bless you all and may Gods best blessings be always yours. Ronald C. O'Bryan P.S. During my time here, I have been treated well by all T.D.C. personnel.

10. Charles Francis Rumbaugh: [Written] I am currently scheduled to be executed before sunrise on the morning of September 11th, 1985. This is my third scheduled execution date and I therefore believe it is highly probable it will be carried out this time. This knowledge does not in any way disturb me; I feel comfortable with myself and my situation. I acknowledge my responsibility for causing a man's death almost 10 1/2 years ago and I am prepared to die for that even though it resulted from a situation I was not in control of and in which I had to either kill or be killed. Regardless of the circumstances, however, I do acknowledge my responsibility because I realize and admit it would not have occurred if I had not been in that place at that time with the intention of committing a robbery; I have no excuse and do not try to claim any.

Because of the offense I committed, my background, my rebellious character, and my alleged remorselessness, society—through it's judicial system—has condemned me to die. Just as I realize and acknowledge that I can proffer no excuse for my actions in causing the death of a human being, so must I state my clear and emphatic belief that neither can society proffer any righteously acceptable or defensible excuse for the imposition of the death penalty. My crime was an individual one committed by me alone and the responsibility is therefore mine alone, whereas society's crimes are concerted ones committed in the name of and by the authority of each and every citizen and therefore the responsibility is that of each and every citizen. Murder is Murder! Just as society condemns me, so must it condemn itself. Just as society labels me a "murderer" for causing the death of a human being, so must it label itself for knowingly, intentionally, premeditatedly and hypocritically causing the deaths of each an every human being throughout this country whom it has put to death. And the only possible "right" that society can claim in the RIGHT of MIGHT!

Just as the State of Texas has indicted me for the offense of Capital Murder, so do I indict each and every adult citizen of the State of Texas for the premeditated murders of nine men thus far and, further, for conspiring to murder over

200 others who are now incarcerated under sentence of death. (The only exception to this indictment are those persons of conscience who recognize the hypocrisy inherent in capital punishment, recognize "legalized" murder for what it really is and actively work in opposition to it.) Just as the State of Texas has convicted me of my crime, so does each and every adult citizen of the State of Texas stand convicted of their crimes. And, finally, just as the State of Texas has condemned me to die, so do I condemn each and every adult citizen of the State of Texas to serve the remainder of their lives contemplating their misdeeds—the rest of their lives contemplating the blood on their hands.

I leave you with one last thought: My life has taught me that violence does indeed beget violence, and capital punishment only perpetuates the vicious cycle and contributes to the list of victims of violence. I have no answers and I have no solutions, but I do know that only through the powers of love, caring, understanding, compassion, and reconciliation can you ever hope to find a solution.

35. Johnny R. Anderson: [Written] My final statement to the people . . .
I just want the public to know that I am not guilty of this crime and am being used as an excape goat, and all the people that were suppose to be involved in this case are out in the free world. I also want the public to know that in Capitol cases, the person getting killed by the state for revenge of the victim and there family, may satisfy the victim's family, but no one looks at what it puts my family through. The state puts my family in the same place as the victim's family. There are a lot of people on death row (that if people could meet would know that either they are not guilty or don't belong on death row). This is not a fair system they use to put people here, and instead of trying to shorten their appeals, you should try and get a specal court to look over all cases that involve the death sentence. Look at all the mistakes the state has made so far in some of these cases, and you will understand how bad the system is. People's lives ar on the life here, (Wake up out there People) some are guilty, but some are not, your killing the not guilty just as much as the state is by not helping find the not guilty one's. How would you like to get locked up for something you know you didn't do, and be killed for it, just because people think they that when you get locked up your guilty and that's the end of it regardless. The higher courts are so full that they are killing people left and right without really looking at the cases or the law, either they will change the law to fit the cases, or they will say when they find out later afterh they kill them and find out they shouldn't of, the one out of Ten is't bad, or try to hide it from the public. People what about that one person and his family?? And the victim's family that helped kill someone that wasn't guilty, through the state, What?? Keep killing people unitl you get the right one and play the odds. You people out there don't understand, any of this, either because you don't care enough to check, or you will have to wait until you're the one on the table getting killed, then as always it will be to late, then you understand how unfair the system really is for all parties involved. And stop killing people that kill people. What kind of masage is this sending to people, (That killing is okay for some people and not others??) That's why death row is full and shows no sign of slowing down, WRONG MASAGE PEOPLE!!!!!!
The excape goat Johnny R. Anderson Ex #000732

36. James Smith: [Portion of spoken last statement, most of which was not recorded]: I have already spoken the truth but because the truth was spoken by one of the accused, the truth was not respected so for that to set me free it must come from the one who spoke a lie. I am not the killer. I myself did not kill anyone. But I go to my death not begging for my life. I will not humiliate myself. I'll let no man break me . . . When people wake up to the reality of execution, the price the will be paid will be a dear one. Hare Krishna.

67. Richard J. Wilkerson: [Written by his sister] This execution is not justice; This execution is an act of revenge! If this is justice, then justice is blind. Take a borderline retarded young male Who for the 1st time ever committed a felony Then contaminate his true tell all confession Add a judge who discriminates Plus an ALL-WHITE jury Pile on an ineffective assistance of counsel And execute the option of rehabilitation Persecute the witnesses And you have created a death sentence or a family lasting over 10 years I will say this again . . . . . This execution isn't justice—but an act of revenge. Killing RJ will not bring Anil back, it only justifies "an eye for an eye and a tooth for a tooth." Its too late to help RJ, but maybe this poem will help someone else out there. [The following statement was also written prior to the execution.] Seeing Through The Eyes of a Death Row Inmate Sometime I wonder why, why he? Why did he go out into the world to see? To be out there and see what really did exist, now his name is written down on the Death Row List. I can only imagine how lonesome he was all by himself. We both knew he had no future left! His hopes and dreams became a fantasy. He often said, "There's nothing left of me." I have asked myself, why did he get involved with drugs? He could never explain why he hung around with thugs? Did it really make him feel like a king— Did he actually think he as capable of getting away with anything? He knew the thought of life wasn't ticking in his head. There's nothing left but the memory of those who lay dead. What was done, cannot be undone. He confessed he was one of the guilty ones. What would he say to the victims family?—I'm sorry and my head wasn't on straight. I hope you will accept my apology, even though its too late. I never knew I would take a life and commit a crime. I regret it because now I have to face the lethal injection while doing death row time. I knew I would pay with struggle and strife, but I never thought the cost would be losing my life.
Richard J. Wilkerson
Written through his sister, Michelle Winn

79. Robert Nelson Drew: [Written] It is now the second of August 1994 and tonight the state of Texas committed murder. The state took the life of Robert Nelson Drew Sr. age 35 for a crime he did not commit and had the evidence to prove it. The state fought for his life/execution with tax payers money that could have been better spent on schools or many other worth while endeavors that the entire state could have benefited from. Instead, one Harris county district attorney is gloating in his victory of not having to admit he made a mistake and sent an innocent man to death row for 11 years of his life. The district attorney would rather murder and innocent person than admit he made this mistake.

I hope that my death will serve as a catalyst to all people world wide to speak up and fight together as one to do away with the crime of judicial murder at the hands of any state. The facts of my case showed that I was and always will be innocent of the crime the state of Texas murdered me for. Yet due to the unjust 30 day low on newly discovered evidence I was unable to get a court to hear the evidence of my innocence. Now, as of April 20th, 1994, this law has been done away with by the court of criminal appeals of Texas and still the district attorney would rather waste the tax payers money to execute an innocent man then agree to a hearing. This tells the truth about the states case, if the state was so sure they were correct in their conviction they would allow a hearing cause they would know they had had nothing to hide. Since the truth of my innocence has come to light the state has fought twice as hard to execute me since they know their case would crumble under their own feet when the judge saw the evidence all presented by competent attorney's and not the incompetent ones they appoint at trial to those of us who were unable to retain our own for one reason or the other.

I think the words of Robert Alton Harris, executed in California, tell it best. "It you're a king or a street sweeper, one day we all dance with the grim reeper." This will include the district attorneys who fought for my judicial murder to be carried out on August second 1994. From this day on they will have the blood of an innocent man on their hands and my name in their lives til the day they stand before a higher power to be judged for the things they've done in their lives on this earth.

But, always remember the words spoken by Jesus Christ, "Forgive them father for they know not what they do." He has the power to forgive what they are doing by taking all the human lives they are taking by judicial murder, 80 in Texas alone since the death penalty was brought back into the law. This includes the murder of me tonight.

I'd like to let all my supporters know I'm very grateful for everything they've done for me over the years. Your kindness and compassion for truth in justice will never go unnoticed by others. I would like you to all remember that if you see another case that makes you feel this way to please stand up and yell long and loud til your heard world wide and justice is served. Not just sitting by is what it takes to change this world and you have to power to do it. Please be heard and fight for the death penalty to be abolished for good. This will be for the good of all humans in the world and not just a couple thousand men and women on death rows world wide. Everyone should remember it could very well be them or one of their loved ones in my place and for this reason everyone should stand now and be heard screaming to the world, "STOP THIS MADNESS, LET NO MORE BLOOD FLOW IN THE NAME OF JUSTICE, JUDICIAL MURDER MUST STOP NOW AND NEVER START AGAIN."

How many innocent people must die at the hands of states before the people all come together to fight for a just cause and do away with this madness? Don't let the politicians ruin your country and what it stands for. Tell them you know the truth and would rather see the two to three million or more that is spent to kill someone, when it would cost less than half a million to keep that person locked up for 40 calendar years or longer, spent on the things needed to ensure the future of the country. This money they have spent to murder an innocent man tonight could have been spent on schools for eh children who are the future of this country. This way it was wasted to murder someone who did nothing, but let the fear of his own death and the drunken haze of a day of drinking cloud his better judgement to not get killed himself to save someone else.

I am truly sorry I was to drunk to stop the killing of that young man that night in 1983, but, should I have been killed for being drunk and not getting myself killed to stop the murder that took place that night? Ask yourself if you'd back the state in this jucidial murder process if you could have seen all the evidence in court and not just what the district attorney wanted you to see. Should people die at the hands of the district attorneys just so they can add to their political endevors to become attorney general or a judge. Do you peole really want to be part of this judicial murder process? You are unless you join the world wide fight now tot do away with this unjust, barbaric, senseless law called the death penalty.

To all my friends I've left behind. I'd like you to always remember the fight must go on and never give up for any reason. Let no man tell you other wise. Always remember that quitters never are winners in anything and if you quit fighting for life and what is right you'll never win the battle. The battle will be won if you continue to fight. The cause is a just one, your own life, so fight with everything you have and win the fight. Carry on and hold your heads high knowing you are going the right thing.

To all my loved ones I left behind. I was taken from this life to satisfy a states governments blood lust but don't ever think of those who di ti cause they are not worthy of your thoughts. Remember I love every one of you from the bottom of my heart and always will. I'll be looking down on you from a better place and I now rest at peace and hope you'll find some comfort knowing these people have not killed me, they killed themselves cause I will never die to those who care and love me for me and not something else. I ask you to remember the good times from years gone by and know we'll be together again.

To all my friends on the "Row," don't give up. Fight his war an dwin it like I know in my heart that you can. Every one or you are worhty of this battle it will take to win, so fight on my brothers and know I'm fighting with you from a better place. Con'd let these bastards get you down.

To my road dog Robert "Shorty" Ramos, keep your head high and remember to do time and don't ever let time do you. Play your own game and don't ever give up the fight. It takes time but it can be won so don't let these bastards ever get you down. Keep yourself well, my brother. Your dog know you can do it so stick with it and you'll win the war.

Remember the good times Shorty and eat some candy for me once in a while. Don't let this shit get you down cause your dog is at peace and in a better place. I did my time in hell and now its time for something better. I'm gone in body but I'll never leave you in spirit, we'll fight together side by side.

To my dearest Judith. You've brought my love and happiness in the time we've been together and that will always be ours if we're together now or later.

Remember our times and smile cause you know I'm looking over you from above. I'll hold you in my arms tenderly one day soon. We'll walk in the summer sun and frolic in the fields of morning glories yet to grow in the fields of tomorrow and those fields will be ours. Give the children and grandchildren my love. Let your mum know I'm at peace but never give up the fight. My love is unconditional and never ending.

To George, your love, understanding, help, care, hard never ending work, and compassion have touched me deeply to depths I had forgotten even I had. Your loved dearly and there is no real way I could tell you in words how deeply grateful I am for everything you and your family have done over the years for me and the cause. Never give up the fight for the death penalty to be abolished once and for all and to never be brought back on the law books in this world again.

To my lawyers, Ron, Bill, Rob and the many others who worked for justice to be done in my case and worked so hard to save my life from this judicial murder. You have my undieing gratitude for everything you've done. Stay involved in capitol cases til the end of this judicial murder has come. Maybe we could've done more, maybe we could've done something differently, we'll never know and I don't want you to think about it. We fought it hard and long and with everything we had. Don't kid yourselves cause the bastards didn't win, they never beat us.

Now that this twelve year nightmare has come to an end let it be rememberd that the state of Texas has taken the life of an innocent man on August second nineteen ninety four and their true colors have been shown for what they are, blood thirsty politicians who will murder the innocent rather then say they made a mistake. May they rest in peace cause every time they close their eye lids I'll appear! I will not go away!!

Peace, Love and Much Respect to All My Comrades, Loved Ones, Fellow Abolishest, And Of Course My Road Dog!!!

Robert "Frenchy" Nelson Drew Sr. – Execution #79, August 2, 1994

85. Raymond Kinnamon: [Spoken last statement: The recording official noted, "portions of last statement of Raymond Kinnamon, #808 that I could hear and understand."] Yes, Warden, I would like to say a few words. I would like to say good-bye to my two boys in Indiana. I would like to tell them that I love them. I love all of my family members. I want my friends and family to keep working on the death penalty here in the State of Texas. I also want to thank my lawyers. I don't understand Judge Poe and Judge Higginbotham (Fifth Circuit) and I don't understand why Governor Richards did nothing. I also want to thank Kent Ramsey, the warden, Mr. Nunneles, etc. Sharon Longmier also treated me god. If any of this makes anyone feel good, then something is wrong with society. Also, thanks to Liz Cohen, Rob Owens, and Marsa Rutenbaum, my lawyers. I appreciate their hard work on my case. I love them all. Good-bye to Joey and all of my friends overseas, and I know there are a few more people I am missing. I'm not trying to delay this; there are just so many people I want to remember. There are so many friends on death row that I can't mention them all. I have never seen so many people who do not want me to be executed. I apologize for anything I have done that is wrong. I am not sure where I am going or if there is an afterlife. I just want one question answered, "What is capital punishment for?" Is it for someone like me to be executed? I also want to thank Kathy Fair, although she is no longer there. I want to thank the radio stations. I want to thank my Aunt Pat and my brother, and I don't want him to let this bother his illness; and Carol and Ron—take care of the boys. This coughing is due to cigarettes and the flu I just got over. There are lots of friends out there on the row that I would like to say good-bye to: Vanderbilt, B.J., Carl Buntion (although he isn't a very popular person on death row because he killed a cop); but he's been a real good friend. The warden wanted me to be short, but shoot, this is my last chance. I want to thank Pete Gaylord for his support and help and old Robert Valentine; he needs to take it easy. I appreciate all of the letters and everything. If I left anyone out, it's due to extenuating circumstances beyond my control. I want to thank everyone back here with me; I don't see how nice guys like them got tied up in something like this. Thank Chaplain Taylor and Jane. I just got your letter. Thanks to Carolyn and Gloria who have been my friends for over four years. I want to remember Patsy Buntion, Gladys, and a lot more friends. I want to thank the prosecutor in my case; it took courage for him to do what he did but he did what he did because he believed in the judicial system. I'm not ready to go, but I have no choice. I sent several letters to my family; they'll be very moving when you get them. I want to say good-bye again to my boys. I know I'm missing somebody, but if there's anything I have left to say, it would be that I wish I had a Shakespearean vocabulary but since I was raised in TDC, I missed out on some of my vocabulary.

If my words can persuade you to discontinue this practice of executing people, please do so. If the citizens don't do away with the death penalty, Texas won't be a safe place to be. I have no revenge because hate won't solve anything. [Last comment from official recording the last statement: "I gave Warden Hodges the phone at this time and he listened for five to ten minutes. When he returned the phone to me, I could hear Kinnamon talking, but evidently the phone was not close to the mike, because I could not understand him."]

86. Jesse Dewayne Jacobs: [Spoken] I would like to say that I see there are a number of you gathered here tonight to witness an execution by the State of Texas. However, I have news for you. There is not going to be an execution. This is premeditated murder by the appointed district attorney and the State of Texas. I am not guilty of this crime. I hope that my death will snowball an avalanche that will stop all executions in the State of Texas and elsewhere. If my death serves this purpose, then maybe it will be worthwhile. I hope my [official record is illegible] I have committed lots of sin in my life but I am not guilty of this crime. I would like to tell my son, daughter, and wife that I love them. Eden, if they want proof of them give it to them. Thanks for being my friend.

118. Clifton Eugene Belyeu: [Written] First of all I want to thank the LORD, my family and my wife Nora for all the support and encouragement they've shown through all this. I love you!! Now I want to thank all of you that came here today to be with me. I know most of you are here to see me suffer and die but your in for a big disappointment because today is a day of joy. Today is the day I'll be set free from this pain and suffering. Today I'm going to HEAVEN to live for all eternity with my HEAVENLY FATHER JESUS CHRIST and as I lay here taking my last breath, I'll be praying for all of you because your here today with anger and hatred in your hears letting satan deceive you into believing that what your doing is right and just. GOD help you, because what your doing here today and what's in your hearts here today makes you no better than any man or woman on death-rows across this country. Today your commiting murder too!!! I pray on my own behalf for forgiveness for any and all of the pain I've caused you, I pray that some day you'll realize your own mistakes and ask GOD to forgive you as I have because there is no peace without GOD's forgiveness.........AMEN

145. Karla Faye Tucker: [Spoken] Yessir, I would like to say to all of you—the Thornton family and Jerry Dean's family—that I am so sorry. I hope God will give you peace with this. Balu, I love you. Ron, give Peggy a hug for me. Everybody has been so good to me. I love all of you very much. I am going to be face-to-face with Jesus now. Warden Baggett, thank all of you so much. You have been so good to me. I love all of you very much. I will see you all when you get there. I will wait for you.

Note: There was a tremendous amount of controversy about the Tucker execution, largely because many believed Tucker had become a Christian and changed her life. Allan B. Polunksy, Chairman of the Texas Board of Criminal Justice, issued the following statement after her execution: "The issues here were not religious conversion or gender but rather culpability and accountability. Karla Faye Tucker brutally murdered two innocent people and was found guilty by the court and afforded all legal processes. Although I believe she finally found God, her religious awakening could in no way excuse or mitigate her actions in the world she just left, but hopefully will provide her redemption in the world she just entered."

160. Jonathan Wayne Nobles: [Spoken] Paula, I love you and I'm sorry. These two weeks have been a huge blessing. Kim, hi, I'm so sorry. Kyra, you made me hope. You received my love; it's yours. I'm so sorry I'm a source of pain. David, thank you for everything. I took so much from you. There's nothing I can do to give it back to you. I love you, I love all of you. Steve, it took me this to get you in a suit coat [laughs]. Don't worry about the phone number. Everything is going to be fine. I love you, man. I love you with all my heart. Father Walsh, my spirit has grown because of you. Larry Fitzgerald, thank you for being my friend. I'll see all of y'all at the church later on. Richard, thank you for everything you brought to Alice to help all of us. To my darling, what would life have been without you? I would still be in the dark night of the soul, I think. Thank you, Dona. Y'all wrap your arms around yourselves and give yourselves a great big hug for me. You know the routine. I want to share my favorite scriptures with y'all. Chaplain, help me through this. [Nobles then recited the text of 1 Corinthians 12:31B—13:13 (NIV).] And now I will show you the most excellent way. If I speak in the tongues of men and angels, but have not love, I am only a resounding gong or a clanging cymbal. If I have the gift of prophecy and can fathom all mysteries and knowledge, and I have a faith that can move mountains, but have not love, I am nothing. If I give all I possess to the poor and surrender my body to the flames, but have not love, I gain nothing.

Love is patient, love is kind. It does not envy, it does not boast, it is not proud. It is not rude, it is not self-seeking, it is not easily angered, it keeps no record of wrongs. Love does not delight in evil but rejoices with the truth. It always protects, always trusts, always hopes, always perseveres.

Love never fails. But where there are prophecies, they will cease; where there are tongues, they will be stilled; where there is knowledge, it will pass away. For we know in part and we prophesy in part, but when perfection comes, the imperfect disappears.

When I was a child, I talked like a child, I thought like a child, I reasoned like a child. When I became a man, I put childish ways behind me. Now we see but a poor reflection as in a mirror; then we shall see face-to-face. Now I know in part; then I shall know fully, even as I am fully known.

And now these three remain: faith, hope, and love. But the greatest of these is love.

I ask God to take my death as sacrifice for all the abuses directed toward the Holy Virgin. I ask this sacrifice in Christ. [Nobles then sang the hymn "Silent Night."]

162. **Daniel Lee Corwin:** [Spoken] I guess the first thing I want to do is thank some very special people, Sara and Sabrina. And for affording me the opportunity that y'all did. It made a real big difference in my life. I thank you. Thank you again from the deepest part of my heart. I'm sorry. The biggest thing I wanted to say was to you and family and I know I haven't had a chance to talk with y'all in any form or fashion or way or manner. And I regret what happened and I want you to know I'm sorry. I just ask and hope that sometime down the line you can forgive me. I think in a lot of ways that without that it becomes very empty and hollow and the only thing we have is hatred and anger. I guess the only thing I have to say about the death penalty is that a lot of times people think of it as one-sided, but it's not. It's two-sided. There is pain on both sides and it's not an issue that people just sit there and voice off and say, "Well this is a good thing or this is a bad thing." But it's something thats you know needs to be looked at and desired in each heart. I just hope that all of you can understand and someday forgive me. I want to thank y'all for affording me the opportunity to talk and meet with y'all. It meant so much. Thank you so much for being with me and my family. Thank you. I love you.

167. **Martin Sauceda Vega:** [Spoken] I really don't have much to say. All I want to say is that when the state introduced my sister and my niece as state witness, it's not that they testified against me. The thing is, my lawyers would not subpoena anyone, so they allowed the state to subpoena them to paint a picture to the jury that my own sister and niece was testifying against me. Linda is innocent of this. I am innocent of this. Now all you all are seeing in this process is a per-

fect example of the ole freaky-deaky Bill Clinton, when he signed that antiterrorism law to shorten the appeals. This is a conspiracy. They used false testimony of a woman that said I had raped her, when the test showed that the foreign pubic hair that was found on her body belonged to no one in that room. They found a drop of sposmosa [sic] in the crotch of her pants that was tied to blood type B. My blood type is A. Now the same woman there they brought to testify during this murder case. That woman was under indictment for possession of methamphetamine, delivery of methamphetamine. She could have gotten out of both those cases. Yet, she swore under oath that she had never been in trouble with the law and none of that mattered. So what does that make this great state? A very high-priced prostitute that sells itself called justice to the highest bidder. I am being charged under article 19.83 of the Texas Penal Code, of murder with the promise of remuneration. That means they got to have three people, the one that paid, the one that killed, and the deceased. And the alleged remunerator is out on the streets. So how come I'm being executed today, without a remunerator? This is a great American justice. So if you don't think they won't, believe me they will. Ain't no telling who gonna be next. That's all I have to say. Especially for the people of the deceased. Sims is innocent and so am I. So the murderer is still out there. Today you are a witness. The state . . . [cough] Bye.

172. **Charles Henry Rector:** [Spoken] the words of the song "God Living with Us 24 Hours"

God Living with Us 24 Hours
Listen people no man can stand all on his own and
No man has to stand alone.
The Father gave his Son so that all mankind never
Have to stand alone.
He's with you the day you are born up until the day
You die, Listen.
God Living with Us twenty-four Hours
Yes Sister, what dwells inside of you
Brother, he dwells inside of me
Yes yes yes, that mighty mighty power
The spirit of God, living with us twenty-four hours

Come on, reach out and touch His hand
Come on, and make a definite friend
Yes He will alway's be there around
Yes He never, never gonna let you down

When you paining, when you in trouble
Look to Him to deal with the problem
All He want from you is your love to be true
Call on Him, He's there inside of you
Yes Sister, what dwells inside of you

Brother, He dwells inside of me
Yes yes yes, that mighty mighty power
The spirit of God, living with us twenty-four hours
Let Him take control, give Him your body
Offer your soul, yes you got the power
The spirit of God, living with us twenty-four hours
Yes yes yes, that mighty, mighty power
Yes Sister, what dwells inside of you
Brother .. he dwells inside of me
Yes yes yes, that mighty mighty power
The spirit of God, living with us 24 hours
Once you had a taste of heaven
Nothing on earth can replace it
Check Him out for yourself, .. yes yes
His love is really something else

188. William Prince Davis: [Spoken] I would like to give thanks to God Almighty, by whose grace I am saved through his son Jesus Christ, without whom I would be nothing today. Because of this mercy and grace I have come a long way. And I would like to thank God and others who have been instrumental. I would like to say to the Lang family how truly sorry I am in my soul and in my heart of hearts for the pain and misery that I have caused from my actions. I am truly sorry. And to my family I would also like to extend to them the same apology for the pain and misery that I have put them through, and I love them dearly from the bottom of my heart, and one day I would like to see them on the other side. Some I will. Some I won't. I would like to thank all of the men on death row who have showed me love through the years but especially the last two or three weeks, and I hold nothing against no man. I am so thankful that I have lived as long as I have. I hope that I have helped someone. I hope that donating my body to science that some parts of it can be used to help someone. And I just thank the Lord for all that he has done for me. That is all I have to say, Warden. Oh, I would like to say in closing, "What about those Cowboys?"

197. James Beathard: [Spoken] I want to start out by acknowledging the love that I've had in my family. No man in this world has had a better family than me. I had the best parents in the world. I had the best brothers and sisters in the world. I've had the most wonderful life any man could have ever had. I've never been more proud of anybody than I have been of my daughter and my son. I've got no complaints and no regrets about that. I love every one of them and have always been loved all of my life. I've never had any doubts about that. Couple of matters that I want to talk about since this is one of the few times people will listen to what I have to say. The United States has gotten to now where they have zero respect for human life. My death is just a symptom of a bigger illness. At some point the government has got to wake up and stop doing things to destroy other countries and killing innocent children. The ongoing embargo and sanctions against places like Iran and Iraq, Cuba and other places. They are not doing anything to change the world, but they are harming innocent children. That's got to stop at some point. Perhaps more important in a lot of ways is what we are doing to the environment is even more devastating, because as long as we keep going the direction we're going the end result is it won't matter how we treat other people, because everybody on the planet will be on their way out. We have got to wake up and stop doing that. Ah, one of the few ways in the world the truth is ever going to get out, or people are ever going to know what's happening as long as we support a free press out there. I see the press struggling to stay existent as a free institution. One of the few truly free institutions is the press in Texas. People like the *Texas Observer,* and I want to thank them for the job they've done in keeping me and everybody else informed. I hope people out there will support them, listen to them, and be there for them. Without it, things like this are going to happen and nobody will even know. I love all of you. I always have; I always will. I would like to address the State of Texas and especially Joe Price, the District Attorney who put me here. I want to remind Mr. Price of the mistake he made at Gene Hathorn's trial when he said that Gene Hathorn was telling the truth at my trial. Mr. Price is a one-eyed hunting dog. He in fact is not a one-eyed hunting dog, and in fact Gene Hathorn lied at my trial. Everybody knew it. I'm dying tonight based on testimony that all parties me, the man who gave the testimony, the prosecutor he used knew it was a lie. I am hoping somebody will call him to the floor for recent comments he's made in the newspaper. It's bad enough that a prosecutor can take truth and spin on it and try to re-doctor it. But when they actually make facts up and present them to the public as trial's evidence. That goes beyond fail; that's completely unforgivable and I hope somebody makes Mr. Price account for or explain the tennis shoes he is talking about that put me here. I'm still completely lost on that and I'm hoping that somebody will go back and verify the trial record and make him accountable for lying to the public and the press that way. That's really all I have to say except that I love my family. And nobody, nobody has got a better family than me. I love you, Booger Bear. I love Doodle Bug, too. Don't let them ever forget me. I'll never forget them. I'll see you on the other side, OK. Bye bye, Debbie. Bye, Bro; bye, Booger Bear. Father Mike, Father Walsh, love you all. That's all, sir.

211. Timothy Gribble: [Written by chaplain] To the Jones Family: Please accept my sincerest apology and requests for what happened to your loved one. It was truly a horrible thing that I did and I regret it deeply. I do not know if this will ease your pain but I truly pray that this will help you find peace. I am sincerely truly sorry. For the Weis Family: The same is true. I regret what happened. I have lived with the guilt and the pain in my heart for taking Donna away from you. There is no way that I can know your pain and sorrow for losing someone so close to you. I truly hope that you will find peace. Please know that I am sorry. I feel that I have to speak out against the practice of the death penalty, although I have no regrets in my case. The death penalty is an unnecessary punishment for society who has other means to protect itself. You cannot rectify death with another death. Whenever the state chooses to take a life and take the power of God into their own hands, whenever our leader's kill in the name of justice, we are all diminished. To my family and friends, father, sister and brother, those that have traveled so far to be here today, please just know that I am at peace. You have all been so good to me through this whole ordeal. I can never find the words to express my love for all of you. Just know that I go with God. Oum—Nama Shiveya I go with God.

212. **Tommy Ray Jackson:** [Spoken] Yes sir, I would like to address the Robinson family. There is nothing I can say here or anything I could probably do. Now you are all probably mad at me and I would probably be in the same situation you all in if anybody I thought killed anybody in my family. Ahh, if I knew who killed Rosalyn I would let you know but, I am going to say this: I am going to heaven with God as my witness. Ros was a personal friend of mine. She was a beautiful person, very educated, her. I'm very tight with the Robinson family. She was proud that she had a father that was a doctor. My family is not here present and that is by my wish and my wish only. Now the tables is turned. You are all here, the Robinson family is here to see me executed. That is something that I would not want for my family. In no form or fashion would I have ever wanted to see Rosalyn dead. I left the scene of where the incident happened. I guarantee you if I would have been there you would not be standing where you are if I would have been there. You all have some very serious look on your face and something very serious fixin' to happen now. I will say this on my own behalf, but then again I know it is not going to make any difference, but what you fixing to witness is not a nice thing. It's not nice. It's not nice. The media. I would just like to address to the media with everybody's permission. I would like to say before I go that it has been said that I have shown no remorse, but if you look at my record and my background, ask anybody that know me that in order for me to show any kind of remorse for killing that ever been done, this one time I can't show no remorse for something that I did not do, and if I did I would be faking. I would totally be faking and believe me there is nothing fake about me. Nothing fake. I've done wrong, sure, I've paid the time. This is one time that I know I cannot show no remorse for something that I did not do. I am at peace, please believe me. Wherefore, I figure that what I am dying for now is what I have done in my past. This is what I am dying for. Not for killing Rosalyn. I don't know what y'all call her but I call her Ros, I call her Ros. That's it.

213. **William Joseph Kitchens:** [Spoken last statement] Yes, sir. James Webb, I don't know which one of you are out there. I can't remember from the trial. I personally just want to let you know if there has ever been any doubt in your mind at all of what happened, I want you to know that Patty was always faithful to you, that I forced her for everything that she did and I am sorry. I just don't know how to tell y'all I am sorry for what I did. There is no way for expressing I am sorry. I just hope that in some kind of way that y'all can move on and find peace in your life. The Lord has given me peace and that is all that I pray for is that ya'll can find that peace. I just want you to know that I am sorry for what I done. I can't change that, all I can do is say I am sorry, that's nothing for what I have done. I can't replace your loss. I am sorry. I just want you to know that I love all of y'all. It's been a pleasure, y'all just keep on with life, it's gonna be good. The Lord's gonna be with us. If it's all right, I just want to say a prayer first. Father, God, I

just thank you for the time that you have given me on this earth, for having mercy on somebody like me for all the despicable things I've done in my life, Father, but you still with your love and your mercy reach down into my heart and changed it before it's too late. I ask that you bestow peace upon the family of Patricia Webb, that you let them know, Father, that you are in a place where they can obtain that peace, and you will help them move on in their life, Father. Help them, Father, to find it in their hearts, not for my sake, but for yours, and their sake too, Father, find it in their heart to forgive me for what I have done. Father, I just ask that you be with my family and comfort them to move on, Father. Father, we are all here today for the mistake that I have made and I thank you for your mercy for sending your Son into this life, that we might come to know you, Father. Father, I pray for these wardens and the officers and the people that deal with all of this, Father, I ask that you touch their hearts, Father, and if there is any wrong to it, that you will forgive them, Father. Just let them know that you love them, Father, and that you are the way. I just thank you and in Jesus' name, I pray, Amen. I love y'all, y'all take care. I am so sorry.

214. **Michael Lee McBride:** [Written] The following is the personal final statement of and by Michael L. McBride. The Beatitudes: Jesus lifted up his eyes on His disciples, and said, "Blessed be the poor: for yours is the kingdom of God. Blessed are ye that hunger now: for ye shall be filled. Blessed are ye that weep now: for ye shall laugh. Blessed are ye, when men shall hate you, and they shall separate you from their company, and shall reproach you, and cast out your name as evil for the Son of Man's sake. Rejoice ye in that day, and leap for joy: for behold, your reward is great in Heaven: for in the like manner did their fathers unto the prophets. But woe unto you that are rich! for ye have received your consolation. Woe unto you that are full! for ye shall hunger. Woe unto you that laugh now! for ye shall moan and weep. Woe unto you, when all men shall speak well of you! for so did their fathers to the false prophets."

The supremacy of love over gifts: I Corinthians, Chapter 13: 4-8: Love is patient, love is kind, and is not jealous, love does not brag and is no arrogant, does not act unbecoming; it does not seek its own, is not provoked, does not take into account a wrong suffered, does not rejoice in unrighteousness, but rejoices with the truth; bears all things, believes all things, hopes all things, endures all things. Love never fails; but if there are gifts of prophecy, they will be done away; if there tongues, they will cease. Now abide faith, hope, love, these three: but the greatest of these is love.

Poem:
Do not stand at my grave and weep,
I am not there I do not sleep.
I am the diamond glints in the snow,
I am the sunlight on the ripened grain.
I am the gentle autumn rain.
When you awaken in the morning's hush,
I am the swift uplifting rush
of quiet birds in circled flight,
I am the soft stars that shine at night.

Do not stand at my grave and cry,
I am not there. I did not die.
Signed
Michael L. McBride #903
May 11, 2000, Huntsville, Texas

215. **James David Richardson:** [Spoken] Can they talk back? Say I pray for it, I accept it. Pray with me. This is still a statement. Ready? Dear Heavenly Father, forgive us, Lord. I ask that you watch over my mama and over my sister. I ask this in the name of Christ. I also repent for all my sins, Lord. I pray that you will bring me home tonight. Please, I ask that I rest in your arms, in the name of Christ Jesus I pray this. I truly believe that Jesus died for my sins that I may be resurrected, Lord, that you would do that much. Please, I ask that you not let me down and that I will be with you today in Heaven. Christ Jesus name I pray this. Donna and everybody else, Mr. Johnson, I ask that y'all will pray for me and that God will bring me home tonight, that he will keep me in heaven, that I will still be in heaven. Please Lord, I don't want to be in heaven, I mean I don't want to be in hell. And, please Lord, I confess my sins. This is your son, Lord Jesus, this is your servant, please, this is your slave. I love you, too. Donna and Mama and Mr. Johnson, I wrote a message. Don't give up, love you all, even the ones that are my enemies. I truly forgive all of y'all in Christ Jesus, we pray. I ask God that he take all the hate out of my heart and away from my soul. Please, please, Lord, don't fail me. I don't know is Margie here now? But if she is, I ask her forgiveness. I ask that you not hold nothing against me or my family from this day forward, and hold no hate toward them. I don't know. I can't hear you, you may forgive me, and you may not. Forgive Mike Allison, forgive McHenry, forgive us all. Whatever the cost may be, I love you. Take care of my mama. Donna, I ask you to take care of my mama, too. Whenever you get mad at her, you remember me. Remember I may be back. Mama, I am going to try to make that promise to you. I gonna ask God to allow his child to come back to see you. Cause I am in Heaven. At time I can come [unintelligible]. OK, Mr. Johnson, you take care, let my mama's will be done. One more prayer, then we may proceed. Heavenly Father, I confess my sins, really I do. Let me know that I will be in heaven tonight. Please let me know. I don't want to be in hell with Satan or anyone else. Please, that is something I need to know. I ask that Jesus give me help. In Jesus precious name, I pray this. I ask that you give me those promises, that you assure me that those promises are real. That I am praying right. In Jesus precious name, I pray this. Good-bye, Mama. Good-bye, Donna.

219. **Thomas Wayne Mason:** [Spoken] I understand that Michael Skains is supposed to be here somewhere. They did everything but make sure I got a fair trial to prove I was innocent. I wasn't the one who had the gun to give to police and all these altered records from the District Attorney's office and the Attorney General's office; that's why Michael Sputnick got fired and ran off when I filed these appeals. Not one of my sell-out lawyers would use this evidence, because they all work as a conspiracy with the court. No doubt about it. Jack King did everything he could to keep me from making arms and showing this evidence. They wait till the hearing was over and then make the arguments in the court or on paper where nobody can

rebut it or contradict the testimony or arguments. There's more than thirty altered and falsified records saying I told so-and-so this or that, but you go look in their record, it does not say Thomas Mason called them at all and told them anything. But that's OK. All this evidence is being saved, so Jack King can laugh all he wants like he's the big hero after this is over with, that's fine. But the person that had the gun, they know was not Thomas Mason, so who's getting the last laugh after all? The guy that got away. But Jack King knows he illegally convicted me of all these falsified, altered records. My sister's got the document that my lawyer filed, but he didn't file with the court. It's got the signature on it. He put this all in one record. So it's going to be saved. It ain't going to be destroyed just because I'm dead. Everybody's got to go sooner or later, and sooner or later every one of y'all will be along behind me. That's all I got to say.

221. **Paul Selso Nuncio:** [Spoken] I have a written statement for the press. It will be released as soon as they can. And I also responded to a comment to me from Sandy, daughter of Ms. Farris. I have felt deeply sorry for the deceased. But I'm sorry that I wasn't the one that did it or anything. She will tell you that when she gets a chance to. When the time comes. I just wish just to be patient when the time for each and every one of ya'll individually have y'all time. But I'm not putting pressure on either one of y'all being having any guilt. I just want to say two things, executing someone that is innocent, cause even though I am, the burden will be wiped away and you will be at ease to know that I know how it is, and they will pay for it when their time comes. And all I have to say is that right now I'm sorry that it happened and I was part, not part in it, but part responsible for not properly getting the word out in time to get the right victim or the right convict or the right person that did it. I just wish to say a little prayer for the family for their appearance and forgiveness in this matter. Our Father, who art in heaven, hallowed by thy name. Thy kingdom come, Thy will be done, on earth as it is in heaven. Give this day your daily bread and forgive us our trespasses as we forgive those who trespass against us. Lead us not into temptation, but deliver us from evil. Our Lord, Amen. And ah, don't be surprised if your mom be the helper of God that would grab my hand and say, "You are now into eternal life with God." This is her being one of the chosen ones to give as proof of innocence. That's what I meant by telling you I don't mean to injure you anymore. When your time comes that she would let you know, if I was innocent or guilty. That about all I have to say. Love you all.
[Written] I wish the public to see my point of inside view that the officers of Death Row of the State of Texas. All the years of 5 or 6 years of my first time being locked up for not doing a crime of this sort. Now, officers of Texas TDCJ are of Terrell Unit, Walls Unit and some of Ellis I are just doing their job for their family. Now there are also respectful inmates death row and population that I've meet, now I say to all of you just realizing what crime is about, don't do it. One way I've thought of was having your friends "inmate" to witness your execution talking about those of population and first timers. I just want to give those officers that respected me while in prison of TDCJ Death Row. May God bless you all of TDCJ and inmates especially the free-world population. With Gods and my words of faith, Paul Selso Nuncio

222. Gary Lee Graham: [Spoken] I would like to say that I did not kill Bobby Lambert. That I'm an innocent black man that is being murdered. This is a lynching that is happening in America tonight. There's overwhelming and compelling evidence of my defense that has never been heard in any court of America. What is happening here is an outrage for any civilized country to anybody anywhere to look at. What's happening here is wrong. I thank all of the people that have rallied to my cause. They've been standing in support of me. Who have finished with me. I say to Mr. Lambert's family, I did not kill Bobby Lambert. You are pursuing the execution of an innocent man. I want to express my sincere thanks to all of y'all. We must continue to move forward and do everything we can to outlaw legal lynching in America. We must continue to stay strong all around the world, and people must come together to stop the systematic killing of poor and innocent black people. We must continue to stand together in unity and to demand a moratorium on all executions. We must not let this murder/lynching be forgotten tonight, my brothers. We must take it to the nation. We must keep our faith. We must go forward. We recognize that many leaders have died. Malcom X, Martin Luther King, and others who stood up for what was right. They stood up for what was just. We must, you must, brothers; that's why I have called you today. You must carry on that condition. What is here is just a lynching that is taking place. But they're going to keep on lynching us for the next hundred years, if you do not carry on that tradition, and that period of resistance. We will prevail. We may lose this battle, but we will win the war. This death, this lynching will be avenged. It will be avenged, it must be avenged. The people must avenge this murder. So my brothers, all of y'all stay strong, continue to move forward. Know that I love all of you. I love the people, I love all of you for your blessing, strength, for your courage, for your dignity, the way you have come here tonight, and the way you have protested and kept this nation together. Keep moving forward, my brothers. Slavery couldn't stop us. The lynching couldn't stop us in the south. This lynching will not stop us tonight. We will go forward. Our destiny in this country is freedom and liberation. We will gain our freedom and liberation by any means necessary. By any means necessary, we keep marching forward. I love you, Mr. Jackson. Bianca, make sure that the State does not get my body. Make sure that we get my name as Shaka Sankofa. My name is not Gary Graham. Make sure that it is properly presented on my grave. Shaka Sankofa. I died fighting for what I believe in. I died fighting for what was just and what was right. I did not kill Bobby Lambert, and the truth is going to come out. It will be brought out. I want you to take this thing off into international court, Mr. Robert Mohammed and all y'all. I want you, I want to get my family and take this down to international court and file a law suit. Get all the video tapes of all the beatings. They have beat me up in the back. They have beat me up at the unit over there. Get all the videotapes supporting that law suit. And make the public exposed to the genocide and this brutality world, and let the world see what is really happening here behind closed doors. Let the world see the barbarity and injustice of what is really happening here. You must get those videotapes. You must make it exposed, this injustice, to the world. You must continue to demand a moratorium on all executions. We must move forward, Minister Robert Mohammed. Ashanti Chimurenga, I love you for standing with me, my sister.

You are a strong warrior queen. You will continue to be strong in everything that you do. Believe in yourself; you must hold your head up, in the spirit of Winnie Mandela, in the spirit of Nelson Mandela. Y'all must move forward. We will stop this lynching. Reverend Al Sharpton, I love you, my brother.

225. **Juan Salvez Soria:** [Spoken] I wish we could pray to Allah, the father of the universe. I ask for your protection and my salvation, my night and my day. I want you to lead me and I will follow. We give praise to Allah the divine and holy prophet. We know that you are Allah, that you are the prophet in these days that is in charge of the human race in this new era of time. These two [unintelligible] to the masters of the temple of the son we have been honored to dwell in our father's house at least for the time in which this finite time has come to its assigned time for one. There is nothing strange, love governs all events, what is [unintelligible], who is who was his mother and father, we extend my love to all my brothers and sister extend to life and my religion, it is Allah. It is going in salvation of the nation I come from South, Central, and North America. [Unintelligible] that would save us. So, I call on to all of my brothers and sisters and to members of the human race that still have some knowledge for what love, divine love, is. That comes learned from your ancient forefathers. Love is brought by this prophet Allah. We extend our love to everyone who believes the faith of Islamic and chooses to love along with all their being. We come to understand what is finite and what is infinite. Again, I say it is an honor to live in my father's house. To see this divine great paradise that which I have come to see with the eye of the spirit, the spirit which was revealed by my prophet which was [unintelligible]. We extend our love to everybody. Extend my love to my divine sister. Sister Dorothy, and my brother Tomas, and we know that our father Allah will bless them in the following days to come. We know that Allah is with us now and forever. They say I am going to have surgery, so I guess I will see everyone after this surgery is performed. It is finished.

233. **Jeffery Dillingham:** [Spoken] I would just like to apologize to the victim's family for what I did. I take full responsibility for that poor woman's death, for the pain and suffering inflicted on Mr. Koslow. Father, I want to thank you for all of the beautiful people you put in my life. I could not have asked for two greater parents than you gave me. I could just ask for two greater people in their life now. It is a blessing that there are people that they love so much but even more so, people that I love so much. I thank you for all the things you have done in my life, for the ways that you have opened my eyes, softened my heart. The ways that you have taught me. For teaching me how to love, for all of the bad things you have taken out of my life. For all the good things you have added to it. I thank you for all of the beautiful promises that you make us in your word, and I graciously received every one of them. Thank you Heavenly Father for getting me off of death row and for bringing me home out of prison. I love you Heavenly Father, I love you Jesus. Thank you both for loving me. Amen.

245. **Jason Eric Massey:** [Spoken] Yes, first I would like to speak to the victims' family. First of all, I would like to say that I do not know any of y'all and that is

unfortunate, because I would like to apologize to each and every one of you individually. I can't imagine what I have taken from y'all, but I do want to apologize and I want to let you know that I did do it. You guys know that I am guilty and I am sorry for what I have done. I apologize and I know that you may not be able to forgive me and I know that you may not be able to forgive me in this life and in this world, but I hope sometime in the future you will be able to find it in you to forgive me. And I want you to know that Christina, she did not suffer as much as you think she did. I promise you that. I give you my word. I know you guys want to know where the rest of her remains are. I put her remains in the Trinity River. I have said that since I have come to death row. I want to apologize to you again. I hope sometime in the future you can forgive me. OK. now I want to speak to my mom and my family. Brother Anderson, Kathy, I want you to know that I appreciate all these years that you have been coming to see me on death row, and Daddy, I love you. I appreciate y'all being here and being strong for me, and Mama, you know I love you, and I appreciate all of these visits, the letters and everything y'all have done for me. Y'all have been wonderful. You too, Granny. I love y'all and you know, I want to apologize to y'all too for what I have done. For all of the pain that I have caused, but all of this pain has brought us closer together and all of this suffering that we have been through has brought us all closer to the Lord and in the end that is what counts. Isn't it? That's what counts in the end; where you stand with Almighty God. I know that God has used this to change my life. And it's all been worth it because of that. If I lie here today where I lie, I can say in the face of death, Jesus is Lord. He has changed my life and I know that when I leave this body, I am going home to be with the Lord forever. That is all I want to say. I love y'all and I won't say goodbye, I will say I will see you again. I love you, Daddy. Tonight I dance on the streets of gold. Let those without sin cast the first stone.

248. Miguel A. Richardson: [Spoken] I love you, I love everyone, I go out with great love and respect. This is a great day to pass on. This so-called dying. This is a great day to approach this glorious event. Approach the present. [mumbling] Thy will be done. [mumbling] I love you all. Don't waste your time arguing and bickering. God loves you all. All that really matters is love. Love is the only thing for us. There is no closure without love. Forgive one another. You got to learn how to forgive and embrace one another. Be one. Our love is just like . . . it is the nectar of God. We have so much to give when we give out of our hearts. The hear is the wishing well that waters the tree. I wish and desire one thing: I wish only the best for all of you. [unintelligible] I love the love in every man and child. Mankind is my family and tribe. I am ready, grumah. A poet once said, ". . . is my country." There is no separation between you and me. There is no enemies, only family. I am a minister of love. I go out loving everyone and everything. God bless my . . . country. I shed tears of love may they nourish everyone. Stop killing, start loving. Stop the violence. Let my death change society. You don't need any more killing. You don't need any minimum, maximum security, death row. You don't need the death penalty. We need more loving fathers and mothers. It is a good day to die. Take, me God, hold me in yours and carry me home.

249. James Joseph Wilkens, Jr.: [Spoken] Sandy, all of you, I am sorry. Please hear me. Please in the name of God forgive me. Please understand. Please find that peace. I am really sorry. Please for your sake forgive me. All of you please. I love my sister, my friends, father. Thank you for loving me and being with me. You are magnificent people. God has blessed me more than I deserve. I would like to end with a prayer. Heavenly Father, as I come to you to praise and thank you that even now I can endure the pain that you endured when you died for me on the cross. You have forgiven me of my sins and travesties. Thank you, Lord, for giving me strength. Give them strength to forgive me. Ask them to have them forgive me in their hearts. I ask you to touch each and every one of them. I am truly repentant. In the name of Jesus Christ I love you. Warden, I am ready to go home, please. Remember God is peace, God is love.

256. Vincent Edward Cooks Tell my family I love y'all. Watch out for Momma. Don't want to talk too much, I will cry. I'll just cry everywhere. I'm sorry, Teach, for not being a better son and not doing better things. It wasn't your fault. You raised me the way you should, at least I won't be there no more. I miss you, too. I see you there, you doing all right? I sent you a letter. Neckbone, there's a sheet, I got your name on it. Keep on writing, now. Write to the, hon. Charles, keep the right, now. You people over there. You know what these people are doing. By them executing me ain't doing nothing right. I don't weigh 180 pounds and 5'7". Take care, love y'all. Did Roger come up here yet? Tell Pat and them I love them. I'm gonna go ahead and let them do what they're gonna do. Help your sister, see ya later Pat, love ya Becca. Do what you do, Warden.

260. Randall Wayne Hafdahl Sr.: [Spoken] Yes, I do. My last full statement is being released in a way other than me right here. All I want to say, I love you all. Approximately twenty-eight years ago, I remember looking down at a bassinet; I saw an angel. I am looking at her right now. I love you, Colleen. Let's get going. The road goes on forever, and the party never ends. Let's rock and roll. Let's go, Warden. Me and you, all of us. Remember wet Willie—keep on smiling, keep on smiling. I love you. It's on the way, I can feel it. It's OK, baby. We have a party to go to. I can feel it now.

[Written] Over the last few days we've had a chance to say it all. If I lived to be a 100, the love we all share couldn't be more beautiful. Than you for loving me. II Timothy 1.7 tells us that God DID NOT instill in us the spirit of fear: but of power, love, and of sound mind . . . For those of you who seek to find fear in my eyes? Look into yourself, that's where you'll find the fear you so desperately search for. I leave this life with a clear conscience and heart; I can say that only because I have spoke the truth over the last 16+ years. I am the only one that can say that truthfully. Chief Neal: as to what you said to me when you had me in the back seat of your car on the night of Nov 11? Thank you for being so determined to only seek a specific conclusion, truth be damned! I say that because the thought of having to die of old age in prison is the worst death any person could endure. To Modina Holmes: I thank you for planting that bullet in the ground, and the cigarette butt, also the knives Danny Helgren had packed in his suit case in the trunk of the car; which you placed in the cab for your photo shoot. I also want to thank you and Chief Neal, because of your actions, it shows me that you are human and can love, the same as I love my Club Brothers. We're a lot more alike than you think. To Wes Clayton: You were nothing but a paid chump. You were brought in to do all the dirty work on this case so as to shield Randy Sherrod, "AKA Daffy Duck" from possibly soiling his reputation if the bottom fell out of this conviction through the appeals. For 16 years now you have been the one I have dreamed of having the chance to meet again: Unrestrained! I really would have loved to have had the chance to take your lying ass to school, boy!

James Farren: You ain't as slick as you think you are. I read that article the Globe printed on the 27th, where you expressed how Eardmann wasn't important because there was at least one witness at trial who testified the first shot disarmed Mitchell and rendered him defenseless. Your sure right about that. Just wonder how many people out there other than me and you know that one witness you used to justify Eardmann was actually Eardmann himself! You know as well as I do the only witness to testify about sequence of shots was Eardmann himself. I have to admit, when it comes to walking the line between a lie and a deception, your good! You sure your not related to Clayton? And to the Mitchell family: I truly am sorry for the tragedy that took place on Nov 11, 85. That's all I can give you. That's all I will give you. Because today your making my family and loved ones a victim just as you have cried to the world you were in this tragedy. I did not deliberately shoot James Mitchell. I had no premeditation in my thoughts when I spun around and fired, no matter how many fantasy motives Clayton and Sherrod fabricated. So today my family becomes a victim. You know, the truth sets you free, and the truth is, if your loved one had acted with any professionalism at all, he would be alive today! And that's all I got to say about it. Scooter, get the beer and get in the truck, take me home baby, we got a party to get ready for. I love y'all. Remember Wet Willy Boocub.

270. Napoleon Beazley: [Spoken] The act I committed to put me here was not just heinous, it was senseless. But the person that committed that act is no longer here—I am. I'm not going to struggle physically against any restraints. I'm not going to shout, use profanity, or make idle threats. Understand though that I'm not only upset, but I'm saddened by what is happening here tonight. I'm not only saddened, but disappointed that a system that is supposed to protect and uphold what is just and right can be so much like me when I made the same shameful mistake. If someone tried to dispose of everyone here for participating in this killing, I'd scream a resounding, "No." I'd tell them to give them all the gift that they would not give me . . . and that's to give them all a second chance. I'm sorry that I am here. I'm sorry that you're all here. I'm sorry that John Luttig died. And I'm sorry that it was something in me that caused all of this to happen to begin with. Tonight we tell the world that there are no second chances in the eyes of justice. Tonight, we tell our children that in some instances, in some cases, killing is right. This conflict hurts us all; there are no sides. The people who support this proceeding think this is justice. The people that think that I should live think that is justice. As difficult as it may seem, this is a clash of ideals, with both parties committed to what they feel is right. But who's wrong if in the end we're all victims? In my heart, I have to believe that there is a peaceful compromise to our ideals. I don't mind if there are none for me, as long as there are for those who are yet to come. There are a lot of men like me on death row—good men—who fell to the same misguided emotions but may not have recovered as I have. Give those men a chance to do what's right. Give them a chance to undo their wrongs. A lot of them want to fix the mess they started but don't know how. The problem is not in that people aren't willing to help them find out, but in the system telling them it won't matter anyway. No one wins tonight. No one gets closure. No one walks away victorious.

277. Javier Suarez Medina: [Spoken] First of all, I would like to apologize to the family members of the Cadena family for whatever hurt and suffering I have caused you. This opportunity has never come up before. It's not that I haven't been remorseful; things just never worked out before. Please forgive me and I hope you find it in your heart to forgive me. The peace you will find will be a temporary peace; true peace will come through finding Christ. I pray through this execution that you will find the peace you seek. Give yourself to Christ and find peace through him. I thought about your loved one very much. He will be waiting in heaven for me. I will be able to talk to him and ask him for forgiveness personally. To my family, I thank you and love you for being there for me and supporting me. This is just a stepping stone to home. The hardest part of all the years I was on death row. To all people that supported me, you will always be in my heart, as I have always been in yours. God bless you. Keep your heads up, see you again soon. Forgive me for the pain I caused you. [Spanish] To all the people of Mexico, I would like to thank them for the help.
I also want to carry each and every one of you in my heart. If you are going to demonstrate, I don't want you to do anything crazy to these people. They have suffered enough. Long lives Mexico. Raise the flag of Mexico with honor. Thanks for everything. I love you. [English] To everyone on death row, keep your heads up and I will see you again. I am truly sorry, may you find peace in this. Forgive me for the pain. God bless you, I love you all, and I'm ready to go home.

282. Ron Scott Shamburger: [Spoken] A lot of people have always asked if there is a heaven, and I say there is. There is a heaven and a hell. They ask, "Who goes to heaven?" I believe that it is those who have placed their faith in Jesus Christ.
Romans 3:25: For all have sinned and come short of the glory of God.
Romans 6:23: The wages of sin is death, but the gift of God is eternal life.
Romans 5:8: While we were yet sinners, Christ died for us.
Romans 10:9: If you confess with your mouth the Lord Jesus Christ, and that He was raised from the dead, thou shalt be saved.
John 3:16: For God so loved the world, that He gave his only begotten Son, that whosoever believeth in Him shall have everlasting life.
A lot of people forget about:
John3:36: If you have the Son, you have life and if you have not the Son, the wrath of God lies on you.
In this life, we sin and we make mistakes:
1 John 1:19: If we confess our sins, He is faithful and just to forgive our sins.
I had a verse that jumped out at me a few days ago. Psalm 99:8 speaks of the

holiness of God and he was to the people a God who forgave, but he took vengeance on his deeds. I am not here because of my faith in the Lord Jesus, but I am here for no other reason than my own actions. To the Bakers, I am really sorry for the pain and sorrow I caused you. I really do not know what to say, but I am sorry—forgive me. And to my parents, I am sorry for the pain I have caused you. Forgive me; thank you for your love.

283. Rex Warren Mays: [Spoken] I would like to say a final prayer: Dear Heavenly Father, I come to you today, Lord, and thank you for this opportunity to be with you in paradise. I ask You for forgiveness for the ones that need to be forgiven. Dear Lord, deliver us from evil and give us the comfort and peace and joy that we need. Dear Lord, I ask you right now to be with each of the witnesses and lift them up and be on solid ground. Let them know what has gone on and may we all see each other again. Amen. I would like to thank each witness: Ms. Cox, Whiteside, Reed, Scott, and Chad. I am going to go and see Jesus tonight and reserve a special place for each one of you. You all have been there when no one else was. Thank you for all of your love and support. Just know that I am ready to go. You all know what I've gone through. I am going to a better place with the Lord. I'm mad for one reason, that I'm leaving you behind, when I am going to a better place. Y'all still have to go through this hell on earth. Just remember the good things and not the bad. You are all loved and respected. Warden, just give me parole and let me go home to be with the Lord.

286. Craig Neil Ogan: [Spoken] I would like to say first of all the real violent crimes in this case are acts committed by James Boswell and Clay Morgan Gaines. We have the physical evidence to prove fabrication and cover-up. The people responsible for killing me will have blood on their hands for an unprovoked murder. I am not guilty; I acted in self-defense and reflex in the face of a police officer who was out of control. James Boswell had his head beat in; possibly due to this he had problems. My jurors had not heard about that. They did not know he had suffered a head injury from the beating by a crack dealer five months earlier; that he was filled with anger and wrote an angry letter to the *Houston Chronicle*. He expressed his frustration at the mayor, police chief and fire chief. He was mad at the world. Three and a half months before I worked on a deal with the DEA, the informant was let off. At the moment he left the courtroom, he became angry with me; Officer Boswell was upset about this. Officer Boswell and an angry woman were in the police car and they were talking in raised voices. In other words, Officer Boswell was angry at the time I walked up. Officer Boswell may have reacted to the . . .

287. William Wesley Chappell: [Spoken] Jane, Grace and all of you all, I know you think I did this, and I'm sure you think this is wonderful in your eyes. But let me tell you something, there were two DNA tests run and none matched me. I wanted a third, but that never happened. Three people at different times confessed to killing these people—your parents. They did not know me. My request is that you get yourselves in church and pray for forgiveness because you are murdering me. I did not kill anyone in my life. If you will look at your house and the police report, there are several bullet patterns shot into the west wall over the bed and the east wall and north wall, and your sister was in the front bedroom while thirty shots were fired. There's no way in hell she would have laid in that bed. If you think I did this, you need to think again. There were three people in the house and have confessed to it. Larry Ashworth in Fort Worth killed seven people. All I was asking for was a DNA and I could not get it. But get in church and get right with God. Jane, you know damn well I did not molest that kid of yours. You are murdering me and I feel sorry for you. Get in church and get saved. I really don't know what else to tell you.

297. Henry Earl Dunn Jr.: [Spoken] To all my family and friends, I want you to know that I love you very much. I appreciate all the good and bad times together. I'll always remember you and love you forever. And to the West family, I hope you can find it in your heart to find forgiveness and strength, to move on and find peace. [Written] The Death Penalty in Texas is broke. When an attorney can be forced to represent you, who is not qualified to represent you under Texas laws, the system does not work. When an attorney can dismiss your appeal process, by missing a filing deadline or for failing to file documents on behalf of a client, that's not Due Process of Law as guaranteed under the Unites States Constitution, the system does not work. When officials of any state, such as the State of Texas, has so much confidence in their justice system, mistakes will be made, and innocent people will be executed. Texas has executed innocent people, and tonight, Texas has shown just how broke and unfair its system is. There is no clemency in Texas, a process that needs to be reviewed, and fixed. Most importantly, the Texas Justice System need to be fixed. I hope the politicians such as Elliot Nashtat, Harold Dutton, Rodney Ellis, and others, continue to do their part in trying to fix the Texas Justice System, and until so is done, continue to work for a moratorium on the death penalty in Texas. The victim of this case is NOT forgotten. To the West family, I hope you find in your hearts forgiveness and peace, and find the strength to move forward and the closure they are looking for. Nicholas West is not forgotten, and never will be forgotten. To my family and friends, Anne Dolatschko, Debbie Bilodeau, and the many supporters around the world, as well as my attorneys, Michael Charlton, who has always been there for me and done everything in their will and power to help me and stand by my side, I love you dearly, and you will always be in my hear forever. Please continue to struggle and fight against the death penalty, as its only use has been for revenge, and it does not deter crime. Its time for a moratorium in the State of Texas.

298. Richard Head Williams: [Spoken] The statement I would like to make is to all my loved ones—and to the Abrahams and Williams families. We came a long way through the tragedy—from hate to love, and I would like to apologize for the pain I have caused all my families on both sides. I am looking at you Mr. Frank: I am sorry, brother, for what happened to your sister and I hope that you would forgive me one day. Ask God to forgive me and ask God to forgive you and allow me to pass through. My brother Farooq, I love you, my brother, and send my love to all my family members. And I was not a monster like they said I was. I made a mistake and this mistake cost—but they won't cost no more. I leave you with all my love and blessings. May Allah bless each and every one of you.

[Written] Hello to all: Tonight I take my last walk as well breath in this world called Earth. I state that to show I'm not saddened or enjoyed to see this moment. Because I leave behind alot of people that loved me, that believe I could had been that someone. If I been given a real chance in life instead of denial or incarceration everytime I was arrested for something the community believed I did. To be here on Texas death Row show all people that we people of American don't care about helping. This is about destroying lives to show they can kill, but they hide behind laws of American. I'm not disappointed of the system or nobody because this is how it's supposed to be. Texans was breed that way to live, think, act. But someone is mad that a system that's supposed to protect and uphold what is just and right, has shown it's just as crooked as I am said to be. Now I lay here dead. But we have gave all Texans the sign that in some instances, and in some cases "KILLING IS ALRIGHT TO DO AS LONG IT'S FOR JUSTICE OF THE AMERICAN PEOPLE". So who win? No one do! Ain't no such thing as a closure! Because we all still will remember who ain't here on them special detes, occasion's ect . . . So no victorious, heros and happiness. but in ALLAH's (GOD) eye justice is his, and we should cry out for his forgiveness. I leave with ALLAH's blessing as well mercy for my soul. I'm free now! Let me rest in peace. Nam-myoho-renge-kyo! Salaamu! Amen! Bro. D'Reehcer Ali Smaillii Muhammd. (formerly known as) Richard Earl Head-Williams III

304. Bruce Charles Jacobs: [Spoken] Can you hear me, Chris? The Lord is my shepherd; I shall not want. He makes me to lie down in green pastures; He leads me beside the still waters. He restores my soul; He leads me in the paths of righteousness for His name's sake. Yea, though I walk through the valley of the shadow of death, I will fear no evil; for Thou art with me; Thy rod and Thy staff comfort me. Thou preparest a table before me in the presence of my enemies; Thou anointest my head with oil; my cup runneth over. Surely goodness and mercy shall follow me all the days of my life; and I will dwell in the house of the Lord forever. I want to thank you for being there with me all these years and supporting me and keeping me in the word. Michael, you take care of her and thank you Father Don and Chris. And I want to thank the media for being nice to me all this time. Bye, Chris. I will see you. Take care of yourselves and you all stay strong. You keep doing your ministry.

306. Hilton Lewis Crawford: [Spoken] First of all, I would like to ask Sister Teresa to send Connie a yellow rose. I want to thank the Lord, Jesus Christ, for the years I have spent on death row. They have been a blessing in my life. I have had the opportunity to serve Jesus Christ and I am thankful for the opportunity. I would like to thank Father Walsh for having become a Franciscan, and all the people all over the world who have become my friends. It has been a wonderful experience in my life. I would like to thank Chaplain Lopez, and my witnesses for giving me their support and love. I would like to thank the nuns in England for their support. I want to tell my sons I love them; I have always loved them—they were my greatest gift from God. I want to tell my witnesses, Tannie, Rebecca, Al, Leo, and Dr. Blackwell that I love all of you and I am thankful for your support. I want to ask Paulette for forgiveness from your heart. One day, I hope you will. It is a tragedy for my family and your family. I am sorry. My special angel, I love you. And I love you, Connie. May God pass me over to the kingdom's shore softly and gently. I am ready.

317. Billy Frank Vickers: [Spoken] Yes. I would just like to say to my family that I am sorry for all the grief I have caused. I love you all. Tell Mama and the kids I love you; I love all of you. And I would like to clear some things up if I could. Tommy Perkins, the man that got a capital life sentence for murdering Kinslow—he did not do it. I did it. He would not even have had anything to do with it if he had known I was going to shoot the man. He would not have gone with me if he had known. I was paid to shoot the man. And Martin, the younger boy, did not know what it was about. He thought it was just a robbery. I am sorry for that. It was nothing personal. I was trying to make a living. A boy on Eastham doing a life sentence for killing Jamie Kent—I did not do it, but I was with his daddy when it was done. I was there with him and down through the years there were several more that I had done or had a part of. And I am sorry and I am not sure how many—there must be a dozen or fourteen I believe all total. One I would like to clear up is Cullen Davis—where he was charged with shooting his wife. And all of these it was never nothing personal. It was just something I did to make a living. I am sorry for all the grief I have caused. I love you all. That is all I have to say.

324. Jasen Shane Busby: [Spoken] Yes I do. I want to tell everyone, my family, thanks for standing by me. I want to tell Mr. and Ms. Gray and everyone that I didn't do what I did to hurt you all. I am sorry that I did what I did. I don't think you know the true reason for doing what I did, but Brandy and I had a suicide pact and I just didn't follow through with it. That did not come out in the trial. I am not trying to hurt you by telling you this. I am trying to tell you the truth. I want Cindy to know that I know she is out there—and Vicente Hernandez that I love them. Thank you for all you have done and I want to make sure you are all right. That is all I want to say. I am ready. See you later. I am ready.

331. Dominique Jerome Green: [Spoken] Yes. Man, there is a lot of people there. There was a lot of people that got me to this point, and I can't thank them all. But thank you for your love and support; they have allowed me to do a lot more than I could have on my own. Sheila, I wish I would have met you seven years ago; it would have been a lot easier. But I have overcame a lot. I am not angry, but I am disappointed that I was denied justice. But I am happy that I was afforded you all as family and friends. You all have been there for me; it's a miracle. I love you. And I have to tell Jessica I am sorry. I never knew it would come to this. Lorna, you know you have to keep my struggle going. I know you just lost your baby, but you have to keep running. Andy, I love you, man. Tell Andre and them that I didn't get a chance to reach my full potential, but you can help them reach theirs. You needed me, but I just did not know how to be there for them. There is so much I have to say, but I just can't say it all. I love you all. Please just keep the struggle going. If you turn your back on me, you turn your back on them. I love you all and I'll miss you all. Thanks for allowing me to touch so many hearts. I never knew I could do it, but you made it possible. I am just sorry. And I am not as strong as I thought I was going to be. But I guess it only hurts for a little while. You all are my family. Please keep my memory alive.

338. Troy Albert Kunkle: [Spoken] Yes sir. I would like to ask you to forgive me. I made a mistake and I am sorry for what I did. All I can do is ask you to forgive me. I love you and I will see all of you in heaven. I love you very much. Praise Jesus. I love you. Our Father, who art in heaven, hallowed be thy name. Thy kingdom come, Thy will be done, on earth as it is in heaven. Give us this day our daily bread, and forgive us our trespasses as we forgive those who have trespassed against us. And lead us not into temptation, but deliver us from evil. Amen.

352. Melvin Wayne White: [Spoken] Tell Beth and them I am sorry, truly sorry for the pain that I caused your family. I truly mean that too. She was a friend of mine and I betrayed her trust. I love you all. Tell Mama I love her. The Lord is my shepherd; I shall not want He maketh me to lie down in green pastures; He leadeth me beside the still waters. He restoreth my soul; He leadeth me in the paths of righeousness for His name's sake. Yea, though I walk through the valley of the shadow of death, I will fear no evil; for Thou art with me. Thou preparest a table before me in the presence of mine enemies; Thou anointest my head with oil; my cup runneth over. Surely goodness and mercy shall follow me all the days of my life; and I will dwell in the house of the Lord forever. Our Father, who are in heaven, hallowed be thy name. Thy kingdom come, thy will be done, on earth as it is in heaven. Give us this day our daily bread, and forgive us our trespasses, as we forgive those who trespass against us. And lead us not into temptation, but deliver us from evil. For Thine is the kingdom, and the power, and the glory, for ever and ever. Amen. All right, Warden, let's give them what they want.

Index